Red Hat® RPM Guide

Red Hat® RPM Guide

Eric Foster-Johnson

Wiley Publishing, Inc.

Red Hat® RPM Guide

Published by
Wiley Publishing, Inc.
10475 Crosspoint Boulevard
Indianapolis, IN 46256
www.wiley.com

Copyright © 2003 by Red Hat, Inc.

Published by Wiley Publishing, Inc., Indianapolis, Indiana

Published simultaneously in Canada

Library of Congress Control Number: 2002114860

ISBN: 0-7645-4965-0

Manufactured in the United States of America

10 9 8 7 6 5 4 3 2 1

1B/QV/QV/QT/IN

About the Author

Eric Foster-Johnson is a veteran software developer who has written more than 16 books on programming, UNIX, Linux, and open-source software. His books include *Graphical Applications with Tcl and Tk*, *Cross-Platform Perl*, *Perl Modules*, and *Teach Yourself Linux*, the latter with Steve Oualline.

Credits

ACQUISITIONS EDITOR
Debra Williams Cauley

PROJECT EDITOR
Sara Shlaer

COPY EDITORS
Chris Jones
Anne Owen

EDITORIAL MANAGER
Mary Beth Wakefield

VICE PRESIDENT & EXECUTIVE GROUP PUBLISHER
Richard Swadley

VICE PRESIDENT AND EXECUTIVE PUBLISHER
Bob Ipsen

VICE PRESIDENT AND PUBLISHER
Joseph B. Wikert

EXECUTIVE EDITORIAL DIRECTOR
Mary Bednarek

PROJECT COORDINATOR
Nancee Reeves

GRAPHICS AND PRODUCTION SPECIALISTS
Beth Brooks
Heather Pope

QUALITY CONTROL TECHNICIANS
Andy Hollandbeck
Susan Moritz
Carl W. Pierce

PROOFREADING AND INDEXING
TECHBOOKS Production Services

COVER IMAGE
© Hulton/Getty

COVER DESIGN
Michael J. Freeland

RED HAT TECHNICAL REVIEW
Chip Turner

RED HAT PRESS LIAISONS
Jeremy Hogan
Kathleen Langhi

SPECIAL RED HAT ASSISTANCE
Ed Bailey
Stephanie Jordan
Jonathan Opp

To Norma, Katya, and Nalana.

Acknowledgments

A very heartfelt thanks goes to the wonderful people at Red Hat. Not only do they make the primary Linux distribution I run, they also provided invaluable help in the creation of this book. Every person I contacted at Red Hat was very helpful and informative. Thanks.

Thanks to my wife Norma for all her help and support on this project.

Foreword

RPM is easy. Despite what you've heard, and perhaps experienced, it really is. The problem, though, is that it just isn't explained as well as it could be. Sure, you could learn just about everything about RPM from the man pages and the Internet, and you could even dig through the hundreds of thousands of lines of code since RPM is Open Source software, but it would take time. Worse, there would be a lot of trial and error, keyboard smashing, teeth grinding, and general frustration.

Never before has a single book covered so much of RPM. From the most basic command-line usage to more complex API interactions, this book covers it. From the creation of RPMs to the creation of tools to manipulate RPMs, for system administrators and developers alike, this is the book you need to learn more about how to best exploit the features of RPM.

When I first began working at Red Hat — the creators of RPM — I expected to immediately be handed the rumored "missing RPM guide" that contained the answers to all of my questions. To the contrary, I found that even inside Red Hat itself there is a lot of confusion over RPM. So, like many others, I struggled to learn more and more, and although I was fortunate to work where so many people knew RPM, it still took time, it still took trial and error, and it still took patience. I wish I'd had this book then.

RPM is worth learning because as a technology it provides a great deal of control over any RPM-based Linux system. At its heart, RPM can perhaps best be thought of as a complexity-management solution for any modern Linux deployment, be it a single system or a cluster of thousands. It has tremendous power; with just one command line, you can verify that your operating system is intact, or remove ten pieces of software you've decided you no longer want. But despite the power of RPM and its sometimes amazing ability to distill incredibly complex actions into simple command lines, there is still much to learn.

That's why this book exists. The cost of the flexibility of RPM is that it can be difficult not only to know how to do something, but even to know if something can be done. Hopefully this book will be your "missing guide."

Chip Turner
Senior Software Engineer
Red Hat Network

Preface

Linux package management grew out of an urgent need to be able to manage multiple systems and the software installed on those systems. Out of these needs came the RPM Package Management system, or RPM for short.

RPM differs from most package-management solutions by the scope of what it solves. RPM allows you to start with pristine sources, create and recreate packages, and verify the contents of packages. You can check the authenticity of signed packages, and you can query to find out what is installed in your system with a plethora of means.

With RPM, you can automate most package-management tasks. This clear focus on automated, unattended usage really sets RPM above other solutions. RPM also helps manage the dependencies between packages, ensuring that the packages you install will actually work together.

This book covers RPM from its basic usage to advanced topics, including programming to the RPM APIs and running RPM on non-Linux systems.

Who Should Read This Book?

This book is aimed at Red Hat and other Linux system administrators who need to use RPM on a day-to-day basis to manipulate the software installed on the systems they control, as well as other Unix administrators who may wish (typically for compatibility or ease-of-management reasons) to implement RPM on their non-Linux systems.

Software developers and advanced system administrators will find this book a valuable reference when writing programs or scripts using the various APIs provided by RPM.

Hardware and Software Requirements

This book uses the latest released version of RPM, 4.1. The vast majority of the text works with other RPM versions due to the compatibility between versions. Most of the examples were run on Red Hat Linux 8.0, but they should work on most versions of Linux.

How This Book Is Organized

This book is divided into four parts. The following paragraphs explain what you'll find in each part.

Part I: RPM Basics

This section introduces the reason we need package-management software and describes the basics of the RPM system, including its driving philosophy. Starting with Chapter 4, this section describes how to use the `rpm` command to install, upgrade, and remove packages. The `rpm` command also supports querying information about packages and verifying packages.

Part II: Creating RPMs

This section explains how to create your own RPMs, from applications developed by your organization to applications written elsewhere but for which no RPM packages are available. Chapters go into detail on the contents of the spec file, which defines how to build the RPM with the `rpmbuild` command. Later chapters delve into advanced topics such as triggers and conditional options. Chapter 14 covers tips and best-practice guidelines to help ensure your RPMs will work on a variety of Linux systems with the least amount of hassle.

Part III: Programming RPM

The entire RPM system is made available through the RPM library, or rpmlib. This section covers how to access RPMs from your scripts and programs. Specific chapters cover Linux shell scripting and C programming, as well as Python and Perl scripting.

Part IV: Extending RPM

This section covers how to use RPM effectively on other (non–Red Hat) versions of Linux along with other operating systems including Solaris and Windows systems. Chapter 21 covers how to customize your RPM environment through the use of RPM settings and macros.

Part V: Appendixes

The appendixes of this book provide additional reference information. This includes the syntax of the `rpm` command, a description of the spec file and RPM package file formats, and a listing of handy development tools and Internet resources.

Conventions Used in This Book

The following sections explain the conventions used in this book.

Typographical conventions

Italic type indicates new terms and provides emphasis. Commands you type from the keyboard and the system's responses are listed in a `fixed-width font` (mono-font). I use **boldface** type to indicate text that you need to type directly from the keyboard.

Code

The same monofont typeface indicates program code and spec file contents, as shown in the following Python code:

```
ts = rpm.TransactionSet()
```

Navigating This Book

This book is designed to be read from beginning to end, although if you have already been introduced to the basics of RPM, you can easily skip over the first set of chapters and return to them at some other time.

Cautions, Notes, and Cross-References appear in the text to indicate important or especially helpful items. Following is a list of these icons and their functions:

 Cautions alert you to problems.

 Notes provide additional or critical information and technical data on the current topic.

 Cross-Reference icons indicate other chapters in the book or sites on the Internet where you can find more information about a particular topic.

Further Information

You can find more help for your specific problems and questions by investigating several Web sites, a mailing list, and a Usenet newsgroup. Appendix E contains a list of resources that you can use to find out more about RPM.

You can contact me via e-mail. But the most effective, and fastest, means to get answers to questions is to read and post to the RPM mailing list. Contact me to provide feedback about the book (positive or negative). This feedback really helps improve any future editions of the book.

Have fun,
Eric Foster-Johnson
erc@pconline.com
January 2003

Contents at a Glance

Contents

Part I

RPM Basics

Chapter 1

Introducing Package Management

IN THIS CHAPTER

- ◆ Issues in software management
- ◆ Examining Linux management tools
- ◆ Introducing the package concept

IN 1991, A YOUNG Finnish graduate student started a new personal hobby. He had acquired an Intel 386 computer and had spent a few weeks exploring it and playing early PC computer games. Eventually, however, he grew bored with the limitations of the MS-DOS environment that had come with his toy and decided that he wanted an operating system for it that he could use more productively. After exploring Minix, a feature-limited teaching operating system, he decided he needed a full-featured OS.

At that time, no full-featured PC operating systems were freely available, so he decided to write his own operating system. Today, that small hobby OS that Linus Torvalds started almost as a whim has become Linux (www.linux.com), a significant new variant of Unix that runs millions of the world's network servers and, increasingly, desktop computers and embedded processors.

Linux has grown up, successfully making the transition from a one-man personal project to a functional, full-featured operating system used by many of the world's major corporations and deployed on millions of corporate and personal systems. Along the way, Linux has had to address many of the same issues any new operating system must face. One of these concerns is how software for Linux, and how the Linux operating system itself, should be installed. How can administrators safely remove software packages without affecting other installed packages? And how can you safely upgrade packages? Answering these questions is what this book is all about.

Installing, Removing, and Upgrading Applications

Applications for most operating systems consist of multiple files that must be copied to specific locations on the computer's file system before each application can be run. This is true for common PC operating systems such as MS-DOS or Microsoft Windows, as well as for Unix and Linux.

In the case of a Unix-like operating system such as Linux, other issues must also be considered. Unix and Linux are multiple-user systems, so they must track ownership of files. Furthermore, Unix and Linux use a system of file permissions. Administrators can grant some users access to files and can control how users may access those files, for example, allowing some users the permission to read only certain files. Administrators can deny other users access to the same files. So, installation of an application on Linux requires consideration of all these details. After files are copied into their appropriate locations, they must be granted correct permissions and correct ownerships.

Similarly, administrators occasionally need to remove installed software from the computer. Maybe the program is no longer needed; maybe it does not work correctly for the needed task, or maybe the space it is using is needed for more important programs. In addition, installed software sometimes needs to be upgraded. Perhaps a new version of the software has come out and the currently installed version needs to be replaced with the presumably improved version. In most respects, software upgrades are the same as the removal of one application (the old version), followed by installation of another application (the new version). Upgrades do, however, have additional issues. Many applications must be configured before they can be used. Ideally, the upgrade for an installed application takes the current configuration into account, preserving old configuration information and applying it to the recently installed version.

All these considerations make installation of a new application onto Unix or Linux a labor-intensive process. To further complicate matters, Unix applications have primarily been distributed as source code. To install a new application, such as the Apache Web server, you download the source code for that application – in this case, from the Apache Project's Web page (http://httpd.apache.org). Typically, the source code is provided in some sort of archive (such as the Zip archival and compression format often used in the Windows world or the tar archive format typically used in the Unix world) that you must then unpack. After unpacking this source code, you have to configure it to support the options and systems you want, compiling it to produce an executable program that can run on your particular operating system (CPU combination).

After compiling the source code, you still have to install the application by putting all of its components (executable programs, documentation, configuration files, and so forth) into the correct locations on your hard drive and setting correct permissions on all those files. You might also need to perform other steps to prepare the system for the software. In the case of Apache, for example, some space needs to be set aside for storage of Web-access logs, and a special user account needs to be created so that the Apache Web server can operate more securely. Finally, you are ready to try running the application you have spent so much time installing.

To help with all these tasks, precompiled software is becoming increasingly prevalent in the Unix and Linux communities, so you might be able to find executable (precompiled binary) copies of the application you wish to install that are appropriate for your particular machine's CPU. In that case, download an archive of the compiled application and unpack it. Then skip the compilation step, since that has already been done for you. The other steps required to install the package (copying files into correct locations, setting file permissions, and doing any needed system or application configuration) are exactly the same as the steps performed to install that application from source code. Once those steps are finished, you are ready to test your freshly installed application.

When you run your newly installed application, you might be thrilled, perhaps discovering that it is something you want to use regularly. On the other hand, you might discover that you have no use for the software you have just installed, deciding that you want to uninstall it.

Uninstallation occurs by reversing the installation steps. Remember any special steps you have performed (such as adding a user account), and undo those. Then remember all the files you have installed and where you have installed them. Manually delete them. As you can see, this can become a pretty tedious exercise.

If you like the application you have installed, you will likely find yourself wanting to upgrade it eventually. The Apache Web server, for example, like any network service, must be upgraded whenever security problems are found and fixed. If you find that you need to upgrade Apache, you need to back up your Apache configuration files and then uninstall Apache. The next step is to install a new version of Apache, applying your Apache-configuration customizations to your new installation of Apache.

All of this is a big pain. There has to be a better way. And there is.

Overcoming the Installation Obstacles

None of the tasks you must perform to install, upgrade, or uninstall applications are especially difficult. However, these steps quickly become daunting when you consider all the files that must be managed. A full Red Hat Linux 7.3 installation provides around 3,000 executable commands and over 160,000 total files (some other Linux distributions are even larger!). Obviously, managing all these files by hand, although theoretically possible, is not technically feasible. On a smaller scale, even management of single applications is not practical. The Postfix e-mail server application, for example, consists of around 275 files scattered in a dozen or so different directories. Imagine trying to remember and manually remove all of those files (and only those files) to uninstall Postfix from your system!

All the steps needed to manage software on Unix or Linux systems are hardly unique to Unix; all operating systems have similar procedures that must be followed to make software usable on the system. For this reason, many approaches have been adopted toward software installation, uninstallation, and upgrading.

Application-level utilities

Some operating systems, such as MS-DOS, have supplied absolutely no built-in tools for software management. Installation of applications on such systems occurs in one of two ways: software is installed manually, using file-copy utilities to put all the application files in the appropriate places on the system, or software is installed using a custom-written installation application (as is usually the case for MS-DOS applications).

Once installed, software can be uninstalled in one of two ways: you can manually delete each file installed for the application (assuming you can even remember them all), or the application might come with a custom uninstallation utility that can be run to remove the application. Upgrading an already installed application on such a system uses a similar procedure. If the application comes with an installation utility capable of handling application upgrades, you can use the utility to perform the upgrade. Otherwise, the software must be manually upgraded using the procedure described previously.

 Note that current versions of Windows such as Windows XP have a central database of installed applications.

Built-in system utilities

Other operating systems have come with built-in utilities that a system administrator can use to manage the system's software. These utilities can be run to install the software on the system; typically, they take some of the work out of manually installing software, dealing with issues such as figuring out which files need to be put where on the system. Once installed, these utilities typically track the files that have been installed. This knowledge can usually be used to uninstall those applications automatically. Since the software knows which files are associated with the application, it can be told to uninstall the application, and it can find and delete all the files that belong to that application.

These built-in utilities typically come in two different forms. One type focuses on managing the installation process, providing custom utilities that can be used to perform the otherwise manual tasks of compiling software and copying files into their final locations. The three major freely available Berkeley Unix, or BSD, operating systems, NetBSD, FreeBSD, and OpenBSD, for example, ship with a software-management system called, variously, *ports* (FreeBSD and OpenBSD) or *packages* (NetBSD).

The ports system is composed of extensions to the normal Unix software-compilation utilities that help it automate and track many of the steps of a standard source-code compilation. When using ports, you still download source code, unarchive it, configure it, compile it, and install it, but the ports software automates many of these steps. Furthermore, the ports system does limited tracking of the files it installs. Although it does not offer more advanced features (such as an interface to search all installed files to see what application supplied that file) or the ability to upgrade installed applications, it does provide the ability to uninstall applications that are installed using ports. These sorts of limitations are typical of management applications that function as the ports system does, by enhancing the compilation and installation phases of application installation. The packages system on NetBSD has similar limitations.

Other system-management utilities focus less attention on compiling an application for installation and more attention on the files that must be installed on the system after the application has been compiled.

For example, the standard System V Unix package-management software supplied with most commercial Unix systems (Sun's Solaris, for example) devotes no attention to management of software compilation at all. Instead, it tracks the individual files associated with each application in a system database.

To install software using the System V tools, you must compile the software. After compiling the software in the standard fashion, prepare a list of the files from that compilation that need to be installed on the system. Be certain to state where the files need to be installed and what permissions and ownerships they need to have once installed. Then run a series of commands that look at this list, find the files listed in it, and archive them into one file, along with a copy of this list that specifies where they should be installed and the ownerships and permissions. This single archive file can then be transferred to other machines, where a System V software-management command can be used to install it. This System V installation command (typically called pkgadd) unpacks the archive, copies the files into their final destinations based on the enclosed listing, and sets permissions and ownerships on the files as specified by the listing. Finally, this pkgadd command registers the list of freshly installed files into a system-wide database of installed files.

Such a system offers several advantages over manual software installation. Software can now be installed and uninstalled easily, and the system-wide database of installed files can be readily searched to locate installed applications and files. However, this sort of system also has severe limitations; it is far less flexible in the software-configuration stages than software such as the FreeBSD ports system, which offers great control over the software-compilation stage of software installation.

Linux Software Management Tools: Packages

Initially, Linux had neither type of software-management tool. In the early days of Linux, you installed Linux by cross-compiling it under a different operating system (Minix), then manually installing the compiled Linux programs into the appropriate locations to produce a working system. As Linux has matured, however, it has acquired software-management tools that have made software installation, removal, and upgrade significantly easier than in the early days. The exact software-management tool used on modern Linux systems varies from distribution to distribution, but both approaches to system management can be found in the tools used by various distributions.

The Gentoo Linux (www.gentoo.org) distribution, for example, uses a software-management system called Portage, which is very similar to the FreeBSD ports system. Like ports, Portage provides great control over software compilation and installation, providing a collection of scripts that automate much of the basic work of downloading and compiling software.

At the other end of the spectrum, the now-defunct deepLinux distribution used a software-management system called deep-package (still available from www2.cddc.vt.edu/linux/distributions/deeplinux/tools. deep-package was intended to be a complete reimplementation of the Solaris pkgadd utility and its helpers. Like the Solaris pkgadd software, deep-package paid no attention to half of the question of how to manage software, focusing entirely on software installation and tracking issues while entirely ignoring the initial compilation of the software.

More typically, however, Linux software-management tools use an approach somewhere between the two extremes represented by Portage and deep-package. Most Linux software-management tools provide software that manages the compilation of software, similarly to the FreeBSD ports tools. However, these software-management tools typically produce *packages* from the software they compile. Much like the archives produced by the System V software-management tools, packages are simply archive files that contain two things: a collection of related files, which together have a common use, and a script that provides all the metadata about those files necessary to install and manage those files.

Typically, packages represent applications. For example, a Postfix package contains the 275 files that make up Postfix and a script that specifies where on the system those 275 files need to be placed, as well as what permissions and ownership those files need. A single command can then take this Postfix package file, extract its 275 archived files, and use the script to place those files correctly on the system.

In addition, most Linux software-management tools have a database component that tracks files and applications that have been installed using the package-management software, helping the package manager do its job of easing the management of installed software.

In the case of my full Red Hat Linux 7.3 installation, this package-management software maintains a database of information regarding all 160,000 files on the system; as applications are installed on the system, this database is updated with information regarding the new application and the locations of its component files. This database is the key component, making it possible to manage the system. Since this database remembers which 275 files compose the Postfix application, it ensures that I can uninstall Postfix with a single command that accesses this database, without my having to remember the locations of all 275 files that make up the Postfix application.

A wide variety of software-management tools are available for Linux to help lessen the work involved with installing, removing, and upgrading applications installed on the system. This book focuses on one of these tools, the RPM Package Management software, or RPM.

 RPM was originally called Red Hat Package Manager. After adoption by other Linux distributions, the name has changed to simply the RPM Package Manager. The RPM initials remain the same.

As the original name implies, RPM was developed by Red Hat, Inc., the major Linux distributor in the United States. Even though the original name seems to point to a Red Hat-only solution, most Linux distributions use the RPM software. The RPM software provides a foundation needed by Linux system administrators throughout the world. You can even use RPM on other operating systems, both Linux and non-Linux, as covered in Chapters 19 and 20, respectively.

The RPM system provides all of the features needed to manage applications, including a database of installed packages with their version numbers, the ability to install, remove, and update packages, and the ability to recompile an application from a source code RPM package.

The remaining chapters in Part I go into depth on what you can do with RPM packages and the commands you need to work with the RPM system:

- Chapter 2 provides an overview of the RPM system, exploring what it was designed for and where it has weaknesses.

- Chapter 3 discusses the technical details of how the RPM system works, where the database of packages gets stored, and what commands should be available for working with RPM packages.

- Chapter 4 continues the discussion by covering the three major tasks you need to perform with RPM packages: installing software, removing software, and upgrading software you have already installed.

- Chapter 5 covers the RPM database, how it works, where it resides, and how you can use it to better manage your system.

◆ Chapter 6 delves into package dependencies, a very important concept. Most major applications depend on a number of other packages. Sometimes these dependencies get very complex, with one package depending on particular versions of other packages. With thousands of packages on your system, this can lead to a big mess. Chapter 6 helps you sort through the issues.

◆ Chapter 7 covers the important issue of transactions, so that you can ensure your system gets updated in an orderly manner and so that you can roll back changes if something does not work out.

◆ Chapter 8 introduces a host of tools that can help you find RPM packages as well as manage the packages on your system. This includes graphical interfaces on top of the RPM system and special Internet search sites devoted just to RPM packages.

Later chapters cover creating RPM packages, programming with RPM, and extending the functionality provided by the base RPM system.

Summary

Modern operating systems have large complex sets of applications, resulting in thousands of files to keep track of for upgrades, installation, and removal of packages. All this complexity has lead Linux vendors to develop a variety of package-management tools.

This chapter briefly introduced the RPM Package Manager, or RPM for short. The next chapter provides an overview of the RPM system, showing how all the parts fit together.

Chapter 2

Introduction to RPM

IN THIS CHAPTER

- ◆ Examining the history of package management
- ◆ Introducing RPM features
- ◆ Getting acquainted with RPM terminology

SEVERAL PACKAGE MANAGERS — SOFTWARE that tracks and manipulates the applications installed on the system — are available for Linux. The most widely used of these Linux package managers is the RPM Package Manager (formerly the Red Hat Package Manager), or RPM for short, the subject of this book

Although RPM was initially developed for Red Hat Linux, a combination of technical features and good timing has resulted in RPM's becoming the de facto standard for packaging software on most Linux distributions. The fact that Red Hat released the source code to the RPM software under an open-source license also helped its adoption.

More recently, the RPM package file format has been adopted as the official standard for Linux as part of the Linux Standards Base, or LSB. Described at www. linuxbase.org/, the Linux Standards Base is an attempt to set a baseline that all Linux distributions should follow. Some vendors have been pulled in kicking and screaming, but the LSB for the most part has really helped the job of system administrators by providing some commonality across distributions, as in the location of certain files. The history of Linux package managers is largely intertwined with the history of Linux distributions.

Strictly speaking, *Linux* refers to a single piece of software, the Unix-like kernel that Linus Torvalds and cohorts have scattered all over the Internet and have been developing since 1991. This Linux kernel is a marvelous piece of software, currently comprising over 3.7 million lines of freely-licensed source code and accompanying documentation. Together, these factors provide a fast, full-featured, stable operating system kernel for use on more than 30 different processor architectures, ranging from embedded systems such as watches and PDAs, to desktop and server systems, all the way up to mainframes and supercomputing clusters.

The Need for Linux Package Management Systems

Although Linux is an excellent core component of an operating system suitable for a wide variety of real-world applications, this Linux kernel by itself is not sufficient for accomplishing most tasks. The technical definition of exactly what constitutes an operating system is a matter of debate.

Despite this controversy, it is clear that most users of Linux require both the Linux kernel and a large suite of accompanying software (a shared C library; traditional Unix utilities such as grep, awk, and sed; an editor, such as vi; a shell, such as the Bourne-Again "bash" shell; and so forth) to complete the various tasks for which they typically employ Linux.

Users expect Linux to include server software such as the Apache Web server, desktop software such as the OpenOffice.org office productivity suite, and a host of other packages. In fact, most Linux users don't make the distinction between the kernel (technically the only part that is "Linux") and all the extra packages (technically "everything else") that comes with a Linux distribution. Most users simply refer to the whole thing as "Linux."

Some Linux distributions include thousands of packages on six or more CD-ROMs. This situation alone cries out for effective package-management software. And this doesn't include the extra packages that don't come with Linux distributions but which organizations need to create an effective working environment.

Furthermore, the Linux kernel and these various software applications are typically made available by their developers in source code formats only, and they can be installed manually only after compiling them from source code.

Most people do not have the technical skills necessary to cross-compile an entire operating system. Even if they do, they usually do not want to devote the time and effort required to bootstrap and compile an operating system just to be able to run Linux.

Fortunately, the early Linux programmers quickly realized the impracticality of source-code only releases early in Linux's development and created what they called *distributions* – collections of precompiled binaries of the Linux kernel and other necessary software that users often wanted. Rather than installing Minix, compiling the Linux kernel and other required software applications under Minix, and installing those compiled binaries of the Linux kernel and essential Linux applications, users could just install these distributions, immediately having a functional Linux environment in which to work.

Early distributions, such as MCC and SLS, initially represented little more than archived snapshots of their developer's hard drive. They offered the user performing the installation little or no control over what applications were put on the system. Whatever the distribution developer had on his hard drive was what the distribution installer got on her hard drive. Even this was much better than rolling your own distribution by hand. SLS, for example, stood for Soft Landing System, and was designed to make the experience of installing Linux easier, hence providing a "soft landing." MCC Interim Linux, from the Manchester Computing Centre, was the first distribution to sport a combined boot/root disk, another attempt to make life easier for those adopting Linux.

Distribution developers quickly realized, however, that more flexibility was needed and began looking for ways to provide choices both during and after installation. The Slackware distribution, for example, divided applications into several functional categories. All users installed the base distribution; users could then selectively install only the additional supplemental categories they needed. If networking support was desired, for example, the networking bundle could be installed. Similarly, if a graphical user interface was desired, the X bundle could be installed, making the X Window System available. This concept offered rudimentary control over what was installed but only at a very coarse level. Installing the X bundle put several applications (multiple X terminal emulators, several different window managers, and so forth) on the system, and all users who installed the bundle got all of those applications whether they wanted them all or not.

The next logical step in distribution evolution was the development of more advanced tools to control what was installed. Several distributions independently developed the notion of application-level installation management. The developers of these distributions realized that Slackware and similar distributions were heading in the right direction, but simply had not made software management granular enough. Slackware allowed installation and uninstallation (after a fashion) of bundles of related applications, but what was really needed was installation and uninstallation on an application-by-application basis.

In late 1993, Rik Faith, Doug Hoffman, and Kevin Martin began releasing the first public betas of the BOGUS Linux distribution. BOGUS was notable for the package management system (pms) software that was used with it for installation and uninstallation of all software on an application-by-application basis. Shortly thereafter, in the summer of 1994, the first public betas of Red Hat Commercial Linux were released. Red Hat initially used Red Hat Software Program Packages (RPP) as the basis of its Linux distribution. Like pms, RPP was a system-management tool that allowed for easy installation and uninstallation of applications. In late 1993, Ian Murdock founded the Debian Gnu/Linux distribution. He began seriously developing its dpkg application-management software by the summer of 1994. Like pms and RPP, dpkg made it possible to manage each application on the system.

RPM Design Goals

All of these early system-management tools took a similar approach. They provided the capability to install an entire application with a single command, to track the files it put on the system, and to remove those files by using another single command. As the preponderance of multiple early tools suggests, this approach to system management was popular. All of these early tools, however, had numerous technical or practical deficiencies. Some tools were designed only for Linux on 32-bit Intel-compatible hardware, even though Linux by this point was already running on other CPUs in addition to the IA32 family. As Linux was spreading to multiple architectures, a package-management system that could produce packages for multiple architectures was needed. Other tools had technical flaws in how they prepared packages, making it difficult to verify that packages had been prepared correctly or to see exactly how the software was prepared.

Because of these concerns, after their initial releases of RPP-based distributions, Red Hat looked closely at both their own RPP software and other software such as BOGUS's pms software. Developers at Red Hat, particularly Marc Ewing and Erik Troan, set out to develop what they initially called the Red Hat Package Manager (RPM). Based on experiences with earlier Linux packaging software and knowledge about packaging tools used on other platforms, Red Hat had several design goals in mind when they developed RPM. These design points include the following features:

- ◆ Ease of use
- ◆ Package-oriented focus
- ◆ Upgradability of packages
- ◆ Tracking of package interdependencies
- ◆ Query capabilities
- ◆ Verification
- ◆ Support for multiple architectures
- ◆ Use of pristine sources

The following sections demonstrate how Red Hat incorporated each of these design goals into RPM.

Ease of use

Perhaps the primary design goal for RPM is that it must be easy to use. Manual software installation has been the primary method of putting software onto Unix boxes for over 30 years now and has worked very well for those three decades. To offer a compelling reason to use the new software, Red Hat's RPM must be significantly easier to use than other Linux package-management tools. For that reason, most tasks that can be handled using RPM were designed to be carried out via a single command. For example, software installation using RPM requires a single command (`rpm -i software_package`), while manual software installation using older manual methods typically requires at least six steps to complete the same task:

1. `tar zxf software_package`

2. `cd software_package`

   3. `./configure`

   4. `make`

   5. `su`

   6. `make install`

Similarly, removal of applications installed using RPM requires a single command (`rpm -e software_package`); manual removal of an installed application requires that each file associated with that application be manually deleted.

Package-oriented focus

Like its predecessors, RPM is intended to operate on a package level. Rather than operating on a single-file basis (as when you manually install software using Unix command-line tools like `mv` and `cp`) or on an entire system basis (as with many PC operating systems, which provide the ability to upgrade entire releases but not to upgrade individual components), RPM provides software that can manage hundreds or thousands of packages.

Each package is a discrete bundle of related files and associated documentation and configuration information; typically, each package is a separate application. By focusing on the package as the managed unit, RPM makes installation and deletion of applications extremely straightforward.

Package upgradability

In addition to its package-oriented focus, RPM is designed to support upgrading packages. Once an application has been installed from an RPM package, a newer version of the same application can be installed using RPM. Doing so upgrades the existing application, removing its old files and replacing them with new files. In addition, however, RPM takes care to preserve any customizations that have been made to that application. The Apache Web server application, for example, is commonly installed on Linux machines that need the ability to serve Web pages.

Apache's configuration information, which specifies things such as which files on the system should be made available as Web pages and who should be able to access those Web pages, is stored in a text file, typically /etc/httpd/conf/httpd.conf. Suppose Apache has been installed using RPM and that you have then customized httpd.conf to specify its configuration. If you upgrade Apache using RPM, as part of the upgrade procedure, the RPM application will take precautions to preserve the customizations you have made to the Apache configuration. In contrast, manual upgrades of applications often overwrite any existing configuration files, losing all site customizations the system administrator has made.

Package interdependencies

Software that manages the applications installed on the system on an application level (such as RPM) does have one potential drawback in comparison with system-wide software management systems (such as PC operating systems like Microsoft's Windows or IBM's OS/2, which allow the entire system to be upgraded but do not generally allow individual components to be upgraded, added, or removed). Software applications often have interdependencies; some applications work only when other applications are installed.

The Postfix and Sendmail mail transfer agent (MTA) applications that are commonly used on Linux boxes to serve e-mail, for example, can both be configured to require users to authenticate themselves (by submitting a correct user name and password) successfully before they can use the e-mail server. This feature is often used to prevent unauthorized access to the e-mail server, preventing unscrupulous advertisers from using the server as a tool to send unsolicited commercial e-mail (or UCE, popularly known as spam). For this optional feature of Postfix and Sendmail to work, however, additional software must be installed. Both applications use another application, Cyrus SASL, which provides the Simple Authentication and Security Layer (SASL) software that Postfix or Sendmail can use to check user names and passwords. In other words, Postfix and Sendmail depend on Cyrus SASL.

For system-wide software management systems, logical interdependencies between system components such as these are easy to track. All required components are included as part of the system, and upgrading the system upgrades all these components, ensuring that all can still interoperate. On Microsoft Windows 2000, IIS (the application used on Windows to serve Web pages) requires several other applications such as EventLog (the Windows application that records system events, much like the Linux syslogd and klogd software) to be present. Since Windows is managed on a system level, not a package level, this dependency is guaranteed to be satisfied. On Linux systems using RPM, however, the situation is different. On Linux, for example, the Postfix application requires the syslogd application, which records system events. However, RPM provides the flexibility to install some applications but not install others or to uninstall others later. When you install Postfix, you have no guarantee that syslogd is already installed. If syslogd is not installed, Postfix will not work correctly.

To avoid problems, Red Hat developers realized that RPMs must also track dependency information about what software they require for correct functionality, and that the RPM install and uninstall applications must use this dependency information. Because of dependencies, installing Postfix using RPM on a system without syslogd installed generates a warning that syslogd must also be installed. Similarly, attempting to uninstall syslogd from a system that already has Postfix installed generates a warning that installed applications require the software that is being deleted. These warnings can be overridden if necessary, but by default RPM enforces these dependencies (refusing, for example, to let you uninstall syslogd without also uninstalling applications that require it, such as Postfix), preventing you from accidentally breaking applications by inadvertently uninstalling other software that they require to operate.

Query capabilities

As part of its implementation, the RPM software maintains a database on the system of all packages that have been installed, and documenting which files those packages have installed on the system. RPM is designed to be queried easily, making it possible for you to search this database to determine what applications have been installed on the system and to see which packages have supplied each file on the system. This feature makes RPM-based systems extremely easy to use, since a single RPM command can be used to view all installed applications on the system.

Package verification

RPM also maintains a variety of information about each installed file in this system database, such as what permissions each file should have and what size each file should be. Red Hat developers designed this database to be useful for software verification. Over time, installed software will fail to work for reasons as mundane as the system administrator setting incorrect permissions on files or as exotic as nuclear decay of one of the computer's atoms releasing an alpha particle that can affect the computer's memory, corrupting that bit of memory and causing errors. Although RPM cannot prevent all errors that cause installed software to fail (obviously, there's not a single thing any software can do to prevent nuclear decay), it can be used to eliminate common errors. When an application fails, you can use the RPM database to make sure that all files associated with that application still have correct Unix file permissions and that no files associated with that application have become altered or corrupted.

Multiple architectures

Most of the RPM design goals mentioned so far are intended primarily to ease the life of system administrators and others who regularly install, remove, and upgrade applications or who need to see what is installed or verify that installed applications have been installed correctly. Some of the design goals for RPM are intended primarily not for those sorts of users of RPM but for users who must prepare software to be installed using RPM.

One of the major limitations of early Linux package management utilities was that they could produce packages suitable only for installation on one type of computer: those that used 32-bit Intel-compatible CPUs. By 1994, Linux was beginning to support other CPUs in addition to the originally supported Intel CPUs. (Initially, Digital's Alpha processor and Motorola's 68000 series of processors were among the first additional CPUs that Linux supported. These days, Linux supports dozens of CPU architectures.) This posed a problem for distribution developers such as Red Hat and Debian and for application vendors who desired to package their software for use on Linux. Because the available packaging methods could not produce packages for multiple architectures, packagers making software for multiple CPUs had to do extra work to prepare their packages.

Furthermore, once the packagers had prepared packages, no method was available to indicate the architecture the packages targeted, making it difficult for end users to know on which machine types they could install the packages.

Red Hat decided to overcome these limitations by incorporating architecture support into RPM, adding features so that the basic setup a packager performs to create a package could be leveraged to produce packages that would run on various CPUs, and so that end users could look at a package and immediately identify for which types of systems it was intended.

Pristine sources

The BOGUS distribution's pms packaging system introduced the use of pristine source code to prepare packages. With Red Hat's early RPP package system and other similar early efforts, software packagers would compile software manually, then run commands to produce a package of that compiled software. Any changes made to the application's original source code were not recorded and would have to be recreated by the next person to package that software. Furthermore, end users wanting to know what changes had been made to the software they were running had no method of accessing that information.

With RPM, Red Hat developed a package system that produced two types of packages: binary and source. *Binary packages* are compiled software that can be installed and used. *Source packages* contain the source code for that software, along with a file documenting how that source code must be compiled to produce that binary package. This feature is probably the single most significant difference between modern Linux packaging software (such as RPM) and the packaging software used on other systems (such as the pkg format that commercial Unix systems use). Source packaging makes the job of software packager easier, since packagers can use old source packages as a reference when preparing new versions of those packages. Source packages are also convenient for the end user, because they make it easily possible to change options with which that software was compiled and to produce a new binary package that supports the features the user needs.

RPM Terminology

When working with RPM, understanding the package concept is key. RPM packages are provided as compressed archive files that contain one or more files, as well as instructions specifying installation information about those files, including the ownerships and permissions that should be applied to each file during installation. The instructions can also contain scripts to be run after installation or before uninstallation. These package files are extremely convenient; they provide a single file that can be easily transferred between machines for installation rather than having to transfer each file to be installed.

To help in installation and management, all package files are labeled with highly identifiable names. Red Hat Linux package files have four-part names, which typically look something like:

```
kernel-smp-2.4.18-3.athlon.rpm
kernel-smp-2.4.18-3.i586.rpm
kernel-smp-2.4.18-3.i686.rpm
kernel-source-2.4.18-3.i386.rpm
rootfiles-7.2-1.noarch.rpm
```

Here, the four parts of each name are separated from each other by dashes or periods. The structure of the package file name is

`name-version-release.architecture.rpm`

The *name* identifies what software is contained within the archive file. Typically, this is a name of an application or package that the archive installs on the system. For example, `kernel-smp` can be installed to provide a very important application, the SMP (symmetric multiprocessing, meaning it supports systems with more than one CPU in them) version of the Linux kernel, on the system. Sometimes, rather than an application, the software is a collection of other files needed on the system. The `rootfiles` package, for example, is not an application but is a collection of basic environmental configuration files for the root user's account (such as /root/ .bashrc, the root user's Bash configuration file) that provides a usable, preconfigured working environment for the root user on Red Hat Linux systems.

The second field in every Red Hat Linux package file's name is the *version* field. This field identifies the version number of the software that is contained in the package file. For example, `kernel-smp-2.4.18` indicates the RPM holds the 2.4.18 release of the SMP version of the Linux kernel, and `rootfiles-7.2` is the 7.2 release of the rootfiles configuration files.

Every Red Hat Linux package file name also has a third component: the *release* field. This field identifies which release of that version of the software the package file contains. Package files contain both software and instructions about how to install that software. As packages of a particular version of software are being prepared, mistakes are sometimes made in these instruction files, or bugs are sometimes fixed within a software version; more recent package files of that software version need to be prepared that correct the problem. The `-1` in the `rootfiles-7.2-1` package shows this is the first release of the 7.2 version of the rootfiles software. The packager of rootfiles version 7.2 got everything right on the first try and had no need to prepare more than one release. The `-3` in the `kernel-smp-2.4.18-3` package, on the other hand, is the third release of the 2.4.18 version of the SMP-capable Linux kernel. This release incorporates new patches to fix bugs present in older releases of the 2.4.18 version of the Linux SMP kernel. The software packager increased the release number so that end users could distinguish the more recent, bug-fixed package file from the older, less bug-free package file.

The final field in Red Hat Linux package file names is the *architecture,* which identifies the system types for which the package file is appropriate. For example, the `kernel-smp-2.4.18-3.athlon` package is intended for use on machines with an AMD Athlon CPU, and `kernel-smp-2.4.18-3.i586` is intended for use on machines with an i586 (Pentium-class) CPU or better. An architecture name of `noarch` indicates this is a special architecture such that the files in the package work on any architecture. Typically, this is because the files are all interpreted scripts, not binary executables, or are documentation.

RPM supports various architectures. Table 2-1 presents the architectures available for different platforms as of RPM version 4.1.

TABLE 2-1 SUPPORTED ARCHITECTURES

Platform	Architectures
Intel compatible 32-bit	i386, i486, i586, i686, athlon
Intel compatible 64-bit	ia64
HPAlpha (formerly Digital, Compaq)	alpha, alphaev5, alphaev56, alphapca56, alphaev6, alphaev67
Sparc/Ultra Sparc (Sun)	sparc, sparcv9, sparc64
ARM	armv3l, armv4b, armv4l
MIPS	mips, mipsel
Power PC	ppc, ppciseries, ppcpseries, ppc64
Motorola 68000 series	m68k, m68kmint
SGI MIPS	Sgi
IBM RS6000	rs6000
IBM S/390	i370, s390x, s390
Platform independent	noarch

When choosing an appropriate architecture for your machine, be aware that more recent architectures typically run software that targets older architectures within the same family; the reverse, however, is not true. For example, within the 32-bit Intel-compatible architectures, a 686-class (Pentium II / III / IV) machine runs files within i386, i486, i586, and i686 RPM package files, but a 386-class (80386) machine runs files within i386 RPM package files only.

Similarly, for the Alpha architecture, more recent Alpha EV68 CPUs can run programs from RPM package files with alphaev67, alphaev6, alphaev56, alphaev5, and alpha architectures, but an older Alpha EV56 machine can run programs from RPM package files with alpha, alphaev5, or alphaev56 architectures only.

Notice that the four fields in RPM package file names are separated from each other by punctuation, either a dash (-) or a period (.). Periods and dashes, however, are also allowed within fields. 7.2 is a valid version number, just as kernel-source is a valid software name. Finally, keep in mind that all RPM package files use an .rpm file-name extension to denote that they are RPMs.

Once installed, package names are slightly different from package file names. Package files, which can be downloaded from the Internet, copied off of CDs, and otherwise easily transferred between machines, always have names that looks like *name-version-release.architecture*.rpm. Installed packages, however, have names that look like *name-version-release*. Once installed, packages are referred to without the architecture field and the .rpm extension. Furthermore, installed packages consist of lots of files, not a single RPM file. For example, the package file kernel-smp-2.4.18-3.i686.rpm after installation is referred to as kernel-smp-2.4.18-3. To simplify usage even further, installed packages can be referred to by their name field only, so this file would become simply `kernel-smp`.

Once installed, the name of the package does not have to be the same as the name portion of the original package file. By convention though, the package name matches the name, version, and release part of the file name.

Usage of the name field by itself to name packages assumes that multiple versions or releases of that particular software are not installed. However, it is in some cases necessary to install different versions or releases of the same package. My desktop at home is a (by now, relatively old) dual Pentium-II system, so it uses an SMP-capable Linux kernel. On it, I have the following Linux SMP kernels installed:

```
$ rpm -q kernel-smp
kernel-smp-2.4.18-4
kernel-smp-2.4.18-3
kernel-smp-2.5.21-4
$
```

This example uses the `rpm -q` command to query for all installed versions of the given package, `kernel-smp`.

Chapter 5 covers querying the RPM database in depth.

I have two different package file releases (release 3 and release 4) of the 2.4.18 version of the Linux kernel, and I have a development kernel, version 2.5.21, installed. On this system, since I have multiple packages installed of the `kernel-smp` software, I have to use the full package name (such as `kernel-smp-2.4.18-4`) whenever I want to work with my installed `kernel-smp` packages.

Summary

The RPM system wasn't created to solve some theoretical problem. Instead, it is the result of years of hard-won practical experience in trying to manage systems with a large number of applications. RPM builds upon older systems that were created to solve some of the problems faced by system administrators. RPM goes further, though, and tries to provide a complete package-management solution. This includes the ability to deal with wrinkles that Linux faces but that many other operating systems do not need to address.

For example, most other operating systems don't support more than one or two processor architectures. Sun's Solaris, for example, supports only the SPARC and Intel architectures. Linux supports these and more. Most other operating systems also don't include nearly so many applications. From the OpenOffice.org office suite to the Apache Web server, Linux distributions are literally packed with applications. As a final point, most other operating systems provide mostly closed-source applications. Linux, on the other hand, includes thousands of open-source applications.

From the perspective of the organizations making Linux distributions, these wrinkles make Linux harder to manage. Luckily for end users, the solution to these problems helps make the RPM system better able to manage user systems:

- The RPM system tags each package with the processor architecture and allows for multiple versions of the same package to be installed on the same system. RPM also packs all the files in a package into one file, called an RPM file, for easy transfer to other systems.

- Most RPM operations such as installing or removing packages require only a single command to run.

- The RPM system supports building RPM packages from a pristine set of sources. This means you can reproduce the commands required to build an application, improving quality.

This chapter introduced the RPM system and the history behind it. The next chapter delves into the RPM basics, including files, database, and commands.

Chapter 3

RPM Overview

IN THIS CHAPTER

- ◆ Understanding the package file
- ◆ Querying the RPM database
- ◆ Running RPM commands

WORKING WITH RPM PACKAGES, files, commands, and databases can be complicated. There are thousands of files, for hundreds if not thousands of packages, installed on your system. You need some way to manage it all. The RPM system can help you do that.

This chapter provides an overview of the components that make up the RPM system for package management: package files, databases, and RPM commands.

Understanding the Package File

RPM provides for installing, upgrading and removing packages. Typically, each package is an application and all the necessary files associated with that application. For example, the Apache Web server comes with a number of configuration files, a large set of documentation files, and the Apache server itself. All of this fits into one RPM package.

One of the main advantages of the RPM system is that each .rpm file holds a complete package. For example, the following file holds the xcopilot package:

```
xcopilot-0.6.6-3.i386.rpm
```

Based on the naming conventions discussed in Chapter 2, this package represents xcopilot package, version 0.6.6, third build of an RPM package, for i386 (Intel) architecture systems.

With a single command, you can copy an .rpm file to another Linux system and install it, getting the complete contents of the package, or you can use other commands to remove or update the package.

RPM file format

RPM files hold a number of tagged data items and a payload, the files to install on your system. The tagged data items describe the package and can contain optional features. For example, the NAME tag holds the package name. The optional PRE tag holds a pre-installation script, a script that the rpm command runs prior to installing the files in the package payload.

Under the covers, RPM package files contain four sections. The first is a leading identification area that marks the file as an RPM package (created with a particular version of the RPM system). The remaining sections are the *signature*, the tagged data (called the *header*), and the *payload*. Each of these sections has important information about the package, although the payload section contains the actual content of the package.

◆ **The signature** appears after the lead or identifier section, which marks the file as an RPM file. Like your signature when you sign a check, the RPM signature helps verify the integrity of the package. No, the signature doesn't check for bugs in software applications. Instead, it ensures that you have downloaded a valid RPM archive.

The signature works by performing a mathematical function on the header and archive sections of the file. The mathematical function can be an encryption process, such as PGP (Pretty Good Privacy), or a message digest in MD5 format.

◆ **The header** contains zero or more tagged blocks of data that pertain to the package. The header contains information such as copyright messages, version numbers, and package summaries.

◆ **The payload** section contains the actual files used in the package. These files are installed when you install the package. To save space, data in the archive section is compressed in GNU gzip format.

Once uncompressed, the data is in cpio format, which is how the rpm2cpio command (introduced in the "Other RPM commands" section later in this chapter) can do its work.

Binary RPMs and Source RPMs

There are two main types of RPM packages: binary (or applications) and source. A binary RPM has been compiled for a particular architecture. For example, the Apache Web server compiled for an Intel Pentium, or i586, architecture won't work on a Sharp Zaurus, which runs an Intel ARM processor. To run on both systems, you would need two separate packages: one for the Pentium i586 and one for the ARM.

In addition to binary RPMs, you can get source code RPMs. These RPMs are packages that provide the source code for other packages. Sounds kind of circular, doesn't it?

Binary RPMs

Binary RPMs hold complete applications or libraries of functions compiled for a particular architecture. Most binary RPMs contain complete applications, such as the Apache Web server or the AbiWord word processor. These application binary RPMs usually depend on a number of system libraries which are, in turn, also provided by binary RPMs.

Chapter 8 covers a number of locations where you can find RPM applications galore. Your Linux installation CDs are also a great source for applications. Most Linux distributions come with more applications than you can imagine using.

Although most binary RPMs are complete applications, others provide libraries. For example, the Simple DirectMedia Layer library (SDL), which provides really cool graphics for many games, can be packaged as an RPM file. A number of programs, mostly games, use this library for enhanced multimedia such as rich graphics. RPMs that provide libraries allow multiple applications to share the same library. Typically, the libraries are packaged into separate RPMs from the applications.

In addition to binary RPMs that hold applications or libraries compiled for a particular architecture, RPM supports the concept of platform-independent binary RPMs. These platform-independent RPMs (called *noarch* as a short form of "no architecture" dependencies) provide applications or libraries that are not dependent on any platform. Applications written in Perl, Python, or other scripting languages often do not depend on code compiled for a particular architecture. In addition, compiled Java applications are usually free of platform dependencies.

Source RPMs

The xcopilot package, mentioned previously, contains the xcopilot application used for synchronization with Palm handheld devices. The source code used to create this application is stored in an xcopilot source RPM, for example:

```
xcopilot-0.6.6-3.src.rpm
```

By convention, source RPMs have a file name ending in .src.rpm. Source RPMs should contain all the commands, usually in scripts, necessary to recreate the binary RPM. Having a source RPM means that you can recreate the binary RPM at any time. This is a very important goal of the RPM system.

Source RPMs have nothing to do with open-source software licenses. Linux is famous for being an open-source operating system. In RPM terms, that means the source code for the Linux kernel and most Linux applications are freely available as source RPMs. But you can also make source RPMs for proprietary programs. The key issue is that you are unlikely to distribute the source RPMs for proprietary packages.

Furthermore, a number of open-source applications are not available as source RPMs. That's a shame, since source RPMs would make these applications easier to install.

While source RPMs hold the commands necessary to create the binary RPM, there may be differences in your Linux environment that would result in rebuilding a binary RPM that is different from the original binary RPM. For example, the compile scripts for some packages may add in optional code depending on which libraries or which versions of libraries are found on your system. Chapter 14 covers many issues in creating RPMs, and Chapters 19 and 20 cover issues related to other versions of Linux and other operating systems, respectively. If you follow the guidelines when making your own RPMs, you should produce source RPMs that reproduce binary RPMs as consistently as possible.

Querying the RPM Database

The RPM database holds information about all the RPM packages installed on your system. You can use this database to query what is installed, to help determine if you have the latest versions of software, and to verify that your system is properly set up, at least from a packaging point of view.

The RPM database itself is stored in the directory /var/lib/rpm, and should contain files like the following:

```
Basenames
Conflictname
__db.001
__db.002
__db.003
Dirnames
Filemd5s
Group
```

```
Installtid
Name
Packages
Providename
Provideversion
Pubkeys
Requirename
Requireversion
Sha1header
Sigmd5
Triggername
```

Chapter 5 covers the database in more detail.

These files make up the RPM database. The file __db.001 and similar files are lock files used by the RPM system. The other files are databases in Berkeley DB format. The most important file is Packages. The Packages file contains the header tag information for each package indexed by an index number for each package. This number slowly grows with time.

The other files, such as Name, Providename, and Group, exist to speed access to particular types of information. Treat your RPM database with care. Back up the files, especially after upgrading, installing, or removing packages.

Only the Packages file is essential. You can recreate the rest of the files using the rpm --rebuilddb command, introduced in Chapter 5.

Running RPM Commands

The primary RPM command is simply rpm. One of the original goals of the RPM system is providing ease of use. In support of this goal, just about everything you want to do with the RPM system can be done with this one command. For most usage, the command-line parameters to the rpm command determine the actions it should take.

Working with the rpm command

The `rpm` command performs the most common package-management functions, along with a host of uncommon functions as well. Table 3-1 lists the main operations you can perform with the `rpm` command and the command-line options to specify the given operations.

TABLE 3-1 THE MAIN RPM OPERATIONS

Operation	Short Option	Long Option
Upgrade/install	-U	--upgrade
Install	-I	--install
Remove	-e	--erase
Query	-q	--query
Verify	-V	--verify
Check signature	-K	--checksig
Freshen (upgrade) already-installed package	-F	--freshen
Initialize database	*None*	--initdb
Rebuild database	*None*	--rebuilddb

Using Table 3-1 as a guide, you can explore the options to the `rpm` command. To install or upgrade a package, use the -U command-line option:

```
# rpm -U filename.rpm
```

For example, to install the xcopilot RPM used as an example in this chapter, run the following command:

```
# rpm -U xcopilot-0.6.6-3.i386.rpm
```

To get extra feedback, you can use a command like the following, with the -h and -v options in conjunction with the -U option:

```
# rpm -Uhv xcopilot-0.6.6-3.i386.rpm
```

When you run this command you will see more output than the default, which is no output unless there are errors. With the -h option, the rpm command will print a series of hash marks, #, to provide feedback that the command is still running. With the -v option, the rpm command provides more verbose messages.

The most common command to install a package is:

`# rpm -Uhv package_file.rpm`

This command upgrades a package with extra output. If the package has not been installed, this command installs the package. See Chapter 4 for more on upgrading and installing.

To remove a package (called *erase* in RPM terminology), use the -e command-line option:

`# rpm -e package_name`

Notice that you install a package file using the file name that ends in .rpm, but uninstall or erase a package without the .rpm extension. This is because you install RPM files, but once installed, you work with the installed packages. The file name and the package name do not have to correspond, but typically (and sanely) they have the same base name.

To list every RPM package installed on your system, use a command like the following.

`$ rpm -qa`

Expect to wait while this command completes. Most Linux systems have numerous packages installed, which will result in many lines of output. To better see the output, you can pipe this command to the more command, as shown following:

`rpm -qa | more`

You will then see the package listing one screen at a time.

Appendix A lists all the options for the rpm command.

Other RPM commands

In addition to rpm, the RPM system includes a few more commands, including rpm
-build and rpm2cpio.

The rpmbuild command helps build RPM packages. I describe its usage in depth
in Part II of this book.

The rpm2cpio command exports an RPM package file into the format that the
cpio command expects. The cpio command works with many tape-backup packages. You can also take advantage of the fact that cpio can list the individual files
in a cpio archive or extract files. To list the files in an RPM package, use a command
like the following:

```
$ rpm2cpio package_file.rpm | cpio -t
```

For example, the following command lists all the files in the xcopilot package:

```
$ rpm2cpio xcopilot-0.6.6-3.i386.rpm | cpio -t
/etc/X11/applink/Applications/xcopilot.desktop
usr/bin/xcopilot
usr/doc/xcopilot-0.6.6
usr/doc/xcopilot-0.6.6/README
usr/include/X11/pixmaps/xcopilot.xpm
usr/include/X11/pixmaps/xcopilot2.xpm
3120 blocks
```

The rpm2cpio command can also help if you want to extract a single file from
the RPM package, using the cpio -ivd command-line options, as follows:

```
$ rpm2cpio xcopilot-0.6.6-3.i386.rpm | cpio -ivd usr/doc/xcopilot-0.6.6/README
```

This command will output local usr/doc/xcopilot-0.6.6 subdirectories and the
README file located under usr/doc/xcopilot-0.6.6.

The -i option tells cpio to extract files. The -d option tells cpio to make any
local subdirectories as needed (usr/doc/xcopilot-0.6.6, in this example), and the -v
option asks cpio to politely output verbose messages about what it does. Of course,
verbose is in the eye of the beholder; with many Unix and Linux commands, verbose output is still somewhat terse.

Summary

The RPM files, the RPM database, and the RPM commands are the primary components that make up the RPM system. This chapter introduces you to the format and types of RPM files, the importance of maintaining the database, and the basic `rpm` command.

The next chapter covers the most frequently used RPM commands. These commands allow you to install, uninstall, and update RPM packages.

Chapter 4

Using RPM

IN THIS CHAPTER

- ◆ Installing and upgrading software
- ◆ Removing software

THIS CHAPTER COVERS THE most common uses for RPM: installing, removing, and upgrading software. These are the most frequently used RPM commands.

The RPM system includes the options you might expect, such as installing a package, but there's a lot more you can do. For example, you can install packages from remote sites using HTTP or FTP to download the package to install. There are quite a few other rpm options you can use to get information and feedback on installation, for example.

The rpm Command

Just about everything you do with RPM requires the rpm command. As a nice added benefit, just about everything you do with RPM requires a single invocation of the rpm command. That means common tasks such as installing and removing software can be done quickly and efficiently. The basics of the rpm command are not very hard, and you can perform the basic tasks within a few minutes of reading this chapter.

Upgrading and Installing Software

To install software, you need something to install. Typically, this is a file packaged as RPM, using a file-name extension of *.rpm*. Of course, this isn't required, but just about every RPM package is stored in a file with a *.rpm* extension. For example, the following file holds an RPM package, ready to be installed:

```
jikes-1.16-1.i386.rpm
```

This package holds an application named *jikes* (a Java language compiler application). From the discussion in the last two chapters, you should be able to determine the version of the program this RPM holds and which release of the RPM package this represents.

Other RPMs hold sources, the program source codes used to create an application or programming library. For example, the following file holds a source RPM:

```
jikes-1.16-1.src.rpm
```

The *src* in the package name is short for source. This file-naming convention is not required, but is used by just about all source code packages. (Following conventions helps other administrators know what to expect.)

Chapters 9 and 12 cover building RPMs from source RPMs.

The rpm command provides three main operations for upgrading and installing packages:

An *upgrade* operation means installing a new version of a package and removing all previous versions of the same package. If you have not installed a package previously, the upgrade operation will install the package.

A *freshen* operation means to install a new version of a package only if you have already installed another version of the package.

An *install* operation installs a package for the first time. It also, through special command-line parameters, allows you to install multiple versions of a package, usually not what you want. So, in the vast majority of cases, you want to run the upgrade operation for all package installations.

The following sections cover the command-line options that apply to these operations.

Upgrading with the rpm command

Almost all installation steps use the rpm command with the -U option, short for upgrade, as introduced in Chapter 3. The basic syntax is:

```
rpm -U package_name
```

For example:

```
rpm -U jikes-1.16-1.i386.rpm
```

You can also use the --upgrade long option in place of -U.

Unless something goes wrong, you won't see any response except for the shell prompt ready for your next command. Options for the `rpm` command, covered shortly, present positive feedback that the package has been installed.

The `rpm` command may print out warnings, such as the one following:

```
warning: pyxf86config-0.3.1-2.i386.rpm: Header V3 DSA
signature: NOKEY, key ID 897da07a
```

This warning comes from the fact that the package was not signed. Chapter 12 covers signing packages. In most cases, warnings such as this one are not that serious. Errors, though, should be treated seriously.

Just about every package you want to upgrade or install requires root, or super user, permissions. That's because most Linux application RPMs hold files that must be installed in a protected directory such as /usr/bin. In addition, RPM requires root access to modify the RPM database. Even if you could modify the system directories such as /usr/bin, you must also be able to modify the RPM database to successfully install or remove packages.

Checking That the Package Is Installed

Use the `rpm -q` command to quickly verify a package has been installed. To verify, you need to use the name of the installed package, *not* the name of the RPM file. You can also use a partial package name, such as *jikes* in this case. For example:

```
rpm -q jikes
```

When you run this command, you should see a response like the following:

```
jikes-1.16-1
```

The response shows that the package named jikes-1.16-1 has been installed. This package name corresponds to the RPM file used in the preceding installation example.

The `rpm -q` command just asks the RPM database if the package has been installed. There may be other issues with the package that this command won't show. For now, though, the `rpm -q` command verifies that package has been installed.

If the package has been not installed, you will see a message similar to the following:

```
package jikes is not installed
```

Getting Feedback During Installation and upgrades

The -h option to the rpm command prints out# signs, also called hash marks (hence the -h). These hash marks provide some confirmation that the rpm command is still running. This is important, since large packages may take a long time to install or upgrade. Run this command like the following:

```
rpm -Uh jikes-1.16-1.i386.rpm
```

You'll see this output:

```
############################################# [100%]
############################################# [100%]
```

The hash marks are printed one at a time as the command does its work. If the package was not created properly, you may see warnings like the following:

```
############################################# [100%]
warning: user cabbey does not exist - using root
warning: user cabbey does not exist - using root
warning: user cabbey does not exist - using root
############################################# [100%]
```

 You can install a package more than once. The rpm command won't complain. The upgrade operation, though, will remove all other versions of a package. This is one more reason to use the -U upgrade option.

In addition to hash marks, you can get more verbose output from the tight-lipped rpm command. The -v option to the rpm command tells the command to print out verbose information as the command runs. Remember, though, that *verbose* is used in the traditional Unix and Linux meaning, which is normally not all that verbose. In the Unix/Linux context, verbose usually means slightly more than nothing. The syntax for the command follows:

```
rpm -Uhv jikes-1.16-1.i386.rpm
```

With the -v command-line option, you will see output more like the following:

```
Preparing...              ############################################# [100%]
   1:jikes                 ############################################# [100%]
```

The most common command to install a package is

`rpm -Uhv package_file.rpm`

That is, upgrade with verbose output and hashes.

To get extra verbose information, use the `-vv` command-line option. Think of this as doubly verbose. Usually, though, this extra information has no meaning unless you are debugging an RPM package you are building. See the chapters in Part II on Creating RPMs for more on how to build RPM packages.

A double-verbose command uses much the same syntax as shown previously:

```
rpm -Uhvv jikes-1.16-1.i386.rpm
```

With the double-verbose option, the output appears as follows:

```
D: ============== jikes-1.16-1.i386.rpm
D: Expected size:        702988 = lead(96)+sigs(100)+pad(4)+data(702788)
D:   Actual size:        702988
D: jikes-1.16-1.i386.rpm: MD5 digest: OK (2dba32192eca23eb480d1d02a9b6c022)
D:      added binary package [0]
D: found 0 source and 1 binary packages
D: opening  db environment /var/lib/rpm/Packages joinenv
D: opening  db index       /var/lib/rpm/Packages rdonly mode=0x0
D: locked   db index       /var/lib/rpm/Packages
D: ========== +++ jikes-1.16-1
D: opening  db index       /var/lib/rpm/Depends create mode=0x0
D:   Requires: rpmlib(PayloadFilesHavePrefix) <= 4.0-1      YES (rpmlib
provides)
D: opening  db index       /var/lib/rpm/Providename rdonly mode=0x0
D: opening  db index       /var/lib/rpm/Pubkeys rdonly mode=0x0
D:   read h#       9 Header V3 DSA signature: NOKEY, key ID 897da07a
D:   Requires: ld-linux.so.2                                YES (db provides)
D:   read h#       9 Header V3 DSA signature: NOKEY, key ID 897da07a
D:   Requires: libc.so.6                                    YES (db provides)
D:   read h#       9 Header V3 DSA signature: NOKEY, key ID 897da07a
D:   Requires: libm.so.6                                    YES (db provides)
D:   read h#     633 Header V3 DSA signature: NOKEY, key ID 897da07a
D:   Requires: libstdc++-libc6.2-2.so.3                     YES (db provides)
D:   read h#       9 Header V3 DSA signature: NOKEY, key ID 897da07a
D:   Requires: libc.so.6(GLIBC_2.0)                         YES (db provides)
D:   read h#       9 Header V3 DSA signature: NOKEY, key ID 897da07a
D:   Requires: libc.so.6(GLIBC_2.1)                         YES (db provides)
```

```
D:   read h#      9 Header V3 DSA signature: NOKEY, key ID 897da07a
D:   Requires: libc.so.6(GLIBC_2.1.3)                      YES (db provides)
D:   Requires: rpmlib(CompressedFileNames) <= 3.0.4-1      YES (rpmlib
provides)
D: closed    db index     /var/lib/rpm/Pubkeys
D: closed    db index     /var/lib/rpm/Depends
D: closed    db index     /var/lib/rpm/Providename
D: closed    db index     /var/lib/rpm/Packages
D: closed    db environment /var/lib/rpm/Packages
D: ========== recording tsort relations
D: ========== tsorting packages (order, #predecessors, #succesors, tree,
depth)D:    0    0    0    0    0 +jikes-1.16-1
D: installing binary packages
D: opening    db environment /var/lib/rpm/Packages joinenv
D: opening   db index     /var/lib/rpm/Packages create mode=0x42
D: getting list of mounted filesystems
D: sanity checking 1 elments
D: opening   db index     /var/lib/rpm/Name create mode=0x42
D:   read h#     707 Header sanity check: OK
D: computing 3 file fingerprints
Preparing...                D: computing file dispositions
D: opening   db index     /var/lib/rpm/Basenames create mode=0x42
######################################### [100%]
        package jikes-1.16-1 is already installed
D: closed    db index     /var/lib/rpm/Basenames
D: closed    db index     /var/lib/rpm/Name
D: closed    db index     /var/lib/rpm/Packages
D: closed    db environment /var/lib/rpm/Packages
```

 Although most Unix and Linux applications use a single minus sign for command-line options, such as rpm -U, many programs use two minus signs to indicate longer option names. For example, with the rpm command, -U and --upgrade are treated the same. You can use the short option, -U, or the long option, --upgrade.

There are long options for virtually every short option. There are also long options that are rarely used, for which there are no short options.

One rarely used feedback option is --percent. The --percent option prints out decimal numbers that show the percentage completed as the rpm command executes. This option is most useful if you wrap the rpm command within some other command, such as a graphical user interface created from a Perl, Python, or Tcl/Tk script.

The basic syntax is:

```
rpm -U --percent jikes-1.16-1.i386.rpm
```

When you run this command, you see output like the following:

```
%% 0.000000
%% 2.661902
%% 5.318614
%% 10.632039
%% 15.945465
%% 18.602177
%% 23.915603
%% 29.229028
%% 34.542453
%% 39.855879
%% 45.169304
%% 50.482729
%% 53.139442
%% 55.796154
%% 61.109580
%% 66.423005
%% 71.736430
%% 74.393143
%% 79.706568
%% 82.363281
%% 87.676706
%% 90.333419
%% 95.646844
%% 98.303557
%% 99.422736
%% 99.910411
%% 99.994892
%% 100.000000
```

These decimal numbers output by the `--percent` option are really meant to be input into another program, perhaps a program that shows a graphical progress meter. Each number output then updates the meter.

Don't trust the numbers too much. Claiming the package is 53.139442 per-cent installed just asks the user to be skeptical that it is exactly that far.

The Installation Task In Detail

You can use the `rpm -U` command or the `rpm -i` command to install a package. When the `rpm` command installs a package, it goes through a number of steps:

♦ Checking the package and the files it wants to install

♦ Performing preinstallation tasks

♦ Uncompressing the files and placing them in the proper locations

♦ Performing post-processing tasks

♦ Updating the RPM Database

When checking the package, `rpm` checks that all the dependencies are installed. Dependencies are packages required by the RPM package you want to install. For example, a database-administration package for a particular database may require that the database itself was already installed.

In addition to checking for dependencies, the `rpm` command checks for conflicting packages. For example, when you are trying to install an older version of a package on top of a newer version, running the `rpm` command alerts you to that conflict. This conflict-checking goes deeper than packages, though. Individual files may conflict if you are trying to install a package that has an older version of a particular file.

After the checks, the `rpm` command executes the preinstallation tasks (covered in depth in Part II). After all this preparatory work, the `rpm` command finally gets down to business and installs the files in the package. These files are stored in compressed format (compressed with gzip compression) inside the RPM file.

After installing the files, there may be some post-processing tasks (also covered in Part II). At the end of its run, the `rpm` command updates the RPM database to reflect the new package information. This update is very important and allows you to track packages.

Taking a Test Drive

The `--test` command-line option tells the `rpm` command to test the installation or upgrade process but not to install the file. For example, the following command performs an upgrade or install of the jikes package, but in test mode only. No files will actually be installed.

```
rpm -U --test jikes-1.16-1.i386.rpm
```

This command will print nothing if the tested installation or upgrade runs smoothly. If, on the other hand, a problem results from the tested installation, you will receive an error message. If the package is already installed, you will see a message like the following:

```
package jikes-1.16-1 is already installed
```

If the file is corrupted, you will see output like the following:

```
chap4.txt: not an rpm package (or package manifest):
```

This example was run against a file that was clearly not an RPM package.

The `test` option can help you determine package dependencies, too.

You can often determine dependencies at a glance – if you know something about the software you are installing. For example, if you know that Ruby is a scripting language, you can guess that packages starting with *eruby*, such as eruby-devel-0.9.8-2.i386.rpm, will depend on a base ruby package.

To show this, query for any ruby packages by using a command like the following:

```
rpm -q ruby
```

If you have not installed a ruby package, you'll see a message like the following:

```
package ruby is not installed
```

Most packages use all lowercase names. Thus, you can expect packages for the Ruby scripting language to start with *ruby*.

Package dependencies can quickly devolve into a nightmare in which one package depends upon another and that package in turn depends on yet another.

This is where the `--test` option comes in handy, since you can check that the dependencies are resolved prior to trying to install. (Note that the `rpm` command will check dependencies on real installs as well. The `--test` option just allows you to check that the installation will succeed prior to trying it.) For example, if you try to install a package named eruby-devel-0.9.8-2.i386.rpm, you may want to run a `--test` option first:

```
rpm -U --test eruby-devel-0.9.8-2.i386.rpm
```

You'll then see a response like the following, presuming you have no ruby packages installed:

```
error: Failed dependencies:
        eruby-libs = 0.9.8 is needed by eruby-devel-0.9.8-2
```

Now you can see that the package in the file eruby-devel-0.9.8-2.i386.rpm depends on another package, eruby-libs in this case. In fact, this package depends on the eruby-libs package having a version number of 0.9.8. These packages are obviously interrelated. From the name eruby-libs, you can guess that the package will be in a file with a name like eruby-libs-0.9.8-2.i386.rpm. (I cheated and used the actual package on the Red Hat installation CDs.)

But you can see how the version numbers of the two files, and the RPM revision levels, match up, as follows:

```
eruby-devel-0.9.8-2.i386.rpm
eruby-libs-0.9.8-2.i386.rpm
```

So, now you think your problems are over. You have the package that eruby-devel-0.9.8-2.i386.rpm depends on: eruby-libs-0.9.8-2.i386.rpm. Just to be careful, though, you can test that package as well, with a command like the following:

```
rpm -U --test eruby-libs-0.9.8-2.i386.rpm
```

Alas, this output leads you further down into dependency nightmare:

```
error: Failed dependencies:
        ruby-libs >= 1.6.4 is needed by eruby-libs-0.9.8-2
        libruby.so.1.6 is needed by eruby-libs-0.9.8-2
```

This short example shows why it makes sense to test packages prior to installing or upgrading them.

Installing or upgrading More Than One Package At A Time

Up to now, all the examples shown have used the rpm command to install or upgrade one package at a time. You can optionally choose to install or upgrade a number of packages at the same time. Just list each file name on the rpm command line. The basic syntax follows:

```
rpm -U package1.rpm package2.rpm .. package100.rpm
```

Simply list all the packages one after another. For example:

```
rpm -U aspell-en-ca-0.33.7.1-16.i386.rpm  aspell-en-gb-0.33.7.1-16.i386.rpm
```

This command installs two packages, the aspell packages for Canadian and British English, respectively.

The --noorder option tells the rpm command not to reorder the packages you are trying to install. Usually, the rpm command will reorder the list of packages in the best order for handling the dependencies. This option really only comes into play when you are installing more than one package where the packages depend on each other. In most cases, you do not want to use this option, since this may mean that packages fail to properly install because necessary packages are not already installed.

Installing in Different Directories

The --prefix and --relocate options should make the rpm command relocate a package to a new location. Not all packages allow relocations, though. The basic format of the command with the --prefix option is:

```
rpm -U --prefix /new/directory package.rpm
```

With the --relocate option, the command format is:

```
rpm -U --relocate /old/directory=/new/directory package.rpm
```

You can also use the --root option to specify a different directory for the rpm command to assume is the system's root, or /, directory. This causes the rpm command to install files under the new root, instead of in system locations under /. This option is most useful for testing the installation of a complete system under a test directory. The command should use the following format:

```
rpm -U --root /tmp --dbpath /var/lib/rpm jikes-1.16-1.i386.rpm
```

The --root option tells the rpm command that the root for this install is in /tmp. Installs with the --root option take place within a chroot() environment. This is often useful for setting up a test environment.

The --dbpath option tells the rpm command that the RPM database is located in the normal location, /var/lib/rpm.

Using the --dbpath and --root options will give you problems unless you have installed all the dependencies in the same virtual root directory. This includes all the standard Linux C libraries. For example, if you just run the example command, you'll see error output like the following:

```
error: Failed dependencies:
        ld-linux.so.2 is needed by jikes-1.16-1
        libc.so.6 is needed by jikes-1.16-1
        libm.so.6 is needed by jikes-1.16-1
        libstdc++-libc6.2-2.so.3 is needed by jikes-1.16-1
        libc.so.6(GLIBC_2.0) is needed by jikes-1.16-1
        libc.so.6(GLIBC_2.1) is needed by jikes-1.16-1
        libc.so.6(GLIBC_2.1.3) is needed by jikes-1.16-1
```

You can use the --badreloc option with the --relocate option to permit relocations on all files in the package. Usually, only those paths to files that are listed as relocatable are supported by the --relocate option.

Forcing the Issue

A number of rpm options cause the rpm command to complain about problems and, in general, fail to install your package. You can use a number of options to run roughshod over the RPM and get it to do what you want.

The --replacepkgs option tells the rpm command to replace, or reinstall, packages it may have already installed.

The --replacefiles option tells the rpm command to overwrite files owned by another package.

The --justdb option tells the rpm command to update the RPM database, not to install the files. You will need to be logged in as the root user to modify the RPM database.

The --nosuggest option tells the rpm command to skip any suggestions for packages that may fill in missing dependencies. You almost never want to use this option.

The --excludepath option tells the rpm command to exclude all files that start with the given path. For example:

```
rpm -U --excludepath /usr/lib eruby-devel-0.9.8-2.i386.rpm
```

This command installs or upgrades all the files in the package, except for those files that would be placed in a directory starting with /usr/lib.

The --allfiles option tells the rpm command to install or upgrade all files in the package, regardless of whether the files exist or not on your hard disk.

The --oldpackage tells the rpm command to allow you to install an older version of a package on top of a more recent one. You don't usually want to do this, but you may need to under the following circumstances:

◆ If the more recent package has some bug or security vulnerability and you need to downgrade to a former version.

◆ If the more recent package won't work with some other package that depends on a particular former version of a package.

The latter case is very common if you upgrade your system in a piecemeal fashion. If a low-level library changes, it may take a while for all the packages that depend on the low-level library to get updated to use the latest version.

Note that when you purchase an upgraded version of Linux, such as Red Hat Linux, all the packages with the product should be properly aligned with each other as to versions. This alignment problem is an issue that the Linux vendors, such as Red Hat, need to take care of. The main problems occur when you need packages beyond those offered with your Linux distribution.

To combine some of these options, you can use --force, which tells the rpm command to turn on the --replacepkgs, --replacefiles, and --oldpackage modes.

The `--nodeps` command-line option tells the `rpm` command to skip the dependencies check and install anyway.

 The `rpm` command complains with good reason. Unless you really, really know what you are doing, don't force the issue by using these command-line options.

Consider the eruby-devel-0.9.8-2.i386.rpm from the previous example. You can force the `rpm` command to install this package, even though it depends on another package that in turn depends on yet another. The following command will force the installation of the package in the eruby-devel-0.9.8-2.i386.rpm file:

```
rpm -U --nodeps eruby-devel-0.9.8-2.i386.rpm
```

Just to be sure, you can query for the package using a command like the following.

```
rpm -q eruby-devel
```

The response should be:

```
eruby-devel-0.9.8-2
```

The package is installed, but it likely won't work, since it really does depend on other packages. These package dependencies aren't for show. You may have a valid reason to force a package to get installed, but you should go back later to try to resolve all the dependencies.

In addition to forcing the `rpm` command not to do certain things, you can use the `--aid` option to have the `rpm` command do something nice for you. The `--aid` option tells the `rpm` command to add all the packages it would suggest into the set of packages to install. The `rpm` command has enough information to suggest a package or packages that ought to contain the dependent files.

The `--aid` option depends on a separate package that contains an RPM database with all packages installed. For Red Hat Linux, this package is rpmdb-redhat. This separate database, built as if all packages were installed (all packages that come with Red Hat Linux in this case), allows the `rpm` command to search for which packages would solve dependencies.

Skipping the Scripts

As part of the package installation, as well as removal, the RPM package may have scripts that the `rpm` command should run. These include pre- and post-installation scripts, as well as pre- and post-uninstallation scripts. These scripts can perform options such as automatically configuring the application based on the target environment. For example, an installation script may try to detect whether a site uses postfix or sendmail for transferring mail messages and configure the newly-installed package accordingly.

In most cases, the rpm command will execute these scripts at the proper time, unless you explicitly turn the command to skip the scripts. The --noscripts option tells the rpm command to skip running the pre- and post-installation scripts.

If you want, you can exercise a finer grain of control. The --nopre option tells the rpm command to skip any pre-installation scripts. The --nopost option tells the rpm command to skip any post-installation scripts.

Similarly, the --nopreun option tells the rpm command to skip any pre-uninstallation scripts, and the --nopostun option tells the rpm command to skip any post-uninstallation scripts.

The --noscripts option is the same as turning on all these options.

Table 4-1 summarizes these options.

TABLE 4-1 SKIPPING SCRIPTS

Option	Usage
--nopre	Skip pre-installation scripts.
--nopost	Skip post-installation scripts.
--nopreun	Skip pre-uninstallation scripts.
--nopostun	Skip post-uninstallation scripts.
--noscripts	Skip all the scripts; same as --nopre, --nopost, --nopreun, and --nopostun.

In general, you never want to disable these scripts. Many RPMs uses these scripts to perform the final steps of the installation, especially the post-installation scripts. For example, the Mozilla Web browser and most network services require some kind of post-processing (using a post-installation script) or the packages will not be properly installed.

In addition to pre- and post-installation scripts, the RPM system supports triggers, a topic covered in detail in Chapter 11.

During installation, you can tell the rpm command not to execute all the triggers or not to execute certain triggers. The --notriggers option tells the rpm command to skip all triggers.

You can gain more fine-grained control with a further set of options in place of --notriggers. The --notriggerin option turns off triggers during installation.

The --notriggerun option turns off uninstallation triggers, and the --notrigger-postun option turns off the post-uninstallation triggers. The --notriggers option is the same as all three, --notriggerin, --notriggerun, and --notriggerpostun.

Table 4-2 summarizes these options.

TABLE 4-2 SKIPPING TRIGGERS

Option	Usage
--notriggerin	Skip installation triggers.
--notriggerun	Skip uninstallation triggers.
--notriggerpostun	Skip post-uninstallation triggers.
--notriggers	Skip all the triggers; same as --notriggerin, -- notriggerun, and -- notriggerpostun.

Ignorance Is Bliss

The rpm command supports several ignore options that tell the command to ignore some aspect of a package it would normally complain about.

The --ignorearch option tells the rpm command to ignore the architecture of the package and install the package, even if the architecture of the package and the architecture of your system do not match. This is a very dangerous option. Linux runs on everything from tiny wristwatches, PDAs such as the Sharp Zaurus, PCs, Macintosh PCs, RISC servers, and all the way up to huge supercomputers and mainframes. If you try to install a binary package compiled for the ARM or PowerPC processor on an Intel-architecture Linux system, the package will at best fail. At worst, it may damage parts of your system.

Similarly, the --ignoreos command-line option tells the rpm command to ignore the operating system. Again, this is likely not a good idea in most situations. Applications compiled for Windows generally won't run on Linux. SCO Unix systems, however, can run some Linux applications, so you may have a valid reason to ignore the operating system. Again, use only with extreme care.

The --ignoresize option tells the rpm command to ignore or skip a check of your hard disk to ensure it has enough space to install the package.

Don't use the --ignoresize option if you have a nearly full hard disk, especially for a root, or /, partition.

The --nodigest option tells the rpm command to skip the test of the digest, the special value that helps verify the package correctness.

The --nosignature option tells the rpm command to skip the test of the digest, the encrypted key, that helps also verify the package correctness.

 Use these rpm command-line options with extreme care and only after carefully considering the circumstances. Wrongful use of these options may damage your operating system.

Documentation? What Documentation?

The --excludedocs command-line option tells the rpm command to ignore any files in the RPM package that are marked as documentation. Considering the general lack of documentation for many Linux applications, you are really asking for trouble by invoking this option. If the documentation takes up a lot of disk space, however, you may want to avoid installing documentation files. This is about the only situation in which this option makes sense.

In reverse of --excludedocs, the --includedocs command-line parameter tells the rpm command to install documentation. This is usually the default, so you rarely need this option.

Upgrading packages

The rpm -U command works for both installation of new packages and for upgrading. When you get beyond simple installations, you begin to see the power of the RPM system where most operations require just one command. The rpm -U command is a very powerful tool and performs some complex operations with just one command. For example, the following commands show the sequence for upgrading the jpilot package, which is used for Palm PDA synchronization.

```
# rpm -q jpilot
jpilot-0.97-1
# rpm -U jpilot-0.99.2-8.i386.rpm
# rpm -q jpilot
jpilot-0.99.2-8
```

Note that the old version of the jpilot package is no longer installed. The rpm --U command removed that package.

Options When Upgrading

You can pass more than one package name on the command line when upgrading. In addition, you can use the installation and upgrade options discussed previously when upgrading.

When upgrading, the `--noscripts` option only turns off the scripts from the new package. If an old package is removed, the uninstallation scripts for the old package still get executed.

When upgrading, you can also use the `--repackage` option, which works the same as when removing packages. The `--repackage` option tells the `rpm` command to create a package, an RPM file, from any packages it would erase. Note that this option will not create a complete package. You will not be able to reinstall a package created by the `--repackage` option. At best, the `--repackage` option provides a backup of the old package, from which you could create a working package. Be careful with the `--repackage` option.

For example, the following command shows how to upgrade a package with the `--repackage` option.

```
rpm -U --repackage jpilot-0.99.2-8.i386.rpm
```

Upgrading and freshening depend on versions of a particular package keeping the same base package name between versions. For most packages this is true, but some packages violate this convention. For example, the Java programming developer's kit (JDK) uses the name jdk-1.3.1_01.i386.rpm for the 1.3.1 version but changes to j2sdk-1_4_0_01-fcs-linux-i386.rpm for the 1.4.0 version.

Watch out for package-name changes like this.

Smart Upgrades

The `rpm` command really shines in the upgrade process. Not only can you upgrade a package with one simple command, but the `rpm` command has some built-in smarts that really help.

When upgrading, the `rpm` command checks each file in the package. It actually compares checksums of the files. An MD5 checksum is a small value computed from the data in a file. Any change to a file results in a different checksum value.

The `rpm` command compares the checksums of three versions of each file: the version of the file from the old package, the version of the file in the new package, and the version of the file on disk.

The `rpm` command looks at all three versions of the files to handle the common case where you may have edited a configuration file on disk. This is where the `rpm` command starts working with some upgrade rules. Note that this special processing only applies to files marked as configuration files within the RPM. Chapter 10 covers how to mark files as configuration files.

If the file on disk is identical to the file in the original package, meaning you have not changed the file, the rpm command simply installs the file from the new version of the package on top of the old file.

If the original package configuration file and the new package file are the same, that is, the file has not changed between the package versions, but the configuration file has been changed on disk, the rpm command leaves that file alone. The rpm command makes the assumption that if the file hasn't changed between versions of the package, and you have modified the file, chances are your file will work with the new package. This takes care of the common case where you have edited an application's configuration files.

But if the file on disk is different from the original version of the file, and the file on disk is different from the new version of the file, the rpm command installs the new version of the file on top of your changed version. This is because the new version of the file is known to work with the new package. The rpm command saves your work by backing up your modified configuration file, renaming the file with a new *.rpmsave* extension. The rpm command also warns you that it is backing up your modified file with a message that tells you the old file name and the new file name.

Freshening up

A *freshen* operation means to install a new version of a package only if you have already installed another version of the package. Thus, a freshen operation is very similar to the upgrade operation except that a freshen requires you to have previously installed the package, while an upgrade can install a package for the first time. The basic syntax for freshening a package is to use the -F option.

```
rpm -F package_name
```

You can also use the --freshen long option in place of -F.

As with upgrading, the options to the rpm command are the same, except for the -F or --freshen option that indicates the operation. These are the options discussed in the sections on upgrading and installing software.

Installing packages

The -i or --install option tells the rpm command to run an installation operation, which, as you'd suspect, installs packages. The basic syntax is:

```
rpm -i filename.rpm
```

For example:

```
rpm -i jikes-1.16-1.i386.rpm
```

You should normally install packages with `rpm -U`, not `rpm -i`. One of the main reasons is that `rpm -i` allows you to install multiple instances of the same (identical) package. This is usually not what you want.

The `rpm -i` command works with the installation options discussed previously. The `-U`, `-F` and `-i` options all accept mostly the same options, except as discussed previously.

Installing over the Internet

All the commands to install packages covered so far assume that you have a local RPM file that you want to install. This is by far the most common case, but you can also use the `rpm` command to install packages available on a network. With the `rpm` command, you can get the packages to install by using the FTP or HTTP network protocols.

With the FileTransfer Protocol (FTP), the `rpm` command connects to an FTP file server, downloads the named package, and installs that package. With the HyperText Transfer Protocol (HTTP) used for Web pages, the `rpm` command connects to a Web server, downloads the named package, and installs that package.

 When using either FTP or HTTP, you need to provide the name of the remote server. An attack on your system can compromise the system of converting server host names into network addresses, thus spoofing the `rpm` command into installing a malicious package from the wrong host.

Installing Using FTP

The key to making the network protocols work with the `rpm` command is that you need to create a URL for the remote file name. The basic format of the command follows:

```
rpm -i ftp://hostname/path/to/file/filename.rpm
```

Note the use of `ftp:` in the URL for the file.
For example, the following downloads a package from an IBM FTP server.

```
rpm -i ftp://www-126.ibm.com/pub/jikes/jikes-1.16-1.src.rpm
```

Many FTP servers require users to log in. If you do not pass a user name and password on the `rpm` command line, the `rpm` command will prompt you for the missing data.

You can add a user name prior to the host name, separating the user name from the host name with an at sign, @. For example:

```
rpm -i ftp://unclejoe@www-126.ibm.com/pub/jikes/jikes-1.16-1.src.rpm
```

In this case, the user name is *unclejoe*.

 These examples do not show valid user names or passwords.

With just a user name, the `rpm` command will prompt you for the password. You can also include the password on the `rpm` command line. Separate the user name from the password with a colon (:).
For example:

```
rpm -i ftp://unclejoe:workers@www-126.ibm.com/pub/jikes/jikes-1.16-1.src.rpm
```

In this case, the user name is *unclejoe* and the password is *workers*.

Open-source Software

Linux and thousands of applications that run on Linux are called *open-source software*. That's because the program source code for Linux and many applications are available.

Many users feel having access to the source code is vital, especially because:

◆ Vendors may stop supporting a package. With the sources, you can — conceivably — maintain the packages yourself, or more likely, others can take up the task and maintain these crucial packages.

◆ Having the source code makes it easier to track down and fix security vulnerabilities, although malicious users also have access to the same source code.

◆ You can enhance and extend packages for which the program sources are available.

Linux applications are available under a variety of open-source licenses. (In fact, it may seem that there are as many licenses as packages.) See the site www. opensource.org/licenses/ for details.

Installing Using HTTP

The `rpm` command supports the HTTP protocol, used by most Web servers, as well as FTP. Similar to accessing a file via FTP, you need to pass the `rpm` command a URL identifying the file. For example:

```
rpm -i http://ftp.redhat.com/pub/contrib/noarch/SRPMS/Squeak-sources-3-1.src.rpm
```

Installing source RPMs

Source RPMs contain the source code used to build an application or programming library and the scripts used to build the software into the application or library. These scripts are called the *recipes* for building the software.

Source RPMs usually contain program source code. They may also contain patches to program sources, scripts to build the program, special files used by desktop environments, icons, and other files considered to be part of the source code, such as programming guides.

 A patch is a file that contains just the differences between one version of a file and another. The differences include the actual text that has changed and enough contextual information that a program can locate where the changes are to take place. Usually, a patch is created with the `diff` command, and the source code is patched with the `patch` command.

In most cases, each binary RPM will have a corresponding source RPM. This is not always true, however.

One source RPM may contain enough shared program code to build multiple application RPMs. Furthermore, the source code is not available for all packages. Commercial applications, for example, rarely come with source code. In this case, obviously, no source RPMs are available. Or, a source RPM for a commercial application may provide no source code, but still provide a way to build the resulting application. See Chapter 10 for more on the source files and options for not including the sources in a source RPM.

Removing Software

The `rpm` command is good for more than just installing and upgrading software packages. Many times, you will need to remove packages as well.

To remove a package, use the `-e` option to the `rpm` command, short for erase. The basic syntax follows:

```
rpm -e package_name
```

When erasing or removing packages, use the package name, not the RPM file name. If you think about this, it makes sense. You don't always have the original RPM files when the time comes to remove a package.

For example:

```
rpm -e jikes-1.16-1
```

This example removes the jikes-1.16-1 package used in previous examples.

 You will need to be logged in as the root user, or super user, to remove most packages. This is because the package files themselves are protected. In addition, the RPM database is protected.

This is only natural, since most RPMs are used to install system-level commands and applications.

When removing a package, the rpm command first checks that no other packages depend on the package you intend to remove. This is very important, since you otherwise can damage your Linux system by inadvertently removing packages needed by the rest of the system.

The rpm command supports the --test option for removing packages as well as when installing. As with installing, the --test option tells the rpm command to test to see whether it can remove the given package but not to force the removal.

For example, if you try to remove the very important-looking syslinux-1.75-3 package, you can use the --test option to see if this works.

For example:

```
rpm -e --test syslinux-1.75-3
```

This command will issue an error such as the following:

```
error: Failed dependencies:
        syslinux is needed by (installed) mkbootdisk-1.4.8-1
```

 When removing packages, you can use the long option name, --erase, in place of -e.

Checking that the package has been removed

As before, you can use the `rpm -q` command to query whether a package is installed. After running the `rpm -e` command, you can run the `rpm -q` command to check whether the package has been removed. If the `rpm -q` command shows that the package is not installed, that tells you the erase operation has worked.

For example:

```
# rpm -q jikes
jikes-1.16-1
# rpm -e jikes-1.16-1
# rpm -q jikes
package jikes is not installed
```

Removing multiple packages at a time

You can remove multiple packages at once by listing each package consecutively on the command line. For example:

```
rpm -e aspell-en-ca-0.33.7.1-16 aspell-en-gb-0.33.7.1-16
```

This command removes the aspell-en-ca-0.33.7.1-16 and aspell-en-gb-0.33.7.1-16 packages.

Options when removing packages

The `--allmatches` option tells the `rpm` command to remove all packages with names that match the names you pass on the command line. If you do not use the `--allmatches` option, the `rpm` command will issue an error if more than one package matches the name or names you pass on the command line.

The `--nodeps` option tells the `rpm` command to skip the test of dependencies. Use this option when you really, really, want to uninstall a package.

Using any option that does not perform the full removal of the package, or skips some of the checks built into the `rpm` command, can result in damage to your Linux system. Use these options with care.

The `--repackage` option, described previously, tells the `rpm` command to create a package, an RPM file, from any packages it would erase. These packages will appear in the default repackage directory, which is normally /var/spool. Note that packages created with the `--repackage` option are not full packages. You cannot install these packages.

Similar to the options when installing or upgrading packages, you can use the --noscripts and --notriggers options when removing packages. The --noscripts option tells the rpm command not to run any uninstallation scripts. You can refine this by using either --nopreun or --nopostun in place of the --noscripts option.

The --nopreun option tells the rpm command not to run the pre-uninstallation scripts. The --nopostun option tells the rpm command not to run the post-uninstallation scripts.

The --notriggers option works in a similar fashion. The --notriggers option tells the rpm command not to execute any triggers. For a finer grain of control, use --notriggerun to prevent any uninstallation triggers and --notriggerpostun to prevent any post-uninstallation triggers.

Other rpm Command Options

Options such as -v (for more verbose output) work with the rpm command for installing, removing, and upgrading packages, as well as most other uses of the rpm command.

Other rpm command options, which work with most RPM actions, include --quiet to turn off most output except for errors, and --root, covered previously.

The --rcfile option tells the rpm command to use one or more other files to initialize the RPM system. These files tell the rpm command the system architecture, operating system, and default location of the RPM database, among a host of other settings.

The term *rc* comes from Unix shells, with initialization files such as .cshrc for the C shell, csh. The term *rc* was originally a shorthand for *run commands*. An *rc* is a file of commands that run when the application starts up. For example, the C shell, csh, runs the commands in file named .cshrc when the shell starts.

In most cases, the application looks in the user home directory for a specific file tied to the application. For the rpm command, this file is .rpmrc. The leading period makes the file hidden for most directory listings.

In addition to the user-level file of commands, most applications supporting this mechanism have a way for site administrators to customize the command for all users. For example, your system may have a file named /usr/lib/rpm/rpmrc (with no leading period) that customizes the rpm command for all users on your system.

The syntax for the `--rcfile` option is

```
--rcfile filename
```

You can also supply more than one file name. This syntax follows:

```
--rcfile filename1:filename2:filename3
```

Separate each file name with a colon.
With Red Hat Linux, the default set of initialization files are:

```
/usr/lib/rpm/rpmrc:/usr/lib/rpm/redhat/rpmrc:~/.rpmrc
```

The ~/.rpmrc means to look in the user's home directory for a file named .rpmrc.

You can use the `--showrc` option to list all the *rc* settings.

See Chapter 21 for more on the `--showrc` option.

The `--version` option tells the `rpm` command to print out the version number of the command and then exit. For example:

```
rpm --version
```

This command prints out a version number, like the following:

```
RPM version 4.1
```

The `--dbpath` option, mentioned previously, tells the `rpm` command to use a different RPM database. This is useful when testing a complete system install, where you want to change the RPM database but don't want that to affect your running Linux system. In this case, you can use a different RPM database and test out your changes. The basic syntax for this option is:

```
--dbpath directory_name
```

The `--pipe` option tells the `rpm` command to send, or pipe, its output to another program. The syntax for this option is:

```
--pipe command_to_send_out_to
```

Summary

This chapter covered the easy part of managing packages, the common actions of installing, removing, and upgrading software.

The `rpm -e` command removes packages. The `rpm -U` command upgrades packages by installing new packages and removing old versions of all the packages upgraded. RPM upgrades also work for installing new packages. The `rpm -F` command freshens packages. This command only upgrades a package if an older version of the package has already been installed. The `rpm -i` command installs packages.

Table 4-3 summarizes the `rpm` command-line options for installing, removing, and upgrading packages.

TABLE 4-3 INSTALLING, REMOVING, AND UPGRADING WITH THE RPM COMMAND

Command	Usage
`rpm -i install_options package_files`	Install packages.
`rpm -e remove_options packages`	Erase, remove, packages.
`rpm -U install_options package_files`	Upgrade or install packages. Use this option for installations.
`rpm -Uvh install_options package_files`	Upgrade or install packages with extra output. This is the recommended command to install packages.
`rpm -F install_options package_files`	Freshen packages.

Unfortunately, modern system management gets more complex than that. The next chapter delves into package dependencies and the nightmare you can get into when one package depends on another that then depends on another, ad infinitum.

Chapter 5

Using the RPM Database

IN THIS CHAPTER

- ◆ Querying the RPM database

- ◆ Getting information on RPM files

- ◆ Finding out which packages own files on your system

- ◆ Verifying installed packages

- ◆ Backing up the RPM database

- ◆ Repairing damaged RPM databases

EVERY PACKAGE YOU INSTALL with RPM is recorded in the RPM database. The RPM system includes commands to query this database to find out which packages are installed and to provide quite a few details about these packages.

This chapter covers querying both the RPM database and RPM package files. Both types of query are important:

- ◆ Query the RPM database to see what is installed, or not installed, on your system.

- ◆ Query package files to see what the files require, as well as what the files provide.

In addition to querying the RPM database, you can use the database to verify packages. Since this database is so important to the management of your Linux system, this chapter covers how to back it up, as well as how to repair a damaged RPM database.

Querying the RPM Database

In Chapter 4, you saw that the `rpm` command usually takes one major command-line option to tell it the operation to perform and a myriad of command-line options to customize the operation. The `rpm` command may also take the name of one or more RPM package files or the name of one or more installed packages. For example, the `rpm -i` command performs an installation operation, and the `rpm -U` command performs an upgrade.

For querying the RPM database, the major command-line option is -q, short for query. This option tells the rpm command to query the RPM database. You can also use the long option --query.

In the last few chapters, you've used the -q option with the rpm command to query just for the presence or absence of installed packages. You can expand the -q option to perform a wide array of queries to find out information about the packages installed on a Linux system.

Querying packages

The basic format of the rpm -q command follows:

```
rpm -q package_name
```

You need to provide the name of a package to query. For example:

```
rpm -q telnet-0.17
```

This command returns the name of the package, if installed. For example:

```
telnet 0.17 20
```

If the package is not installed, you'll see a message like the following:

```
package telnet-0.17 is not installed
```

You can provide the whole package name to the rpm command, which includes the name, the version, and the RPM package number, as discussed in Chapter 3. You can also just provide the name and version number, as shown previously, or just the base name of the package.

For example, the following command uses just the base name of the package:

```
$ rpm -q telnet
telnet-0.17-20
```

 The rpm -q command expects a package name. Although it supports some amount of customized queries, you really need to know which packages you want the rpm command to report on.

You can provide more than one package name; the rpm command reports on each package, as shown following.

```
$ rpm -q telnet telnet-server
telnet-0.17-20
telnet-server-0.17-20
```

You need to change the way you query if you want to perform searches when you do not know the full package name in advance. The following sections cover options for creating various queries.

Querying everything

Up to now, we have used the rpm command to query only for specific packages. The -a option tells the rpm command to query for all packages. You can also use the longer option, -all, in place of -a.

For example:

```
rpm -qa
```

This command returns every package installed on your system, quite a few packages. The packages are returned one per line, as shown following.

```
words-2-17
kudzu-0.99.23-1
openldap-2.0.11-13
rpm-4.0.3-1.03
kernel-smp-2.4.7-10
quota-3.01pre9-3
expat-1.95.1-7
groff-perl-1.17.2-3
perl-DateManip-5.39-5
perl-libnet-1.0703-6
perl-URI-1.12-5
perl-XML-Parser-2.30-7
perl-XML-Twig-2.02-2
a2ps-4.13b-15
4Suite-0.11-2
XFree86-xfs-4.1.0-3
ghostscript-6.51-12
tcl-8.3.3-65
portmap-4.0-38
bind-utils-9.1.3-4
ftp-0.17-12
micq-0.4.6.p1-2
```

This output has been modified to meet size constraints. Try the `rpm -qa` command to see the full output for your system.

There may be over a thousand packages on your system. Even so, the `rpm -qa` command executes surprisingly fast.

Refining the query

When you query all the installed packages, you get too much output for most purposes, other than to get a general idea of the magnitude of packages installed on your system. But if you cannot remember a package name, there's no real option, other than writing your own RPM query program.

You can take advantage of the power of the Linux shells, though, and the wonderful ability to pipe the output of one command into another to work around this problem. With the large amount of output, you may want to pipe the output to the `more` or `less` programs, and display the output one page at a time.

 For more information on the `more` or `less` commands, view the online manuals with the `man more` and `man less` commands.

Even with `more` and `less`, the `rpm -qa` command outputs too much information to be really useful, unless you can somehow filter the information automatically.

Piping the Output To grep

The Linux (and Unix) `grep` command provides a powerful tool for filtering through lots of textual data. If you pipe the output of the `rpm -qa` command into the `grep` command, you have a powerful search engine – Linux – at your fingertips.

For example, if you know that most packages that use the Python scripting language have a *py* in their names, you can find all these packages by using a command like the following:

```
rpm -qa | grep py
```

This command outputs packages such as the following:

```
python-2.2.1-17
pygtk2-1.99.12-7
pyxf86config-0.3.1-2
```

```
rpm404-python-4.0.4-8x.27
python-devel-2.2.1-17
gnome-python2-gtkhtml2-1.99.11-8
orbit-python-1.99.0-4
gnome-python2-canvas-1.99.11-8
gnome-python2-bonobo-1.99.11-8
gnome-python2-1.99.11-8
pyOpenSSL-0.5.0.91-1
rpm-python-4.1-1.06
pygtk2-devel-1.99.12-7
kdesdk-kspy-3.0.3-2
mod_python-3.0.0-10
gnome-python2-gconf-1.99.11-8
libxslt-python-1.0.19-1
python-tools-2.2.1-17
libxml2-python-2.4.23-1
pygtk2-libglade-1.99.12-7
python-optik-1.3-2
kfloppy-3.0.3-3
```

You can also use the --pipe option to the rpm command, introduced in Chapter 4. With this option, your command becomes:

```
rpm -qa --pipe "grep py"
```

Chapter 17 covers programming with the RPM system with the Python scripting language.

You can take advantage of some of the options that the grep command supports, including -i for ignoring the case of the string to match, --regexp to pass a regular expression to grep, and -v, to output only those entries that do not match the search string.

If you are unfamiliar with grep, the online manual pages for the grep command provide a listing of the command-line options available for grep as well as a short tutorial on regular expressions supported by grep.

Table 5-1 lists some of the common package-naming conventions. Remember that these are just conventions, not hard-and-fast rules. You can use these conventions in concert with rpm queries.

TABLE 5-1 COMMON NAMING CONVENTIONS ON LINUX

Convention	Usually indicates
Starts with g	GNOME desktop application or a GNU application, especially GNU C programming tools and libraries
Starts with j	Cross-platform Java application
Starts with k	KDE desktop application, Linux kernel package, or Kerberos security package
Starts with py	Python application
Starts with rh	Red Hat application, usually for configuring your system
Starts with tk	Graphical Tcl application
Starts with x	X Window System graphical desktop application
Ends with wm	Window manager for controlling the layout of windows on the screen

Querying with Wildcards

In addition to using other Linux commands, the rpm command supports some search options. You can pass a wildcard to rpm -qa (but not just rpm -q, you need the -a to look for all packages). For example:

```
$ rpm -qa "send*"
sendmail-cf-8.11.6-3
sendmail-8.11.6-3
```

The quotation marks around "send*" are to prevent the Linux shell from expanding the wildcard character, *, to try to match a list of file names in the local directory. By passing the command-line parameter as "send*", the rpm program gets to see the * character. Otherwise, the shell expands the parameter and the program, rpm in this case, never sees the *.

This command searches for all package names starting with *send*. You can reverse this with an exclamation mark. For example:

```
$ rpm -qa '!send*'
```

This command works sort of like grep -v and searches for all packages that do not start with *send*.

There are quite a few other Linux commands you can use in pipelines with the rpm -qa command to better filter and display the data, such as wc -l to count the number of packages that you query. You can also use a number of other query options to find out more specialized information from the RPM database.

 If you aren't familiar with grep or other Linux commands, pick up a Linux tutorial such as (insert shameless plug) *Teach Yourself Linux* by Steve Oualline and Eric Foster-Johnson, available from Wiley Publishing, Inc.

Finding which packages own files

One of the common problems with package management comes when you want to track a given file on your system back to the package that "owns" the file (that is, the package that, when installed, installed the particular file).

The -qf option tells the rpm command to query for all packages that own a particular file. You can also use the longer option, --file, in place of -f. The basic syntax follows:

```
rpm -qf filename
```

For example, the grep command used in previous examples is really a file. (Just about all Linux commands are a file of some sort, be it a shell script or an executable application.) You can use a few Linux commands to determine which package provides this handy program.

First, we need the exact path to the file. For Linux commands, you can use the which command, if the program is in your path. (The grep program must be in your path, or commands with grep will fail.)

Try the following command:

```
which grep
```

This command returns the path to grep:

```
/bin/grep
```

We can now check which package owns this file with the following command:

```
# rpm -qf /bin/grep
grep-2.4.2-7
```

You can also use the Linux back-tick operator to perform this check with one command.

```
# rpm -qf `which grep`
grep-2.4.2-7
```

If you use the bash shell, you can use the $(*command parameters*) syntax in place of the back tick, or `, characters. For example:

```
# rpm -qf $(which grep)
grep-2.4.2-7
```

If no package owns a given file, you'll see output like the following:

```
# rpm -qf mail
file mail is not owned by any package
```

Often, the package that owns a file does not have an intuitive name. The ssh command, for example, is owned by the openssh-clients package, as shown following:

```
# rpm -qf `which ssh`
openssh-clients-3.1p1-2
```

As you can see, the name of a command does not always correspond directly to the name of the package that provides that command. This is where the rpm -qf command proves very useful. Otherwise, you would just have to know that OpenSSH is the project responsible for this command.

Symbolic Links

The rpm -qf command follows symbolic links. This was not always true with older versions of the rpm command, but the modern rpm command can now trace package ownership to files placed in linked directories.

For example, the directory /usr/lib/X11 is a link to the real directory, /usr/X11R6/lib/X11. You can track the package ownership of a file in that directory, XKeysymDB, for example, by using the following command:

```
# rpm -qf /usr/lib/X11/XKeysymDB

XFree86-4.2.0-72
```

This file, XKeysymDB, really resides in /usr/X11R6/lib/X11.

Getting Information on Packages

The query options for the rpm command include a whole set of options that return information about the files that make up a package, the scripts, and other parts of the original package. The following sections cover these options.

Describing packages

The -i option with an rpm query command tells the rpm command to output descriptive information about the package. You can also use the longer option, --info, in place of -i. The basic syntax is:

rpm -qi *package*

The order of the command-line options is very important. Remember that the rpm command has the following general syntax:

rpm -MajorOperation -extra_options packages_or_files

The rpm -i command installs packages. The rpm -q command queries packages. The rpm -qi command outputs the descriptive information on packages. If you make a mistake and place the *i* in front of the *q*, you are telling the rpm command to perform a different operation.

When you run this command, being very careful with the order of the options, you'll see output like the following, which describes the tcsh shell package.

```
# rpm -qi tcsh-6.10-6
Name        : tcsh                     Relocations: (not relocateable)
Version     : 6.10                           Vendor: Red Hat, Inc.
Release     : 6                          Build Date: Sun 24 Jun 2001 10:45:29
 PM CDT
Install date: Fri 14 Dec 2001 10:45:39 AM CST     Build
Host: porky.devel.redhat.com
Group       : System Environment/Shells    Source RPM: tcsh-6.10-6.src.rpm
Size        : 764000                         License: distributable
Packager    : Red Hat, Inc. <http://bugzilla.redhat.com/bugzilla>
URL         : http://www.primate.wisc.edu/software/csh-tcsh-book/
Summary     : An enhanced version of csh, the C shell.
Description :
Tcsh is an enhanced but completely compatible version of csh, the C
```

```
shell.  Tcsh is a command language interpreter which can be used both
as an interactive login shell and as a shell script command processor.
Tcsh includes a command line editor, programmable word completion,
spelling correction, a history mechanism, job control and a C language
like syntax.
```

From this description, you can find out a lot about a package, such as where it comes from. Note how the description also names the source RPM used to build the package programs.

The sections on custom queries following in this chapter show how you can query for any information stored in a package header, including all of the information shown with the rpm -qi command, as well as any other header tag.

Package groups

RPM packages can be placed into groups, merely arbitrary names for a set of packages. The rpm -qi command, shown previously, lists the group for a package, if there is one. For the tcsh package shown in the previous example, the package is System Environment/Shells.

The -g option to the rpm -q command tells the rpm command to list all the packages in a given group. You can also use the longer option, --group, in place of -g. The basic syntax follows:

```
rpm -qg group_name
```

For example:

```
# rpm -qg "System Environment/Shells"
bash-2.05b-5
sh-utils-2.0.12-3
ash-0.3.8-5
tcsh-6.12-2
```

This group has a space in its name, so you need quotation marks to pass the group name as one parameter to the rpm command.

Listing the files in a package

The -1 (ell) option queries all the files in a package. You can also use the longer option, --list, in place of -1. The basic syntax is:

```
rpm -ql package
```

For example, to query the files in the tcsh package, you'll see the following:

```
# rpm -ql tcsh
/bin/csh
/bin/tcsh
/usr/share/doc/tcsh-6.10
/usr/share/doc/tcsh-6.10/FAQ
/usr/share/doc/tcsh-6.10/Fixes
/usr/share/doc/tcsh-6.10/NewThings
/usr/share/doc/tcsh-6.10/complete.tcsh
/usr/share/doc/tcsh-6.10/eight-bit.txt
/usr/share/doc/tcsh-6.10/tcsh.html
/usr/share/doc/tcsh-6.10/tcsh.html/header.html
/usr/share/doc/tcsh-6.10/tcsh.html/index.html
/usr/share/doc/tcsh-6.10/tcsh.html/lists.html
/usr/share/doc/tcsh-6.10/tcsh.html/tcsh.man
/usr/share/doc/tcsh-6.10/tcsh.html/tcsh.man2html
/usr/share/doc/tcsh-6.10/tcsh.html/top.html
/usr/share/locale/de/LC_MESSAGES/tcsh
/usr/share/locale/el/LC_MESSAGES/tcsh
/usr/share/locale/es/LC_MESSAGES/tcsh
/usr/share/locale/fr/LC_MESSAGES/tcsh
/usr/share/locale/it/LC_MESSAGES/tcsh
/usr/share/locale/ja/LC_MESSAGES/tcsh
/usr/share/man/man1/tcsh.1.gz
```

 You can pass more than one package name to this option, but it won't tell you which package owns which file. Use the --filesbypkg option to list files by package (see the related sidebar).

The -v (verbose) option can give you more information on the files when used with the various query options. For example:

```
# rpm -qlv tcsh
lrwxrwxrwx 1 root root        4 Jun 24  2001 /bin/csh -> tcsh
-rwxr-xr-x 1 root root   288604 Jun 24  2001 /bin/tcsh
drwxr-xr-x 2 root root        0 Jun 24  2001 /usr/share/doc/tcsh-6.10
-rw-r--r-- 1 root root     8306 Aug 25  2000 /usr/share/doc/tcsh-6.10/FAQ
-rw-r--r-- 1 root root    64761 Nov 19  2000 /usr/share/doc/tcsh-6.10/Fixes
-rw-r--r-- 1 root root     6518 Oct  2  1998 /usr/share/doc/tcsh-6.10/NewThings
-rw-r--r-- 1 root root    41328 Nov 19  2000 /usr/share/doc/tcsh-6.10/complete.tcsh
-rw-r--r-- 1 root root     4668 Jun 24  2001 /usr/share/doc/tcsh-6.10/eight-bit.txt
drwxr-xr-x 2 root root        0 Jun 24  2001 /usr/share/doc/tcsh-6.10/tcsh.html
-rw-r--r-- 1 root root      124 Jun 24  2001 /usr/share/doc/tcsh-
6.10/tcsh.html/header.html
lrwxrwxrwx 1 root root        8 Jun 24  2001 /usr/share/doc/tcsh-
6.10/tcsh.html/index.html -> top.html
-rw-r--r-- 1 root root      911 Jun 24  2001 /usr/share/doc/tcsh-
6.10/tcsh.html/lists.html
-rw-r--r-- 1 root root        0 Jun 24  2001 /usr/share/doc/tcsh-
6.10/tcsh.html/tcsh.man
-rw-r--r-- 1 root root    22542 Jun 24  2001 /usr/share/doc/tcsh-
6.10/tcsh.html/tcsh.man2html
-rw-r--r-- 1 root root      693 Jun 24  2001 /usr/share/doc/tcsh-
6.10/tcsh.html/top.html
-rw-r--r-- 1 root root    45861 Jun 24  2001 /usr/share/locale/de/LC_MESSAGES/tcsh
-rw-r--r-- 1 root root    47566 Jun 24  2001 /usr/share/locale/el/LC_MESSAGES/tcsh
-rw-r--r-- 1 root root    47413 Jun 24  2001 /usr/share/locale/es/LC_MESSAGES/tcsh
-rw-r--r-- 1 root root    47156 Jun 24  2001 /usr/share/locale/fr/LC_MESSAGES/tcsh
-rw-r--r-- 1 root root    48264 Jun 24  2001 /usr/share/locale/it/LC_MESSAGES/tcsh
-rw-r--r-- 1 root root    18682 Jun 24  2001 /usr/share/locale/ja/LC_MESSAGES/tcsh
-rw-r--r-- 1 root root    62399 Jun 24  2001 /usr/share/man/man1/tcsh.1.gz
```

This information is the same as a long listing on the files.

As you can see, the -l option results in quite a lot of output. In some cases, though, you aren't interested in documentation and other miscellaneous files in the package. It's the commands and libraries that cause the most package-related problems. To help with this, you can use a series of rpm options to list only certain types of files.

Listing the configuration files for a package

The -c option tells the rpm -q command to list the configuration files for a package. You can also use the longer option, --configfiles, in place of -c. The basic syntax is:

```
rpm -qc package_name
```

Listing Files By Package

The --filesbypkg option outputs the files by package, so you can make some sense of a list of files from more than one package.

For example:

```
# rpm -q --filesbypkg file openssh-clients
file                    /usr/bin/file
file                    /usr/share/magic
file                    /usr/share/magic.mgc
file                    /usr/share/magic.mime
file                    /usr/share/man/man1/file.1.gz
file                    /usr/share/man/man5/magic.5.gz
openssh-clients         /etc/ssh/ssh_config
openssh-clients         /usr/bin/sftp
openssh-clients         /usr/bin/slogin
openssh-clients         /usr/bin/ssh
openssh-clients         /usr/bin/ssh-add
openssh-clients         /usr/bin/ssh-agent
openssh-clients         /usr/bin/ssh-keyscan
openssh-clients         /usr/share/man/man1/sftp.1.gz
openssh-clients         /usr/share/man/man1/slogin.1.gz
openssh-clients         /usr/share/man/man1/ssh-add.1.gz
openssh-clients         /usr/share/man/man1/ssh-agent.1.gz
openssh-clients         /usr/share/man/man1/ssh-keyscan.1.gz
openssh-clients         /usr/share/man/man1/ssh.1.gz
```

Use this option without -l, because the -l option will also list the files alone, without any package name.

For example:

```
# rpm -qc bash
/etc/skel/.bash_logout
/etc/skel/.bash_profile
/etc/skel/.bashrc
```

This command lists the configuration files for the bash package. Some packages don't have configuration files, as shown following:

```
# rpm -qc python
#
```

In this case, the rpm command provides no output. Other packages have a lot of configuration files, such as the sendmail mail transfer agent, as shown following:

```
# rpm -qc sendmail
/etc/aliases
/etc/mail/Makefile
/etc/mail/access
/etc/mail/domaintable
/etc/mail/helpfile
/etc/mail/local-host-names
/etc/mail/mailertable
/etc/mail/sendmail.mc
/etc/mail/statistics
/etc/mail/trusted-users
/etc/mail/virtusertable
/etc/rc.d/init.d/sendmail
/etc/sendmail.cf
/etc/sysconfig/sendmail
/usr/lib/sasl/Sendmail.conf
```

As with the -l option, the -v option provides more information on each file, as shown following:

```
#rpm -qcv bash
-rw-r--r-- 1 root    root    24 Jul  9 2001 /etc/skel/.bash_logout
-rw-r--r-- 1 root    root   191 Jul  9 2001 /etc/skel/.bash_profile
-rw-r--r-- 1 root    root   124 Jul  9 2001 /etc/skel/.bashrc
```

Listing the documentation files for a package

Similarly to the -c option, the -d option tells the rpm -q command to list just the documentation files for a package. The basic syntax is:

```
rpm -qd package_name
```

For example:

```
# rpm -qd tcsh
/usr/share/doc/tcsh-6.10/FAQ
/usr/share/doc/tcsh-6.10/Fixes
/usr/share/doc/tcsh-6.10/NewThings
/usr/share/doc/tcsh-6.10/complete.tcsh
/usr/share/doc/tcsh-6.10/eight-bit.txt
/usr/share/doc/tcsh-6.10/tcsh.html/header.html
/usr/share/doc/tcsh-6.10/tcsh.html/index.html
/usr/share/doc/tcsh-6.10/tcsh.html/lists.html
```

```
/usr/share/doc/tcsh-6.10/tcsh.html/tcsh.man
/usr/share/doc/tcsh-6.10/tcsh.html/tcsh.man2html
/usr/share/doc/tcsh-6.10/tcsh.html/top.html
/usr/share/man/man1/tcsh.1.gz
```

 You can add the -v option to all of the file-listing options to get more information.

You can also use the longer option, --docfiles, in place of -d.

Listing the state of the files in a package

The -s option to the rpm -q command lists the state of each file in a package. The basic syntax follows.

```
rpm -qs package_name
```

For example:

```
# rpm -qs tcsh
normal       /bin/csh
normal       /bin/tcsh
normal       /usr/share/doc/tcsh-6.10
normal       /usr/share/doc/tcsh-6.10/FAQ
normal       /usr/share/doc/tcsh-6.10/Fixes
normal       /usr/share/doc/tcsh-6.10/NewThings
normal       /usr/share/doc/tcsh-6.10/complete.tcsh
normal       /usr/share/doc/tcsh-6.10/eight-bit.txt
normal       /usr/share/doc/tcsh-6.10/tcsh.html
normal       /usr/share/doc/tcsh-6.10/tcsh.html/header.html
normal       /usr/share/doc/tcsh-6.10/tcsh.html/index.html
normal       /usr/share/doc/tcsh-6.10/tcsh.html/lists.html
normal       /usr/share/doc/tcsh-6.10/tcsh.html/tcsh.man
normal       /usr/share/doc/tcsh-6.10/tcsh.html/tcsh.man2html
normal       /usr/share/doc/tcsh-6.10/tcsh.html/top.html
not installed /usr/share/locale/de/LC_MESSAGES/tcsh
not installed /usr/share/locale/el/LC_MESSAGES/tcsh
not installed /usr/share/locale/es/LC_MESSAGES/tcsh
not installed /usr/share/locale/fr/LC_MESSAGES/tcsh
not installed /usr/share/locale/it/LC_MESSAGES/tcsh
not installed /usr/share/locale/ja/LC_MESSAGES/tcsh
normal       /usr/share/man/man1/tcsh.1.gz
```

You can also use the longer option, `--state`, in place of -s.

You can combine the `-s` option with other file filters, such as `-d`, for listing only the documentation files for a package.

Table 5-2 lists the states that the `rpm` command supports.

TABLE 5-2 RPM FILE STATES

State	Usage
Normal	The file has been installed.
not installed	The file from the package is not installed.
Replaced	The file has been replaced.

Sometimes files in a package may have been skipped during installation with options such as `--excludedocs`. This can lead to non-normal states. You may have also modified files installed from a given package.

See Chapter 4 for more on installing RPMs.

Listing the scripts in a package

RPM packages can have preinstallation, postinstallation, preuninstallation, and postuninstallation scripts. These are scripts that the `rpm` command will execute before and after installing a package, as well as before and after removing the package. The `--scripts` option to the `rpm -q` command lists the scripts associated with a package. The basic syntax follows:

```
rpm -q --scripts package_name
```

For example:

```
# rpm -q --scripts tcsh
postinstall scriptlet (through /bin/sh):
if [ ! -f /etc/shells ]; then
    echo "/bin/tcsh" >> /etc/shells
    echo "/bin/csh" >> /etc/shells
```

```
else
    grep '^/bin/tcsh$' /etc/shells > /dev/null || echo "/bin/tcsh" >> /etc/shell
s
    grep '^/bin/csh$' /etc/shells > /dev/null || echo "/bin/csh" >> /etc/shells
fi
postuninstall scriptlet (through /bin/sh):
if [ ! -x /bin/tcsh ]; then
    grep -v '^/bin/tcsh$' /etc/shells | grep -v '^/bin/csh$'> /etc/shells.rpm
    mv /etc/shells.rpm /etc/shells
fi
```

The simple scripts shown here add an entry to the /etc/shells file and clean up the entry when uninstalled.

Cleaning up any changes your package makes on uninstallation is a very good idea. See the chapters in Part II, "Creating RPMs," for details on making your own well-behaved packages.

Other packages have more complex scripts, as shown following:

```
# rpm -q --scripts sendmail
preinstall scriptlet (through /bin/sh):
/usr/sbin/useradd -u 47 -d /var/spool/mqueue -r -s /dev/null mailnull >/dev/null
 2>&1 || :
postinstall scriptlet (through /bin/sh):
#
# Convert old format to new
#
if [ -f /etc/mail/deny ] ; then
    cat /etc/mail/deny | \
        awk 'BEGIN{ print "# Entries from obsoleted /etc/mail/deny"} \
                {print $1" REJECT"}' >> /etc/mail/access
    cp /etc/mail/deny /etc/mail/deny.rpmorig
fi
for oldfile in relay_allow ip_allow name_allow ; do
    if [ -f /etc/mail/$oldfile ] ; then
        cat /etc/mail/$oldfile | \
                awk "BEGIN { print \"# Entries from obsoleted /etc/mail/$oldfile
\" ;} \
            { print \$1\" RELAY\" }" >> /etc/mail/access
        cp /etc/mail/$oldfile /etc/mail/$oldfile.rpmorig
    fi
```

```
done

#
# Oops, these files moved
#
if [ -f /etc/sendmail.cw ] ; then
    cat /etc/sendmail.cw  | \
      awk 'BEGIN { print "# Entries from obsoleted /etc/sendmail.cw" ;} \
           { print $1 }' >> /etc/mail/local-host-names
    cp /etc/sendmail.cw /etc/sendmail.cw.rpmorig
fi
#
# Rebuild maps (next reboot will rebuild also)
#
{ /usr/bin/newaliases
  for map in virtusertable access domaintable mailertable
  do
    if [ -f /etc/mail/${map} ] ; then
      /usr/bin/makemap hash /etc/mail/${map} < /etc/mail/${map}
      sleep 1
    fi
  done
} > /dev/null 2>&1

/sbin/chkconfig --add sendmail
preuninstall scriptlet (through /bin/sh):
if [ $1 = 0 ]; then
   /etc/rc.d/init.d/sendmail stop >/dev/null 2>&1
   /sbin/chkconfig --del sendmail
fi
postuninstall scriptlet (through /bin/sh):
if [ "$1" -ge "1" ]; then
    /etc/rc.d/init.d/sendmail condrestart >/dev/null 2>&1
fi
exit 0
```

In this case, the main script is the post-install script, which tries to convert old-format data into the new format, thereby helping users upgrade to the newer release.

Listing what has changed

The --changelog option lists what has changed, as described in a file that logs changes, from previous versions of a given package. The change log is just a convention, so not all packages will sport this nifty feature. In addition, the change log for many packages documents the changes in the RPM packaging, not the changes in the underlying application. If a change log is available, however, this can prove a very good way to help determine whether you want to upgrade to a new version of a package.

For example, a network server application may have been updated to fix some security problems. In that case, you likely want to upgrade. Other changes may not affect your site, leading you to decide not to upgrade.

The basic format of the command is:

```
rpm -q --changelog package_name
```

For example, the following shows the beginning of the log-change log for the bash package, with names and e-mail addresses changed to protect the innocent:

```
# rpm -q --changelog bash
* Fri Aug 23 2002 Bob Marley <bob@marley.com.>

- re-bzip the docs, something was corrupted

* Thu Aug 22 2002 Peter Tosh <peter@tosh.com> 2.05b-4

- Fix history substitution modifiers in UTF-8 (bug #70294, bug #71186).
- Fix ADVANCE_CHAR at end of string (bug #70819).
- docs: CWRU/POSIX.NOTES no longer exists, but ship POSIX.

* Wed Aug 07 2002 Jimmy Cliff <jimmy@cliff.com> 2.05b-3

- Fixed out of memory problem with readline.

* Tue Jul 23 2002 Jimmy Cliff <jimmy@cliff.com> 2.05b-2

- @code 80 last:Added symlink for sh.1 in man1 section so that man sh works
(#44039).
```

Combining queries

The rpm command is very flexible in allowing you to combine queries. Just start the command with rpm -q and add the various options either on their own, such as -q with -s and -f, or together, such as -qsf.

The following sections show a few handy combinations of the options you can use for real-world package-management tasks.

Listing Package Description and Documentation Files

To find information on a package and where it is documented, use the -qdi option to the rpm command (a combination of the -q, -d, and -i options):

```
# rpm -qdi grep
Name        : grep                    Relocations: /usr
Version     : 2.5.1                       Vendor: Red Hat,
Inc.
Release     : 4                        Build Date: Sat 20 Jul
2002 01:08:48 AM CDT
Install date: Sat 05 Oct 2002 12:21:58 PM CDT      Build
Host: stripples.devel.redhat.com
Group       : Applications/Text        Source RPM: grep-2.5.1-
4.src.rpm
Size        : 475770                      License: GPL
Signature   : DSA/SHA1, Tue 03 Sep 2002 04:17:47 PM CDT, Key ID
219180cddb42a60ePackager    : Red Hat, Inc.
<http://bugzilla.redhat.com/bugzilla>
Summary     : The GNU versions of grep pattern matching utilities.
Description :
The GNU versions of commonly used grep utilities. Grep searches
through textual input for lines which contain a match to a specified
pattern and then prints the matching lines. GNU's grep utilities
include grep, egrep, and fgrep.

You should install grep on your system, because it is a very useful
utility for searching text.
/usr/share/doc/grep-2.5.1/ABOUT-NLS
/usr/share/doc/grep-2.5.1/AUTHORS
/usr/share/doc/grep-2.5.1/ChangeLog
/usr/share/doc/grep-2.5.1/NEWS
/usr/share/doc/grep-2.5.1/README
/usr/share/doc/grep-2.5.1/THANKS
/usr/share/doc/grep-2.5.1/TODO
/usr/share/info/grep.info-1.gz
/usr/share/info/grep.info-2.gz
/usr/share/info/grep.info-3.gz
/usr/share/info/grep.info.gz
/usr/share/man/man1/egrep.1.gz
/usr/share/man/man1/fgrep.1.gz
/usr/share/man/man1/grep.1.gz
```

It's often hard to track down the documentation for a given package. Some packages use Unix manual pages; others use info files, and still others provide HTML for other formatted manuals. Some have no real documentation at all.

Listing the State of Configuration Files

To find the state of all the configuration files for a given Linux command, use a command with the -qcsf option with the name of the file, as shown here, or the -qcs option with the name of a package.

For example:

```
# rpm -qcsf /bin/bash
normal          /etc/skel/.bash_logout
normal          /etc/skel/.bash_profile
normal          /etc/skel/.bashrc
```

Listing the Most Recently Installed Packages

To list the most recently installed packages, use the following command with the --last option. This is very useful if you recently installed or upgraded a number of packages and something unexpected happens. If you cannot remember the package names, you can use the --last option to list out packages in reverse order of installation.

You can pipe the output of a query to the head command to show only the last ten packages that were installed or upgraded, as shown following:

```
# rpm -qa --last | head
comps-8.0-0.20020910         Sat 05 Oct 2002 01:17:30 PM CDT
tkinter-2.2.1-17             Sat 05 Oct 2002 01:16:58 PM CDT
tix-8.2.0b1-74               Sat 05 Oct 2002 01:16:52 PM CDT
tclx-8.3-74                  Sat 05 Oct 2002 01:16:44 PM CDT
python-tools-2.2.1-17        Sat 05 Oct 2002 01:16:41 PM CDT
mx-2.0.3-6                   Sat 05 Oct 2002 01:16:34 PM CDT
libxslt-python-1.0.19-1      Sat 05 Oct 2002 01:16:31 PM CDT
librpm404-devel-4.0.4-8x.27 Sat 05 Oct 2002 01:16:27 PM CDT
itcl-3.2-74                  Sat 05 Oct 2002 01:16:12 PM CDT
gnumeric-1.0.9-2             Sat 05 Oct 2002 01:15:46 PM CDT
```

You can pass options to the head command to show more or fewer than ten lines. In general, starting with the last ten packages can help you track down something you installed the day before.

Creating custom queries

The --qf or --queryformat option allows you to create custom queries with the rpm command, although in a rather difficult manner. You need to pass a query format string, the syntax of which originates with the C printf function and requires precision.

The basic syntax of the query format is %{tag_name}. (The percent sign is about the only part that comes from the C printf function.) You can combine tag names to display more than one item per package. You can also add formatting options following C language conventions.

For example, to list all package names, use a command like the following:

```
# rpm -qa --qf "%{NAME}"
redhat-menusglibccracklibgdbmgmplibacllibjpeglincpcreshadow-
utilslibtermcapfreetypeinfofileutilspsmiscntpmountcracklib-dictskrb5-libscyrus-
saslusermodeXftlibpnglibxmllibbonobopythonpygtk2pyxf86configredhat-config-
usersredhat-config-keyboardrpm404-pythongnome-vfs2libgnomeuiashbind-utilscyrus-
sasl-plaindos2unixethtoolfingergroffautofskbdconfiglesslibtool-
libslockdevmailcapMAKEDEVmouseconfignetpbmntsysvORBitpartedppppsutilsrdaterhnlibrp
mrshsetuptoolstatserialtarlilopciutilstimeconfigunzipkernel-pcmcia-
csanacronXFree86
```

This command used the simplest format, which is just the value of the tag in the package headers; in this case, the package names. Because we used no other formatting, this command outputs all the package names smashed together. To deal with this problem in the output, you can place a \n, the C language convention for a newline character, at the end of the format string. This fixes the output considerably.

For example (showing just the first few entries):

```
# rpm -qa --qf "%{NAME}\n"
redhat-menus
glibc
cracklib
gdbm
gmp
libacl
libjpeg
linc
pcre
shadow-utils
libtermcap
freetype
info
fileutils
psmisc
ntp
mount
cracklib-dicts
krb5-libs
```

```
cyrus-sasl
usermode
Xft
```

This command provides a custom query that is essentially the same as the `rpm -qa` command. You'll likely not use this command in favor of the simpler `rpm` option, but you can use this example as a guide for creating your own custom queries.

 A great many of the command-line options to the `rpm` command are defined as popt aliases. These popt aliases define the `rpm` command-line options in terms of longer query format strings. See Chapter 21 for more information on popt.

You can add items to the query string and use C language conventions for formatting and controlling the amount of space provided for each item output.

For example, the following command prints the name and platform for all packages, showing the first few entries, formatted with 20 characters for each item:

```
rpm -qa --qf "%-20{NAME} %-20{PLATFORM}\n"
redhat-menus         noarch-redhat-linux-gnu
glibc                i686-redhat-linux-gnu
cracklib             i386-redhat-linux
gdbm                 i386-redhat-linux-gnu
gmp                  i386-redhat-linux-gnu
libacl               i386-redhat-linux-gnu
libjpeg              i386-redhat-linux
linc                 i386-redhat-linux-gnu
pcre                 i386-redhat-linux
shadow-utils         i386-redhat-linux-gnu
libtermcap           i386-redhat-linux
freetype             i386-redhat-linux-gnu
info                 i386-redhat-linux-gnu
fileutils            i386-redhat-linux-gnu
psmisc               i386-redhat-linux
ntp                  i386-redhat-linux-gnu
mount                i386-redhat-linux-gnu
cracklib-dicts       i386-redhat-linux
krb5-libs            i386-redhat-linux-gnu
cyrus-sasl           i386-redhat-linux-gnu
usermode             i386-redhat-linux-gnu
Xft                  i386-redhat-linux-gnu
```

Working With Query Format Tags

To build queries with the `--queryformat` option, you need to know what tags you can use. To list the names of the available query format tags, use the `--querytags` option, which returns a large set of tags, truncated here for space:

```
# rpm --querytags
NAME
VERSION
RELEASE
SUMMARY
DESCRIPTION
BUILDTIME
```

Each of these tags also has a version with a `RPMTAG_` prefix, such as `RPMTAG_NAME`. You can use this tags with or without the `RPMTAG_` prefix. For example:

```
$ rpm -q --qf "%{RPMTAG_NAME}\n" sendmail
sendmail
```

Note how this command uses the `-q` option to query for one package, instead of `-qa` to query for all packages. You can use query formats with any of the `rpm` queries.

The next sections cover the available tags based on the type of the information stored in the tag.

Querying for Package Information

Many of the query format tags refer to package-information data stored in the RPM header, introduced in Chapter 3. Table 5-3 lists the package-information tags.

TABLE 5-3 PACKAGE-INFORMATION QUERY TAGS

Tag	Holds
NAME	Package name
VERSION	Version number
RELEASE	Release number
SUMMARY	One-line summary of the package contents
DESCRIPTION	Descriptive text about the package
BUILDTIME	Time package was built
BUILDHOST	Host package was built on

Tag	Holds
SIZE	Size of all the regular files in the payload
LICENSE	License package was released under
GROUP	Descriptive group or category name for the package
OS	Operating system package was built for
ARCH	Architecture, such as i386
SOURCERPM	The associated source RPM
CHANGELOGTIME	Array of changelog times
CHANGELOGNAME	Array of changelog names
CHANGELOGTEXT	Array of changelog text entries
PREIN	Pre-install script
POSTIN	Post-install script
PREUN	Pre-uninstall script
POSTUN	Post uninstall script
PLATFORM	Platform

All of these tags, except for the CHANGELOGTIME, CHANGELOGTEXT, and CHANGELOGNAME tags, are single-value tags.

Formatting Arrays

Many of the header entries are arrays, so the header tags can hold more than one item. For example, RPM packages can have more than one file in the payload.

To specify a format for each item in an array, use square brackets. For example:

```
$ rpm -q --queryformat "[%-50{FILENAMES} %{FILESIZES}\n]" sendmail
/etc/aliases                                       1295
/etc/aliases.db                                    12288
/etc/mail                                          4096
/etc/mail/Makefile                                 748
/etc/mail/access                                   331
/etc/mail/access.db                                12288
/etc/mail/domaintable                              0
/etc/mail/domaintable.db                           12288
/etc/mail/helpfile                                 5588
/etc/mail/local-host-names                         64
```

This example lists the files and file sizes within a package, with the listing of files truncated for size.

If you want to mix array tags with non-array tags, you can use an equals sign, =, in front of the tag name to specify that the given tag should be repeated for each item in the array. For example:

```
$ rpm -q --queryformat "[%-15{=NAME} %-50{FILENAMES}\n]" sendmail jikes
sendmail      /usr/lib/sendmail
sendmail      /usr/sbin/mailstats
sendmail      /usr/sbin/makemap
sendmail      /usr/sbin/praliases
sendmail      /usr/sbin/sendmail.sendmail
sendmail      /usr/sbin/smrsh
sendmail      /usr/share/man/man1/mailq.sendmail.1.gz
sendmail      /usr/share/man/man1/newaliases.sendmail.1.gz
sendmail      /usr/share/man/man5/aliases.sendmail.5.gz
sendmail      /usr/share/man/man8/mailstats.8.gz
sendmail      /usr/share/man/man8/makemap.8.gz
sendmail      /usr/share/man/man8/praliases.8.gz
sendmail      /usr/share/man/man8/rmail.8.gz
sendmail      /usr/share/man/man8/sendmail.8.gz
sendmail      /usr/share/man/man8/smrsh.8.gz
sendmail      /var/spool/clientmqueue
sendmail      /var/spool/mqueue
jikes         /usr/bin/jikes
jikes         /usr/doc/jikes-1.18/license.htm
jikes         /usr/man/man1/jikes.1.gz
```

This example, also truncated for size, lists the package name along with the file name for the files contained in these two packages.

Special Formatting

Some of the tags within an RPM package header contain special binary information that usually makes no sense when printed out. To help with these header tags, you can use special RPM formatting options, using a syntax like the following:

```
%{tag:special_format}
```

For example, to print the INSTALLTIME tag, use %{INSTALLTIME:date}, which specifies to print the INSTALLTIME tag in date format. For example:

```
$ rpm -q --qf "%{NAME}-%{VERSION}-%{RELEASE} %{INSTALLTIME:date}\n" jikes
jikes-1.18-1 Fri 06 Dec 2002 09:19:30 PM CST
```

This example prints the NAME-VERSION-RELEASE of the package, along with the INSTALLTIME in date format.

Most tags in a header are optional. You can print the value of these tags, but you may get nothing. To help deal with this, you can use a conditional operator based loosely on the C language ternary operator. The basic syntax is:

```
%|tag?{print_if_present}:{print_if_absent}|
```

With the normal %{tag} syntax, this conditional syntax gets complicated really fast. You need to break the elements down. For example:

```
$ rpm -q --qf "%{NAME} %|EPOCH?{%{EPOCH}}:{(no Epoch)}|\n" perl
perl 1
```

If the package has a value for the EPOCH tag, you will see output as shown in this example, which indicates that the perl package has an EPOCH of 1. Most packages do not have an EPOCH defined, in which case you will see output like the following:

```
$ rpm -q --qf "%{NAME} %|EPOCH?{%{EPOCH}}:{(no Epoch)}|\n" sendmail
sendmail (no Epoch)
```

See the "Getting Information on Package Files" section in this chapter for more on querying RPM package files.

Other special-formatting options are described in the following sections on the dependency and file information tags.

Querying for Package Dependencies

A number of tags provide package dependency information. Each of these tags comes in triples, which are formatted similarly. For example, for the capabilities a package requires, you have the REQUIRENAME, REQUIREVERSION, and REQUIREFLAGS tags.

The REQUIRENAME tag holds an array of required capability names. The REQUIRE-VERSION tag holds an array of the versions of the required capabilities. The REQUIREFLAGS tag ties the two together with a set of bit flags that specify whether the requirement is for a version less than the given number, equal to the given number, greater than or equal to the given number, and so on.

Table 5-4 lists the dependency tags.

TABLE 5-4 DEPENDENCY QUERY TAGS

Tag	Holds
CONFLICTFLAGS	Array of flags for the capabilities this package conflicts
CONFLICTNAME	Array of capabilities that this package conflicts
CONFLICTVERSION	Array of version numbers that this package conflicts
REQUIREFLAGS	Array of flags for the capabilities this package requires
REQUIRENAME	Array of capabilities that this package requires
REQUIREVERSION	Array of version numbers that this package requires
OBSOLETENAME	Array of capabilities that this package obsoletes
OBSOLETEFLAGS	Array of flags for the capabilities this package obsoletes
OBSOLETEVERSION	Array of version numbers that this package obsoletes
PROVIDENAME	Array of capabilities that this package provides
PROVIDEFLAGS	Array of flags for the capabilities this package provides
PROVIDEVERSION	Array of version numbers that this package provides

---

Each of these tags is an array. The PROVIDENAME, PROVIDEVERSION, and PROVIDEFLAGS tags work similarly for the capabilities this package provides. The CONFLICTNAME, CONFLICTVERSION, and CONFLICTFLAGS tags specify the conflicts, and, the OBSOLETENAME, OBSOLETEVERSION, and OBSOLETEFLAGS tags specify the obsolete dependencies.

The depflags special-formatting option prints out the flag tags, such as REQUIREFLAGS, in human-readable format. For example, the following command lists the requirements for a package:

```
$ rpm -q --qf \
   "[%{REQUIRENAME} %{REQUIREFLAGS:depflags} %{REQUIREVERSION}\n]" sendmail
rpmlib(VersionedDependencies) <= 3.0.3-1
chkconfig >= 1.3
/usr/sbin/useradd
/bin/mktemp
fileutils
gawk
sed
sh-utils
procmail
```

```
bash >= 2.0
/bin/sh
rpmlib(PayloadFilesHavePrefix) <= 4.0-1
rpmlib(CompressedFileNames) <= 3.0.4-1
```

For those requirements that have specific version numbers, this command prints out the version number along with the operator, such as >= for a version greater than or equal to the given number.

Note that for many of the requirements, there is no specific version information.

 In addition to normal capabilities, most packages will have some RPM-related requirements as well, which specify any required RPM versions, for example, rpmlib(CompressedFileNames).

Querying for File Information

The file-information tags hold data on the files within the package payload, that is, the files the rpm command installs when you install the package. These tags are arrays, with one value per file.

Table 5-5 lists the file-information tags.

TABLE 5-5 FILE-INFORMATION QUERY TAGS

Tag	Holds
OLDFILENAMES	Array of full file names, used in older packages
FILESIZES	Array of sizes for each file
FILEMODES	Array of permissions for each file
FILERDEVS	Array of rdev values for each file
FILEMTIMES	Array of modified times for each file
FILEMD5S	MD5 checksum for each file
FILELINKTOS	Array of link information for each file
FILEFLAGS	Array of flags for each file
FILEUSERNAME	Array of user names for the file owners
FILEGROUPNAME	Array of group names for the file owners

Continued

TABLE 5-5 FILE-INFORMATION QUERY TAGS *(Continued)*

Tag	Holds
FILEDEVICES	Array of devices for each file
FILEINODES	Array of inodes for each file
FILELANGS	Array of language flags for each file
DIRINDEXES	Array of values that matches the DIRNAMES with the BASENBAMES
BASENAMES	Array of file base names
DIRNAMES	Array of directories that matches up with BASENAMES

The OLDFILENAMES tag is used when the files are not compressed, when the REQUIRENAME tag does not indicate rpmlib(CompressedFileNames).

The FILESIZES tag specifies the size of each file in the payload, while the FILEMODES tag specifies the file modes (permissions) and the FILEMTIMES tag holds the last modification time for each file.

The BASENAMES tag holds an array of the base file names for the files in the payload. The DIRNAMES tag holds an array of the directories for the files. The DIRINDEXES tag contains an index into the DIRNAMES for the directory. Each RPM must have either OLDFILENAMES or the triple of BASENAMES, DIRNAMES, and DIRINDEXES, but not both.

When listing file information, use the square bracket array syntax with your query formats. You can use the perms special formatting option for the file modes. For example:

```
$ rpm -q --qf "[%-15{=NAME} %-36{FILENAMES} %{FILEMODES:perms}\n]" jikes
jikes          /usr/bin/jikes                       -rwxr-xr-x
jikes          /usr/doc/jikes-1.18/license.htm      -rw-r--r--
jikes          /usr/man/man1/jikes.1.gz             -rw-r--r--
```

Other Query Format Tags

In addition to all these tags, there are a number of other miscellaneous tags, many of which are listed in Table 5-6.

TABLE 5-6 OTHER QUERY TAGS

Tag	Holds
ARCHIVESIZE	Uncompressed size of the payload section
COOKIE	Holds an opaque string
RPMVERSION	Holds the version of the RPM tool used to create the package
OPTFLAGS	Compiler optimization flags used to build the package
PAYLOADFORMAT	Must be cpio for LSB-compliant packages
PAYLOADCOMPRESSOR	Must be gzip for LSB-compliant packages
PAYLOADFLAGS	Must be 9 for LSB-compliant packages
RHNPLATFORM	Holds an opaque string
FILEVERIFYFLAGS	Bitmask that specifies which tests to perform to verify the files after an install

For example, you can list the version of RPM that created a package with a command like the following:

```
$ rpm -qp --qf "%{name} - rpm %{rpmversion}\n" *.rpm
acroread - rpm 2.5.5
canvas - rpm 3.0.3
jikes - rpm 4.0.2
SDL - rpm 2.5.1
ted - rpm 2.5.5
```

See Appendix D for a listing of all the tags in an RPM file.

Other queries

If what you've seen so far isn't enough, the rpm command supports a number of extra queries, mostly of use to developers at Red Hat.

Table 5-7 summarizes these extra queries.

TABLE 5-7 EXTRA QUERIES

Option	Meaning
`--dump`	Dumps out extra information on files
`--fileid` *md5_id*	Queries for the package with the given MD5 digest
`--hdrid` *sha1_header_id*	Queries for the package with the given header identifier number, in SHA1 format
`--last`	Reorders the output of the `rpm` command to show the most recently-installed packages first
`--pkgid` *md5_id*	Queries for the package with the given MD5 package ID
`--querybynumber` *number*	Queries for the given entry, by number, in the RPM database
`--tid` *transaction_id*	Queries for the package or packages with the given transaction ID

Getting Information on Package Files

In addition to querying the RPM database about installed packages, the `rpm` command provides the handy ability to extract information from RPM files. This is very useful for determining whether you want to install a given package or not. It also helps with the simple task of figuring out what a package's purpose, especially if names like *kudzu*, *anaconda*, or *dia* don't immediately tell you what the corresponding packages provide.

The `-p` option tells the `rpm` command to provide information on the given package file. The basic syntax is:

```
rpm -qp option_query_options filename.rpm
```

You can use the longer option, `--package`, in place of `-p`. You can also pass more than one RPM file to the command.

The query information options shown previously for installed packages also work for RPM files. For example, to list the configuration files for a package, combine the `-q`, `-p`, and `-c` options with the name of a package file, as shown following:

Querying Package Files Remotely

As shown in Chapter 4, you can access RPM package files over a network using FTP or HTTP connections. To query remote files, use the same rules as shown in Chapter 4, with the following syntax:

```
rpm -qf ftp://username:password@hostname:port/path/to/rpm/file
rpm -qf ftp://username@hostname:port/path/to/rpm/file
rpm -qf ftp://hostname:port/path/to/rpm/file
rpm -qf http://hostname:port/path/to/rpm/file
```

If your system resides behind a firewall with a proxy server, use the options in the following table to name the proxy. Note that these proxy options only work with the TIS Firewall toolkit.

Network Proxy Option	Meaning
--ftpproxy proxy_hostname	Names the proxy system
--ftpport proxy_port_number	Network port number on the proxy system
--httpproxy proxy_hostname	Names the proxy system
--httpport proxy_port_number	Network port number on the proxy system

---

```
# rpm -qpc telnet-server-0.17-23.i386.rpm
/etc/xinetd.d/telnet
```

To list all the files in an RPM package, combine the -q, -p, and -l options:

```
# rpm -qpl telnet-server-0.17-23.i386.rpm
/etc/xinetd.d/telnet
/usr/sbin/in.telnetd
/usr/share/man/man5/issue.net.5.gz
/usr/share/man/man8/in.telnetd.8.gz
/usr/share/man/man8/telnetd.8.gz
```

Verifying Installed RPM Packages

You can do a lot more than just query packages in the RPM database. You can ask the rpm command to verify packages with the -V (or --verify) option.

The basic syntax is:

```
rpm -V verify_options package_name
```

For example:

```
# rpm -V telnet
#
```

If everything checks out, you'll get no response. The rpm command reports problems only. For example, if you have an installation of the telnet-server package that is missing some files, the rpm -V command will let you know, as shown following:

```
# rpm -V telnet-server
missing   c /etc/xinetd.d/telnet
missing     /usr/sbin/in.telnetd
missing   d /usr/share/man/man5/issue.net.5.gz
```

In this example, the c and d stand for configuration and documentation files, respectively.

 The rpm -V command will also report missing dependencies.

Verifying your entire system

To verify your entire system, use the -a option.
    For example:

```
# rpm -Va
SM5....T c /usr/share/info/dir
.......T c /etc/krb5.conf
.......T   /usr/share/pixmaps/gnome-default-dlg.png
.......T   /usr/share/pixmaps/gnome-error.png
.......T   /usr/share/pixmaps/gnome-info.png
.......T   /usr/share/pixmaps/gnome-question.png
.......T   /usr/share/pixmaps/gnome-warning.png
S.5....T c /etc/sysconfig/pcmcia
.....U..   /dev/winradio0
```

Each line that the rpm command outputs indicates a problem with the given file. The rpm command uses letter codes to show the type of the problem. Table 5-8 lists the letter codes with their meanings.

TABLE 5-8 RPM VERIFY OUTPUT CODES

Code	Meaning
S	File size differs.
M	File mode differs.
5	The MD5 checksum differs.
D	The major and minor version numbers differ on a device file.
L	A mismatch occurs in a link.
U	The file ownership differs.
G	The file group owner differs.
T	The file time (mtime) differs.

Controlling the verification

You can use a number of options to tell the verification command specifically what to check for or not check for. Table 5-9 lists these options.

TABLE 5-9 CONTROLLING THE VERIFICATION

Option	Usage
--nodeps	Don't verify dependencies.
--nodigest	Don't verify the package or header digests.
--nofiles	Don't verify the file attributes.
--noscripts	Don't try to verify the scripts.
--nosignature	Don't verify the package or header signatures.
--nolinkto	Don't verify the link file attribute.
--nomd5	Don't verify the MD5 digest file attribute.
--nosize	Don't verify the file size attribute.
--nouser	Don't verify the file owner attribute.

Continued

TABLE 5-9 CONTROLLING THE VERIFICATION *(Continued)*

Option	Usage
--nogroup	Don't verify the file group owner attribute.
--nomtime	Don't verify the file mtime attribute.
--nomode	Don't verify the file mode attribute.
--nordev	Don't verify the file rdev attribute.
-a	Verify all packages in a given group.
-g *group*	Verify all packages in a given group.
-p *file*	Verify the given RPM file.

 Chapter 12 covers another option for verifying a package file, the rpm -K command.

The --nofiles option is often used with the -Va option to verify the whole system but skip tests of file attributes. This command is used so often it has become an idiom for RPM usage, especially for debugging RPM problems. Run a command like the following:

```
$ rpm -Va --nofiles
```

Working with the RPM Database

As mentioned in Chapter 3, the RPM database is stored in /var/lib/rpm. The files in that directory are Berkeley DB files, as shown by the file command:

```
# file /var/lib/rpm/*
/var/lib/rpm/Basenames:      Berkeley DB (Hash, version 7, native byte-order)
/var/lib/rpm/Conflictname:   Berkeley DB (Hash, version 7, native byte-order)
/var/lib/rpm/__db.001:       data
/var/lib/rpm/__db.002:       X11 SNF font data, LSB first
/var/lib/rpm/__db.003:       X11 SNF font data, LSB first
/var/lib/rpm/Dirnames:       Berkeley DB (Btree, version 8, native byte-order)
```

```
/var/lib/rpm/Filemd5s:        Berkeley DB (Btree, version 8, native byte-order)
/var/lib/rpm/Group:           Berkeley DB (Hash, version 7, native byte-order)
/var/lib/rpm/Installtid:      Berkeley DB (Btree, version 8, native byte-order)
/var/lib/rpm/Name:            Berkeley DB (Hash, version 7, native byte-order)
/var/lib/rpm/Packages:        Berkeley DB (Hash, version 7, native byte-order)
/var/lib/rpm/Providename:     Berkeley DB (Hash, version 7, native byte-order)
/var/lib/rpm/Provideversion:  Berkeley DB (Btree, version 8, native byte-order)
/var/lib/rpm/Requirename:     Berkeley DB (Hash, version 7, native byte-order)
/var/lib/rpm/Requireversion:  Berkeley DB (Btree, version 8, native byte-order)
/var/lib/rpm/Sha1header:      Berkeley DB (Btree, version 8, native byte-order)
/var/lib/rpm/Sigmd5:          Berkeley DB (Btree, version 8, native byte-order)
/var/lib/rpm/Triggername:     Berkeley DB (Hash, version 7, native byte-order)
```

Each file is a separate database in Berkeley DB format, except for a few __db data files. (These are not really X11 font files, just plain data files. The file command is confused by the data in the files.)

If something goes wrong with your RPM database, you can first try to rebuild it. If that fails, you may need to initialize a new database, although that is generally not needed. First and foremost, however, you should back up this database.

Backing up the RPM database

As mentioned before, the RPM database resides in the /var/lib/rpm. You can back up the RPM database by using commands such as the following:

```
# cd /var/lib
# tar cvf rpmdb.tar ./rpm
# gzip rpmdb.tar
```

The Berkeley DB Library

Available from SleepyCat Software at www.sleepycat.com/, the Berkeley DB library provides a simple database API. This is not a traditional relational database. Instead, data values are stored in what amounts to a persistent hash table of name/value pairs. This type of database is very quick to look up a named entry (such as a package name) but is not so quick for iterating over all the entries.

One of the nice things about this library is that it is available in an open-source format, and you can get programming API libraries for C, C++, Java, Python, Perl, and Tcl languages.

The RPM database is really a number of Berkeley DB databases, each designed for a different type of query.

These commands create a tar archive from the contents of the rpm directory (where the RPM database is stored) and compress the file with the `gzip` command.

 Adding the `z` option to the `tar` command can create a compressed archive directly, without the need for the `gzip` command.

Rebuilding the RPM database

If the RPM database has been corrupted in some way, you can use the `--rebuilddb` option to tell the `rpm` command to rebuild your database.

For example:

```
rpm --rebuilddb
```

This command rebuilds the RPM database from the installed packages, the file named Packages in the /var/lib/rpm directory. Only the Packages file is required. All the other files can be recreated from the Packages file. If your database is OK, this command won't do much, other than shrink the size of your RPM database by removing unused entries. This command will take some time to execute, though.

 Before running this command, back up your RPM database.

To check that the `rpm --rebuilddb` command has not damaged the RPM database, you can check with a file listing, query all packages, and then check the results of the `rpm --rebuilddb` command with another file listing when done.

Another useful technique that can help with a corrupted RPM database is to use the db_dump and db_load utilities that come with RPM (from the SleepyCat DB database library). Use db_dump to dump the Packages file. Then, use db_load to reload the Packages file. The act of dumping and restoring may fix a corrupted file. As always, back up your RPM database prior to performing these commands.

Creating a new RPM database

If all else fails, use the `--initdb` option to tell the `rpm` command to create a new empty RPM database. In almost all cases, you do not want to create a new RPM database, since this database will be empty. It will not have any knowledge about the packages you have already installed on your system. That could lead to a lot of problems, since you have the files installed, but the RPM system just doesn't know about them.

The basic syntax follows.

```
rpm --initdb
```

 This command should not damage an existing database.

If the RPM system cannot be rebuilt, you may have to reinstall the operating system to recreate a clean system. In general, if things are this far gone, reinstalling may be your best answer instead of wiping the RPM database and creating an empty database.

You can also use the --dbpath option to tell the rpm command to create an RPM database in a different directory.

For example:

```
mkdir /tmp/rpm
rpm --initdb --dbpath /tmp/rpm
```

These commands create a temporary directory and an RPM database in the /tmp/rpm directory.

After running this command, you can examine the files created.

```
# ls -l /tmp/rpm
total 288
-rw-r--r--   1 root     root        8192 Oct 10 20:29 __db.001
-rw-r--r--   1 root     root     1310720 Oct 10 20:29 __db.002
-rw-r--r--   1 root     root      360448 Oct 10 20:29 __db.003
-rw-r--r--   1 root     root       12288 Oct 10 20:29 Packages
```

This shows an empty RPM database.

Summary

This chapter covers the rpm command options to query the RPM database and RPM package files. You can determine the packages installed on your system, as well as which packages are responsible for the files on your system.

The RPM database maintains a lot of information about the files and packages on your system. Thus, it is crucial for managing your Linux systems. You should back up the RPM database before and after any installation, upgrade, or removal of packages.

You can also use the `--rebuilddb` option to the `rpm` command to rebuild a damaged RPM database.

Chapter 6

Package Dependencies

PACKAGES AREN'T BUILT IN a vacuum. Web applications, for example, build on system networking libraries, system-encryption libraries, and system-file input and output libraries.

This chapter covers dependencies between packages, along with ways to discover and manage those dependencies.

Understanding the Dependency Concept

A *dependency* occurs when one package depends on another. You might think it would make for an easier-to-manage system if no package depended on any others, but you'd face a few problems, not the least of which would be dramatically increased disk usage.

Packages on your Linux system depend on other packages. Just about every package with an application, for example, depends on the system C libraries, since these libraries provide common facilities that just about every program uses. Network applications typically depend on low-level networking libraries. These dependencies really work in your favor, since a security bug fix in the network libraries can update all applications that make use of the updated libraries.

Furthermore, sharing software means that each package has less code to maintain and thus improved quality. Code sharing has been in the computer lexicon since the 1960s.

Although quite a few packages depend on system-level libraries, some packages depend on applications defined in other packages. The Emacs text editor package, for example, depends on the Perl scripting language, specifically, the `perl` command. Database client programs usually depend on the database server applications.

The RPM database tracks dependency information, so it can, for example, stop attempts to remove packages that other packages depend on or inform users of dependent packages upon installation.

Capabilities

In RPM terminology, each package provides capabilities. A *capability* is simply a text string that the package claims it provides. In most cases, a capability names a file or a package. But the capability can be any arbitrary text string.

Other packages can then depend on certain capabilities. (You can use this concept in building your own packages.) Each package lists the capabilities it requires as well as the capabilities it provides.

Package dependencies and capabilities are very important when creating spec files for building your own RPM packages, the subject of Chapter 10.

When you install a package, the capability information is stored in the RPM database. When you remove a package, the `rpm` command checks the RPM database. If the package you are trying to remove provides a capability that another package needs, the command will generate an error. If you try to remove a package that other packages depend on, you'll see an error like the following:

```
# rpm -e setup
error: Failed dependencies:
    setup is needed by (installed) basesystem-8.0-1
    setup >= 2.0.3 is needed by (installed) initscripts-6.95-1
    setup >= 2.5.4-1 is needed by (installed) filesystem-2.1.6-5
    setup is needed by (installed) xinetd-2.3.7-2
    setup is needed by (installed) dump-0.4b28-4
```

To verify that the package has not been removed, you can query for the package after trying to remove it, as shown following:

```
# rpm -q setup
setup-2.5.20-1
```

This shows that the `rpm` command has not removed the setup package due to the errors.

Chapter 4 covers ways to force the rpm command to do what you want, although this can cause problems if you try to force the issue and remove a crucial package. In virtually all cases, you should not use any of the force options, as this can cause problems with the RPM system, since the force options are purposely ignoring safety checks performed by the rpm command.

Many capabilities that packages require are system libraries, especially shared libraries. Shared libraries, which usually have a *.so* file extension (short for *shared object*), provide a memory-efficient means for applications to share program code. These libraries may also have a *.so.number* extension, such as libc.so.6.

Shared libraries on Windows are called DLLs, short for Dynamic Link Libraries. The implementations differ, but the Windows DLL concept is similar to Linux and Unix shared objects.

Shared libraries have been part of Linux for a long time and have nothing to do with the RPM system. Shared libraries accessed by a program, however, represent natural dependencies. Because so many programs depend on shared libraries, the RPM system can automatically handle many shared-library dependencies.

To list the shared libraries that a program accesses, use the ldd command, for example:

```
$ ldd /bin/grep
    libc.so.6 => /lib/i686/libc.so.6 (0x42000000)
    /lib/ld-linux.so.2 => /lib/ld-linux.so.2
(0x40000000)
```

Other dependencies include version-specific dependencies.

Version dependencies

An application may depend on a capability provided by another package. It may also depend on the capability that a specific version of another package provides. For example, some add-ons to the Apache Web server depend on the version of Apache. The Apache 2.0 version made a number of changes that affect add-on packages. Some Apache add-on packages depend on version 1.3; others depend on version 2.0.

Most package dependencies assume some level of compatibility and require a version at or above a given version number (for example, version 2.0 or later).

 You'll see more version dependencies when applications make major changes, such as the change from 1.3 to 2.0 for the Apache Web server.

Conflicts

Some packages may provide capabilities that interfere with those in other packages. This is called a *conflict*. Installing conflicting packages is an error. For example, the httpd package (the Apache Web server) conflicts with the thttpd package. Both packages want to provide the primary Web server for a system.

The RPM system will prevent you from installing packages that conflict with other packages. You can force the issue, using the techniques described in Chapter 4, and override the RPM system. But in most cases, you should not install packages that conflict.

Obsoletes

The RPM system supports one more type of dependency, called *obsoletes*. This refers to a capability that a package provides that makes another capability obsolete. For example, a new version of the perl interpreter may make an older version obsolete. In most cases, the obsoletes dependency should be used when the name of a package changes. For example, the apache Web server package became the httpd package. You would expect the new package, httpd, to obsolete the old package name, apache.

This brings the total to four types of dependencies that the RPM system tracks:

◆ *Requires,* which tracks the capabilities a package requires

◆ *Provides,* which tracks the capabilities a package provides for other packages

◆ *Conflicts,* which describes the capabilities that if installed, conflict with capabilities in a package

◆ *Obsoletes,* which describes the capabilities that this package will make obsolete

Packages advertise this dependency information. Each dependency holds the type, such as requires, a capability, such as a shared library, and optionally a version number, such as requiring the python package at a version number greater than or equal to 2.2.

You can check package dependencies by using, as you'd guess, the rpm command.

Checking for Dependencies

The `rpm -q` command queries the RPM database or RPM package files. With the right options to this command, you can check for the four types of package dependencies as well. These options are based on the concept of capabilities introduced previously.

You can query what capabilities a package requires. You can also query what capabilities a package provides. You can query for the obsoleting and conflicting information as well. Furthermore, given a capability, you can query which packages require this capability as well as which packages provide this capability.

There are quite a few more options you can use with the `rpm -q` command for querying packages. See Chapter 5 for more on querying packages and package files.

Determining the capabilities a package requires

The first and most important step is to determine what capabilities a package requires. If all the required capabilities are met, you can safely install the package (barring other things that can go wrong, such as conflicts). The requires dependencies are by far the most important.

The `--requires` option to the `rpm -q` command lists the capabilities a given package requires. The basic syntax is:

```
rpm -q query_options --requires packages
```

For example:

```
$ rpm -qp --requires sendmail-8.12.5-7.i386.rpm
/usr/sbin/alternatives
rpmlib(VersionedDependencies) <= 3.0.3-1
chkconfig >= 1.3
/usr/sbin/useradd
/bin/mktemp
fileutils
gawk
sed
sh-utils
procmail
bash >= 2.0
/bin/sh
/bin/sh
```

```
/bin/sh
/bin/sh
/bin/sh
rpmlib(PayloadFilesHavePrefix) <= 4.0-1
rpmlib(CompressedFileNames) <= 3.0.4-1
/bin/bash
libcrypto.so.2
libcrypt.so.1
libc.so.6
libc.so.6(GLIBC_2.0)
libc.so.6(GLIBC_2.1)
libc.so.6(GLIBC_2.1.3)
libc.so.6(GLIBC_2.2)
libdb-4.0.so
libgdbm.so.2
libhesiod.so.0
liblber.so.2
libldap.so.2
libnsl.so.1
libnsl.so.1(GLIBC_2.0)
libresolv.so.2
libresolv.so.2(GLIBC_2.0)
libresolv.so.2(GLIBC_2.2)
libsasl.so.7
libssl.so.2
```

This example tests an RPM package file, sendmail-8.12.5-7.i386.rpm, for the
requires dependency, in other words, what capabilities the package requires. The
sendmail package depends on a lot of other parts of the system, as you can see in
the response to the command shown previously. Most of the dependencies are for
system libraries (all the dependencies ending in *.so* or *.so.number*). This package
requires other capabilities (packages in this case). It also requires the chkconfig
package at a specific version, version 1.3 or higher, and the bash package at version
2.0 or higher. The sendmail package also requires a particular version of the RPM
system (the rpmlib dependency).

Always check what a package requires before installing the package. You
can also use the --test option when trying to install the package to first
test whether the installation can proceed. See Chapter 4 for details on
installing packages and the --test option. The rpm command will perform
all these checks for you anyway. Checking in advance, though, with the
--test option, helps avoid dependency hell with circular dependencies.

You can also check for what an installed package requires with the `--requires` option. For example:

```
rpm -q --requires sendmail
```

You can use the `-R` short option in place of the `--requires` option. This command returns the same data as the previous command but queries an installed package rather than an RPM package file.

You might assume that applications have the most dependencies, which is true. But even source packages may depend on other packages, often the packages needed to build the sources into an application. For example, the following command lists the capabilities required by a source RPM:

```
$ rpm -qp --requires telnet-0.17-23.src.rpm
ncurses-devel
```

Some packages require particular versions of other packages, for example:

```
rpm -qp --requires xcdroast-0.98a9-18.src.rpm
imlib-devel >= 1.9.13-9
gtk+-devel >= 1.2.10
desktop-file-utils >= 0.2.92
rpmlib(CompressedFileNames) <= 3.0.4-1
```

This example shows that the xcdroast source package requires the imlib-devel capability (in this case, a package) at version 1.9.13-9 or higher, the gtk+-devel package at version 1.2.10 or higher, and the desktop-file-utils package at version 0.2.92 or higher. This is a more stringent requirement than just depending on the given packages being installed. This RPM is also an older RPM package, based on the requirement for the rpmlib to be prior or equal to 3.0.4-1.

Some packages may require a particular version of the rpmlib, or RPM library. For example, the setup package contains special system configuration files, including the default password file, /etc/passwd.

```
$ rpm -q --requires setup
rpmlib(PayloadFilesHavePrefix) <= 4.0-1
rpmlib(CompressedFileNames) <= 3.0.4-1
```

As shown in this example, this package depends only on capabilities of the RPM system itself. The particular requirements shown here specify how the `rpm` command should treat the package payload, including how the files are listed in the package and what type of compression is used.

Determining the capabilities a package provides

Packages require capabilities, and they can provide capabilities for other packages to require. To list the capabilities a package provides, use the `--provides` option. These capabilities can be arbitrary names, shared libraries (*.so* files), and the package name itself. The basic syntax is:

```
rpm -q query_options --provides packages
```

For example, the tcsh shell package provides two capabilities, at a particular version number, as shown following:

```
$ rpm -q --provides tcsh
csh = 6.12
tcsh = 6.12-2
```

Other packages provide a lot more, including shared libraries. The httpd package provides a long list of capabilities, as shown following:

```
$ rpm -q --provides httpd
webserver
httpd-mmn = 20020628
libapr.so.0
libaprutil.so.0
mod_access.so
mod_actions.so
mod_alias.so
mod_asis.so
mod_auth_anon.so
mod_auth_dbm.so
mod_auth_digest.so
mod_auth.so
mod_autoindex.so
mod_cern_meta.so
mod_cgi.so
mod_dav_fs.so
mod_dav.so
mod_deflate.so
mod_dir.so
mod_env.so
mod_expires.so
mod_headers.so
mod_imap.so
mod_include.so
```

```
mod_info.so
mod_log_config.so
mod_mime_magic.so
mod_mime.so
mod_negotiation.so
mod_proxy_connect.so
mod_proxy_ftp.so
mod_proxy_http.so
mod_proxy.so
mod_rewrite.so
mod_setenvif.so
mod_speling.so
mod_status.so
mod_suexec.so
mod_unique_id.so
mod_userdir.so
mod_usertrack.so
mod_vhost_alias.so
httpd = 2.0.40-8
```

Checking for conflicts

Use the --conflicts option to check what conflicts with a given package. The basic syntax is:

```
rpm -q query_options --conflicts packages
```

For example:

```
# rpm -q --conflicts httpd
thttpd
```

This command tells you that the httpd package (the Apache Web server) conflicts with the thttpd package. Both packages provide a similar capability. By marking the conflict, the httpd package tells you that you cannot normally install both the httpd and thttpd packages on a system. This information comes from the httpd package, which has an entry in the package that indicates the conflict. The conflict is not guaranteed. These packages may work together, but the creator of the httpd package felt that httpd would not work with the thttpd package and helpfully let us all know.

The RPM system will report on the conflicts and indicate an error if you try to install conflicting packages. The idea of conflicts really gives package creators a way to alert users to potential problems and to tell us that one package likely won't work with another.

The force options discussed in Chapter 4 allow you to override conflicts, if absolutely necessary. In most cases, though, a conflict presents you with the choice to install one or the other of the packages, but not both.

Determining which packages require a certain capability

In addition to querying capabilities and requirements of a particular package, you can query the capabilities themselves. This function allows you to check which packages require a given capability.

The `--whatrequires` option tells the `rpm` command to report on which packages in the RPM database require a certain capability. The basic syntax is:

```
rpm -q query_options --whatrequires capability
```

Some packages are not required by anything:

```
$ rpm -q --whatrequires tcsh
no package requires tcsh
```

 Don't worry about the poor tcsh package being lonely. Because other packages do not require this package, you can easily remove the tcsh package without affecting the rest of your system.

This example shows a package name as the capability. Shared libraries are also considered capabilities. You can query on these as well. For example:

```
$ rpm -q --whatrequires librpm-4.1.so
rpm-4.1-1.06
net-snmp-5.0.1-6
rpm-python-4.1-1.06
rpm-devel-4.1-1.06
rpm-build-4.1-1.06
```

This example shows that the core RPM library is used by a number of RPM-related packages, along with, oddly enough, the net-snmp system-management package.

The capability you query for must be an explicit capability. For example, you will get different results if you query for the bash package or the command, /bin/bash. If you query for the bash package, you will see the packages that explicitly require the capability *bash*. For example:

```
$ rpm -q --whatrequires bash
gpm-1.19.3-20
info-4.0b-3
initscripts-6.40-1
sendmail-8.11.6-3
sysklogd-1.4.1-4
vixie-cron-3.0.1-63
ypbind-1.8-1
ypserv-1.3.12-2
```

If you instead query for the capability /bin/bash, that is, the file /bin/bash, you will see a different list of packages. For example:

```
$ rpm -q --whatrequires /bin/bash
apmd-3.0final-34
at-3.1.8-20
autofs-3.1.7-21
autofs-3.1.7-21
bash-2.05-8
bind-9.1.3-4
cipe-1.4.5-6
crontabs-1.10-1
dialog-0.9a-5
gpm-1.19.3-20
hotplug-2001_04_24-11
initscripts-6.40-1
ipchains-1.3.10-10
iproute-2.2.4-14
kudzu-0.99.23-1
logwatch-2.1.1-3
man-1.5i2-6
mkbootdisk-1.4.2-3
mkinitrd-3.2.6-1
mutt-1.2.5i-17
openssh-server-3.1p1-2
pine-4.44-1.72.0
rpm-build-4.0.3-1.03
rusers-server-0.17-12
sendmail-8.11.6-3
shapecfg-2.2.12-7
sharutils-4.2.1-8
sysklogd-1.4.1-4
tetex-1.0.7-30
ucd-snmp-4.2.1-7
```

```
vixie-cron-3.0.1-63
xinetd-2.3.3-1
ypbind-1.8-1
ypserv-1.3.12-2
```

There is no short form for the --whatrequires option.

Other capabilities, especially system-level shared libraries, are used by a large number of packages. For example:

```
# rpm -q --whatrequires libcrypt.so.1 | sort
autofs-3.1.7-21
cvs-1.11.1p1-3
cyrus-sasl-1.5.24-23
cyrus-sasl-devel-1.5.24-23
cyrus-sasl-plain-1.5.24-23
fetchmail-5.9.0-1
ircii-4.4Z-7
krbafs-1.0.9-2
nss_ldap-172-2
openldap12-1.2.12-4
openldap-2.0.11-13
openldap-clients-2.0.11-13
pam-0.75-19
pam_krb5-1.46-1
passwd-0.64.1-7
perl-5.6.0-17
pine-4.44-1.72.0
pwdb-0.61.1-3
python-1.5.2-35
rsh-0.17-5
rsh-server-0.17-5
screen-3.9.9-3
sendmail-8.11.6-3
shadow-utils-20000902-4
sh-utils-2.0.11-5
SysVinit-2.78-19
tcsh-6.10-6
util-linux-2.11f-17
vim-enhanced-5.8-7
wu-ftpd-2.6.1-20
xinetd-2.3.3-1
ypserv-1.3.12-2
yp-tools-2.5-1
```

Quite a few packages require encryption and decryption (the purpose of this library), making this library crucial to operating the system. Many of the packages listed here are in turn depended on by even more packages.

To help trace back capabilities, you can combine the queries. For example:

```
$ rpm -q --provides sendmail
smtpdaemon
sendmail = 8.11.6-3
$ rpm -q --whatrequires smtpdaemon
fetchmail-5.9.0-1
mutt-1.2.5i-17
```

The first command lists the capabilities that the sendmail package provides, including the generic capability of *smtpdaemon*. You can then list which packages require this particular capability, as shown in the second command. This is a big help for wading through a mess of packages depending on packages depending on yet more packages.

Determining which package provides a certain capability

To complete the circle, you can query for which package provides a certain capability. This knowledge allows you to trace a requirement back to the package that provides it.

The --whatprovides option tells the rpm command to list the capabilities a package provides. Use the --whatprovides option with the -q, or query, option to the rpm command. (There is no short form for the --whatprovides option.)

The basic syntax follows:

```
rpm -q --whatprovides capability
```

For example, to query what package provides the capability webserver, use the following command:

```
$ rpm -q --whatprovides webserver
httpd-2.0.40-8
```

In this case, the capability is identified by an arbitrary string, webserver. This is a generic name for a given capability, serving Web pages.

You can also trace individual files using the --whatprovides option. For example:

```
$ rpm -q --whatprovides /etc/skel/.bashrc
bash-2.05-8
```

The `rpm -qf` command, covered in the last chapter, is an easier way to get to the same information when tracking which package provides a particular file. For example:

```
rpm -qf /etc/skel/.bashrc
bash-2.05-8
```

If you are querying particular files, use `rpm -qf`. If you are querying capabilities, use `--whatprovides`.

Triggers

A *trigger* is a script that gets run when a package is installed or uninstalled. Triggers allow packages that depend on other packages to properly configure themselves when those other packages are installed or removed.

The `--triggers` option to the `rpm` command lists any trigger scripts in a given package. For example:

```
$ rpm -q --triggers sendmail
triggerpostun script (through /bin/sh) -- sendmail < 8.10.0
/sbin/chkconfig --add sendmail
```

This shows that the sendmail mail transfer agent (mail-sending program) provides a short trigger script.

In contrast, the anonftp (anonymous file transfer) package has a fairly complex set of triggers, as shown following:

```
$ rpm -q --triggers anonftp
triggerin script (through /bin/sh) -- glibc
copy() { file="`ls --sort=time $1 |head -n 1`"; ln -f "$file" "$2" 2>/dev/null |
| cp -df "$file" "$2"; }
# Kill off old versions
rm -f /var/ftp/lib/ld-* /var/ftp/lib/libc* /var/ftp/lib/libnsl* /var/ftp/lib/lib
nss_files* &>/dev/null || :
# Copy parts of glibc, needed by various programs in bin.
LIBCVER=`basename $(ls --sort=time /lib/libc-*.so |head -n 1) .so |cut -f2- -d-`
copy /lib/ld-${LIBCVER}.so /var/ftp/lib
copy /lib/libc-${LIBCVER}.so /var/ftp/lib
copy /lib/libnsl-${LIBCVER}.so /var/ftp/lib
copy /lib/libnss_files-${LIBCVER}.so /var/ftp/lib
md5sum /var/ftp/lib/lib*-*.so /var/ftp/lib/libtermcap.so.*.*.* 2>/dev/null >/var
/ftp/lib/libs.md5
chmod 0400 /var/ftp/lib/libs.md5
```

```
# Use ldconfig to build symlinks and whatnot.
[ ! -e /var/ftp/etc/ld.so.conf ] && touch /var/ftp/etc/ld.so.conf
/sbin/ldconfig -r /var/ftp
triggerin script (through /bin/sh) -- fileutils
copy() { file="`ls --sort=time $1 |head -n 1`"; ln -f "$file" "$2" 2>/dev/null |
| cp -df "$file" "$2"; }
copy /bin/ls /var/ftp/bin
md5sum `ls /var/ftp/bin/* |grep -v bin.md5` >/var/ftp/bin/bin.md5
chmod 0400 /var/ftp/bin/bin.md5
triggerin script (through /bin/sh) -- cpio
copy() { file="`ls --sort=time $1 |head -n 1`"; ln -f "$file" "$2" 2>/dev/null |
| cp -df "$file" "$2"; }
copy /bin/cpio /var/ftp/bin
md5sum `ls /var/ftp/bin/* |grep -v bin.md5` >/var/ftp/bin/bin.md5
chmod 0400 /var/ftp/bin/bin.md5
triggerin script (through /bin/sh) -- tar
copy() { file="`ls --sort=time $1 |head -n 1`"; ln -f "$file" "$2" 2>/dev/null |
| cp -df "$file" "$2"; }
copy /bin/tar /var/ftp/bin
md5sum `ls /var/ftp/bin/* |grep -v bin.md5` >/var/ftp/bin/bin.md5
chmod 0400 /var/ftp/bin/bin.md5
triggerin script (through /bin/sh) -- gzip
copy() { file="`ls --sort=time $1 |head -n 1`"; ln -f "$file" "$2" 2>/dev/null |
| cp -df "$file" "$2"; }
copy /bin/gzip /var/ftp/bin
ln -sf gzip /var/ftp/bin/zcat
md5sum `ls /var/ftp/bin/* |grep -v bin.md5` >/var/ftp/bin/bin.md5
chmod 0400 /var/ftp/bin/bin.md5
triggerin script (through /bin/sh) -- libtermcap
copy() { file="`ls --sort=time $1 |head -n 1`"; ln -f "$file" "$2" 2>/dev/null |
| cp -df "$file" "$2"; }
rm -f /var/ftp/lib/libtermcap.so.*.*.* &>/dev/null || :
copy '/lib/libtermcap.so.*.*.*' /var/ftp/lib
md5sum /var/ftp/lib/lib*-*.so /var/ftp/lib/libtermcap.so.*.*.* 2>/dev/null >/var
/ftp/lib/libs.md5
chmod 0400 /var/ftp/lib/libs.md5
# Use ldconfig to build symlinks and whatnot.
[ ! -e /var/ftp/etc/ld.so.conf ] && touch /var/ftp/etc/ld.so.conf
/sbin/ldconfig -r /var/ftp
triggerin script (through /bin/sh) -- ncompress
copy() { file="`ls --sort=time $1 |head -n 1`"; ln -f "$file" "$2" 2>/dev/null |
| cp -df "$file" "$2"; }
copy /usr/bin/compress /var/ftp/bin
md5sum `ls /var/ftp/bin/* |grep -v bin.md5` >/var/ftp/bin/bin.md5
```

```
chmod 0400 /var/ftp/bin/bin.md5
triggerpostun script (through /bin/sh) -- anonftp  4.0
if [ "$2" != 1 ] ; then
        # The user has multiple glibc packages installed.  We can't read the
        # user's mind, so don't do anything.
        exit 0
fi
copy() { file="`ls --sort=time $1 |head -n 1`"; ln -f "$file" "$2" 2>/dev/null |
| cp -df "$file" "$2"; }
# Kill off old versions
rm -f /var/ftp/lib/ld-* /var/ftp/lib/libc* /var/ftp/lib/libnsl* /var/ftp/lib/lib
nss_files* &>/dev/null || :
# Copy parts of glibc, needed by various programs in bin.
LIBCVER=`basename /lib/libc-*.so .so | cut -f2- -d-`
copy /lib/ld-${LIBCVER}.so /var/ftp/lib
copy /lib/libc-${LIBCVER}.so /var/ftp/lib
copy /lib/libnsl-${LIBCVER}.so /var/ftp/lib
copy /lib/libnss_files-${LIBCVER}.so /var/ftp/lib
copy /bin/ls /var/ftp/bin
copy /bin/cpio /var/ftp/bin
copy /bin/tar /var/ftp/bin
copy /bin/gzip /var/ftp/bin
ln -sf gzip /var/ftp/bin/zcat
copy /usr/bin/compress /var/ftp/bin
rm -f /var/ftp/lib/libtermcap.so.*.*.* &>/dev/null || :
copy '/lib/libtermcap.so.*.*.*' /var/ftp/lib
# Use ldconfig to build symlinks and whatnot.
[ ! -e /var/ftp/etc/ld.so.conf ] && touch /var/ftp/etc/ld.so.conf
/sbin/ldconfig -r /var/ftp
# Generate md5sums for verifyscript
md5sum /var/ftp/lib/lib*-*.so /var/ftp/lib/libtermcap.so.*.*.* 2>/dev/null >/var
/ftp/lib/libs.md5
chmod 0400 /var/ftp/lib/libs.md5
md5sum `ls /var/ftp/bin/* |grep -v bin.md5` >/var/ftp/bin/bin.md5
chmod 0400 /var/ftp/bin/bin.md5
```

Reading through the scripts indicates that this package seems to be triggered by the glibc standard C programming library package. You can confirm this by using the --triggeredby option to the rpm command, as shown following:

```
$ rpm -q --triggeredby glibc
anonftp-4.0-9
```

The anonftp package needs to be notified on changes to the glibc package, so that the anonftp package can properly set up its application. It actually uses part of glibc and is therefore highly susceptible to changes in the glibc package. Thus, the use of triggers provides essentially an extended form of dependencies. The anonftp package in this example depends so much on the glibc package that it needs to execute scripts whenever the glibc package changes.

Summary

Linux comes with many packages. Most of these packages depend on some other packages installed on your system. In RPM terms, packages provide capabilities and depend on capabilities that other packages provide. When the rpm command checks the RPM database for dependencies, it checks to ensure that all the capabilities that a given package requires are met by other installed packages.

You can trace the capabilities a package requires with the --requires option to the rpm command. You can see what capabilities a package provides for others with the --provides option.

Once you know a capability, you can query which package provides that capability with the --whatprovides option to the rpm command. And you can see which packages require that capability with the --whatrequires option.

Triggers are an extended form of dependencies. A trigger is a script that gets executed when other packages are installed or removed. This allows a package with a high dependence on another package to track changes in that package and reconfigure itself as needed.

The next chapter delves into transactions, which provide a safe means to install a set of packages. With transactions, either all the packages get installed, or none.

Chapter 7

Transactions

IN THIS CHAPTER

- ◆ Understanding transactions
- ◆ Querying for packages based on transactions
- ◆ Rolling back transactions
- ◆ Saving old packages when upgrading

WHEN PACKAGES DEPEND ON other packages, you may have to install multiple packages to add a single application. Some of the packages may install cleanly; others may not. But you have to install all of the packages to get the complete application. The designers of the RPM system understood this problem and added the concept of transactions to RPM.

This chapter covers transactions and how they can help you cleanly install a set of dependent packages. But transactions won't solve all your problems. You still have to resolve conflicts and dependencies by using the techniques provided in the last three chapters.

Understanding Transactions

A *transaction* is a way to delimit a set of operations. All the operations can be undone, often called *rolled back*. Once rolled back, the system is back in the same state it was prior to the transaction. If all the operations succeed, though, the system will be in a new state. The key issue is that all of the operations must complete successfully, or you can roll back the entire transaction. The assumption is that if any of the operations fail, the system will be in an inconsistent or erroneous state. Transactions are a way to prevent that.

Transactions are common when working with databases, but they are just as important when working with packages.

Starting with RPM version 4.0.4, transactions and rollbacks became a workable part of any administrator's toolkit. With RPM, the rpm command sets up a transaction any time you attempt to install, remove, or upgrade more than one package. The rpm command automatically makes a transaction.

When do you need transactions?

Whenever you install or remove packages, the RPM system assigns a transaction and a transaction ID to the set of packages. You can then perform operations on the packages that share the same ID, including rolling back the transaction.

 Rollbacks work only for package *upgrades* with the 4.1 version of the RPM system, not package installs.

The RPM system saves an image of the RPM package header for each package installed or removed. You can use this image, along with RPM transaction IDs, to back out of transactions should something go wrong when setting up your system.

The main advantage of transactions with RPM, though, is the fact that the rpm command automatically sets up a transaction for all the packages on each command line and does not perform the operation if any package fails. This ability to automatically set up transactions for each call to the rpm command eliminates many errors when working with packages.

Use a transaction when you need to be sure that a set of packages install properly.

Backing out of transactions

With RPM, backing out of a transaction involves two operations: rolling back the transaction and reinstalling the former packages to restore the previous system state. In the simplest case, the rpm command handles all the tasks for you. If you try to install, upgrade, or remove multiple packages and any package fails, the rpm command will restore the system state for you.

This automatic support for transactions is a great help to system administrators, but it only applies when you first install, upgrade, or remove the packages. If you have upgraded your system and later discover problems, then you can also use the --rollback option to roll the system back from a set of upgrades in a limited set of circumstances.

Transactions with the rpm Command

To set up an RPM transaction, you don't have to do much. All you need to do is pass more than one RPM package on the rpm command line. For example, to set up a transaction for installing three packages, use a command like the following:

```
rpm -ihv package1.rpm package2.rpm package3.rpm
```

If any of the packages fail to install, the rpm command will not install any packages. All of the packages will be installed, or none.

This way, if you have a number of packages that together perform some function, such as an Integrated Development Environment (IDE), along with program-language compilers and other software-development tools, you can ensure that all get installed.

As an example, say you need to install the gnorpm package, which provides a graphical front end for the rpm command, and the rpmrebuild package, which allows you to create RPMs from already-installed packages.

 The gnorpm command is covered in Chapter 8. The rpmrebuild package is covered in the "Saving Old Packages" section in this chapter.

You can install these packages with a transaction by using the following command:

```
# rpm -ihv gnorpm-0.9-1.i386.rpm rpmrebuild-1.0-0.noarch.rpm
Preparing...
######################################### [100%]
        package gnorpm-0.9-1 is already installed
```

The rpmrebuild package can be installed. (We know this since the rpm command did not issue an error about this package.) But because it was on the same command line as the gnorpm package, the transaction failed. No packages were installed.

To check that the rpmrebuild package was not installed (that is, to check that the transaction worked as expected), you can use the rpm -q command to see if the rpmrebuild package was installed or not. To do so, use a command like the following:

```
# rpm -q rpmrebuild
package rpmrebuild is not installed
```

This shows that the rpmrebuild package was not installed, even though the package could be installed on its own. To check that the package could be installed, you can use the --test option, as shown following:

```
# rpm -i --test rpmrebuild-1.0-0.noarch.rpm
#
```

This command shows that the rpmrebuild package would install successfully on its own. If there were problems, the rpm command would have issued an error message.

This example shows that when you try to install multiple packages with the `rpm` command, should any fail, the `rpm` command will not install any.

The `rpm` command works similarly for removing packages and upgrading packages. When removing packages, you'll see an error like the following if any of the packages on the command line cannot be removed:

```
# rpm -e setup jikes-1.17
error: Failed dependencies:
        setup is needed by (installed) basesystem-8.0-1
        setup >= 2.0.3 is needed by (installed) initscripts-6.95-1
        setup >= 2.5.4-1 is needed by (installed) filesystem-2.1.6-5
        setup is needed by (installed) xinetd-2.3.7-2
        setup is needed by (installed) dump-0.4b28-4
```

The setup package could not be removed because it had several capabilities needed by other packages. You can check that the jikes package was not removed by using the `rpm -q` command, even though it had no failed dependencies:

```
# rpm -q jikes
jikes-1.17-1
```

This package was not removed because it appeared as part of the same command that failed, so none of the operations were performed.

When upgrading, you will also see an error message if any of the package upgrades fail. For example:

```
# rpm -Uhv jikes-1.14-1.i386.rpm autoupdate-3.1.5-1.noarch.rpm
error: jikes-1.14-1.i386.rpm cannot be installed
```

You can then check that the jikes package, in this example, was not downgraded to the earlier version with the `rpm -q` command:

```
# rpm -q jikes
jikes-1.17-1
```

Transaction IDs

The `rpm` command gives every package installed a transaction ID. The transaction ID is a Unix time stamp (number of seconds since January 1, 1970). You can then perform some operations on packages based on the transaction ID.

The fact that a transaction ID uses a Unix timestamp may change in the future.

All the packages installed at the same time are given the same transaction ID. This means that you can perform operations on a set of packages, the packages that were installed together.

But there's also a downside to this. All the packages installed when you first installed or upgraded your Linux system are given the same transaction ID. This means you cannot selectively act on these packages using the transaction ID, because you will likely get far more packages than you want to work on.

Viewing RPM Transaction IDs

To view the install transaction ID (a date code) for a given package, you can use a command like the following:

```
$ rpm -q --qf "%-20{NAME} %-20{INSTALLTID}\n" jikes
jikes                   1035589778
```

This command uses the --qf or --queryformat option to specify the data to return from the RPM query command. In this case, the command requests the name of the package as well as the transaction ID (TID) for installation.

Chapter 5 describes the --queryformat option.

There is also a transaction ID for removal, the REMOVETID. You can also query for this ID. For example, if a package hasn't been removed, you'll see an entry like the following:

```
$ rpm -qa --qf "%-20{NAME} %-20{REMOVETID}\n" termcap
termcap             (none)
```

Viewing the Packages Associated with a Transaction ID

Once you have a transaction ID, you can use the --tid option, short for transaction ID, to query for the package associated with a given transaction, using a command like the following:

```
$ rpm -q --tid 1035589778
jikes-1.17-1
```

This example uses the transaction ID that the earlier query example returned. If you installed more than one package at the same time, you will see a listing of all the packages that share the transaction ID.

For example, to see many packages with one transaction ID, you can query for packages installed when you installed or upgraded your version of Linux. First, query for the transaction ID of a package you know was installed with the Linux distribution, such as setup on a Red Hat system:

```
$ rpm -q --qf "%-20{NAME} %-20{INSTALLTID}\n" setup
setup                1033838323
```

Second, use this transaction ID and query for all packages with this ID, using code like the following:

```
$ rpm -q --tid 1033838323 | more
redhat-menus-0.26-1
glibc-2.2.93-5
cracklib-2.7-18
gdbm-1.8.0-18
gmp-4.1-4
libacl-2.0.11-2
libjpeg-6b-21
linc-0.5.2-2
pcre-3.9-5
shadow-utils-20000902-12
libtermcap-2.0.8-31
freetype-2.1.2-7
info-4.2-5
fileutils-4.1.9-11
psmisc-20.2-6
ntp-4.1.1a-9
mount-2.11r-10
cracklib-dicts-2.7-18
krb5-libs-1.2.5-6
cyrus-sasl-2.1.7-2
usermode-1.63-1
Xft-2.0-1
```

 Be sure to replace the transaction ID shown here with the transaction ID obtained by querying your system.

This example shows just a few of the packages installed when the Red Hat Linux was installed.

With these options, you can find the transaction IDs for given packages and can use the rpm command to install, remove, or otherwise modify the packages that share a transaction ID.

Rolling back transactions

The --rollback option to the rpm command allows you to roll back upgrades based on a time. Use a command like the following:

```
# rpm -U --rollback "3 months ago"
```

The --rollback option is very limited in what it can do. The --rollback option works only for packages that have been upgraded. You cannot rollback the initial installation of a package. This is to prevent you from accidentally rolling back all packages.

The --rollback option works best if you want to restore the system to a previous state, prior to performing any other RPM operations; that is, soon after you upgraded a package and decide that it isn't working right. If you have modified the RPM system after performing the transaction you want to rollback, there may be unintended consequences if any new package depends on the packages you want to roll back. In addition, the --rollback option only works in limited situations but does not always report when these conditions are not met. The rpm command may simply do nothing, or it may remove packages you do not expect.

Before running the --rollback option, back up your RPM database as described in Chapter 5.

Because of all these limitations, rollbacks do not work in all situations. In place of the --rollback option, you can use the query shortcuts introduced in Chapter 5 and find the packages you have installed recently (if that is what you want to roll back). In this case, you can use the rpm command to remove the packages you want to get rid of and reinstall the packages you want to restore.

In many cases, this manual approach is safest, and you will have a clearer understanding about what was installed or upgraded on your system.

Saving Old Packages

When installing, removing, or upgrading, you can use the --repackage command-line option to save a version of something like the old package to a file, making a backup of the older package contents.

The package created by the --repackage option is not a complete RPM package. You can use the rpmbuild command to make it into a complete package, but by itself, it will not be a complete package.

You can later reinstall the old files, once they have been made into a complete package. This can be quite useful if something goes wrong or the upgraded package has bugs. You can fall back to the old package if needed.

By default, the --repackage option puts the old package in the /var/spool/repackage directory. Other common directories are /var/spool/up2date or /var/tmp. Your RPM configuration determines the directory used by this option.

The up2date name comes from the Red Hat service for keeping a system up to date with regard to package versions.

For example, say you have a package, jikes (a Java programming language compiler used in previous examples) that you want to upgrade. But you are worried that the new version may not work properly.

First, check the version you have. For example:

```
# rpm -q jikes
jikes-1.14-1
```

This shows you are at version 1.14 of the jikes Java compiler. You can then upgrade to version 1.17 while repackaging the old version, as shown following:

```
# rpm -Uhv --repackage jikes-1.17-glibc2.2-1.i386.rpm
Preparing...               ######################################### [100%]
Repackaging...
   1:jikes                 ######################################### [100%]
Upgrading...
   1:jikes                 ######################################### [100%]
```

This upgrade has kept a copy of the old package in the /var/spool/repackage directory. You can verify this with the following command:

```
$ ls -l /var/spool/repackage/
total 692
-rw-r--r--   1 root     root       703037 Oct 25 18:49 jikes-1.14-1.i386.rpm
```

You can see a version of the old package, with the old version number.

This is not the same as the original package. This is not a complete package.

The repackaged RPM contains a snapshot of the package's files as they were on your hard disk, not as they were when you originally installed the package. Thus, the contents may differ if the files have changed on your hard disk. In addition, the --repackage option may not properly sign the package as the original was.

In addition to the --repackage option with the rpm command, you can use a free tool called rpmrebuild to make snapshots of any installed packages.

Written by Eric Gerbier, rpmrebuild allows you to create an RPM from the installed, and perhaps modified, version of a package. You don't have to upgrade, remove, or install a new package, as you do with the --repackage option.

Download rppmrebuild from http://rpmrebuild.sourceforge.net/.

Summary

Transactions allow you to install multiple packages as a group and know that either all the packages will succeed in installing or none of them will. This is very important if you have a set of interlocking packages that you need to install.

All the packages you install, remove, or upgrade on the same command line are automatically made part of a transaction. The rpm command will ensure that all packages can be installed, removed, or upgraded, and will not perform the operation unless all will succeed.

All packages installed or removed are given a transaction ID, which uses a Unix timestamp (the number of seconds since January 1, 1970). All packages installed or removed at the same time are given the same transaction ID. You can then query by transaction IDs to perform operations on all the packages installed together.

The --repackage option tells the rpm command to make a backup RPM of the current package when you are installing or upgrading a more recent version or removing the package. By default, the backup RPM is placed in the /var/spool/repackage directory. Note that a package created this way is not exactly the same as the original package. Files may have changed on disk. In addition, packages created with the --repackage option are not really valid RPM packages. You cannot install these packages without performing extra operations to create a real RPM package from the repackaged data.

Chapter 8

RPM Management Software

YOU CAN FIND A VARIETY OF SOFTWARE packages to ease the work of managing RPM-based systems. These utilities can help you find a specific software application packaged using RPM or search through a collection of RPM-packaged software to locate applications with specific features. Similarly, several utilities provide features to ease long-term system-management tasks. These applications provide features such as automatic updating of existing installed software with more recent versions or simplification of software installation by automating installation of any required software dependencies.

This chapter covers a number of tools for finding packages in RPM format, as well as tools to help manage the RPMs on your system.

Locating RPMs

RPM provides a powerful tool for managing software installed on a system. With a single command, an entire application can be installed on the system in a ready-to-run configuration. With a different command, the entire application can be removed without having manually to track down all of the associated files scattered throughout the hard drive. For RPM to work, however, the software being managed must be packaged in the proper RPM format. RPM packages can be easily prepared if necessary, but you can save time by using the wide variety of software already available in the RPM format. The only trick to using this RPM-packaged software is finding it.

As you start to search for RPM packages on the Internet, you'll find thousands of packages available. Many of these packages are built specifically for various Linux distributions, such as Conectiva, SuSE, Red Hat, or Mandrake. In many cases, the Linux distribution won't matter, but in general it's best to download packages built for your version of Linux, such as Red Hat.

Although the examples in this book assume Red Hat Linux as a base, just about everything applies to all versions of Linux that use the RPM system, unless noted otherwise.

Internet search engines are popular, but they aren't very helpful for finding RPM packages, especially because lots of Web pages have the term rpm (including those covering revolutions per minute). A more efficient approach is to use one of the RPM-specific Internet search tools such as rpmfind.

rpmfind and rpm2html

One popular free tool for locating RPMs is rpmfind, written by Daniel Veillard. This tool provides a command-line utility that can search for packages by name or description, displaying or optionally downloading any matching packages it finds. It can even provide a list of the dependencies that those matching packages require to run and can download those required dependencies as well.

When searching for packages, rpmfind can search both the software already installed on the local system and remote databases, including the databases located at `http://rpmfind.net/`.

 The databases at `http://rpmfind.net/` are, in turn, created by another utility: rpm2html. Both are covered in the sections following.

Commonly, rpmfind is used to search for packages by name, though it can be used to search package descriptions for key words. For example, I might want to find new e-mail clients to install on my system. I happen to know that one popular Linux e-mail client is Ximian's evolution, so I search for that.

The basic syntax for rpmfind follows:

```
rpmfind package_name
```

For example, to search for evolution, use a command like the following:

```
$ rpmfind evolution
Resource evolution already installed
$
```

Before accessing the Internet, rpmfind searches my local system and finds that I already have evolution installed, so it does not even bother searching for copies to download. It looks like I'm forgetful, not remembering that I already have evolution installed. At this point, I might realize that I already have the software I need, or I might decide to search for a similar application, such as exmh, another popular Unix e-mail client.

To search for exmh (which in this example has not been installed), use a command like the following:

```
$ rpmfind exmh
Installing exmh will require 7301 KBytes

### To Transfer:
ftp://ftp.redhat.com/pub/redhat/linux/7.2/en/os/i386/RedHat/RPMS//nmh-1.0.4-9.i3
86.rpm
ftp://ftp.redhat.com/pub/redhat/linux/7.2/en/os/i386/RedHat/RPMS//exmh-
2.4-2.noarch.rpm
Do you want to download these files to /tmp [Y/n/a/i] ? : a
transferring
ftp://ftp.redhat.com/pub/redhat/linux/7.2/en/os/i386/RedHat/RPMS//nmh-
1.0.4-9.i386.rpm
saving to /tmp/nmh-1.0.4-9.i386.rpm
transferring
ftp://ftp.redhat.com/pub/redhat/linux/7.2/en/os/i386/RedHat/RPMS//exmh-
2.4-2.noarch.rpm
saving to /tmp/exmh-2.4-2.noarch.rpm
rpm -U /tmp/nmh-1.0.4-9.i386.rpm /tmp/exmh-2.4-2.noarch.rpm
$
```

Here, rpmfind searches my local system for exmh. Since exmh is not installed there, rpmfind searches the databases at http://rpmfind.net/ and does two things: it finds exmh, and it learns that exmh depends upon another package: nmh. After double-checking and learning that nmh is not installed on my local system, rpmfind gives me a choice regarding whether I should download both of those packages; rpmfind gives me four possible answers:

```
Do you want to download these files to /tmp [Y/n/a/i] ? : a
```

My possible answers were:

Y   Yes, do download the files.

N   No, do not download the files.

A   Get all. By default, run in Automatic mode, trying to upgrade packages after they are downloaded

I   Install packages after download.

Any user can download packages, but usually only the root user can install
packages. Unless you are logged in as root, rpmfind will likely fail to install
the downloaded RPMs.

Because I select the "a" answer, rpmfind downloads all necessary packages to
/tmp and tries to upgrade the packages automatically by running the following
command:

```
rpm -U /tmp/nmh-1.0.4-9.i386.rpm /tmp/exmh-2.4-2.noarch.rpm
```

In this case, the `rpm -U` command silently fails, since I am not running it as root
and do not have permission to install software.

If the name of a package is unknown, rpmfind also supports searching by key-
words. The `--apropos pattern` option tells rpmfind to search through all package
descriptions in the databases for the pattern. If I do not know the names of any
e-mail clients, I might use this code for my search:

```
$ rpmfind --apropos "mail client"
Searching the RPM catalog for mail client ...
1:
ftp://ftp.redhat.com/pub/redhat/linux/7.2/en/os/i386/RedHat/RPMS//netscape-
communicator-4.78-
2.i386.rpm
netscape-communicator : A Web browser, news reader and e-mail client.
2:
ftp://ftp.redhat.com/pub/redhat/linux/7.2/en/os/i386/RedHat/RPMS//sylpheed-
0.5.0-3.i386.rpm
sylpheed : A GTK+ based, lightweight, and fast email client.
<snip>
364: ftp://ftp.pld.org.pl/PLD-1.0/dists/ra/PLD/SRPMS/SRPMS/sylpheed-
0.7.4-1.src.rpm
sylpheed : GTK+ based fast e-mail client
```

From my search, rpmfind returns the following output (with most of the entries
edited out for space):

```
Found 364 packages related to mail client
$
```

With this command, rpmfind connects to the databases at http://rpmfind.net/
and returns the location of all packages whose description contains the text "mail

client". Notice that 364 packages are found; there are lots of e-mail clients available for Linux! That number, however, is slightly misleading. Some of the packages found are prepared for the distribution I am running (Red Hat Linux version 7.2), but others are not. Result #364, for example, appears to be the Polish(ed) Linux Distribution 1.0 package of sylpheed, the same software offered to me packaged for my Red Hat Linux version 7.2 system in Result #2.

Use caution when working with rpmfind. By default, it connects to the databases on the server `http://rpmfind.net/` and queries them. These databases are indexes of all RPM-based distributions, and of all versions of each RPM-based distribution, and of all architectures, and of both source and binary RPMs for all these distributions!

To help you avoid being overwhelmed with results (such as the 364 results I obtain when I search for "mail client"), options are available to fine-tune rpmfind's searches in various ways. Common options are presented in Table 8-1.

TABLE 8-1 SEARCH OPTIONS FOR RPMFIND

Option	Result
`-v`	Increases verbosity of output (can be used multiple times)
`-s server`	Connects to a specific rpmfind database server
`--sources package`	Looks for source RPMs of the package
`--apropos key word(s)`	Looks by keyword instead of package name
`--dist dist`	Restricts packages to a specific distribution
`--latest package`	Finds the most current version of package available
`--upgrade package`	Finds the most current dependencies available for package

The rpmfind databases that rpmfind searches are created using the utility rpm2html. If you desire, rpm2html can be used to set up a local mirror of the databases at rpmfind.net or to make a custom database of locally available RPMs for in-house use.

rpm2html

The rpm2html utility generates HTML Web pages that describe RPM packages. Very simple in concept, rpm2html has proven very useful over the years.

With rpm2html, each package is displayed as a single HTML page that describes the package using information much like that returned by the `rpm -qi` command, covered in Chapter 4. The HTML page also lists the capabilities the package requires and those it provides. This shows the needed dependency information. Finally, the page includes a download link to download the RPM file.

All packages of the same name, such as the exmh e-mail client, are collected on summary pages. The summary page tries to list all RPMs for all Linux distributions that provide the given package. For exmh, for example, the database as of this writing includes 71 versions of the exmh package, for Conectiva Linux, Mandrake Linux, Yellow Dog PowerPC Linux, and so on. The summary page also links to the URL in the RPMs that is listed as the home page for the application.

Used together with its database, rpm2html provides a powerful RPM-centric search engine. You can find more on rpm2html at `rpmfind.net/linux/rpm2html/` or just access an RPM search site such as `rpmfind.net`.

In addition to rpm2html, the program pdbv creates a set of cross-linked HTML files that list the packages on your system. Pdbv doesn't support searching and wasn't built as a front end for search sites, so it is simpler than rpm2html. Instead, pdbv just creates a set of HTML pages that list data that you can query with the `rpm` command, including the package descriptions, the capabilities required and provided, as well as all the files in the package.

The primary advantage of pdbv is that it runs relatively quickly to provide you a snapshot of your system.

RPM sites on the Internet

In addition to the command-line RPM search tools, a number of Web sites provide handy front ends to databases of available packages. These Web sites make it easy to query for packages and also provide snapshots of what is happening in Linux development, especially with the sites that list recently created RPMs.

The following sections list some of the more popular sites.

 As with anything on the Internet, sites come and go. I've used `rpmfind.net` for years, but it is always possible that any of these sites may suddenly disappear.

rpmfind.net

The rpmfind utility is associated with an online database available at www. rpmfind.net. You can search this site and see the results in the same format as that created by the rpm2html utility. In essence, this site acts as an HTML front end to the rpmfind query commands. By providing a search engine accessible from a Web browser, instead of the command line as used by the rpmfind utility, the rpmfind.net site is easy to search and also displays the data in an easier-to-read format.

Use the rpmfind command when you know you want to install something. Use the rpmfind.net Web site when you want to browse through the lists of available RPMs.

 You can download the rpmfind command RPM from the rpmfind.net site.

freshrpms.net

The site name, freshrpms.net, is a play on the popular but oddly named Linux site freshmeat.net. The freshmeat.net site provides listings of newly-updated applications for Linux and other operating systems. The freshrpms.net site provides a similar service devoted to freshly-made RPMs.

 You don't always want the most recently made RPMs. Sometimes it's good to wait a while and see if others have faced problems with a given RPM before downloading it.

One of the best features of the freshrpms.net site is that it also provides links to the RPM spec files for the packages it references. This is a very useful source of examples when you try to build RPMs.

 See Chapter 10 for more on RPM spec files.

RPM PBone Search

The site http://rpm.pbone.net/ provides a database of RPM packages you can search. This site also lists quite a few recently created RPMs. In fact, much of the focus here lies in finding the latest updates to the applications you run.

The feature I like most about the PBone search is the ability to specify which Linux distributions to search by using a set of check boxes. Although in theory most Linux RPMs should work on most Linux distributions, I prefer to get something made for and tested on my version of Linux.

Other Sites

Table 8-2 lists additional sites where you can find RPMs. As with all listings of Internet sites, these may come and go.

TABLE 8-2 MORE RPM SITES

Site	Holds
`http://plf.zarb.org/`	The Penguin Liberation Front has RPMs that for legal reasons cannot be included in the Mandrake Linux distribution.
`www.math.unl.edu/~rdieter/Projects/`	Rex Dieter's RPM site
`www.rpmhelp.net/`	Mandrake Linux RPMs
`www.aucs.org/rpmcenter/`	Edwin Chan's Red Hat RPMs
`www.owlriver.com/projects/links/`	Owl River Company RPMs

Graphical RPM Management

Once appropriate RPMs have been obtained, they have to be installed before the application they provide can be used. You can use the rpm command-line utility to do this. The rpmfind utility also has the capability to launch the rpm utility automatically to install any software located. In addition to these two tools, however, several graphical applications are available that provide basic RPM package-management capabilities. Most of these programs offer easy-to-use GUIs that can be used to install and uninstall packages, to query packages, and to verify installed packages.

Even though Linux and Unix fans generally aren't bothered by command-line tools such as rpm, many newcomers to Linux fret over the seeming difficulty of the command line. They are more used to graphical applications and, in many cases, are more productive in a graphical environment. Keeping with the Linux tradition of freedom of choice, you can use the command-line tools such as the rpm command or pick from a variety of graphical tools.

Nautilus

Nautilus provides a visually appealing file manager that is part of the GNOME desktop. Nautilus acts as a normal file manager that can also display some types of files, such as images. In addition, you can launch applications that Nautilus knows about when you double click files. Figure 8-1 shows Nautilus in action.

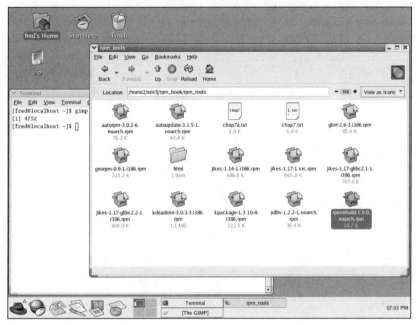

Figure 8-1: Browsing RPM files with Nautilus

If you double click an RPM file (a file ending with the extension *.rpm*), Nautilus will install the RPM file. First, though, Nautilus will prompt you for the root password, since you must be logged in as root to install RPMs. Figure 8-2 shows Nautilus prompting for a password.

After some time processing, you should see the Completed System Preparation window, as shown in Figure 8-3.

When you install RPMs with Nautilus, it really runs the Red Hat Package Management tool.

Nautilus only supports RPM functionality starting with Red Hat Linux 8.0.

This functionality may not be supported in other versions of Linux.

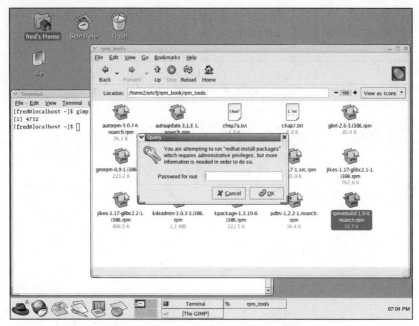

Figure 8-2: You must be logged in as root to install packages.

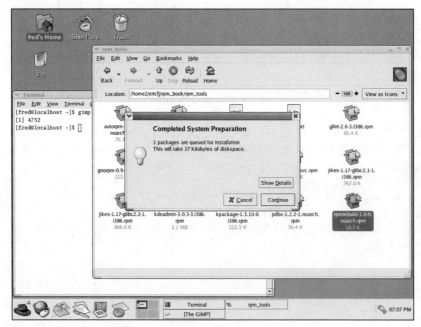

Figure 8-3: Installing RPM files with Nautilus

Red Hat Package Management

The `redhat-config-packages` application (say that three times fast) comes new with Red Hat Linux 8.0. You can use the Python program in this package to manage the packages that come with Red Hat Linux, using an interface that is very similar to the Red Hat Linux installation program. This similarity may make it easier for many users to manage their packages, although I found the program a bit short on explanations.

To run this program, you first have to do a bit of searching to find it. It appears under the System Settings menu from the main Red Hat Start menu under the default Bluecurve desktop. Select the Packages choice to launch this program. You can also start the program from the command line with the following command:

```
# redhat-config-packages
```

This program takes a long time to read in all the information and start up. Once started, the interface provides the same categories and much the same look as the Red Hat Linux installer, as shown in Figure 8-4.

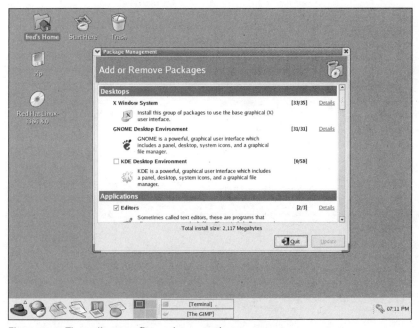

Figure 8-4: The redhat-config-packages package manager

The packages tool divides the packages into groups. Inside each group, the packages are divided into two sets: standard and extra packages. (Red Hat places the packages into these categories, striving to make a reasonable division among the many packages that come with Linux.) If you click the check box for a group, the tool will queue up all the standard packages within that group for installation. If you uncheck a check box for a group that was checked before, the tool will queue up all the installed packages in that group for removal, both standard and extra.

 Installing or removing all the packages in a group when you don't know what is in the group is not a good idea.

To delve into a group and see what is inside, click the Details link associated with that group. Clicking the Details link will bring up a window where you can check individual packages for installation and uncheck individual packages for removal. Figure 8-5 shows the details of the Web Server group.

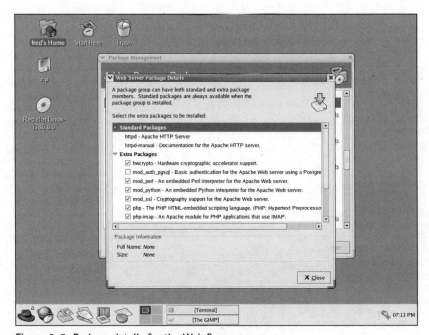

Figure 8-5: Package details for the Web Server group

Once you have selected all the packages you want to install, and unselected all the packages you want to remove, click the Update button on the main window of the package-management tool. After some processing, you should see the Completed System Preparation window, which lists the amount of disk space required for the new packages and the amount that will be freed by the packages to be removed. Figure 8-6 shows this window.

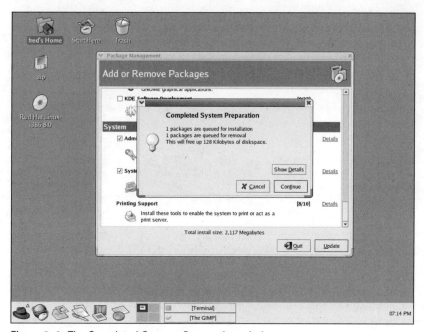

Figure 8-6: The Completed Systems Preparation window

Click the Show Details button to see a complete list of all the packages to be installed and removed.

If the packages you choose to install depend on any other packages, the package-management tool will automatically add these packages to the list to be installed. More important, if any packages installed on your system depend on any of the packages you have marked for removal, the tool will add those additional installed packages to the list to be removed. Always examine the Show Details window to see what will really be installed and removed.

Figure 8-7 shows the window with the package details.

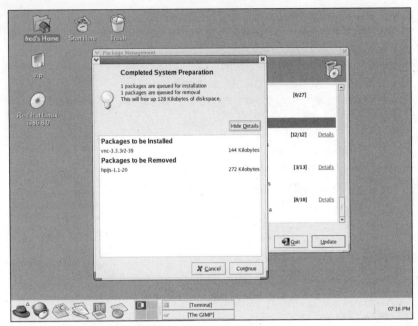

Figure 8-7: The Show Details window

The package-management tool worries me. It has an absolutely beautiful look, but it tries to do too much, especially when removing packages. Always use this program with care. I much prefer to just launch it with single packages from the Nautilus file manager.

KPackage

One popular graphical RPM management tool is KPackage, supplied with the KDE Desktop. (You can find this product at www.kde.org.) KPackage offers basic package-management functionality. It can install and uninstall packages and display information about installed and available packages' contents and headers. In addition, KPackage supports a wide variety of package formats in addition to RPMs. Be aware, however, that KPackage cannot automatically resolve dependencies. When you are installing new software packages, any dependencies required by that software must first be manually installed.

When started, KPackage presents a basic two-paned interface. The left-hand panel lists Installed packages already on the system, Updated packages available to update the system, New packages available for installation, and All packages (both installed and available for installation/upgrade). When displaying package lists, KPackage organizes the displayed packages into categories based on their group.

The right-hand panel lists information about the package currently selected in the left-hand panel. Information displayed includes the package Properties, listing the package's header, and the File List of files that package owns. Figure 8-8 shows this panel on the right side of the interface.

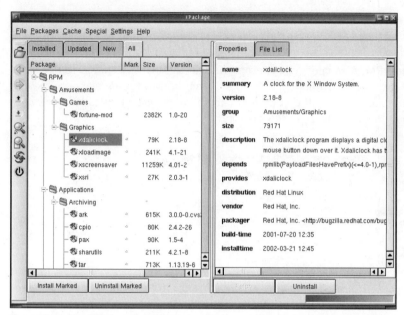

Figure 8–8: The KPackage interface, showing properties of the selected package

After packages have been selected, they can be installed or uninstalled, as shown in Figure 8-9:

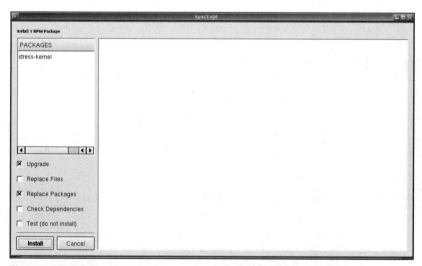

Figure 8–9: KPackage installs the selected package on your command.

In addition to supporting RPM, KPackage can be used on systems that use other packaging methods. Current versions of KPackage support Debian's dpkg and the BSD projects' package formats as well as RPM.

Gnome-RPM

The GNOME Desktop (www.gnome.org) provides another graphical RPM-management tool, Gnome-RPM. Also known as gnorpm, Gnome-RPM is very similar to KPackage in terms of its basic functionality, although Gnome-RPM can manage only RPMs.

When started, Gnome-RPM presents a hierarchical list of installed packages, arranged by group, as shown in Figure 8-10:

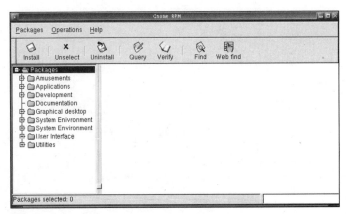

Figure 8-10: The main Gnome-RPM window

After a specific package has been selected, you can query to see its details, as shown in Figure 8-11:

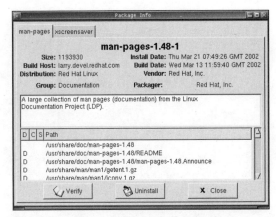

Figure 8-11: Querying the details for a package

With Gnome-RPM, you can also filter the list of packages to see only the list of uninstalled RPMs, as shown in Figure 8-12.

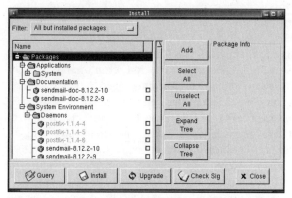

Figure 8–12: Filtering to see only the uninstalled packages

Like KPackage, when installing new software, Gnome-RPM lacks the ability to automatically install any dependencies needed by that software.

Extending RPM Management

RPM makes it very easy to install and uninstall software from systems. One simple command installs an entire application onto the computer, and another removes all files associated with an application. Using RPM to install and uninstall software can become tedious in some situations, however. Manually installing software on one system is no great task, but what if that same software package needs to be installed on all the computers in the department? Or on all the computers in a company? Suddenly, that one `rpm -i` command has become a major chore!

Similarly, keeping one system up-to-date with the latest vendor errata, although an extremely important administrative task, is not terribly time-consuming or difficult – simply download all the errata and associated packages from the vendor; then use the command `rpm -Fvh` to install the packages on the system, freshening all installed software with the latest updates of that software.

If several machines are being managed, though, the task becomes slightly more difficult. Now the vendor errata and packages must be manually copied to each machine, and `rpm -Fvh` must be run on each machine to update it. If many machines are being managed, and those systems are running different versions of the operating system (so that they require different errata), the task becomes even more complicated. Separate errata packages must be downloaded for every operating system version in use; then the appropriate errata collections must be pushed to each machine and manually freshened. To make life as a system administrator even more frustrating, sometimes vendor-supplied errata cannot be installed using the freshen option. A package supplied as one RPM in the initial operating-system release might be split into two RPMs for the errata, for example. When this happens, freshen cannot be used. Instead, the administrator must determine what software is currently installed on the system, and the errata for that software must be manually installed. Typically, this involves several rounds of comparing output from `rpm -qa` with the list of current errata, using `rpm -Uvh` to upgrade only the appropriate errata for that system.

Worse yet, errata updating should ideally be done on an automatic basis. While rpm commands can be scheduled using system utilities such as cron or at, obviously this cannot be done when the rpm commands to be scheduled need to be interactive.

Installation of new packages can pose problems as well. New software will often have logical dependencies upon other software that is also not currently installed. Although RPM does track software dependencies, it does not magically find all dependencies an application needs, nor does it automatically install them along with the initial application. Instead, all required "helper" applications must be searched out and manually installed. Then the desired software can be installed.

These and similar problems are very common in the real world. Typically, system administrators manage as many as 200 or more systems. Manually logging into 200 systems and executing an `rpm -i` command every time another application is needed is not practical. Even when managing one system, downloading errata and manually installing it regularly quickly becomes tedious.

Like any regular system-administration task, it should be automated. When installing new software on machines, managing dependencies and downloading and installing required support software becomes tiresome as well.

To aid with these common problems, a variety of helper applications are available for RPM. These management aids can perform functions such as automatically managing dependencies. When an application is being installed using one of these helpers, the utility also finds and installs any required dependencies. Similarly, when errata are being installed, these management aids can automatically determine which errata are needed by the current system, even in situations in which `rpm -F` does not work. Some of these tools can even be used to manage clusters of computers. Running one command applies the RPM install or delete on the entire group of machines. All of these commands are designed with scriptability in mind, making them perfect for use automatically via tools such as cron or at.

AutoRPM

One popular tool to lessen the work involved with administering RPM-based systems is AutoRPM. Written by Kirk Bauer, AutoRPM is available under a free MIT-style license from the home page `www.autorpm.org`.

A Perl script, AutoRPM provides several features that make it especially useful. First, it can create local mirrors of RPM repositories. Typically, this feature might be used to create a local archive of errata for a Linux distribution. AutoRPM can also compare all currently installed RPMs against a list stored elsewhere. This list can be either an FTP site or a directory on the local system. After comparing the currently-installed RPMs against the list, AutoRPM can then update any packages from the list site that are newer than what is installed on the local system. This way, you can define one site or directory as the master site of the package versions that need to get installed on all systems and let AutoRPM ensure that all computers on your network are up to date.

Together, these two functions make AutoRPM very convenient for keeping systems current with all errata the vendor releases. They can also be used to create a method of distributing software to a network of systems. For example, every workstation in the department can run AutoRPM, configured to watch a common directory on a local NFS server. Installing new software on every workstation in the department occurs simply by copying an RPM of the software into that directory, letting AutoRPM do the rest of the work.

AutoRPM is designed to be used both automatically from cron and interactively from the command line. By default, AutoRPM runs via a nightly cron job and downloads all updates for software currently installed on the system. It then stores these updates in a local directory, typically /var/spool/autorpm, and e-mails an administrator a notification on the new updates. The administrator can then log onto the system and manually install the updates using the rpm command. AutoRPM can also be easily configured to install automatically any new packages it downloads. If AutoRPM is so configured, the system administrator does not even have to log in and run rpm commands to keep the system up-to-date!

In interactive mode, AutoRPM provides a basic set of commands, listed in Table 8-3.

TABLE 8-3 BASIC AUTORPM COMMANDS

Command	Usage
?	Displays help on the various commands
Help	Displays help on the various commands
Info	Displays information about an RPM
Fullinfo	Displays complete information about an RPM
Install	Installs RPMs onto the system
Add	Adds RPMs to the queue of RPMs to be processed
Remove	Deletes RPMs from the queue of RPMs waiting to be processed
List	Displays all RPMs currently in the queue waiting to be processed
Cd	Changes the local directory
Auto	Executes commands defined in the system-wide configuration file
Set	Displays or modifies current AutoRPM settings
Abort	Exits without saving changes
Exit	Exits and saves changes

The commands that manipulate RPMs (such as `install`, used to install an RPM) accept as arguments both paths to RPM files on the local system, and also URLs pointing to RPMs on an FTP repository. In addition, they support wild cards and directory accesses, so a command such as `install ftp://ftp.redhat.com/pub/redhat/linux/updates/current/*` can be used to install all errata for the current release of Red Hat Linux.

In addition to interactive mode, AutoRPM provides a noninteractive mode, suitable for use through cron. In noninteractive mode, invoked by the command `autorpm --notty auto`, AutoRPM consults the configuration file /etc/autorpm.conf to decide what to do. By default, /etc/autorpm.d/autorpm.conf is configured to download, but not automatically install, all errata for the release of Red Hat Linux running on the local system. Editing this file makes it possible to use AutoRPM to download all errata – or errata for other Linux distributions – or to install errata automatically once downloaded.

Typically, AutoRPM is used to automate installation of errata updates and other software on all machines in the enterprise. To do this, one machine is selected to serve as a file server. On it, AutoRPM is configured to download and install all errata. The directory where the errata are stored on that server is then exported to the other machines in the enterprise, which also run AutoRPM. These other machines have AutoRPM configured to install all files that the file server exports. Using a configuration such as this, all machines in the enterprise get all security updates automatically installed. In addition, installing a desired new software application on all hosts in the enterprise can be done simply by copying an RPM of the application onto the file server, making it available for the AutoRPM nightly updates to access and install automatically.

AutoUpdate

AutoUpdate, written by Gerald Teschl, is another Perl script that can be used to automate RPM downloads or installations. Available freely under the terms of the GNU GPL from `www.mat.univie.ac.at/~gerald/ftp/autoupdate`, AutoUpdate is very similar to AutoRPM in terms of both functionality and potential applications. Unlike AutoRPM, AutoUpdate offers no interactive capability. However, AutoUpdate does have the capability to manage dependencies correctly; when using AutoUpdate to install software that depends upon other uninstalled software, AutoUpdate attempts to resolve the dependencies and to install all necessary software packages.

AutoUpdate bases all decisions about what software to download or install upon its configuration file, /etc/autoupdate.d/autoupdate.conf. By default, AutoUpdate provides several additional configuration files pre-defined for downloading updates for the most popular RPM-based Linux distributions (Red Hat Linux, Mandrake Linux, Caldera/SCO OpenLinux, and SuSE Linux). The autoupdate.conf file can be modified to configure AutoUpdate to install software automatically.

Table 8-4 lists the five commands that compose all the utilities provided by AutoUpdate:

TABLE 8-4 AUTOUPDATE COMMANDS

Command	Usage
autodld	Downloads updated versions of all installed software
autoget	Downloads specific RPMs from remote sites
autoupd	Installs more recent versions of currently installed software
autoins	Installs specific applications
automerge	Merges new RPMs into an existing directory of RPMs, removing any old versions
autopurge	Removes old RPMs from an existing directory of RPMs.

These tools can access remote files by using a variety of methods. Like AutoRPM, AutoUpdate can download files if given an FTP URL. AutoUpdate can also access HTTP URLs and local files. Its additional dependency-tracking functionality and support for additional file-access methods make it suitable for use in cases where AutoRPM might be inappropriate. AutoUpdate cannot be used interactively, however, making AutoRPM more useful for nonautomated purposes.

The Red Hat Network and up2date

Some vendors of RPM-based Linux distributions also provide utilities that can help with management of the distributions they create. Red Hat has created two complementary products, the Red Hat Network (RHN) and up2date, which together provide much the same functionality for managing Red Hat Linux installations as tools such as AutoUpdate and AutoRPM, as well as offering more advanced features.

Red Hat Network is a subscription-based service offered by Red Hat that makes software available for installation via the network. (A free evaluation is also available.) After registering machines with Red Hat Network, administrators can pull updates or new software for installation to those registered machines. In addition, administrators have access to a Web-based administrative console from which they can view the systems they manage and can push software out to those systems.

Red Hat offers two tiers of access to Red Hat Network. Basic Service subscriptions to Red Hat Network provide the ability to manage single systems. Multiple machines can be subscribed by the same administrator for Basic Service level Red Hat Network access, but they must all be managed independently. The administrator must push out errata to each machine separately. Workgroup Service subscriptions provide the same functionality as Basic Service subscriptions, but they also provide the ability to group multiple machines for simultaneous administration. All errata updates for all machines subscribed to Workgroup Service can be pushed out by a single action, for example. Furthermore, Workgroup Service subscriptions can allow management by multiple administrators if desired, making it possible for large organizations to share responsibilities among administrators.

When using Red Hat Network to manage machines with Workgroup Service subscriptions, Red Hat also offers two optional services: Red Hat Network Proxy Server and Red Hat Network Satellite. The Red Hat Network Proxy Server is, as its name suggests, a proxy server for the Red Hat Network. Using it, errata pushed out via Red Hat Network is downloaded by the organization (only once) to a central server in-house. All machines in that organization subscribed to Red Hat Network get their updated software from that in-house proxy server, significantly reducing the network bandwidth requirements needed to keep large organizations up to date.

In addition, the Red Hat Network Proxy Server can be used to provide all subscribed machines with software not provided with Red Hat Linux. Custom "channels" of supplemental software can be created on the Proxy Server, and machines can be subscribed to those channels as desired. Using this feature, different departments in the organization with different software needs can create independent channels for each department, ensuring that machines get only the software needed on them. Similarly, distinct channels can be created for separate classes of machines, ensuring that servers get only software appropriate for server machines and that desktops only get only software that desktop machines need.

The Red Hat Network is normally centrally administered through Red Hat. Machines subscribed to the Red Hat Network have a system profile on file with Red Hat that details the system's essential configuration information (what software is installed on it, what CPU architecture it contains, and so forth) needed to determine which software errata are appropriate for that system. Similarly, the Web console through which machines subscribed to Red Hat Network can be administered is also located on a Red Hat server. Customers wishing to use Red Hat Network services, but not wanting the dependency upon Internet access to Red Hat, can create an in-house Red Hat Network by using the Red Hat Network Satellite. This solution is often practical for customers who need to keep system information confidential or for customers whose systems are not able to access the Internet.

Red Hat provides several interfaces for administering machines subscribed to the Red Hat Network. A Web-management console is available at `https://rhn.redhat.com/`. Administrators of machines subscribed to any level of the Red Hat Network can simply log into this Web site and perform a variety of package-management operations from their Web browsers. In addition to viewing other things, administrators can see what software is currently installed, select and install Red Hat Linux errata or new software, or schedule a time for automatic installation of Red Hat Linux errata.

When using Red Hat Network, rhnsd is a client-side daemon that should be run on subscribed systems. It periodically launches a helper utility, rhn_check, which connects to the Red Hat Network servers and checks for any actions (such as a scheduled installation of errata) that an administrator has selected in the Web console. If any actions have been scheduled for that client machine, rhn_check on the client initiates those actions. By default, rhnsd runs rhn_check every two hours. This time can be increased to check for configuration changes as frequently as every hour if necessary.

In addition, Red Hat provides client-side tools that can be used in a more inter-active fashion to connect to the Red Hat Network from subscribed systems. The up2date program provides a graphical and command-line tool that can be used to install packages from Red Hat Network servers. When installing a new package, up2date automatically installs any necessary dependencies the package requires, making it a very convenient tool for adding software to the system. up2date can also be run in update mode, thus telling it to install all updates available for the software already installed on the system. Commonly used options with up2date include those listed in Table 8-5.

TABLE 8-5 OPTIONS FOR THE UP2DATE COMMAND

Option	Usage
--configure	Start a dialog for configuring up2date options
-d	Download packages but do not install them
-f	Force packages to be installed, even if they have been marked to be skipped
-i	Download and install packages
-l	List available updated versions of already installed packages
--showall	List all available packages, including packages not currently installed at all
-k	List local directories containing packages
--nosig	Disable GPG package signature checking
--src	Download both source and binary RPMs
--nosrc	Do not download source RPMs
-p	Update the list of installed packages associated with this computer in the Red Hat Network database
--whatprovides	Ask the RHN servers which packages will resolve the listed dependencies
--solvedeps	Ask the RHN servers which packages will resolve the listed dependencies, then downloads and installs those packages
--tmpdir	Specify the temporary directory to which packages should be downloaded

Continued

TABLE 8-5 **OPTIONS FOR THE UP2DATE COMMAND** *(Continued)*

-u	Update all software currently installed on the system to the latest available version
--nox	Short for No X, this disables the X-based GUI, instead using only the command-line interface
-v	Provide more verbose output

Current

The up2date command, the Red Hat Network client software, is open-source software released by Red Hat under the terms of the GNU GPL. Red Hat Network Proxy Server and Red Hat Network Satellite, the server applications with which up2date interacts, are not freely available, open-source applications. For this reason, an effort is underway to develop servers available under the terms of the GNU GPL that can be used with up2date clients. The main program in this effort is called current, which refers to keeping your systems current.

The current server can be downloaded from `http://current.tigris.org`. Although not yet as functional as Red Hat Network Proxy Server or Red Hat Network Satellite, current can already be used to create a RPM repository from which up2date-using clients can retrieve and install software. More advanced features, such as support for multiple "channels" of software, will be added to current in future releases.

urpmi and RpmDrake

Mandrake provides a set of software similar to the combination of up2date and Red Hat Network or current that can be used with the Mandrake Linux distribution. Links to the source code for the Mandrake applications can be found at `www.linux-mandrake.com/cooker/urpmi.html`. This suite of applications is typically referred to as urpmi and includes both the `urpmi` command and several helper applications. `urpmi` itself is a command that acts as a wrapper around the `rpm` command. When given the name of a package to install, urpmi determines what dependencies, if any, required by the application are not already resolved and offers to install the packages necessary to fulfill those dependencies.

When installing packages, urpmi can install from a variety of sources: FTP repositories, Web servers, local or NFS directories, and removable media such as CD-ROMs. The helper application `urpmi.addmedia` is used to add package sources, and the corresponding utility `urpmi.removemedia` is used to remove package sources no longer desired.

Mandrake's urpmi program includes one very handy feature. It comes with an autoirpm helper utility that can be used to configure the system to install packages on demand. This is done by running the command `autoirpm.update-all`, an application that scans all packages available for installation via urpmi. For every package available through urpmi, autoirpm.update-all determines what executable programs it provides, and it creates a symbolic link from that executable's name to the autoirpm script. Attempting to execute such a symbolic link executes autoirpm, which in turn automatically uses urpmi to install the associated package. The result: on-demand installation of packages when users on the system attempt to execute the programs that those packages provide.

Two different interfaces are available for urpmi. The `urpmi` command starts up urpmi in command-line mode, and the `gurpmi` command (or `urpmi --X`) starts urpmi in a graphical X-based mode. In addition, Mandrake provides a more full-featured graphical application: RpmDrake. RpmDrake provides the same package-management capabilities as urpmi, including the capability to install all required dependencies whenever installing any new packages.

apt-rpm

Another free RPM management utility is available that provides many of the features of both vendor solutions such as up2date or urpmi and of third-party utilities such as autoUpdate or KPackage. This tool is apt-rpm, a port of the Debian Project's excellent apt (Advanced Package Tool) software.

The Debian Project (`www.debian.org/`) is a nonprofit volunteer group that develops a Linux distribution, Debian GNU/Linux. The group uses a different package format, dpkg, which was developed independently of and simultaneous to Red Hat's creation of RPM. The two formats, dpkg and RPM, are very similar in terms of utility and functionality. In addition to having created a package format, the Debian Project later developed a collection of software, apt, which could be used to manage and install dpkg-format software. And, since Debian distributions are typically installed over the Internet, this apt software has to supply advanced distributed package management functionality.

In many respects, Debian's implementation of apt is very similar to the functionality provided by Red Hat's up2date/Red Hat Network products or Mandrake's urpmi software. On Debian systems, apt is a client tool used to select and install new software packages or to update existing packages already installed on the system. To do this, it accesses a user-configured list of resources that supply new packages; these resources are typically the Debian Project's FTP or Web servers, though they can also be CD-ROMs or local or remote file systems. For apt to be able to download packages from a resource such as a CD-ROM or an FTP server, that resource must supply two things: the software packages being downloaded and a database supplying metadata about all the packages in the repository. These resource databases are essential for apt to operate. For this reason, apt can only be used to update systems from apt-capable repositories.

Although apt was created by the Debian Project and designed for dpkg-format software packages, nothing about apt requires that it inherently be usable only with dpkg-format packages. Because of this, and because of its powerful capabilities,

Conectiva, a Brazilian Linux distribution vendor (`www.conectiva.com`), extended apt to support management of RPM packages in addition to dpkg packages. Conectiva's work, commonly referred to as apt-rpm, makes the apt client software available for use on any RPM-based Linux distribution. Conectiva also provides its customers with access to apt-capable FTP servers. A related project, apt4rpm (`http://apt4rpm.sourceforge.net/`), supplies the necessary utilities that can be used to make any RPM repository apt-capable. By creating apt-capable servers using apt4rpm and then installing apt-rpm on the client systems, any RPM-based distribution, such as Red Hat Linux, Mandrake Linux, Caldera/SCO OpenLinux, or SuSE Linux, can then be easily managed using apt.

The `freshrpms.net` site, mentioned previously, provides a touted apt repository.

Administrators managing multiple dispersed machines as well as those used to Debian administration often find it useful to configure their machines to use apt; its dependency tracking is far better than any other tool, except for Red Hat's up2date/RHN combination. To use apt, administrators must install it on their machines and have access to an apt-capable RPM repository for the distribution they use. Several public FTP sites that support apt are now available for most of the major RPM-based distributions. Also, the administrator can create another apt-capable repository.

Configuration of machines to use apt is simple. The apt and libapt RPMs simply need to be installed. Although binaries are sometimes available, the best success can usually be obtained by building binary RPMs from the latest Conectiva apt SRPM (source RPM), available at `ftp://ftp.conectiva.com/pub/conectiva/ EXPERIMENTAL/apt/`.

Once apt and libapt RPMs are installed, the sources.list file in /etc/apt needs to be modified to reference the apt-capable software site that will be used. For example, to configure a machine to access the apt-capable Red Hat Linux 7.2 software distributed by the Tuxfamily.org server, the /etc/apt/sources.list file needs to list:

```
rpm http://apt-rpm.tuxfamily.org/apt redhat-7.2-i386/redhat os
rpm http://apt-rpm.tuxfamily.org/apt redhat-updates-7.2/redhat os
```

These two lines, respectively, access the Red Hat Linux 7.2 and Red Hat Linux 7.2 errata RPMs being served by the system `apt-rpm.tuxfamily.org`. If you also want access to source RPMs, the following lines are necessary as well.

```
rpm-src http://apt-rpm.tuxfamily.org/apt redhat-7.2-i386/redhat os
rpm-src http://apt-rpm.tuxfamily.org/apt redhat-updates-7.2/redhat os
```

In addition to, or instead of, using public apt-capable servers, many sites want to create their own apt servers. If apt is being used to manage all the machines in the enterprise, a custom apt server might be needed that contains apt-accessible RPMs of all the custom software used in the enterprise. This can be done using the tools provided by the apt4rpm package (`http://apt4rpm.sourceforge.net`).

Once apt has been installed on clients, and the clients have been configured to access an apt-capable server, keeping systems updated is simple. The command `apt-get update` updates the client system's apt database of available software, after which the command `apt-get upgrade` upgrades all currently installed software to the latest version available in the software repository. By listing a site that provides vendor errata updates in /etc/apt/sources.list and then setting up a nightly cron job to run the `apt-get upgrade` command, administrators can be sure that client systems always have the latest errata installed. You can use a similar technique to ensure that all client systems are always up to date with the latest custom in-house applications. To do this, set up your own apt server and ensure that the latest custom applications are placed on the apt server.

In addition, apt simplifies interactive installation of RPMs on systems that are using it. The command `apt-get install` *package* retrieves the named RPM from the apt-capable software repository and installs it. If the package requires any dependencies that are not already resolved, apt will ask for confirmation, then download and install the package and all dependencies. Similarly, `apt-get remove` `package` uninstalls the named RPM. If any other packages depend on it, it will prompt for confirmation, then uninstall the named RPM and all of its dependencies.

In addition to these command-line utilities, several graphical front-end tools for manipulating apt are currently being ported for use with apt-rpm. Because of its ease of use for automating installation of system errata and necessary custom software, and because of the excellent dependency tracking it provides for interactive installation and uninstallation of software, apt-rpm can be excellent for managing RPM-based systems.

The poldek

Also similar to the Debian apt tool, a utility called the poldek works like apt-get. The poldek was designed to quickly scan through dependencies and install a number of packages at once. You can specify all the packages to install in a file.

The poldek automatically downloads any needed dependencies. The poldek can download files over the Internet and also help create the packages for storage on CD-ROMs. The poldek optimizes the set of packages to reduce the number of times users have to switch CDs.

For more on the poldek, see `poldek.pld.org.pl`.

Summary

This chapter has covered a number of tools for finding packages in RPM format, as well as tools to help manage the RPMs on your system. The `rpm` command does a great job of installing, removing, and upgrading packages. You can use it or choose from one of the many graphical RPM management tools shown in this chapter.

The rpmfind utility helps find RPM packages on Internet servers. You can use rpmfind to find the latest version of the packages installed on your system.

The Nautilus file manager allows you to browse files on disk, and it installs any RPM files you double-click.

Red Hat Linux 8 comes with a new package-management tool available from the System Settings menu. Be careful with this tool, though, as it automatically installs — and removes — dependent packages.

AutoRPM and AutoUpdate provide utilites that you can run periodically to ensure that your systems are up to date. The Red Hat Network and up2date also provides this capability.

The Debian GNU/Linux apt system provides many of the same capabilities as RPM, along with the network-updating capabilities of up2date and the Red Hat Network. You can use special apt packages that adapt apt for RPM-based Linux distributions and get the best of both the RPM system and the apt system.

The next chapter starts the major section on creating RPMs. The RPM system reduces a lot of the burden of administering Linux systems. You can take advantage of this when building any sort of software for distribution — or even when managing your own system.

Part II

Creating RPMs

Chapter 9

Creating RPMs:
An Overview

IN THIS CHAPTER

- ◆ Preparing to build RPMs
- ◆ Planning for RPMs
- ◆ Explaining the build process
- ◆ Using build files
- ◆ Seeing the results
- ◆ Verifying your RPMs

THUS FAR IN THIS BOOK, ALL THE commands presented have been used to manage or query packages. With this chapter, though, you start creating RPMs of your own. Even if you do not produce applications on your own, you may want to create RPM packages out of software you use, if only for the ease of management that the RPM system provides.

Creating RPMs allows you to create a consistent set of applications for use on all systems in your organization and easily manage those applications. You may create RPMs of applications developed in house or RPMs of applications developed elsewhere that you need to customize for your environment. Making RPMs of the customized applications reduces work and makes the customizations consistent.

This chapter introduces the RPM system from the point of view of creating RPMs and demonstrates the steps and planning necessary to make your own packages. As such, this chapter introduces the RPM-building topics covered in depth in the remaining chapters in this part.

Preparing to Build RPMs

The RPM-building task starts with gathering all the material you want to bundle into an RPM package and then defining the RPM directives to make your package. The final steps are to build and test an RPM. This sounds easy, and for the most part it is fairly straightforward.

The main problems arise when you try to define the many RPM directives for your package. In addition, some of the elements in an RPM can be complex, such as upgrade scripts.

The main tasks in building RPMs are:

1. Planning what you want to build

2. Gathering the software to package

3. Patching the software as needed

4. Creating a reproducible build of the software

5. Planning for upgrades

6. Outlining any dependencies

7. Building the RPMs

8. Testing the RPMs

The sections in this chapter cover the initial planning stages and provide an overview of the process of building RPMs. The remaining chapters in Part II go in depth into the process of building RPMs.

Planning what you want to build

The first step in the entire RPM-building process is simply to decide exactly what you want to make into an RPM. Is this an application, a programming library, a set of system configuration files, or a documentation package? If this is an application, is it customized or patched? Think these issues over and decide what you want to package as an RPM.

In most cases, you want to create both a source package and a binary package containing the built sources. You need a binary package because that holds the RPM you want to install on other systems. You need the source package so you can recreate the binary package at any time. And, if the sources get updated, you can quickly make a new binary RPM from the updated sources if you have already defined a source RPM.

Most packages start with a source RPM, although you have the option to skip making a source RPM. It is a good idea to make the source RPM, however, because it makes it easier to reproduce the final binary RPM. One of the key goals of the RPM system is to allow for reproducible builds, and making source RPMs is just one step to help towards this goal.

Creating a source RPM also allows you to transfer the entire set of sources for a package to another system, since the source RPM is just one file and it contains all the program sources along with the instructions, called a spec file, for building the binary RPM. Furthermore, creating a source RPM makes it easier to create binary RPMs on different processor architectures or different versions of Linux.

Not all programs are portable to multiple-processor architectures. But many Linux programs can simply be recompiled on another architecture to make a binary program for that architecture. That's because there are a lot of common APIs for Linux applications and because most programs are not processor dependent. This is not true of all programs, so your mileage may vary.

Source packages are not that hard to make, and they provide a single package, and single file, that holds all the sources necessary to build your binary package. In addition, once you have a source RPM, it is very easy to build a binary RPM.

Binary packages are likely the real reason you want to make an RPM. You can package an application, a programming library, or almost anything you want. Armed with a binary RPM, you can transfer one file to another machine and install the application there, taking full advantage of the RPM system.

Gathering the software to package

Whether you are writing your own software or merely packaging software found elsewhere, the next step is to gather the software you want to bundle into an RPM. This includes the applications or libraries you want to package, as well as the program source code.

In general, you'll be doing one of three things:

◆ Packaging your own software

◆ Packaging someone else's software

◆ Packaging someone else's stuff after first customizing or patching the software

In all cases, you need to gather the software together and decide whether you want everything to go into one bundle or a number of bundles.

As covered in Chapter 2, a major tenet of the philosophy behind RPM is to start with pristine – unmodified – sources. You may need to patch or customize the sources for your environment, but you can always go back to the original sources.

Starting with pristine sources provides a number of advantages, including the following:

◆ You clearly separate any changes you have made to the software from the original software.

◆ You make it easier to get an upgrade of the original sources, since your changes are cleanly separated from the original sources. With each new release of the software, you can determine which of your changes, if any, are still needed. This is especially important if you are packaging an application created by another organization into an RPM.

◆ You have a reproducible way to recreate everything in the package. Since you start with unmodified sources, you can always go back to the beginning of the process and start again. Thus, your RPMs don't depend on any actions taken beforehand, such as patching, that you may later forget to do because the steps are not automated as part of the RPM-building process.

Start with pristine sources; then patch as needed. A patch is an automated set of modifications to the source code. Use the diff command to build a patch and the patch command to apply the patch (that is, to modify the source code). Keep the original sources separate from any patches you need to make the software work in your environment.

See the online manual pages for the patch and diff commands for more information on how to create and apply a patch.

Creating a reproducible build of the software

The RPM system will automate the steps to create an application, as long as you configure the RPM with the proper steps, such as which make targets to run. Unfortunately, configuring the proper steps is not always easy. So before trying to make an RPM, you need to figure out how to build the application or library you plan to package into an RPM. Once you have figured out how to build the application or library, you can set up a reproducible build. The RPM system can then automate this build.

To build the software, you'll need to use a variety of Linux tools. The specific tools you need depend largely on where the original software came from. The following sections outline some of the more common techniques for preparing and building Linux software.

Unpacking Software

Many applications are downloaded in compressed tar format, often called a tarball. A *tarball* is merely an archive file built by the tar command that has been compressed, usually using the gzip command.

In most cases, these files have a name such as the following:

```
filename.tar.gz
filename.tgz
filename.tar.Z
```

For the first two cases, use the gunzip command to unzip the file; then use the tar command to extract the file, for example:

```
$ gunzip filename.tgz
$ tar xf filename.tar
```

 In the case of a file name ending in .Z, use the `uncompress` program instead of `gunzip`.

Once you have unpacked the sources, start looking around at the files.

Reading the README

Many applications come with a very handy file named README, or something similar, such as README.txt. As the name implies, you should read this file. The README file answers some of the most common questions about a particular application.

 You really should read any file named README or any variant of README.

Other useful files include those named INSTALL or some close variant. Read these files, too. Usually, the README or the INSTALL file will tell you what you need to do to build the software.

Once you have extracted the source code files and read all the available documentation, the next step is to build, usually compile, the application or library.

Building Programs with Linux Build Tools

Most applications or libraries need to be built into executable programs or compiled archived libraries. This process of building can be as simple as just compiling, but is usually more involved. Most Linux applications and libraries use a build tool called `make` to manage the building of the source code and creation of the executable programs. The `make` command uses a file, normally named Makefile, that contains the rules for building the software. You will usually find a Makefile in each directory in the source code.

Each Makefile contains a set of targets that define things that `make` can build. Each *target* defines the commands to run to build a particular thing (`make` targets are purely arbitrary, although some conventions are usually followed). Some combination of the targets results in a built application. The `make` program runs the targets that you specify on the command line, or the Makefile rules indicate it needs to run based on the targets you specify on the command line.

You need to tell `make` the target to build the application or library you want to package into an RPM. Each target is defined within the Makefile. The conventional `make` targets to build and install a program are:

```
make
make install
```

When you call the `make` command without the name of a target, `make` builds the default target, named `all`. This target usually compiles the program or library. The `install` target should install the program.

The names of these `make` targets are conventions shared by many but not all programs. Other common targets include `clean`, which should clean up any files built.

The commands in the Makefile may be specific to a given system. For example, the traditional command for compiling C programs is `cc`, short for C Compiler. You may have the `gcc` command (GNU C Compiler) instead. The options passed to the C compiler may differ depending on the architecture of the system. Other commands may exist but be located in different locations. `SuSE Linux`, for example, puts a lot of programs in /opt.

These system-dependent issues mostly apply to various versions of Unix. Most modern Linux systems are fairly similar. Because many packages, such as sendmail, have a long Unix history, you'll find all sorts of complications in the Makefiles or many Makefiles provided with many applications. If we could just convince everyone to give up all non-Linux operating systems, this task would be much simpler.

Because the Makefiles are platform specific, a number of tools have been developed to create the proper Makefile, usually by running a program that knows about your system's architecture. The simplest of these tools is the manual approach. You may download a program and find files such as Makefile.amiga, Makefile.solaris, and Makefile.linux. You need to copy the file for your system architecture to the name Makefile.

The following sections discuss other tools for creating Makefiles.

IMAKE   A program called imake is used mostly for X Window graphical applications, and typically older X Window applications. The `imake` command uses a file named Imakefile that contains rules used to build a platform-specific Makefile. This allows X Window applications, which run on many architectures and operating systems, to come with fairly generic build scripts.

When you see an Imakefile, use the following general set of commands to compile and install an application:

```
$ xmkmf
$ make
$ make install
```

These commands work for most X Window applications. The xmkmf command is a script that runs the imake command to create a Makefile. If the xmkmf command is not available or if this command does not work, you may need to run a command such as the following:

```
make Makefile
```

Or, if there are multiple directories of source code, try the following command:

```
make Makefiles
```

For more on imake, see www.dubois.ws/software/imake-stuff/.

THE CONFIGURE SCRIPT   Most Linux programs, especially server-side or command-line programs, use a script called configure. The configure script outputs a platform-specific Makefile.

If you see a script named configure in the source files, try the following commands to build and install the program:

```
$ ./configure
$ make
$ make install
```

The ./configure command runs the script in the local directory, which outputs a Makefile configured for your system. The make command builds the program and the make install command installs the program.

The configure script is created by a set of tools including automake and autoconf, which use generic files usually named configure.in and makefile.am, among other files, to create the generic configure script.

In many cases, you'll need to pass parameters to the configure script. One of the most common parameters is --prefix, which tells the configure script the name of the starting directory from which to base all other paths. This is the root directory for building the application.

For more on the configure system, autoconf, and automake, see
www.airs.com/ian/configure/.

BUILDING PERL MODULES   Perl is a scripting language used heavily on Linux systems, especially by administrators. Most Perl modules and packages use the following set of commands to create a system-specific Makefile and to build the module:

```
$ perl Makefile.PL
$ make
$ make test
$ make install
```

If you see a file named Makefile.PL, chances are these are the commands to run to build the application or module.

The goal of all these steps is to figure out how to make a reproducible build of the application or library you want to package in RPM format. Once you have a build, the next step is to plan for upgrades.

Planning for upgrades

Any application or library you package in RPM format is likely to get upgraded sometime. When this happens, you'll need to make a new RPM. This new RPM must handle not only installing the package, but also handling any upgrade issues. You need to think about the following issues:

◆ How to install the RPM for the new version of the software. Are there any necessary install scripts?

◆ How to remove the previous RPM package. If your package has an install script, then you may need an uninstall script to cleanly remove any changes made to the system by the install script. The RPM system handles the removal of the files in the package. You need to handle the task of undoing any changes made to the system during installation.

At this point in time, the main effort is to keep these issues in mind and plan ahead, since these issues will come up with any upgrade.

Outlining any dependencies

Often, the hardest task is getting make to build a program properly. One potential problem is assuring that all the dependencies are included. As you work with make, keep track of any other libraries that the program you are trying to build requires. These libraries will become dependencies when you get to the stage of making the RPM.

In most cases you do not want to include the dependencies in your RPM. Instead, each dependency should have its own RPM for each necessary library. In many cases, you should be able to find RPMs for these dependencies. Keep track of the packages that provide the dependencies.

After you have built the application, planned for upgrades and outlined dependencies, you can make an RPM.

Building RPMs

In previous chapters, just about everything you want to do with RPMs is accomplished with the rpm command. Building RPMs is one exception. Just about everything you want to do to build an RPM is done by the rpmbuild command, often with a single command.

 Older RPM manuals refer to using the -b option to the rpm command to create RPMs. Don't use that option. Instead, always use the rpmbuild command. The reason for this change is that starting with version 4.1, RPM no longer maps the rpm -b command to the real command, rpmbuild.

When building RPMs, go through the following steps:

1. Set up the directory structure.

2. Place the sources in the right directory.

3. Create a spec file that tells the rpmbuild command what to do.

4. Build the source and binary RPMs.

The following sections provide details for these steps.

Setting up the directory structure

The RPM system expects five directories, as listed in Table 9-1.

TABLE 9-1 RPM DIRECTORIES

Directory	Usage
BUILD	The `rpmbuild` command builds software in this directory.
RPMS	The `rpmbuild` command stores binary RPMs it creates in this directory.
SOURCES	You should put the sources for the application in this directory.
SPECS	You should place the spec file for each RPM you plan to make in this directory.
SRPMS	The `rpmbuild` command places source RPMs in this directory.

The RPMS directory usually has a number of architecture-specific subdirectories, such as the following (on an Intel architecture system):

```
$ ls RPMS
athlon
i386
i486
i586
i686
noarch
```

By default, Red Hat Linux systems expect RPMs to be built in the /usr/src/redhat directory.

 This directory is obviously specific to Red Hat Linux. On other Linux distributions, you'll likely see directories such as /usr/src/OpenLinux for SCO (formerly Caldera) OpenLinux.

Within the /usr/src/redhat directory, you'll see the subdirectories listed in Table 9-1, as follows:

```
$ ls /usr/src/redhat
BUILD
```

```
RPMS
SOURCES
SPECS
SRPMS
```

At first, it seems rather odd to be using a system directory to build RPMs. But remember that the RPM system was originally built to create Linux distributions. You can also change the default directories by modifying your rpmrc settings.

See Chapter 21 for more on the use of the rpmrc settings.

For now, it is easiest to just change to the /usr/src/redhat directory and work from this location. To start, you will need to change ownership or permissions on these files so you can build RPMs while logged in as a normal user.

Never, ever build RPMs while logged in as root. Mistakes in building packages can have serious consequences if you are logged in as root.

To build RPMs, you really need only two things:

♦ Your sources in the SOURCES directory

♦ Your spec file in the SPECS directory

Placing your sources into the directory structure

You can place all the source files directly in the /usr/src/redhat/SOURCES directory. In most cases, however, it is easier to create a tarball of the sources you want to build and place the tarball file in the /usr/src/redhat/SOURCES directory. The RPM specifications for commands necessary to extract the sources from such a file are trivial. Furthermore, the tarball, when extracted, should create a subdirectory specific to your package. This keeps your source code separate from other packages that also have source code in the SOURCES directory.

The best strategy is to start in a directory of your own making, create the tarball file from the sources, and then copy the tarball file to the /usr/src/redhat/SOURCES directory.

The convention for these tarball files is *package-version*.tar.gz. For example:

```
jikes-1.17.tar.gz
```

Place a file like this into the /usr/src/redhat/SOURCES directory. This file should include all the sources, all the build scripts, and any documentation you want to install as part of the package.

Creating the spec file

The spec file, short for specification file, defines all the actions the `rpmbuild` command should take to build your application, as well as all the actions necessary for the `rpm` command to install and remove the application. Each source RPM should have the necessary spec file for building a binary RPM.

The spec file is a text file. The normal naming convention is to name the file with the package name and a .spec filename extension. For example, the jikes package spec file would be named jikes.spec.

Inside the spec file, format the information on the package using a special syntax. This syntax defines how to build the package, version numbers, dependency information, and everything else you can query about a package. This syntax differs slightly depending on the sections in the spec file. The following sections describe these spec file sections and the necessary syntax in each section.

The introduction section

The introduction section contains information about the package, the type of information shown with the `rpm -qi` command. For example:

```
Summary: java source to bytecode compiler
%define version 1.17
Copyright: IBM Public License, http://ibm.com/developerworks/oss/license10.html
Group: Development/Languages
Name: jikes
Prefix: /usr
Provides: jikes
Release: 1
Source: jikes-%{version}.tar.gz
URL: http://ibm.com/developerworks/opensource/jikes
Version: %{version}
Buildroot: /tmp/jikesrpm


%description
The IBM Jikes compiler translates Java source files to bytecode. It
also supports incremental compilation and automatic makefile generation,
and is maintained by the Jikes Project:
http://ibm.com/developerworks/opensource/jikes/
```

In this example, you can see the Source: definition of a compressed tar archive associated with a particular version number. This also names a Buildroot: setting that defines where the files will get built into a working program. You can see the description of the package that will get printed with the rpm -qi command.

The prep section

The prep section, short for prepare, defines the commands necessary to prepare for the build. If you are starting with a compressed tar archive (a tarball) of the sources, the prep section needs to extract the sources.

For example:

```
%prep
%setup -q
```

The prep section starts with a %prep statement.

This example uses the %setup RPM macro, which knows about tar archives, to extract the files. In most cases, this will be all you need in your spec file prep section.

The build section

The spec file build section contains the commands to build the software. Usually, this will include just a few commands, since most of the real instructions appear in the Makefile. For example:

```
%build
./configure CXXFLAGS=-O3 --prefix=$RPM_BUILD_ROOT/usr
make
```

The build section starts with a %build statement. The commands shown for this build section run the configure script, covered in the previous section on Linux build tools, and then run the make command with the default maketarget. If things unfold as they should, this procedure builds the software.

The install section

The spec file install section holds the commands necessary to install the newly built application or library. In most cases, your install section should clean out the Buildroot directory and run the make install command. For example:

```
%install
rm -fr $RPM_BUILD_ROOT
make install
```

The install section starts with an %install statement.

The clean section

The clean section cleans up the files that the commands in the other sections create:

```
%clean
rm -rf $RPM_BUILD_ROOT
```

The clean section starts with a %clean statement

The files section

Finally, the files section lists the files to go into the binary RPM, along with the defined file attributes. For example:

```
%files
%defattr(-,root,root)
/usr/bin/jikes
%doc /usr/doc/jikes-%{version}/license.htm
%doc /usr/man/man1/jikes.1*
```

The files section starts with a %files statement
The %doc macro marks certain files as documentation. This allows the RPM to distinguish the files holding documentation from the other files in the RPM.

 This example skips the install and uninstall script sections, as well as a verification section. There are also no triggers defined in this RPM spec file. All of these topics are covered in Chapters 10 and 11.

Once you have written your spec file, and placed the files in the SOURCES and SPECS directories under /usr/src/redhat, you'll see files like the following:

```
$ ls -CF /usr/src/redhat/*
/usr/src/redhat/BUILD:

/usr/src/redhat/RPMS:
athlon/   i386/   i486/   i586/   i686/   noarch/

/usr/src/redhat/SOURCES:
jikes-1.17.tar.gz

/usr/src/redhat/SPECS:
jikes.spec

/usr/src/redhat/SRPMS:
```

That is, with a clean system and no other RPMs being built, you'll see a spec file in /usr/src/redhat/SPECS and the sources in /usr/src/redhat/SOURCES. In this example, the sources are in a compressed `tar` archive. (For this, the RPM spec file, jikes.spec needs to have a command in the prep section to extract the files.)

You should now be ready to build an RPM.

Building RPMs with the rpmbuild command

To build RPMs with the `rpmbuild` command, use the following basic syntax:

```
rpmbuild -bBuildStage spec_file
```

The `-b` option tells `rpmbuild` to build an RPM. The extra *BuildStage* option is a special code that tells the `rpmbuild` command how far to go when building. Table 9-2 lists these options:

TABLE 9-2 OPTIONS FOR BUILDING WITH RPMBUILD

Option	Usage
-ba	Build all, both a binary and source RPM
-bb	Build a binary RPM
-bc	Build (compile) the program but do not make the full RPM, stopping just after the %build section
-bp	Prepare for building a binary RPM, and stop just after the %prep section
-bi	Create a binary RPM and stop just after the %install section
-bl	Check the listing of files for the RPM and generate errors if the buildroot is missing any of the files to be installed
-bs	Build a source RPM only

For example, to set up all the necessary files and prepare for building, run the following command:

```
rpmbuild -bp specfile
```

This example runs through the %prep section, and stops immediately after this section. With the jikes package, for example, you'll see a result like the following:

```
$ rpmbuild -bp /usr/src/redhat/SPECS/jikes.spec
Executing(%prep): /bin/sh -e /var/tmp/rpm-tmp.72435
+ umask 022
+ cd /usr/src/redhat/BUILD
+ LANG=C
+ export LANG
+ cd /usr/src/redhat/BUILD
+ rm -rf jikes-1.17
+ /usr/bin/gzip -dc /usr/src/redhat/SOURCES/jikes-1.17.tar.gz
+ tar -xf -
+ STATUS=0
+ '[' 0 -ne 0 ']'
+ cd jikes-1.17
++ /usr/bin/id -u
+ '[' 500 = 0 ']'
++ /usr/bin/id -u
+ '[' 500 = 0 ']'
+ /bin/chmod -Rf a+rX,g-w,o-w .
+ exit 0
```

After running this command, the source files are extracted into the /usr/src/red-hat/BUILD directory, under the jikes-1.17 subdirectory. Using a subdirectory keeps the sources for this package from intermixing with the sources for other packages.

Running a directory listing on the /usr/src/redhat/BUILD/jikes-1.17 subdirectory shows what the spec file %prep section commands have done. For example:

```
$ ls -1 /usr/src/redhat/BUILD/jikes-1.17
acinclude.m4
aclocal.m4
AUTHORS
ChangeLog
config.guess
config.sub
configure
configure.in
COPYING
depcomp
doc
INSTALL
install-sh
jikes.spec
Makefile.am
```

```
Makefile.in
missing
mkinstalldirs
NEWS
README
src
TODO
```

From these sources, you see a `configure` script. The `configure` script gives a good indication of how the software needs to be built. This example also shows a README file. You know what to do with these files.

The actual source code is in the /usr/src/redhat/BUILD/jikes-1.17/src directory. The user documentation is stored in the /usr/src/redhat/BUILD/jikes-1.17/doc directory.

To build a binary RPM, use the `-bb` option to the `rpmbuild` command. For example:

```
$ rpmbuild -bb /usr/src/redhat/SPECS/jikes.spec
```

Don't build packages when you are logged in as the root user. Log in as a normal user instead. This is to limit the damage caused to your system if the spec file or the Makefile contains errors that delete system files, for example. If you are logged in as the root user, you will have permission to perform these destructive acts. If you are logged in as a normal user, though, these RPM spec file and Makefile errors will fail to run, because you don't have permission to modify system files.

This command results in a lot of output, most coming from the `configure` script. (This script examines the C programming environment on your system.) When the `rpmbuild` command completes, you'll see the binary RPM in the proper subdirectory of the RPMS directory. You can see the RPM with a directory listing, for example:

```
$ls /usr/src/redhat/RPMS/i386:
jikes-1.17-1.i386.rpm
```

To stop execution just after the %install section, use a command like the following:

```
rpmbuild -bi specfile
```

For example:

```
# rpmbuild -bi /usr/src/redhat/SPECS/jikes.spec
```

To build a source RPM out of the files you have (in this case a `tar` archive of the sources and the spec file), use a command like the following:

```
rpmbuild -bs specfile
```

For example:

```
$ rpmbuild -bs /usr/src/redhat/SPECS/jikes.spec
```

When done, you'll see the source RPM in the /usr/src/redhat/SRPMS directory:

```
$ ls /usr/src/redhat/SRPMS
jikes-1.17-1.src.rpm
```

To clean out the files created by building these RPMs, use the `--clean` option to the `rpmbuild` command:

```
rpmbuild --clean specfile
```

For example:

```
$ rpmbuild --clean /usr/src/redhat/SPECS/jikes.spec
Executing(--clean): /bin/sh -e /var/tmp/rpm-tmp.21908
+ umask 022
+ cd /usr/src/redhat/BUILD
+ rm -rf jikes-1.17
+ exit 0
```

Chapter 12 covers a number of addition options for the `rpmbuild` command that you can use to customize the build.

Verifying Your RPMs

After you've built an RPM, you can use the techniques from Chapter 5 to verify the RPM. You can also use the `-bl` option to the `rpmbuild` command to verify the list of files in the RPM. Use a command like the following:

```
rpmbuild -bl spec_file
```

For example:

```
$ rpmbuild -bl /usr/src/redhat/SPECS/jikes.spec
Processing files: jikes-1.17-1
error: File not found: /tmp/jikesrpm/usr/bin/jikes
error: File not found: /tmp/jikesrpm/usr/doc/jikes-1.17/license.htm
error: File not found by glob: /tmp/jikesrpm/usr/man/man1/jikes.1*
Provides: jikes


RPM build errors:
    File not found: /tmp/jikesrpm/usr/bin/jikes
    File not found: /tmp/jikesrpm/usr/doc/jikes-1.17/license.htm
    File not found by glob: /tmp/jikesrpm/usr/man/man1/jikes.1*
```

This example shows a number of errors. The -bl option checks that all the necessary files are located within the buildroot directory. The buildroot directory is a location that acts like the final installed root directory. From the previous example, this package was not properly built yet.

In a situation like this, you can start over, or use the --short-circuit option to restart the build from a given section in the spec file. As you create an RPM, you will need to go back and forth restarting the build as you detect and fix errors.

You can also use the rpm command with options such as -V for verification on a fully-built package. For example:

```
$ rpm -Vp /usr/src/redhat/RPMS/i386/jikes-1.17-1.i386.rpm
S.5....T   /usr/bin/jikes
.......T d /usr/doc/jikes-1.17/license.htm
..5....T d /usr/man/man1/jikes.1.gz
```

In this case, you see some file sizes and times differ. These differences can be explained by the fact that the original package was compiled on a different system and older version of Red Hat Linux than the version compiled locally.

See the "Verifying Installed RPM Packages" section in Chapter 5 for more on the -V option.

Summary

This chapter introduced the task of building RPMs, whether building RPMs from your own applications or from software you have gathered elsewhere. In both cases, the steps for building the RPMs are the same.

In most cases, you should build an RPM of the sources for your application, an RPM that can be used to reproduce the build of the application. Create a second RPM that holds the binary application. Once you set up the commands and define the spec file for the binary RPM, making a source RPM is trivial.

Use the `rpmbuild` command to create RPMs. This command uses an RPM spec file to define the commands and settings for creating the RPM.

The next chapter delves into the spec files that define the RPM directives for your packages.

Chapter 10

Working with Spec Files

THE PREVIOUS CHAPTER INTRODUCED the concepts of how to build RPMs, and briefly covered the spec file, which controls how RPM packages are built and installed. This chapter delves into how to create spec files and the next chapter covers advanced spec file topics such as using conditional commands and making relocatable packages.

A spec file defines all the commands and values that are required for creating a package, everything from the name and version number to the actual commands used to build the program you are packaging.

This chapter covers the spec file syntax and how to write spec files. It goes in depth into defining information about your package, controlling how the software will be built, defining what exactly should go into the package, and customizing your build with RPM macros.

Reading Spec Files

The first step to learning more about spec files is to read through some of the huge number of spec files for the source RPMs that come with your Linux distribution. Looking at these files will show two things right away:

♦ You will see that the spec file syntax is not really as complicated as it appears.

♦ You will see how many others have solved problems similar to those you need to solve.

I've used real-world examples throughout this book, to show how the RPMs you need to deal with actually work. Some of the more interesting packages include anything that has a client and a server component, anything with networking or e-mail, and anything that installs a system service. All these types of packages solve problems that you will commonly face. Some useful spec files to look at are those for anonftp, telnet, vnc, and sendmail. To get these spec files, you need to install the corresponding source RPMs for each of these packages.

As you read through spec files, you'll start to see common patterns in how packages are defined, named, the macros used, and common elements in the build sections of the spec files. You'll also see how network services are installed on Linux, as well as example install and uninstall scripts. The next sections provide more information on the things to look for within spec files.

Furthermore, even with the plethora of options RPM provides, if you know shell scripting basics and something about how C programs are normally built, with `configure` scripts and `make` commands, you will find most spec files relatively easy to understand.

The following sections go into the details of writing your own spec files. Keep your example spec files handy as you read through these sections.

Writing Spec Files

Spec files are text files containing RPM directives. These directives use a simple syntax of a tag name, a colon, and a value:

```
TagName: value
```

For example:

```
Version: 1.15
```

This example sets the package version to 1.15. The name of the item is not case sensitive, so tag names of *version*, *Version*, or *VERSION* all set the same value. This syntax works for most settings, including Name, Release, and so on.

In addition to this directive syntax, you can define macros using the RPM `%define` syntax. For example:

```
%define major 2
```

This example defines a macro named `major` with a value of 2. Once defined, you can access macros using the `%{macro_name}` or just `%macro_name` syntaxes. For example:

```
source: %{name}-%{version}.tar.gz
```

See the section "Defining Spec File Macros" later in this chapter for more options for macros.

Major sections in the spec file are also delimited with % markers. For example, the build section starts with %build on a line by itself.

 The multiple uses of the % sign aren't really that confusing in practice. Read through some spec files and you should find most of the commands are easily understood.

Blank lines separate sections in the spec file, which makes sense for readability as well.

Comments

To help document your work, you can include comments (to yourself and others reading the spec file). Any line starting with a hash character, #, holds a comment. RPM will ignore comments.

```
# This is a comment.
```

In spec files, comments are mostly to help explain your syntax choices to yourself should you view the spec file later. Comments are a good thing. You should comment heavily, especially for any choice that deviates from the norm. For example, if you provide special C compiler options for building the package, add comments to describe why you picked the options and how necessary they are. Such comments help immensely should you need to port the RPM to another architecture or modify how it was built.

 Avoid single percent signs, %, in comments. For example:

```
# Added new commands to %prep
```

The rpmbuild command may report an error of a second %prep section. To get around this problem, use two percent signs, such as %%prep, in spec file comments.

Storing spec files on disk

As discussed in Chapter 9, the rpmbuild command expands source RPMs to the /usr/src/redhat directory. Under this directory, the RPM system assumes five subdirectories, listed in Table 10-1.

TABLE 10-1 DEFAULT RPM DIRECTORIES

Directory	Usage
BUILD	Where the rpmbuild command builds software
RPMS	Where the rpmbuild command stores binary RPMs it creates
SOURCES	Where you should put the sources for the application
SPECS	Where you should place the spec file
SRPMS	Where the rpmbuild command places source RPMs

The spec files you create should be stored in the SPECS directory while building RPMs. (You can store your spec files permanently in any location you desire.)

These directories are the default directories. See Chapter 21 for changing RPM default values. In addition, these are the defaults for Red Hat Linux. See Chapters 19 and 20 for discussions on other versions of Linux and other non-Linux operating systems, respectively.

With the knowledge of the spec file syntax covered in the preceding sections, you can start to write spec files. The first step is to define the basic package information.

Defining Package Information

Most of the package information you need to enter into a spec file fleshes out the information you can query for a given package, such as the name, version, and release information, along with a longer description and a one-line summary.

This gets a little more complicated when you set build locations, name source files, and name patches. The following sections cover how to specify the package information.

Describing the package

The first part of the spec file defines macros (covered in the section "Defining Spec File Macros"), and describes the package. Starting with the basics, you need a name, version, and release. You also should provide a longer description. For legal reasons, you may need to include ownership and copyright information.

Naming the Package

The most important part of the package description is the NVR, or Name-Version-Release information, because this information is so crucial for the RPM system to compare versions and track dependencies.

Set the name with the `Name:` directive. For example:

```
Name: myapp
```

The name should not contain any spaces or other whitespace characters such as tabs or newlines. Remember, RPM files are named, by default, *name-version-release*.rpm, or *name-version-release-architecture*.rpm, so use valid characters for file names.

The version number is used in version comparisons. The RPM comparison algorithm is fairly complex, but can get fooled by strange version numbers. So, your best bet is to stick to dotted numerics, such as 1.5 or 2.3.1.1.4 or 1.0. Version numbers such as these will compare best from within the RPM system. For example:

```
Version: 1.1.2
```

You cannot use a dash in the version number, as RPM uses the dash to separate the Name-Version-Release elements. You can use a dash in the package name, though.

The release number should start at 1 for the first RPM you build for a given version of the package, and count up from there. For example:

```
Release: 1
```

The release differentiates newer updates of the RPM itself, even if the underlying application hasn't changed. (The application may be compiled with different compiler options, though.) For most usage, simply start at 1 and each time you modify the spec file and recreate the package, increment the release number.

If the version number is not enough to allow for comparisons, for example, if the version numbering scheme has changed radically between releases, you can define an `Epoch:` directive. For example:

```
Epoch: 3
```

If you renumber your versions, use an Epoch setting to clarify the version history. For example, Sun Microsystems went from SunOS 4.1 to Solaris 2. The `Epoch:` helps RPM properly handle strange version number changes. Define the `Epoch:` as a whole number such as 1, 2, or 3.

Avoid using the Epoch: directive if at all possible. It is far better to use a sane version-numbering scheme than to try to resolve the mess with epoch values. The main problems with using epoch values are that epochs are hidden from users in most cases, and using epochs can lead to very strange-looking tasks such as a newer package with a version number that looks older than the older package.

The older Serial: directive also works similarly to the Epoch: directive. For example:

```
Serial: 6
```

Like the Epoch:, the Serial: directive should be a number that counts upward. Modern packages should use the Epoch: directive instead of Serial:, since Serial: has been deprecated.

The Group: directive provides a classification for your packages. If at all possible, use a category name that already exists for other packages, such as System Environment/Shells for a Linux shell. For example:

```
Group: System Environment/Shells
```

Many graphical installation tools divide packages by these categories, so you want to fit into the existing group names if possible. (See Chapter 5 for more on querying group information from RPMs.) The official list of groups is located in the file /usr/share/doc/rpm-4.1/GROUPS for RPM 4.1, and in a similar location for other RPM versions.

The Distribution: directive is used by Linux distribution vendors such as Red Hat to identify that the package is part of a given distribution, or was built for a particular distribution. Most packages created outside of the Linux vendors don't provide this directive.

```
Distribution: Red Hat Linux
```

The Icon: directive names an icon file stored in the RPM. The file format should be XPM or GIF, with an extension of .xpm or .gif, respectively. Some packaging tools will use this icon in a package display.

Specifying Company Information

For legal reasons, you probably want to specify the organization behind the RPM, any copyright or licensing information, as well as a URL to find out more information. Even if you are not concerned about corporate legal issues, you may want to identify where the package came from. Use the following directives to provide this information.

The `Vendor:` directive names the company or organization behind an RPM. For example:

```
Vendor: The Really Cool Company
```

The `URL:` directive provides a URL to your company or organization home page, or perhaps to a URL for a particular application. For example:

```
URL: http://mycompany.yow/products/coolstuff
```

Similarly, the `Packager:` directive provides an optional name and e-mail address for the person who created the RPM:

```
Packager: Bob Marley <marley@reggae.com>
```

The `License:` and `Copyright:` directives provide legal information about your package. Older packages tended to use `Copyright:` as a statement of the package's license, not copyright. For example:

```
Copyright: BSD
License: LGPL
```

The `Copyright:` directive is now deprecated in favor of `License:`.

Filling in the Description

The `Summary:` directive provides a one-line short description of the package. You should not exceed much more than 50 characters when writing your summary. For example:

```
Summary: A program that does exactly what you want
```

 The `Summary:` directive of the spec file replaces the older `Description:` directive.

The `%description` section allows for longer text describing your package. Fill in as many lines as you need after the `%description` section. For example:

```
%description
This is a really cool package. It contains the really cool
program that provides a maximum return on investment,
or ROI, for achieving your crucial business objectives
utilizing world-class high-caliber componentized software
```

```
implemented with world-class quality and performance
metrics.
```

The %description section supports a limited amount of formatting. Blank lines are assumed to separate paragraphs. Some graphical user interface installation programs will reformat paragraphs into a nicer-looking font and change the display width.

Lines in the %description section that start with whitespace, such as a space or tab, will be treated as preformatted text and displayed as is, normally with a fixed-width font.

Specifying the Platform Architecture

Spec files can announce that a package can run on more than one operating system or is tied to a particular version of a particular operating system.

For example, the Excludearch: directive states that a package should not be built on the given architecture or architectures. For example:

```
ExcludeArch: sparc s390 s390x
```

This example excludes the SPARC and S/390 mainframe architectures. You can provide more than one architecture in the directive, separated by spaces or commas.

Similarly, the Exclusivearch: directive states that a package can only be built on the given architecture or architectures. For example:

```
ExclusiveArch: i386 ia64 alpha
```

This example identifies the package as only working on the Intel i386, IA-64, and Alpha architectures.

The Excludeos: and Exclusiveos: directives restrict the operating system. For example:

```
Excludeos: windows
```

This example states that the package should not be built on Windows. In contrast, the Exclusiveos: directive names only the operating system or systems that the package can be built on. For example:

```
Exclusiveos: linux
```

Chapters 19 and 20 cover RPMs on other versions of Linux and other operating systems, respectively.

Setting build locations

RPM supports two build-related directories with very similar names, the build directory and the buildroot.

The *build directory* is the location where RPM actually builds the software, compiling source code, running the configure script, and so on. Normally, you do not need to worry about the build directory as the rpmbuild command properly changes to this directory as needed.

The *buildroot*, on the other hand, acts as a staging area that looks like the final installation directory. The name buildroot refers to the fact that the final installation directory is usually the root directory, /. The install section of the spec file (covered in the section "Installing the software") installs files into the buildroot directory in the proper subdirectories, as if the files were really under the system root directory, /. This allows the buildroot directory to hold all the final installed files for a package, so you can see what will really be installed by the package.

You should always set the buildroot by defining a Buildroot: entry in your spec file. For example:

```
Buildroot: %{_tmppath}/%{name}-%{version}-root
```

This example sets the buildroot under the temporary directory named in the %_tmppath macro. The subdirectory is named based on the name and version of the package. For example, for a package named ypbind and a version 1.12, with a %_tmppath value of /tmp, the final buildroot directory would be:

```
/tmp/ypbind-1.12-root
```

Once you set a buildroot, your scripts run from the spec file and commands within the spec file can access the buildroot using the RPM_BUILD_ROOT environment variable. You normally need to access the RPM_BUILD_ROOT environment variable in the install section of the spec file (covered in the section "Installing the software").

 You can override the buildroot with the --buildroot command-line parameter to the rpmbuild command.

The buildroot replaces the older, and now obsolete directive, Root:.

Naming source files

Most packages have one or more bundles of source code, which you need to name in the spec file. In most cases, you will have a compressed tar archive of source files.

These may be files developed by your organization or downloaded from an Internet site. You can define one or more source tags, counting from 0. For example:

```
Source0: telnet-client.tar.gz
Source1: telnet-xinetd
Source2: telnet.wmconfig
```

In this example, `Source0:` refers to a compressed `tar` archive. The `rpmbuild` program will extract the files into the buildroot directory. The Source1: and Source2: directives name individual source files. You can name compressed `tar` archives or individual files as needed.

If you just have one Source directive, you can skip the 0. For example:

```
Source: telnet-client.tar.gz
```

You can also use FTP or HTTP URLs to name sources. For example:

```
Source0: ftp://ftp.somesite.yow/pub/linux/%{telnet_version}.tar.gz
```

 The URLs listed in source directives are for convenience and future reference only. RPM will not download these files.

The files named by the Source directives will get included into the source RPM. Sometimes you need to keep some sources out of the source RPM. This could be for proprietary sources you cannot ship, or simply due to size. The `Nosource:` directive tells RPM to skip a source file from the source RPM.

 Using the `Nosource:` or `Nopatch:` directives, covered following, mean you are creating a source RPM that cannot be rebuilt unless you also have the sources or patches, respectively, that were used to create the original RPM.

If the package contains a `Nosource:` or `Nopatch:` directive, `rpmbuild` will use a file-name extension of *.nosrc.rpm* instead of *.src.rpm*.

Naming patches

Patches are named similar to sources, using a similar syntax. For example:

```
Patch1: telnet-client-cvs.patch
Patch2: telnetd-0.17.diff
Patch3: telnet-0.17-env.patch
Patch4: telnet-0.17-issue.patch
Patch5: telnet-0.17-sa-01-49.patch
Patch6: telnet-0.17-env-5x.patch
Patch10: telnet-0.17-pek.patch
```

Note that you can have Patch directives are not numbered sequentially, such as the `Patch10:` directive in this example. In addition, you must apply each patch manually using `%patch` directives.

The patch files may be individual files or compressed (with `gzip`) patch files.

See the patch and diff online manual pages for more on patches.

Patches are important because they allow you to start with pristine sources, the source code for the original application. You can then apply patches as needed to get a working application, more clearly separating the work needed to create an RPM from the original application source code.

Chapter 14 discusses packaging guidelines and best practices. Starting from pristine sources is one of the best practices.

Similar to the sources directives, you can define a `Nopatch:` directive, which defines a patch that is applied to the sources, but is not included in the source RPM.

Controlling the Build

After describing information about the package, the crucial step comes when you need to build the package. The spec file should contain all the commands needed to build the application or library you want to package. But, and this is the important part, most of the build process should be run from a Makefile or other conventional way to build applications. Using a build tool such as make means that you can test the application outside of the RPM system. You don't need an RPM to build the application. Instead, you use the RPM to package the application.

Chapter 9 covers make and other Linux build tools.

In RPM terms, building the package is split into four steps:

1. Preparing for building, including unpacking the sources

2. Building

3. Installing the application or library

4. Cleaning up

The next sections cover how to control the build run by rpmbuild by defining commands within your spec files.

Preparing for the build

The %prep section defines the commands to prepare for the build. In most cases, you can run the simple %setup macro. For example:

```
%prep
%setup -q
```

This command changes to the build directory, typically /usr/src/redhat/BUILD, and then extracts the source files. This macro expects that at least one of the source files will create the necessary subdirectory under /usr/src/redhat/BUILD. This subdirectory should be named with the package name and version, such as telnet-1.0.1. If you are not using a compressed tar archive that will automatically create the right subdirectory, add the -c option to the %setup macro. The -c option creates the subdirectory for extracting the sources.

The -q command-line option runs in quiet mode with minimal output. The -T option disables the automatic extraction of compressed tar files. You can set the name of the build subdirectory with the -n option.

Normally, the %setup macro deletes the subdirectory prior to extracting the sources. You can disable the directory deletion with the -D option.

Table 10-2 summarizes the %setup command-line parameters. Many of these options apply mostly for subpackages, a topic covered in Chapter 11.

TABLE 10-2 COMMAND-LINE PARAMETERS FOR %SETUP

Parameter	Usage
-a *number*	Only unpack the source directive of the given number, such as -a 0 for source0:, after changing to the directory.
-b *number*	Only unpack the source directive of the given number, such as -b 0 for source0:, before changing to the directory.
-c	Create directory before unpacking, used if your sources will not create the directory as part of unpacking.
-D	Do not delete the directory before unpacking.
-n *name*	Name the directory as *name*.
-q	Run quietly with minimal output.
-T	Disable the automatic unpacking of the archives.

Like the %setup macro, the %patch directive applies a patch to the sources. Use this macro in your %prep section if you have patches. You need a %patch directive for each patch.

The %patch directive accepts -p and -s and other command-line parameters for the underlying patch command. The -p option, with a number, such as -p0, tells the patch command to remove that many slashes from the file names within the patch. A -p0 option tells the patch command to remove no slashes, a -p1 option tells patch to remove one slash, and correspondingly, one directory level from the files in the patch. The -s option tells the patch command to run silently (quietly) and output only errors. You can also pass other options for the patch command.

Use these options if you need them for the patch command when manually patching the sources. Otherwise, you can set up your %prep section as follows, for a spec file with two patches:

```
%prep
%setup -q
%patch1
%patch2
```

Use numbers to identify which patch to apply. For example, %patch0 corresponds to the patch file named with the Patch0: directive.

You must define a separate %patch directive for each patch. In most packages, this format, %patch1, %patch2, and so on, is used.

The %patch directive without a number corresponds to %patch0.

See the patch and diff online manual pages for more on patches.

In addition to the options supported by the patch command, you can use special options to the %patch directive to control how the directive works. The -P option tells the %patch directive to apply a given patch. For example, to only apply the patch named with the Patch2: directive, use the following %patch directive:

```
%patch -P 2
```

This is an uppercase P. The lowercase p performs a different function, described earlier in this section. The -P option is rarely used. Instead, patches are normally applied with %patch0, %patch1, and so on directives.

Building the software

The %prep section prepares for the build, which the %build section performs. You need to fill in the %build section with all the commands necessary to build the software. In most cases, this consists simply of the following commands:

```
%build
./configure
make
```

In this case, the %build section runs two commands, ./configure to run the configure script, and make to build the software. For most applications, this may be all you need. You can use the %configure macro in place of the call to the ./configure script. For example:

```
%build
%configure
make
```

Most spec files should use the %configure macro, since it automatically sets many environment variables that are often used within the configure script, especially path-related values such as the online manual path, the temporary directory, and so on. You can use the rpm --eval to see how the %configure macro expands. For example:

```
$ rpm --eval '%configure'

CFLAGS="${CFLAGS:--O2 -march=i386 -mcpu=i686}" ; export CFLAGS ;
CXXFLAGS="${CXXFLAGS:--O2 -march=i386 -mcpu=i686}" ; export CXXFLAGS ;
FFLAGS="${FFLAGS:--O2 -march=i386 -mcpu=i686}" ; export FFLAGS ;
[ -f configure.in ] && libtoolize --copy --force ;
./configure i386-redhat-linux \
        --prefix=/usr \
        --exec-prefix=/usr \
        --bindir=/usr/bin \
        --sbindir=/usr/sbin \
        --sysconfdir=/etc \
        --datadir=/usr/share \
        --includedir=/usr/include \
        --libdir=/usr/lib \
        --libexecdir=/usr/libexec \
        --localstatedir=/var \
        --sharedstatedir=/usr/com \
        --mandir=/usr/share/man \
        --infodir=/usr/share/info
```

 The vast majority of the work of building the software should remain in the Makefile where it belongs. The commands in the spec file should invoke the targets defined in the Makefile. Don't place too much logic in your RPM spec file as this makes it harder to test the application or library you plan to package.

If you intend to support relocatable packages, covered in Chapter 11, you will likely need to pass a --prefix option to the configure script. For example:

```
%build
./configure --prefix=$RPM_BUILD_ROOT/usr
make
```

You can also pass other options to the configure script, as needed, for compiling the application.

Installing the software

The %install section should install the software built in the %build section. If your Makefile contains all the instructions to install, you can define an %install section as follows:

```
%install
make install PREFIX=$RPM_BUILD_ROOT/usr
```

In most cases, you need to pass some parameter to make or install or another command to install all files into the buildroot directory, as shown in this example with the $RPM_BUILD_ROOT environment variable. You need to look within the Makefile to determine if the make variable should be PREFIX, prefix, or something else.

Sometimes, you want to call the install command instead of make to perform the installation. For example:

```
%install
install -m755 myapp $RPM_BUILD_ROOT/usr/bin/myapp
```

This example uses a hypothetical application name of myapp.

Many packages use the %makeinstall macro, which runs the make install command. For example:

```
%install
rm -rf $RPM_BUILD_ROOT
%makeinstall
```

This example also cleans the files from the buildroot. Use the rpm --eval command to see how the %makeinstall macro expands. For example:

```
$ rpm --eval '%makeinstall'

  make \
        prefix=/usr \
        exec_prefix=/usr \
        bindir=/usr/bin \
        sbindir=/usr/sbin \
        sysconfdir=/etc \
        datadir=/usr/share \
        includedir=/usr/include \
        libdir=/usr/lib \
        libexecdir=/usr/libexec \
        localstatedir=/var \
        sharedstatedir=/usr/com \
```

```
        mandir=/usr/share/man \
        infodir=/usr/share/info \
install
```

 RPM 4.2 adds a %check section after the %install.

Cleaning up after the build

The %clean section should clean up after the build and installation, removing compiled files and other files created as part of the build. If you use a buildroot, discussed previously, then you can provide a %clean section like the following:

```
%clean
rm -rf $RPM_BUILD_ROOT
```

Defining installation scripts

In addition to the sections described previously for controlling the build of the package software, you can define more scripts in your RPM spec files. RPM supports a script run prior to installation, %pre, and a script run after installation, %post. The same concepts apply when a package is erased, or uninstalled. The %preun script is run just before the uninstall and the %postun script just after the uninstall.

 Chapter 11 covers triggers, another form of script that gets run when packages are installed or removed.

Start your scripts with the RPM section marker for the given script, such as %pre for the pre-install script. Then, place the shell commands you want to run. For example, the following define %post, %preun, and %postun scripts from the ypbind networking package:

```
%post
/sbin/chkconfig --add ypbind
```

```
%preun
if [ "$1" = 0 ] ; then
    /sbin/service ypbind stop > /dev/null 2>&1
    /sbin/chkconfig --del ypbind
fi
exit 0

%postun
if [ "$1" -ge 1 ]; then
    /sbin/service ypbind condrestart > /dev/null 2>&1
fi
exit 0
```

Few packages need to perform any work prior to installation, so the %pre script is rarely used.

In this example, the chkconfig command is called to update the runlevel information for system services after installation and prior to removal. This is an example where just installing the application, ypbind in this case, is not enough. Since this application acts as a system service, more work needs to be done to finish the installation with the %pre script or clean up the service on removal with the %preun script.

 Do not try to write interactive scripts. Many users install RPMs automatically. In such cases, or if the user runs a graphical RPM tool, any information your scripts output will be lost. User input will not be available.

The rpm command will pass one argument to your scripts, shown as $1 in the previous example, which holds a count of the number of versions of the package that are installed. Table 10-3 lists the counts for specific cases.

TABLE 10-3 INSTALL AND UNINSTALL SCRIPT COUNT VALUES

Action	Count
Install the first time	1
Upgrade	2 or higher (depending on the number of versions installed)
Remove last version of package	0

The previous script example accesses the count using the shell variable $1.

Filling the List of Files

The %files section holds a list of all the files that RPM should install from the package. This list should be exhaustive, so that the RPM system knows exactly what your package installs. There are some options, though, to name all the files within a directory to help with packages containing hundreds of files.

In the default case, each line under the %files section names a separate file with its full path. For example:

```
%files
/usr/X11R6/bin/xtoolwait
/usr/X11R6/man/man1/xtoolwait.1
```

This example lists two files, /usr/X11R6/bin/xtoolwait and /usr/X11R6/man/man1/ xtoolwait.1, presumably an online manual files.

Using wildcards

In addition to naming each file on a line, you can use glob-style wildcards. For example:

```
%files
/usr/X11R6/bin/xtoolwait
/usr/X11R6/man/man1/xtoolwait.*
```

This example states that all files in /usr/X11R6/man/man1 that start with xtool- wait. should be included in the package.

Naming directories of files

In addition to using wildcard globs, you can specify whole directories as part of your package. For example:

```
%files
/usr/X11R6/bin/xtoolwait
/etc/xtoolwait
```

This example names all the files in the directory /etc/xtoolwait as part of the package. Be very careful when listing this directory. Do not include a system directory such as /usr/bin, as RPM will assume your package owns all of /usr/bin, which contains hundreds of commands. This can be a problem when you try to remove a package.

It is OK to name a subdirectory that your package owns. For example, while /etc is a system directory, /etc/xtoolwait is a reasonable directory for the xtoolwait package to control.

If you just want to include an empty directory in the package, and not the files within the directory, use the %dir directive in front of the directory name. For example:

```
%files
/usr/X11R6/bin/xtoolwait
%dir /etc/xtoolwait
```

This example states that the package contains the /usr/X11R6/bin/xtoolwait program and the empty directory /etc/xtoolwait.

In addition to the straight list of files or directories, RPM provides other options, starting with marking certain files as documentation or configuration files.

Marking files as documentation or configuration files

RPM keeps special track of files within a package that hold documentation or configuration data. You need to identify these files with special directives.

The %doc directive marks a file as a documentation file. For example:

```
%files
/usr/X11R6/bin/xtoolwait
%doc /usr/X11R6/man/man1/xtoolwait.*
```

This example lists all the included files in /usr/X11R6/man/man1 as documentation files.

If you don't include the full path to a documentation file or files, the RPM system will create a special documentation directory for the package, and place those files into that directory. For example:

```
%doc README NEWS
```

This example places the files README and NEWS into a newly created package-specific directory, typically a subdirectory under /usr/share/doc or /usr/doc.

The %docdir directive names a directory that holds documentation. All files under that directory in the package will get automatically marked as documentation files. For example:

```
%files
/usr/X11R6/bin/xtoolwait
%docdir /usr/X11R6/man/man1
/usr/X11R6/man/man1/xtoolwait.*
```

In addition to the marked directories, the standard Linux documentation directories, such as /usr/man, are automatically assumed to be documentation directories.

Similar to the %doc directive, the %config directive marks a file as configuration. For example:

```
%files
/sbin/ypbind
%config /etc/rc.d/init.d/*
%config /etc/yp.conf
%doc README NEWS
```

A special option to the %config directive, noreplace, tells RPM not to overwrite, or replace a configuration file. For example:

```
%files
/sbin/ypbind
%config /etc/rc.d/init.d/*
%config(noreplace) /etc/yp.conf
%doc README NEWS
```

Use this option to help protect local modifications. If you use %config(noreplace), the file will not overwrite an existing file that has been modified. If the file has not been modified on disk, the rpm command will overwrite the file. But, if the file has been modified on disk, the rpm command will copy the new file with an extra file-name extension of *.rpmnew*.

Similarly, %config(missingok) means that the file does not have to exist on disk. You can use this modifier for files or links that are created during the %post scripts but will need to be removed if the package is removed.

Another special modifier, %ghost, tells the rpm command that the file should not be included in the package. You can use this to name the needed attributes for a file that the program, when installed, will create. For example, you may want to ensure that a program's log file has certain attributes.

Setting file attributes

When your package is installed, you can control the file attributes as well as the files that get included into the package. This is very useful since most packages are installed by the root user and you don't always want the root user owning the files.

The %attr directive allows you to control the permissions for a particular file. The format is:

```
%attr(mode, user, group) filename
```

For example:

```
%attr(0644, root, root) /etc/yp.conf
```

This example sets the file permissions to 644, the user and the group to `root`. If you don't need to specify a value, use a dash, -, to leave the setting as is for the file. For example:

```
%attr(-, root, -) /etc/yp.conf
```

Note that you can combine directives, one after another. For example:

```
%config %attr(-, root, -) /etc/yp.conf
```

You can also use spaces instead of commas as delimiters. For example:

```
%attr(0700 root root) %dir /var/tux
```

In addition to using `%attr` to set the attributes for a file, you should use the `%defattr` directive to set the default attributes for all files in the package. For example:

```
%files
%defattr(-,root,root)
/usr/X11R6/bin/xtoolwait
/usr/X11R6/man/man1/xtoolwait.*
```

Just about every spec file uses the `%defattr` directive as this directive eliminates a lot of work you need to do to set file attributes individually. In addition, using the `%defattr` directive is considered a best practice when creating packages.

You can also mark files for a particular language. For example, from the tcsh shell package:

```
%files
%defattr(-,root,root)
%doc FAQ Fixes NewThings complete.tcsh eight-bit.txt tcsh.html
%{_bindir}/tcsh
%{_bindir}/csh
%{_mandir}/*/*
%lang(de)    %{_datadir}/locale/de/LC_MESSAGES/tcsh*
%lang(el)    %{_datadir}/locale/el/LC_MESSAGES/tcsh*
%lang(en)    %{_datadir}/locale/en/LC_MESSAGES/tcsh*
%lang(es)    %{_datadir}/locale/es/LC_MESSAGES/tcsh*
%lang(et)    %{_datadir}/locale/et/LC_MESSAGES/tcsh*
%lang(fi)    %{_datadir}/locale/fi/LC_MESSAGES/tcsh*
```

```
%lang(fr)    %{_datadir}/locale/fr/LC_MESSAGES/tcsh*
%lang(it)    %{_datadir}/locale/it/LC_MESSAGES/tcsh*
%lang(ja)    %{_datadir}/locale/ja/LC_MESSAGES/tcsh*
%lang(pl)    %{_datadir}/locale/pl/LC_MESSAGES/tcsh*
%lang(ru)    %{_datadir}/locale/ru/LC_MESSAGES/tcsh*
%lang(uk)    %{_datadir}/locale/uk/LC_MESSAGES/tcsh*
```

This example marks certain files as only being of use with particular languages, such as ja for the Japanese text and fr for the French text.

Verifying the %files section

You can use the `%verify` directive to control which tests RPM uses when verifying a package.

See Chapter 5 for more on package verification.

The `%verify` directive names the tests to include or not include. Table 10-4 lists the tests.

TABLE 10-4 PACKAGE VERIFICATION TESTS

Test	Usage
Group	Verifies the group of the file
Maj	Verifies the file's major device number
Md5	Verifies the file's MD5 checksum
Min	Verifies the file's minor device number
Mode	Verifies the file mode, or permissions
Mtime	Verifies the file's last modification time
Owner	Verifies the owner of the file
Size	Verifies the file's size
Symlink	Verifies a symbolic link

With the %verify directive, you can name test, such as shown following:

```
%verify(owner group size) /etc/yp.conf
```

This example limits the tests to owner, group, and size. (The default is to perform all the tests.) You can also use the word *not* to specify that RPM should not run one or more tests. For example:

```
%verify(not owner) /etc/yp.conf
```

This example turns off just the owner test.

Filling the list of files automatically

The -f option to the %files section allows you to read in a list of file names from a file. This file is assumed to look like the contents of the %files section, holding one file name per line. You can also include the various directives for files such as %attr or %doc. For example:

```
%files -f list_of_filenames.txt
```

You can combine this list with filename entries, such as the following:

```
%files -f xconfig_files.txt
%defattr(-,root,root)
/usr/X11R6/bin/xtoolwait
/usr/X11R6/man/man1/xtoolwait.1
```

This example reads in a list of file names from the file named xconfig_files.txt and also includes two additional files.

This list of files works best if you cannot determine the file names in advance. The build may create different files based on various macro values. In addition, you may not know the final paths for the files until build time.

Handling RPM build errors for unpackaged files

Starting with RPM 4.1, rpmbuild will exit if all files in the $RPM_BUILD_ROOT directory are not found in the %files section (or in a file that lists file names used with the -f option). This is officially known as a Fascist build policy and you can turn it off with the following macros.

The %_unpackaged_files_terminate_build macro, if set to 1, tells rpmbuild to exit if it finds files that are in the $RPM_BUILD_ROOT directory but not listed as part of the package. Set this macro to 0 to turn off the Fascist build policy. For example:

```
%define _unpackaged_files_terminate_build    0
```

You can also control the flag that specifies whether missing documentation files cause `rpmbuild` to exit. Set the `%_missing_doc_files_terminate_build` macro to 0 to turn off this feature:

```
%define _missing_doc_files_terminate_build  0
```

See the "Defining Spec File Macros" section later in the chapter for more on using macros.

 You can also store this setting in a macro file so that it applies for all packages you build. See Chapter 21 for more on macro files.

While the Fascist build policy may be an annoyance, it can prove very useful. Chances are your spec file has an error if you have files in the `$RPM_BUILD_ROOT` directory that are not listed in the `%files` section. The Fascist build policy helps catch these errors. In addition, since the error outputs a list of files in the `$RPM_BUILD_ROOT` directory that are not listed in the `%files` section, you can often paste this list into your `%files` section.

Adding Change Log Entries

The change log usually appears at the end of a spec file and is marked with `%changelog`. It holds messages for each significant change. You should add a change log entry for each major change to the application. For example, if you download a new version of the software you are packaging, add a change log entry for the new version:

```
%changelog
* Fri Jun 21 2002 Bob Marley <marley@reggae.com>
- Downloaded version 1.4, applied patches

* Tue May 08 2001 Peter Tosh <tosh@reggae.com> 1.3-1
- updated to 1.3
```

Defining Spec File Macros

The RPM system defines a lot of handy macros so that your spec files can work regardless of where system directories are located. You simply use the macro, such as %_bindir, in place of hard-coded paths. The %_bindir macro, for example, identifies the default directory for binary executables, /usr/bin.

Use these macros wherever possible to avoid hard-coded paths and settings.

Built-in macros

RPM includes a host of built-in macros, including the following useful directories:

```
%_prefix           /usr
%_exec_prefix      %{_prefix}
%_bindir           %{_exec_prefix}/bin
%_sbindir          %{_exec_prefix}/sbin
%_libexecdir       %{_exec_prefix}/libexec
%_datadir          %{_prefix}/share
%_sysconfdir       %{_prefix}/etc
%_sharedstatedir   %{_prefix}/com
%_localstatedir    %{_prefix}/var
%_libdir           %{_exec_prefix}/lib
%_includedir       %{_prefix}/include
%_oldincludedir    /usr/include
%_infodir          %{_prefix}/info
%_mandir           %{_prefix}/man
```

Spec file-specific macros

Most of the pre-defined RPM macros hold directory paths or architecture information. RPM also includes a set of useful macros that you can use to help debug problematic spec files and well as perform common tasks in spec files. Table 10-5 lists these debugging and special spec file macros.

TABLE 10-5 SPECIAL SPEC-FILE MACROS

Macro	Usage
%dump	Prints out macro values
%{echo:*message*}	Prints *message* to stderr
%{error:*message*}	Prints *message* to stderr and returns BADSPEC
%{expand:*expression*}	Like eval, expands *expression*
%{F:*file_exp*}	Expands *file_exp* to a file name
%global *name value*	Defines a global macro

Macro	Usage
`%{P:patch_exp}`	Expands *patch_exp* to a patch file name
`%{S:source_exp}`	Expands *source_exp* to a source file name
`%trace`	Toggles the printing of debugging information
`%{uncompress:filename}`	Tests if file *filename* is compressed. If so, uncompresses and includes in the given context. If not compressed, calls cat to include file in given context.
`%undefine macro`	Undefines the given macro
`%{warn:message}`	Prints *message* to stderr

To see the current list of macros, put a `%dump` at the start of your spec file.

Defining new macros

In addition to the built-in macros, you can define your own to make it easier to manage your packages. Define a new spec file macro with the following syntax:

```
%define macro_name value
```

For example:

```
%define major 2
%define minor 2
%define patchlevel 7
```

You can then use a macro with the `%macro_name` or `%{macro_name}` syntax. For example:

```
Version: %{major}.%{minor}.%{patchlevel}
```

You can also expand the results of running shell commands using a `%(command)` syntax with parenthesis instead of curly braces. For example:

```
%define today %(date)
```

Specifying parameters to macros

Most macros perform simple text substitution. You can also pass parameters to macros, and access those parameters within your macros, similarly to how shell scripts get command-line parameters.

Chapter 15 covers shell scripting with RPM.

With parameters, you can expand the normal definition of a macro to the following:

```
%define macro_name(options) value
```

Any text within the parenthesis is passed to getopt(3), and acts as parameters to the macro. This is performed when the macro is expanded. You can also pass options to the macro using the *%macro_name* syntax (without curly braces). For example:

```
%foo 1 2 3
```

This example passes the parameters 1, 2, and 3 to the macro foo. Inside the macro, you can use a shell script-like syntax to access the parameters through special macros. Table 10-6 lists these macros.

TABLE 10-6 PARAMETER MACROS INSIDE A MACRO EXPANSION

Macro	Holds
%0	The name of the macro
%*	All the parameters to the macro, except for any processed options
%#	The number of parameters
%1	The first parameter
%2	The second parameter
%3	The third parameter, and so on with %4, %5 and beyond
%{-p}	Holds -p if the -p parameter was passed to the macro; otherwise holds nothing

Macro	Holds
%{-p*}	Holds the value passed with the -p parameter, if the -p parameter was passed to the macro; otherwise holds nothing
%{-p:*text*}	Holds *text* if the -p parameter was passed to the macro; otherwise holds nothing

Note that all parameters listed in Table 10-6 hold the remaining parameters after getopt(3) processing. You can use these macros within the definition of your own macros. You can also nest macros, such as the following:

```
%define mypatch() patch %{-p:-p%{-p*}}
```

This macro expands to the patch command if no -p parameter was passed. If you pass a -p parameter, such as -p 1, then the macro expands to -p with the value of the -p parameter:

```
patch -p1
```

 This type of syntax is used heavily with the patch command.

Creating XML Spec Files

RPM spec files are text files containing structured information. It is a natural progression to write RPM spec files using XML. The tool rpmxmlbuild will build an RPM package from an XML-formatted spec file.

For example, Listing 10-1 holds a spec file in XML format.

Listing 10-1: An XML spec file

```
<?xml version="1.0"?>
<spec distribution="RPM Test" vendor="rpm.org"
     name="bash" version="2.05a" release="02test"
     copyright="GPL"
     url="http://www.gnu.org/software/bash/bash.html">
```

Continued

Listing 10-1: An XML spec file *(Continued)*

```
<source name="%{name}-%{version}.tar.bz2"
    size="1434025" md5="c29b50db808003e39558a0f6354f4cad"
    path="%{name}-%{version}">
</source>

<buildrequires>
    <require name="bash" />
    <require name="gcc" />
    <require name="make" />
</buildrequires>

<!-- packages -->
<package group="System/Base" autoreqprov="no">
    <requires>
        <require name="glibc" />
    </requires>
    <summary>The Bash package contains the bash program.</summary>
    <description>%{summary}
Bash is the Bourne-Again SHell, which is a widely used command interpreter
on Unix systems. Bash is a program that reads from standard input, the
keyboard. A user types something and the program will evaluate what he has
typed and do something with it, like running a program.</description>
    <files list="%{name}.files.lst" />
</package>

<package name="bash-doc" group="Documentation/System/Base" autoreqprov="no">
    <requires>
        <require name="%{name}" />
    </requires>
    <summary>Documentation for the bash package.</summary>
    <description>%{summary}</description>
    <pre script="%{name}-doc.pre.sh" />
    <files list="%{name}-doc.files.lst" />
</package>

<!-- scripts to create the package -->
<prep script="%{name}.prep.sh">
    <setup />
    <script>echo &quot;Prep completed&quot;</script>
</prep>
<build script="%{name}.build.sh" />
<install script="%{name}.install.sh" />
<clean script="%{name}.clean.sh" />
```

```
<!-- changelog -->
<changelog>
      <changes date="Mon Aug 26 2002" version="2.05a-02test"
        author="" author-email="">
      <change>Added setup macro to extract files</change>
      <change>Initial version ready for jbj</change>
   </changes>
 </changelog>
</spec>
```

 This is an experimental feature. Future releases of RPM will likely provide more support for XML spec files.

Summary

This chapter covers spec files, the files that define how to build packages. Start your spec file by defining package information, such as the name, version, and release number. You can also add a detailed description to help administrators decide whether to install your packages.

You need to name all of the source and patch files used to build the package. In most cases, the source files are compressed `tar` archives. After naming all the sources and patches, you need to control how the `rpmbuild` command should build your package. This comes in four sections.

The `%prep` section prepares for the build by extracting the source files and applying patches. The `%build` section defines the commands to build the software, normally something as simple as running a configure script and then the `make` command. The `%install` section contains the commands for installing the software. And, the `%clean` section provides commands to clean up after the build.

For these sections, you can use handy RPM macros for common tasks, such as running the `configure` script or the `make install` command. You can also define scripts the `rpm` command should run before and after installing, as well as before and after removing the package.

Spec files contain a listing of all the files that should go into the package, as well as where those files should be placed on the user's hard disk.

You can define RPM macros in your spec files to make commands that can work with different directory structures as well as simplify common commands.

While it may seem that this chapter described a great many options for making spec files, there's more to come. The next chapter covers advanced spec file topics such as triggers, conditional builds, and specifying dependencies.

Chapter 11

Advanced RPM Packaging

IN THIS CHAPTER

- ◆ Defining package dependency information

- ◆ Setting triggers

- ◆ Writing verification scripts

- ◆ Creating subpackages

- ◆ Creating relocatable packages

- ◆ Defining conditional builds

THE PREVIOUS CHAPTER INTRODUCED the RPM spec file, which controls how RPM packages are built and installed. This chapter delves into advanced spec file topics such as using conditional commands and making relocatable packages, starting with how to specify package dependencies.

Defining Package Dependencies

Dependencies are one of the most important parts of the RPM system. The RPM database tracks dependencies between packages to better allow you to manage your system. A *dependency* occurs when one package depends on another. The RPM system ensures that dependencies are honored when upgrading, installing, or removing packages. From that simple concept, RPM supports four types of dependencies:

- ◆ Requirements, where one package requires a capability provided by another

- ◆ Provides, a listing of the capabilities your package provides

- ◆ Conflicts, where one package conflicts with a capability provided by another

- ◆ Obsoletes, where one package obsoletes capabilities provided by another, usually used when a package changes name and the new package obsoletes the old name

Chapter 6 covers more on dependencies. The obsoletes dependencies are usually only used when a package is renamed, such as the apache package becoming the httpd package, starting in Red Hat Linux 8.0. The httpd package obsoletes the apache package.

You can list all of these dependencies in your spec file. The most commonly used dependency information, though, is what a package requires.

Naming dependencies

In your spec files, you can name the dependencies for your package. The basic syntax is:

```
Requires: capability
```

In most cases, the *capability* should be the name of another package. This example sets up a *requires* dependency. This means that the package requires the given capability. Use a similar syntax for the other kinds of dependencies:

```
Provides: capability
Obsoletes: capability
Conflicts: capability
```

You can put more than one capability on the dependency line. For example:

```
Requires: bash perl
```

You can use spaces or commas to separate the capabilities. For example:

```
Requires: bash, perl
```

Specifying the Version of the Dependencies

You can also add version information, for example:

```
Requires: bash >= 2.0
```

This states that the package requires the capability bash (a package) at version 2.0 or higher. The same logic applies to the other types of dependencies. For example:

```
Conflicts: bash >= 2.0
```

This example states that the package conflicts with all versions of bash 2.0 or higher.

Table 11-1 lists the version comparisons you can use.

TABLE 11-1 DEPENDENCY VERSION COMPARISONS

Comparison	Meaning
package < version	A package with a version number less than *version*
package > version	A package with a version number greater than *version*
package >= version	A package with a version number greater than or equal to *version*
package <= version	A package with a version number less than or equal to *version*
package = version	A package with a version number equal to *version*
package	A package at any version number

RPM supports an extended version number syntax for comparisons. The full format follows:

```
Epoch:Version-Release
```

For example:

```
1:5.6.0-17
```

In this case, the epoch is 1, the version 5.6.0, and the release is 17. In most cases, you will need just the version number. The epoch allows for handling hard-to-compare version numbers. The release number is almost never used. This makes sense, in that it ties a dependency to a particular build of the RPM package, rather than a version of the software itself. This type of dependency would only be useful if you drastically changed the way you build a package.

Creating Virtual CAPABILITIES

Dependencies are based on capabilities, most of which are packages. You can create virtual capabilities, which are just names you define. For example, the sendmail package provides a virtual capability named *smtpdaemon*. For example:

```
Provides: smtpdaemon
```

This capability refers to the general SMTP Internet service for sending e-mail messages. There is no file of this name. Instead, it is just a capability, arbitrary text. Other packages require this capability, such as the fetchmail mail retrieval and forwarding application, and mutt, an e-mail client program.

By using a virtual capability, other packages can provide the capability, and most importantly, client applications can require the capability without worrying which package provides the ability to send e-mail messages. For example, the exim and postfix packages, mail transport agents like sendmail, can provide the same capability.

 Of course, you want to ensure that these packages specify that they conflict with each other.

Naming Dependencies on Script Engines and Modules

Scripting languages such as Perl and Tcl allow for add-on modules. Your package may require some of these add-on modules. RPM uses a special syntax with parenthesis to indicate script module dependencies. For example:

```
Requires: perl(Carp) >= 3.2
```

This indicates a requirement for the Carp add-on module for Perl, greater than or equal to version 3.2.

Setting prerequisites

A *prerequisite* is similar to a require dependency, except that a prerequisite must be installed prior to a given package. Specify a prerequisite as follows:

```
PreReq: capability
```

You can include version-number dependencies, such as:

```
PreReq: capability >= version
```

In most usage, a PreReq: acts just like Requires:, in fact, the PreReq: directive exists just to allow for a manual order to dependencies. RPM guarantees that the PreReq: package will be installed prior to the package that names the PreReq: dependency.

Naming build dependencies

Your package, once built, has a set of dependencies. These dependencies are important for anyone installing the package. But there are also dependency issues when trying to build packages. Build dependencies allow you to specify what is necessary to build the package. While you may think this would be the same as what is needed to install a package, this is normally not true. Linux distributions tend to divide up software into runtime and development packages. For example, the python package contains the runtime for executing scripts written in Python. The python-devel package provides the ability to write extensions to the Python language.

RPM allows you to define build-time dependencies in your spec files using the following directives:

```
BuildRequires:
BuildConflicts:
BuildPreReq:
```

These directives act like `Requires:`, `Conflicts:`, and `PreReq:`, respectively, except that the dependencies are needed to build the package, not install it. For example, your package may require a C compiler to build, or may need a special build tool or developer library.

Generating dependencies automatically

Because so many dependencies are related to shared libraries, the RPM system will automatically generate provide dependencies for any file in your packages that is a shared object, or `.so`, file. RPM will also automatically generate require dependencies for all files in the `%files` list that require shared libraries. To do this, RPM uses the `ldd` command, which determines the shared libraries used by an application.

In addition, the find-requires and find-provides scripts in /usr/lib/rpm can determine Perl, Python and Tcl script dependencies and other dependencies, such as Java package dependencies, automatically. The find-requires script determines requires dependencies automatically, and the find-provides script determines provides dependencies.

Chapter 14 covers a common problem of handling circular dependencies using prerequisites, along with how to turn off the automatic generation of dependencies.

Setting Triggers

Triggers provide a way for one package to take action when the installed status of another package changes. A *trigger* is a script you define in your package's spec file that gets run by the RPM system when the status of another named package changes. If your package depends in some way on another package, a trigger can allow your package to deal with changes to the other package.

Triggers are not a replacement for package dependencies. Instead, triggers are useful when you need to change a package's installation based on other packages installed on the system. For example, if your package is a mail client program, your package will need to have a mail transfer agent, or MTA. Linux supports a number of different mail transfer agents, such as sendmail, vmail, exim, qmail, and postfix.

Typically a system will have one mail transfer agent installed. In most cases, a mail client won't care which MTA is installed, as long as one is installed. (In fact, most of these packages should be marked that they conflict with one another, ensuring that a given system can only have one.)

The %triggerin script is run when a given target package is installed or upgraded. The %triggerin script is also run when your package is installed or upgraded, should the target package be already installed. Similarly, the %triggerun script is run if the target package is removed. It is also run if your package is removed and the target package is installed. The %triggerpostun script is run after the target package has been removed. It is not run if your package is removed.

To define one of these scripts, you need to list the name of the target package; for example:

```
%triggerin -- tcsh
script commands...
```

This example sets up a trigger for the tcsh package. If the tcsh package is installed or upgraded, RPM will run the script. If your package is installed or upgraded and the tcsh package is presently installed, RPM will also run the script.

Define the %triggerun script similarly:

```
%triggerun -- tcsh
script commands...
```

You can also use version numbers in the trigger script definition to only run the script in the case of a particular version. For example:

```
%triggerpostun -- vixie-cron < 3.0.1-56
/sbin/chkconfig --del crond
/sbin/chkconfig --add crond
```

This example, from the vixie-cron scheduling package, runs a post-uninstall trigger for the same package, but for older versions. To define trigger scripts for particular versions, use the same syntax as for requires dependencies for naming the version number and comparisons.

Triggers are run through /bin/sh, the most commonly used shell script engine. With the -p option, though, you can specify a different script interpreter. For example, to write a Perl script, define your trigger like the following:

```
%triggerpostun -p /usr/bin/perl -- vixie-cron < 3.0.1-56
system("/sbin/chkconfig --del crond");
system("/sbin/chkconfig --add crond");
```

With subpackages, defined following, you can use a -n option to tie the trigger script to a subpackage. For example:

```
%triggerpostun -n subpackage_name -- vixie-cron < 3.0.1-56
/sbin/chkconfig --del crond
/sbin/chkconfig --add crond
```

Inside your trigger scripts, $1, the first command-line argument, holds the number of instances of your package that will remain after the operation has completed. The second argument, $2, holds the number of instances of the target package that will remain after the operation. Thus, if $2 is 0, the target package will be removed.

The anonftp package, mentioned in Chapter 6, has a lot of triggers. Many of these set up a number of commands to be locally available to the anonftp package. This networking package is also closely tied to the version of the C library, glibc, as shown in Listing 11-1.

Listing 11-1: Anonftp package trigger scripts

```
%triggerin -- glibc
copy() { file="`ls --sort=time $1 |head -n 1`"; ln -f "$file" "$2" 2>/dev/null |
| cp -df "$file" "$2"; }
# Kill off old versions
rm -f /var/ftp/lib/ld-* /var/ftp/lib/libc* /var/ftp/lib/libnsl* /var/ftp/lib/lib
nss_files* &>/dev/null || :
# Copy parts of glibc, needed by various programs in bin.
LIBCVER=`basename $(ls --sort=time /lib/libc-*.so |head -n 1) .so |cut -f2- -d-`
copy /lib/ld-${LIBCVER}.so /var/ftp/lib
copy /lib/libc-${LIBCVER}.so /var/ftp/lib
copy /lib/libnsl-${LIBCVER}.so /var/ftp/lib
copy /lib/libnss_files-${LIBCVER}.so /var/ftp/lib
md5sum /var/ftp/lib/lib*-*.so /var/ftp/lib/libtermcap.so.*.*.* 2>/dev/null >/var
/ftp/lib/libs.md5
```

Continued

Listing 11-1 *(Continued)*

```
chmod 0400 /var/ftp/lib/libs.md5
# Use ldconfig to build symlinks and whatnot.
[ ! -e /var/ftp/etc/ld.so.conf ] && touch /var/ftp/etc/ld.so.conf
/sbin/ldconfig -r /var/ftp


%triggerin -- fileutils
copy() { file="`ls --sort=time $1 |head -n 1`"; ln -f "$file" "$2" 2>/dev/null |
| cp -df "$file" "$2"; }
copy /bin/ls /var/ftp/bin
md5sum `ls /var/ftp/bin/* |grep -v bin.md5` >/var/ftp/bin/bin.md5
chmod 0400 /var/ftp/bin/bin.md5


%triggerin -- cpio
copy() { file="`ls --sort=time $1 |head -n 1`"; ln -f "$file" "$2" 2>/dev/null |
| cp -df "$file" "$2"; }
copy /bin/cpio /var/ftp/bin
md5sum `ls /var/ftp/bin/* |grep -v bin.md5` >/var/ftp/bin/bin.md5
chmod 0400 /var/ftp/bin/bin.md5


%triggerin -- tar
copy() { file="`ls --sort=time $1 |head -n 1`"; ln -f "$file" "$2" 2>/dev/null |
| cp -df "$file" "$2"; }
copy /bin/tar /var/ftp/bin
md5sum `ls /var/ftp/bin/* |grep -v bin.md5` >/var/ftp/bin/bin.md5
chmod 0400 /var/ftp/bin/bin.md5


%triggerin -- gzip
copy() { file="`ls --sort=time $1 |head -n 1`"; ln -f "$file" "$2" 2>/dev/null |
| cp -df "$file" "$2"; }
copy /bin/gzip /var/ftp/bin
ln -sf gzip /var/ftp/bin/zcat
md5sum `ls /var/ftp/bin/* |grep -v bin.md5` >/var/ftp/bin/bin.md5
chmod 0400 /var/ftp/bin/bin.md5


%triggerin -- libtermcap
copy() { file="`ls --sort=time $1 |head -n 1`"; ln -f "$file" "$2" 2>/dev/null |
| cp -df "$file" "$2"; }
rm -f /var/ftp/lib/libtermcap.so.*.*.* &>/dev/null || :
copy '/lib/libtermcap.so.*.*.*' /var/ftp/lib
md5sum /var/ftp/lib/lib*-*.so /var/ftp/lib/libtermcap.so.*.*.* 2>/dev/null >/var
/ftp/lib/libs.md5
chmod 0400 /var/ftp/lib/libs.md5
# Use ldconfig to build symlinks and whatnot.
```

```
[ ! -e /var/ftp/etc/ld.so.conf ] && touch /var/ftp/etc/ld.so.conf
/sbin/ldconfig -r /var/ftp


%triggerin -- ncompress
copy() { file="`ls --sort=time $1 |head -n 1`"; ln -f "$file" "$2" 2>/dev/null |
| cp -df "$file" "$2"; }
copy /usr/bin/compress /var/ftp/bin
md5sum `ls /var/ftp/bin/* |grep -v bin.md5` >/var/ftp/bin/bin.md5
chmod 0400 /var/ftp/bin/bin.md5


%triggerpostun -- anonftp  4.0
if [ "$2" != 1 ] ; then
        # The user has multiple glibc packages installed.  We can't read the
        # user's mind, so don't do anything.
        exit 0
fi
copy() { file="`ls --sort=time $1 |head -n 1`"; ln -f "$file" "$2" 2>/dev/null |
| cp -df "$file" "$2"; }
# Kill off old versions
rm -f /var/ftp/lib/ld-* /var/ftp/lib/libc* /var/ftp/lib/libnsl* /var/ftp/lib/lib
nss_files* &>/dev/null || :
# Copy parts of glibc, needed by various programs in bin.
LIBCVER=`basename /lib/libc-*.so .so | cut -f2- -d-`
copy /lib/ld-${LIBCVER}.so /var/ftp/lib
copy /lib/libc-${LIBCVER}.so /var/ftp/lib
copy /lib/libnsl-${LIBCVER}.so /var/ftp/lib
copy /lib/libnss_files-${LIBCVER}.so /var/ftp/lib
copy /bin/ls /var/ftp/bin
copy /bin/cpio /var/ftp/bin
copy /bin/tar /var/ftp/bin
copy /bin/gzip /var/ftp/bin
ln -sf gzip /var/ftp/bin/zcat
copy /usr/bin/compress /var/ftp/bin
rm -f /var/ftp/lib/libtermcap.so.*.*.* &>/dev/null || :
copy '/lib/libtermcap.so.*.*.*' /var/ftp/lib
# Use ldconfig to build symlinks and whatnot.
[ ! -e /var/ftp/etc/ld.so.conf ] && touch /var/ftp/etc/ld.so.conf
/sbin/ldconfig -r /var/ftp
# Generate md5sums for verifyscript
md5sum /var/ftp/lib/lib*-*.so /var/ftp/lib/libtermcap.so.*.*.* 2>/dev/null >/var
/ftp/lib/libs.md5
chmod 0400 /var/ftp/lib/libs.md5
md5sum `ls /var/ftp/bin/* |grep -v bin.md5` >/var/ftp/bin/bin.md5
chmod 0400 /var/ftp/bin/bin.md5
```

Writing Verification Scripts

RPM automatically handles package verification, checking to see that the proper files are installed, and testing the files themselves for the proper size and other attributes. You may need to do more in your package, though, to ensure everything is properly set up. With RPM, you can:

- Control the tests used to verify each file, as described in Chapter 10

- Create a verify script that performs other tests

If you need to perform some other test to verify your package, such as check that a configuration file has a particular setting (and that the setting is valid), you can fill in the %verifyscript in the spec file. The %verifyscript acts much like the %pre or %post scripts, except that the %verifyscript gets executed during package verification. Fill in a %verifyscript as follows:

```
%verifyscript
your script commands ...
```

Common %verifyscript actions are to check for an entry in a system configuration file, such as an init-time startup script or /etc/shells (which lists the available shells). These are files owned by other packages that may need to be properly modified for a package to be properly installed. If your package has a similar circumstance, write a %verifyscript. In your script, send all error output to stderr.

 See Chapter 5 for more on package verification.

Creating Subpackages

A spec file may define more than one package. This type of additional package is called a *subpackage*. Subpackages exist to handle cases where you don't want to associate one spec file with one package. Instead, you can define multiple packages within the spec file, as needed. For example, you may want to build the runtime and developer packages together, or the client and server portions of an application using subpackages. Splitting large documentation sets into separate subpackages is also common.

With subpackages, you get:

- One spec file
- One source RPM
- One set of build commands
- Multiple binary RPMs, one per package or subpackage

In most cases, subpackages are created as a means to partition the files produced by a package into separate packages. For example, you will often see development libraries and header files split into a separate package from the main application package. Sometimes documentation is split out into a separate package, or client and server applications are divided into separate packages. In the end, though, this usually results in shifting files into subpackages and nothing more.

To define a subpackage within a spec file, you start with the %package directive. For example:

```
%package sub_package_name
```

By default, the name of the subpackage will be the name of the package, a dash, and the subpackage name provided with the %package directive. For example:

```
%package server
```

This example names a subpackage *server*, which is a real subpackage inside the *telnet* package. In this case, the name for the server subpackage will be *telnet-server*, that is, the naming format is *package-subpackage*.

If you don't want this naming format, you can use the -n option to the %package directive to define an entirely new name, using the following syntax:

```
%package -n new_sub_package_name
```

For example:

```
%package -n my-telnet-server
```

With the -n option, you specify the full name for the subpackage. The RPM system will not prefix the name with the enclosing package name.

Providing information for subpackages

When you define a subpackage, you need to provide as many of the package information directives as you need, including at the least Summary:, Group:, and %description directives. Anything not specified will use the parent package's value, such as the version. Place these directives after the `%package` directive. For example:

```
%package server
Requires: xinetd
Group: System Environment/Daemons
Summary: The server program for the telnet remote login protocol.
```

The `%description` directive for subpackages requires the name of the subpackage using the following syntax:

```
%description subpackage
```

For example:

```
%description server
Telnet is a popular protocol for logging into remote systems
over the Internet. The telnet-server package includes a telnet
daemon that supports remote logins into the host machine. The
telnet daemon is enabled by default. You may disable the telnet
daemon by editing /etc/xinetd.d/telnet.
```

If you used the `-n` option with the `%package` directive, you need to repeat the `-n` option with the `%description` directive. For example:

```
%description -n my-telnet-server
Telnet is a popular protocol for logging into remote systems
over the Internet. The telnet-server package includes a telnet
daemon that supports remote logins into the host machine. The
telnet daemon is enabled by default. You may disable the telnet
daemon by editing /etc/xinetd.d/telnet.
```

The same concept works for the `%files` section. You need a separate `%files` section for each subpackage. For example:

```
%files server
%defattr(-,root,root)
%{_sbindir}/in.telnetd
%{_mandir}/man5/issue.net.5*
%{_mandir}/man8/in.telnetd.8*
%{_mandir}/man8/telnetd.8*
```

Again, if you used the `-n` option with the `%package` directive, you need to repeat the `-n` option with the `%files` section. For example:

```
%files -n my-telnet-server
%defattr(-,root,root)
%{_sbindir}/in.telnetd
%{_mandir}/man5/issue.net.5*
%{_mandir}/man8/in.telnetd.8*
%{_mandir}/man8/telnetd.8*
```

Defining scripts for subpackages

Much as you define separate %files and %description sections for subpackages, you can also define install and uninstall scripts for subpackages. The syntax is similar to that for the %files and %description sections:

```
%pre subpackage
```

For example, Listing 11-2 shows the scripts from the VNC package.

Listing 11-2: VNC package install and uninstall scripts

```
%post server
if [ "$1" = 1 ]; then
  /sbin/chkconfig --add vncserver
fi

%preun server
if [ "$1" = 0 ]; then
  /sbin/service vncserver stop >/dev/null 2>&1
  /sbin/chkconfig --del vncserver
fi

%postun server
if [ "$1" -ge "1" ]; then
  /sbin/service vncserver condrestart >/dev/null 2>&1
fi
```

Building subpackages

The build sections in the spec file serve double duty. These sections are used for building the main package as well as subpackages. This is one reason why there are so many options on the %setup macro.

The %setup macro allows for selectively unpacking the sources, rather than the default option of unpacking all the sources. For example, the following %setup macro definition gives rpmbuild specific instructions for unpacking one source file:

```
%setup -D- T -a 1
```

In this example, the -D option disables the automatic deletion of the directory where the sources will be unpacked. This means any previous contents of this directory, perhaps for other subpackages, will be left alone. The -T option disables the automatic unpacking of the source files, and the -a 1 option specifies to only unpack the first source file. You may need to use options like these when working with subpackages, though, in most cases, subpackages are just means to partition the package files into separate packages. In cases like this, you will likely not need any of these special %setup options.

Chapter 10 covers the %setup macro and lists the available options.

Creating Relocatable Packages

A *relocatable* package allows a user to specify where to install the package. For example, if you build a package for Red Hat Linux, the normal directory for binary executable programs is /usr/bin. Other versions of Linux, though, may place executable programs into /opt/bin, for example. If your package forces the use of /usr/bin, then your package won't work on these other systems.

Chapter 19 covers using RPM on other versions of Linux.

With a relocatable package, though, you allow the user to redefine the top-level directories for your package, such as changing from /usr/bin to /opt/bin in the previous example. Making relocatable packages is generally considered a good thing, as you make the user's life easier.

To set up a relocatable package, you need to:

◆ Set up the prefix directives for the top-level directories

◆ Define the files under the prefix directories

Setting up the prefixes

The Prefix: directive names a top-level directory as a prefix you can relocate to another directory. For example:

```
Prefix: /usr
```

This states that all files under /usr can be relocated to other directories by simply mapping /usr to some other directory, such as /opt, on the rpm command line when installing or upgrading the package.

You can define more than one Prefix: directive to list more than one top-level directory.

Define the files section

When you use a Prefix: directive in your spec file, all files in the %files section must be under the directory named with the Prefix: directive. For example, from the jikes compiler package:

```
Prefix: /usr

...

%files
%defattr(-,root,root)
/usr/bin/jikes
%doc /usr/doc/jikes-%{version}/license.htm
%doc /usr/man/man1/jikes.1*
```

In this example, all the files are under the /usr directory. All files in the %files section must be located under one of the Prefix: directories. If you have more than one top-level directory, such as /usr and /etc, define more than one Prefix: directive. For example:

```
Prefix: /usr
Prefix: /etc
```

Chapter 4 covers how to install or upgrade packages into different directories using the --relocate and --prefix options.

Problems creating relocatable packages

Not all packages work well as relocatable packages. Some packages have files that simply must go into a certain location and are therefore not relocatable. Some packages have programs that are hard-coded to look for files in a particular location and therefore cannot be relocated elsewhere. Other packages have symbolic links that also may not be relocatable. Furthermore, your package may provide software that is referenced by other packages, in the known directories. Relocating such a package will disable other software packages, packages you may not even know about.

If your packages face any of these problems, chances are that making the package relocatable is not a good idea. In addition, if you use the %doc directive with local file names, remember that RPM will make a package-specific documentation directory, normally under /usr/doc. For example:

```
%doc README NEWS
```

This may defeat your attempts to create a relocatable package, unless you have a Prefix: directive with /usr, because the normal location is under /usr/doc, and all files in the %files section must start with one of the directories named with Prefix: directives.

Defining Conditional Builds

With the ability to define macros inside spec files, and also to use macros defined elsewhere, you gain a lot of control over how your package gets built. You can go further, though, and use special directives to perform only certain commands based on certain conditions. This adds a powerful capability to your spec files, and also makes it much easier to do things like build for multiple versions of Linux or other operating systems, as well as handle various backwards-compatibility issues.

To define conditional build commands, you need to create conditional constructs in your package's spec file. In addition, you need to define macros that the conditional constructs use to determine whether or not to execute a set of spec file directives.

 See Chapter 21 for more on macro file locations, and Chapters 19 and 20 for more on using RPM on other versions of Linux and other operating systems, respectively.

RPM supports a number of ways to make parts of your spec file enabled or disabled based on certain conditions. These include conditional macros, conditional blocks, and special directives based on the system architecture.

Defining conditional macros

You can use a special syntax to test for the existence of macros. For example:

```
%{?macro_to_test: expression}
```

This syntax tells RPM to expand the *expression* if the macro `macro_to_test` exists. If the macro `macro_to_test` does not exist, nothing will be output. You can also reverse this test. A leading exclamation point, !, tests for the non-existence of a macro:

```
%{!?macro_to_test: expression}
```

In this example, if the `macro_to_test` macro does not exist, RPM will expand the *expression*.

If you want, you can omit the expression and just test for the existence of the macro. If it exists, RPM will use the value of the macro. If the macro does not exist, RPM will use nothing. For example:

```
%build
./configure %{?_with_ldap}
make
```

In this case, if the `_with_ldap` macro exists, the value of that macro will get passed on the command line to the `configure` script. If the `_with_ldap` macro does not exist, nothing extra will be passed on the command line to the `configure` script. This is very important when creating commands to build or install packages.

Many of the macros you will test this way are set up with the `--with` command-line parameter. See Chapter 19 for details.

Using conditional blocks

The `%if` macro enables all the directives up to the `%endif` directive, if the condition is true. This is much like scripting languages. For example:

```
%if %{old_5x}
%define b5x 1
%undefine b6x
%endif
```

In this case, if the %old_5x macro has a value, the test will be true and all the directives inside the block will get executed.

A %else allows you to specify what to do if the test is not successful. For example:

```
%if %{old_5x}
%define b5x 1
%undefine b6x
%else
%define b6x 1
%undefine b5x
%endif
```

In this case, if the %old_5x macro has a value, then all the directives up to the %else will get executed. Otherwise, if the %old_5x macro has no value, the directives from the %else to the %endif will get executed.

Again, use an exclamation point to negate the test. For example:

```
%if ! %{old_5x}
%define b5x 1
%undefine b6x
%endif
```

You can use a && for an AND test. For example:

```
%if %{old_5x} && %{old_6x}
%{error: You cannot build for .5x and .6x at the same time}
%quit
%endif
```

Using architecture-based conditionals

In addition to the general-purpose %if conditional directive, you can use special directives that test for processor architecture and operating system.

The %ifarch directive enables all the directives up to the %endif directive, if the processor architecture matches the values you pass to the %ifarch directive. For example:

```
%ifarch sparc
%define b5x 1
%undefine b6x
%endif
```

This block will only get executed if the processor architecture is SPARC.

Chapter 21 covers RPM architecture and operating system names.

You can pass more than one architecture name, separated by commas or spaces. For example:

```
%ifarch sparc alpha
%define b5x 1
%undefine b6x
%endif
```

This example tests if the processor architecture is SPARC or Alpha.

As with the %if directive, you can also use an %else, to cover all cases where the test is not true. For example:

```
%ifarch sparc alpha
%define b5x 1
%undefine b6x
%else
%define b6x 1
%undefine b5x
%endif
```

This example tests if the processor architecture is SPARC or Alpha. If so, the directives from the %ifarch to the %else are executed. If not, the directives from the %else to the %endif are executed.

The %ifnarch directive reverses the %ifarch test. That is, %ifnarch tests if the architecture is not one of the values listed. The following example tests if the processor architecture is not an i386 or an Alpha.

```
%ifnarch i386 alpha
%define b5x 1
%undefine b6x
%endif
```

The %ifos directive tests for the operating system. For example:

```
%ifos linux
%define b5x 1
%undefine b6x
%endif
```

This example tests if the operating system is Linux. You can reverse the test with the %ifnos directive. For example:

```
%ifnos irix
%define b5x 1
%undefine b6x
%endif
```

This example tests if the operating system is not Irix.

Summary

This chapter covers advanced topics in creating packages. Dependencies are very important. You need to specify which packages or capabilities your package requires, so the RPM system can ensure that all requirements are met before allowing users to install the package. If you do not specify the dependencies properly, you are defeating the integrity of the RPM system.

In addition to specifying what your package requires, it is also important to specify other dependency information. For example, if your package conflicts with another package, you need to very clearly state this. E-mail and Web server packages often conflict with other servers of the same type.

You can specify both package dependencies as well as build dependencies. For example, you may need certain developer libraries to build your package, but not to install it. These are build dependencies.

To help manage dependencies between packages and system configuration issues, you can set up trigger scripts. A trigger is a script in your package that gets executed when another package is installed or removed. If your package, for example, is an e-mail client program, it may need to execute a script should the e-mail server package change. This is a great usage for triggers.

If your package has a complicated installation, the normal RPM verification won't be sufficient. To help the RPM system ensure the integrity of all the packages, you can write a verify script in your spec file to perform any extra commands necessary to verify your package has been properly installed.

Relocatable packages allow users to install your packages in different locations than originally planned. This is very useful when working with more than one version of Linux, or with other operating systems. For example, most Linux commands are stored in /usr/bin, at least for Red Hat Linux. Other Linux distributions, or other operating systems may specify that programs added to the original set should be stored in /opt/bin and not /usr/bin, for example. Making your package relocatable helps users in these situations.

Conditional directives in your spec file allow you to control the build on different processor architectures and operating systems. The %if directive tests if a value is set. If so, then all the directives up to the %endif directive are executed. If you need to execute a different set of directives, use %else. In this case, if the %if test is true, RPM executes the directives up to the %else. If the test is not true, RPM executes the directives up to the %endif.

Once you have your spec file defined, the next step is to start building packages. The next chapter covers options for the rpmbuild command and how you can use rpmbuild to make your packages.

Chapter 12

Controlling the Build with rpmbuild

IN THIS CHAPTER

- ◆ Building with the `rpmbuild` command
- ◆ Building RPMs without an external spec file
- ◆ Working with source RPMs
- ◆ Optimizing builds
- ◆ Signing built RPMs

THE PRECEDING CHAPTERS IN THIS Part cover details on how to put together RPMs. This chapter rounds out the discussion by delving into more details on the `rpmbuild` command.

You can customize how `rpmbuild` creates RPMs, and you can use RPM commands to test and debug your package.

Building RPMs with the rpmbuild Command

The `rpmbuild` command provides a workhorse command for building RPMs in all sorts of ways. The basic syntax, as shown in Chapter 9, is:

```
rpmbuild -bBuildStage spec_file
```

The *BuildStage* is a letter, such as *c*, to prepare and compile the application, executing through the `%build` section, or *i*, to execute through the `%install` section. This allows you a good deal of flexibility for building the entire RPM or stopping at some point prior to a full build.

There's more to the `rpmbuild` command, though. Quite a few additional options allow you to further customize the build.

As mentioned in Chapter 9, previous versions of the RPM system used the rpm command with a -b, for build, option. This option is no longer supported. Use the rpmbuild command to build RPMs.

Customizing the build

You can customize the rpmbuild command with the options listed in Table 12-1.

TABLE 12-1 EXTRA BUILD OPTIONS FOR THE RPMBUILD COMMAND

Option	Usage
--buildroot *directory*	Override the default root directory for building with directory, generally not very useful since most packages already name a buildroot
--clean	Remove the build tree after building
--nobuild	Just test the spec file and do not run the build
--rmsource	Remove the sources after the build
--rmspec	Remove the spec file after the build
--short-circuit	With the -bc or -bi options, jump directly to the given stage and resume the build from that stage
--sign	Sign the package with a GPG signature
--target *platform*	Build for the given platform. May not work if you don't have the other platform build commands, such as cross compilers, set up. Can work for Intel platforms with i386, i686, and so on.

Testing the build

One of the most useful options is --nobuild, which tells the rpmbuild command to not build anything. This may seem silly, but the --nobuild option is very useful for testing whether your RPMs can be built. With the --nobuild option, the rpmbuild command parses the spec file and checks for errors, but does not run any of the build stages.

The --buildroot allows you to specify a different top-level directory for building, overriding the BuildRoot tag in the spec file. This means you can build in a separate location, which is helpful in case there are mistakes. Using a separate directory means the build won't get mixed with anything else in the build root directory.

Debugging the build

The --short-circuit option tells the rpmbuild command to restart at a particular location in the build. Rather than working its way through all the steps up to the build stage you ask for, the --short-circuit option allows the rpmbuild command to restart just at the step you ask for.

This works with the -bc and -bi options only, as well as the -tc and -ti options covered later in this chapter.

For example, if you run the rpmbuild -bc command to stop after the %build section, you can use the --short-circuit option to restart the build at the %build section. If you found a problem in the %build section and corrected it, you can quickly get going again by restarting the build at the %build section rather than extracting all the sources yet again.

This option is most useful when you are compiling a package, hit an error, and fix that error. Without the --short-circuit option, you'll likely end up spending a lot of time recompiling the code you have already compiled.

During normal development of an RPM package, you will likely execute each build section, one at a time, stop, fix any errors and restart where you left off. You'll go through this cycle a number of times before the RPM finally builds right.

Never distribute an RPM made with the --short-circuit option. Instead, once you have everything working, start from scratch and rebuild the RPM. This is to avoid any problems with a partially-created RPM.

Cleaning up

The --clean option tells the rpmbuild command to remove the build tree when complete. This helps ensure that the next time you run the rpmbuild command, you are starting from a known situation.

For example:

```
$ rpmbuild --clean /usr/src/redhat/SPECS/jikes.spec
Executing(--clean): /bin/sh -e /var/tmp/rpm-tmp.98247
+ umask 022
+ cd /usr/src/redhat/BUILD
+ rm -rf jikes-1.17
+ exit 0
```

You can use the `--clean` option alone, as shown previously, or in concert with another option such as `-bi` to build and install a binary RPM. In the latter case, the `rpmbuild` command will clean the built files after the rest of the command finishes.

Similarly, the `--rmsource` option tells the `rpmbuild` command to remove the sources after completing the command. You can call this option with another option, such as `-bi` for building and installing a binary RPM (and then removing the sources), or alone on the command line to remove the sources only.

For example:

```
rpmbuild --rmsource jikes.spec
```

 The abbreviation *rm* is short for remove. It comes from the Linux `rm` command, used for removing files.

The `--rmspec` option tells the `rpmbuild` command to remove the spec file when done with the command. As with the `--rmsource` option, you can use the `--rmspec` option in conjunction with another `rpmbuild` option or on its own to just remove the spec file.

For example:

```
rpmbuild --rmspec jikes.spec
```

 The file you are removing with this command is the spec file you are passing to the command. Be careful, because you cannot undo this operation and you have now lost your spec file, except inside your source package.

Building for other platforms

The `--target` option tells the `rpmbuild` command to build a package for another platform. You need to pass the name of the platform. For example:

```
rpmbuild -bi --target i486-redhat-linux
```

The basic format is:

```
cpu-vendor-os
```

For example, i686-redhat-linux specifies a 686 CPU with Red Hat Linux. Other CPUs include ppc for PowerPC and sparc for Sun SPARC.

The --target option sets the target architecture at build time. Chapter 4 covers how you can use the --ignoreos and --ignorearch options when installing RPMs to ignore the operating system and architecture that is flagged within the RPM. Of course, this works only if you are installing on a compatible architecture.

On the surface level, the --target option overrides some of the macros in the spec file, %_target, %_target_arch, and %_target_os. This flags the RPM for the new target platform.

Under the covers, setting the architecture macros is not enough. You really cannot create a PowerPC executable, for example, on an Intel-architecture machine, unless you have a PowerPC cross compiler, a compiler that can make PowerPC executables.

Set the target with care. Make sure you can really build executable programs for that architecture.

If you try to compile a system that uses the GNU configure system to configure the build, your target will likely be ignored. For example, if you try to build the aforementioned jikes package with a target of ppc-ibm-aix, to specify IBM's Unix, called AIX, on a PowerPC architecture, you will see the target ignored as the configure system detects that it's running on Linux on an i686 architecture.

For example:

```
$ rpmbuild -bc --target ppc-ibm-aix /usr/src/redhat/SPECS/jikes.spec
Building target platforms: ppc-ibm-aix
Building for target ppc-ibm-aix
Executing(%prep): /bin/sh -e /var/tmp/rpm-tmp.94955
+ umask 022
+ cd /usr/src/redhat/BUILD
+ LANG=C
+ export LANG
+ cd /usr/src/redhat/BUILD
+ rm -rf jikes-1.17
+ /usr/bin/gzip -dc /usr/src/redhat/SOURCES/jikes-1.17.tar.gz
+ tar -xf -
+ STATUS=0
+ '[' 0 -ne 0 ']'
+ cd jikes-1.17
```

```
++ /usr/bin/id -u
+ '[' 500 = 0 ']'
++ /usr/bin/id -u
+ '[' 500 = 0 ']'
+ /bin/chmod -Rf a+rX,g-w,o-w .
+ exit 0
Executing(%build): /bin/sh -e /var/tmp/rpm-tmp.15710
+ umask 022
+ cd /usr/src/redhat/BUILD
+ cd jikes-1.17
+ LANG=C
+ export LANG
+ ./configure CXXFLAGS=-O3 --prefix=/tmp/jikesrpm/usr
checking for a BSD-compatible install... /usr/bin/install -c
checking whether build environment is sane... yes
checking for gawk... gawk
checking whether make sets ${MAKE}... yes
checking whether to enable maintainer-specific portions of
Makefiles... no
checking build system type... i686-pc-linux-gnu
checking host system type... i686-pc-linux-gnu
checking for g++... g++
```

As you can see, the command starts out with the target as the platform, but the configure script soon overrides that, as shown at the end of the truncated output.

Building RPMs without an External Spec File

Most of the options for the rpmbuild command require an RPM spec file. This file defines all the necessary parameters for the RPM to build. If you've downloaded an application, though, you may not have all the information needed to build a spec file. In addition, writing the spec file is the most time-consuming task when building RPMs. If you are lucky, the provider of a given application may have already created a spec file and included the spec file within the source distribution.

Options for working with tar archives

A special set of options aims toward building RPMs with spec files stored in tar archives, also called tarballs. *Tarballs* are files combined with the tar (tape archiver) utility and then optionally compressed, usually with the gzip command. Because this format is used so often for Unix and Linux software, you can use a set of -t options to the rpmbuild command that mimic the -b options.

The basic syntax follows:

```
rpmbuild -tBuildStage compressed_tar_archive
```

The -t option is a lot like the -b option covered in Chapter 9, except -t tells rpm-build to build an RPM from a compressed tar archive instead of from an RPM spec file. You still need a spec file. These commands just assume that the spec file is located within the tar archive. The extra *BuildStage* option is a special code that tells the rpmbuild command how far to go when building. Table 12-2 lists these options:

TABLE 12-2 OPTIONS FOR BUILDING WITH RPMBUILD WITH TAR ARCHIVES

Option	Usage
-ta	Build all, both a binary and source RPM
-tb	Build a binary RPM
-tc	Stop after the %build section
-tp	Stop after the %prep section
-ti	Stop after the %install section
-tl	Check the listing of files for the RPM
-ts	Build a source RPM only

These command-line options work with a tar archive or a compressed tar archive.

The expected archive structure

To build a package this way, the tar archive must have enough of an expected structure, such as a configure script and a Makefile with the expected make targets. The most crucial element is that the tar archive must have the package spec file. That's because the rpmbuild command doesn't know how to build every program in the universe. Instead, rpmbuild expects to find a spec file to tell it what to do. If you see an error like the following, then your tar archive likely is missing the spec file:

```
$ rpmbuild -tc vixie-cron*tar.gz
error: Name field must be present in package: (main package)
error: Version field must be present in package: (main package)
```

```
error: Release field must be present in package: (main package)
error: Summary field must be present in package: (main package)
error: Group field must be present in package: (main package)
error: License field must be present in package: (main package)
```

These errors show expected tags from the missing spec file.

Working with Source RPMs

Most of your work with the rpmbuild command will likely be to create binary RPMs after you have the sources for an application and a spec file. You can also get a lot of mileage out of source RPMs, whether you build them or download them.

Chapter 10 covers the spec file in depth.

Because they are RPMs themselves, source RPMs act like other RPMs. For example, you can use the rpm -i command to install a source RPM. This installs the sources provided by the source RPM, not the actual application. Normally, when you install a source RPM on a Red Hat Linux system, the package gets installed into /usr/src/redhat.

This directory is obviously specific to Red Hat Linux. On other Linux distributions, you'll likely see directories such as /usr/src/OpenLinux for SCO (formerly Caldera) OpenLinux.

Installing a source RPM is not exactly the same as installing a binary RPM. For example, the rpm command does not update the RPM database when you install a source RPM. In addition, listing the files in a source RPM only shows the relative paths, not the full paths.

Once installation is complete, you can use the rpmbuild command to create a binary RPM from the sources in the source RPM, using the -b command-line options introduced in Chapter 9. The next sections show more shortcuts with source RPMs.

Rebuilding binary RPMS from source RPMs

As a shortcut, you do not have to install a source RPM to create a binary RPM. Instead, you can build the binary RPM directory using the --rebuild option.

The --rebuild option tells the rpmbuild command to rebuild a binary RPM from a source RPM file. The basic syntax is:

```
rpmbuild --rebuild package.src.rpm
```

This command builds a binary RPM out of a source RPM with a minimum of fuss. For example:

```
$ rpmbuild --rebuild unix2dos-2.2-17.src.rpm

Installing unix2dos-2.2-17.src.rpm
Executing(%prep): /bin/sh -e /var/tmp/rpm-tmp.15828
+ umask 022
+ cd /usr/src/redhat/BUILD
+ LANG=C
+ export LANG
+ cd /usr/src/redhat/BUILD
+ rm -rf unix2dos-2.2
+ /bin/mkdir -p unix2dos-2.2
+ cd unix2dos-2.2
+ /usr/bin/gzip -dc /usr/src/redhat/S  OURCES/unix2dos-2.2.src.tar.gz
+ tar -xf -
+ STATUS=0
+ '[' 0 -ne 0 ']'
++ /usr/bin/id -u
+ '[' 500 = 0 ']'
++ /usr/bin/id -u
+ '[' 500 = 0 ']'
+ /bin/chmod -Rf a+rX,g-w,o-w .
+ echo 'Patch #0 (unix2dos-mkstemp.patch):'
Patch #0 (unix2dos-mkstemp.patch):
+ patch -p1 -b --suffix .sec -s
+ echo 'Patch #1 (unix2dos-2.2-segfault.patch):'
Patch #1 (unix2dos-2.2-segfault.patch):
+ patch -p1 -b --suffix .segf -s
+ echo 'Patch #2 (unix2dos-2.2-manpage.patch):'
Patch #2 (unix2dos-2.2-manpage.patch):
```

```
+ patch -p1 -b --suffix .man -s
+ perl -pi -e 's,^#endif.*,#endif,g;s,^#else.*,#else,g' unix2dos.c unix2dos.h
+ exit 0
Executing(%build): /bin/sh -e /var/tmp/rpm-tmp.60650
+ umask 022
+ cd /usr/src/redhat/BUILD
+ cd unix2dos-2.2
+ LANG=C
+ export LANG
+ gcc -O2 -march=i386 -mcpu=i686 -ounix2dos unix2dos.c
+ exit 0
Executing(%install): /bin/sh -e /var/tmp/rpm-tmp.35128
+ umask 022
+ cd /usr/src/redhat/BUILD
+ cd unix2dos-2.2
+ LANG=C
+ export LANG
+ rm -rf /var/tmp/unix2dos-root
+ mkdir -p /var/tmp/unix2dos-root/usr/bin /var/tmp/unix2dos-
root/usr/share/man/man1
+ install -m755 unix2dos /var/tmp/unix2dos-root/usr/bin
+ install -m444 unix2dos.1 /var/tmp/unix2dos-root/usr/share/man/man1
+ /usr/lib/rpm/redhat/brp-compress
+ /usr/lib/rpm/redhat/brp-strip
+ /usr/lib/rpm/redhat/brp-strip-comment-note
Processing files: unix2dos-2.2-17
Executing(%doc): /bin/sh -e /var/tmp/rpm-tmp.12033
+ umask 022
+ cd /usr/src/redhat/BUILD
+ cd unix2dos-2.2
+ DOCDIR=/var/tmp/unix2dos-root/usr/share/doc/unix2dos-2.2
+ export DOCDIR
+ rm -rf /var/tmp/unix2dos-root/usr/share/doc/unix2dos-2.2
+ /bin/mkdir -p /var/tmp/unix2dos-root/usr/share/doc/unix2dos-2.2
+ cp -pr COPYRIGHT /var/tmp/unix2dos-root/usr/share/doc/unix2dos-2.2
+ exit 0
Finding  Provides: /usr/lib/rpm/find-provides
Finding  Requires: /usr/lib/rpm/find-requires
PreReq: rpmlib(PayloadFilesHavePrefix) <= 4.0-1 rpmlib(CompressedFileNames)
<= 3.0.4-1
Requires(rpmlib): rpmlib(PayloadFilesHavePrefix) <= 4.0-1
rpmlib(CompressedFileNames) <= 3.0.4-1
Requires: libc.so.6 libc.so.6(GLIBC_2.0) libc.so.6(GLIBC_2.1)
Checking for unpackaged file(s): /usr/lib/rpm/check-files /var/tmp/unix2dos-root
Wrote: /usr/src/redhat/RPMS/i386/unix2dos-2.2-17.i386.rpm
```

```
Executing(%clean): /bin/sh -e /var/tmp/rpm-tmp.47653
+ umask 022
+ cd /usr/src/redhat/BUILD
+ cd unix2dos-2.2
+ rm -rf /var/tmp/unix2dos-root
+ exit 0
Executing(--clean): /bin/sh -e /var/tmp/rpm-tmp.47653
+ umask 022
+ cd /usr/src/redhat/BUILD
+ rm -rf unix2dos-2.2
+ exit 0
```

With the --rebuild option, the rpmbuild command installs the source RPM for you and then performs the preparation, compile, and installation stages of building a binary RPM. Unless there are errors, you should have a new binary RPM file.

When complete, the rpmbuild --rebuild command cleans out the built files in the build directory, as if the --clean option were used. The rpmbuild --rebuild command also removes the installed sources and spec file upon completion.

Recompiling binaries from source RPMs

If you just want to recompile the files in a source RPM, you can use the --recompile option. The --recompile option tells the rpmbuild command to recompile the binary application from a source RPM.

For example:

```
rpmbuild --recompile package.src.rpm
```

This is the same as installing the source RPM and then running rpmbuild -bc --clean with the package spec file.

 There is no difference between --recompile and --rebuild in RPM 4.1. RPM 4.2 fixes this problem.

SRPMs? Finding source RPMs

Often, source RPMs are abbreviated as SRPMs. In fact, if you see a directory named SRPM or SRPMS, chances are the directory holds source RPMs. (Red Hat uses this convention for its Linux distributions.)

The SRPMS directories on Red Hat CD-ROMs or on the Red Hat FTP Internet site, ftp.redhat.com, indicate directories that hold source RPMs.

Signing Built RPMs

Signing RPMs adds an extra level of trustworthiness to your RPMs. A digital signature helps establish that the package comes from you, really you, and not from someone masquerading as you. Unfortunately, the RPM system requires a bit of set up work before you can sign RPMs.

Checking that the GPG software is installed

To sign packages, you need to ensure that you have the gpg command installed and configured. To check that this command is installed, use a command like the following:

```
$ rpm -qf `which gpg`
gnupg-1.0.7-6
```

This shows that the command is available.

Configuring a signature

To configure a signature, you first need to create a new key with the gpg command, using the --gen-key option, as shown following:

```
$ gpg --gen-key
gpg (GnuPG) 1.0.7; Copyright (C) 2002 Free Software Foundation, Inc.
This program comes with ABSOLUTELY NO WARRANTY.
This is free software, and you are welcome to redistribute it
under certain conditions. See the file COPYING for details.

gpg: Warning: using insecure memory!
gpg: please see http://www.gnupg.org/faq.html for more information
gpg: keyring `/home2/ericfj/.gnupg/secring.gpg' created
gpg: keyring `/home2/ericfj/.gnupg/pubring.gpg' created
Please select what kind of key you want:
    (1) DSA and ElGamal (default)
    (2) DSA (sign only)
    (4) ElGamal (sign and encrypt)
    (5) RSA (sign only)
Your selection? 1
DSA keypair will have 1024 bits.
About to generate a new ELG-E keypair.
              minimum keysize is  768 bits
              default keysize is 1024 bits
    highest suggested keysize is 2048 bits
What keysize do you want? (1024)

Requested keysize is 1024 bits
Please specify how long the key should be valid.
         0 = key does not expire
      <n>  = key expires in n days
      <n>w = key expires in n weeks
      <n>m = key expires in n months
      <n>y = key expires in n years
Key is valid for? (0)

You need a User-ID to identify your key; the software constructs the user id
from Real Name, Comment and Email Address in this form:
    "Heinrich Heine (Der Dichter) <heinrichh@duesseldorf.de>"

Real name: Eric Foster-Johnson
Email address: please_no_spam@nospam.com
Comment: Example for Red Hat RPM Guide
You selected this USER-ID:
    "Eric Foster-Johnson (Example for Red Hat RPM Guide) <erc@no_spam.com>"
Change (N)ame, (C)omment, (E)mail or (O)kay/(Q)uit?
O
You need a Passphrase to protect your secret key.
```

```
Enter passphrase:
We need to generate a lot of random bytes. It is a good idea to perform
some other action (type on the keyboard, move the mouse, utilize the
disks) during the prime generation; this gives the random number
generator a better chance to gain enough entropy.
++++++++++++++++++++++++++++++++++++++++++++++++++++++++++++++++++++++++++++++++
++++++++++++++++++++++++++++++++++++++..+++++..++++++++++>+++++++++++........+++++
gpg: /home2/ericfj/.gnupg/trustdb.gpg: trustdb created
public and secret key created and signed.
key marked as ultimately trusted.

pub  1024D/01681C24 2002-11-05 Eric Foster-Johnson (Example for Red Hat RPM
Guide) <please_no_spam@nospam.com>
     Key fingerprint = 8C14 A2E9 47D1 301B 2153  7CDF BEE5 9C10 0268 1D24
sub  1024g/1A15D6C8 2002-11-05
```

You can choose the default options for most choices. You need to enter a real name, an e-mail address, and a pass phrase. Remember the pass phrase. You will need to enter the pass phrase every time you wish to sign a package.

Once you have a key, the next step is to set up some RPM macros. There are a number of places you can do this, but using the .rpmmacros file in your home directory is one of the easiest. Edit this file as shown in the following example:

```
%_signature gpg
%_gpg_path /home2/ericfj/.gnupg
%_gpg_name EricFJ (Eric Key) <erc@no_spam.com>
%_gpgbin /usr/bin/gpg
```

Add lines like these to the $HOME/.rpmmacros file. (Create this file if it does not exist.)

 Chapter 21 covers RPM macros and the $HOME/.rpmmacros file.

Inside the file, change the %gpg_path macro to the .gnupg directory under your home directory (or the root user's home directory). Change the %_gpg_name macro to the name you have entered into the gpg program.

Signing with the rpmbuild command

The `--sign` option tells the `rpmbuild` command to sign the created package. You need to have configured the RPM system for your signature as shown in the previous sections.

When you then build an RPM, you will be prompted for your pass phrase prior to the package build. For example, the following shows this prompt (and truncates the rest of the rpmbuild messages that follow):

```
$ rpmbuild -bb --sign xtoolwait-1.2.spec
Enter pass phrase:
Pass phrase is good.
```

Signing with the rpm command

In addition to the `--sign` option for the `rpmbuild` command, you can sign packages that have already been created using the `rpm` command. The `--addsign` and `--resign` options generate new signatures and insert them into the passed-in package file. The basic syntax is:

```
rpm --addsign package.rpm
rpm --resign package.rpm
```

The `--addsign` option adds another signature to the RPM. RPM versions prior to 4.1 allowed you to sign a package with multiple keys, which causes problems for automatic verification. Because of that, use the `--resign` option, which removes the old signature and inserts a new signature into the package.

Verifying signatures

You can verify the RPM signature to ensure that the package has not been modified since it has been signed. Verification also checks that the package is signed by the key that matches the claimed vendor.

To verify the signature in an RPM, use the `-K` option to the `rpm` command. The basic syntax is:

```
rpm -K package.rpm
```

This is the `rpm` command, not the `rpmbuild` command.

This command accepts the options shown in Table 12-3 to turn off checking for certain types of signatures.

TABLE 12-3 OPTIONS TO TURN OFF SIGNATURE CHECKING

Option	Usage
--nogpg	Don't check for GPG signatures
--nomd5	Don't check for MD5 signatures
--nopgp	Don't check for PGP signatures

You can also use the --checksig option, which is the same as -K. When you run this command on a package that has a verifiable key, you will see output like the following:

```
# rpm -K xtoolwait-1.3-3.src.rpm
xtoolwait-1.3-3.src.rpm: (sha1) dsa sha1 md5 gpg OK
```

This verifies that the package has not been changed from when it was first signed. It also verifies that the signature matches the public key from the vendor of the package. This goes a long ways toward verifying that the package is indeed legitimate.

To get more information, add a -v (verbose) option. For example:

```
$ rpm -Kv vixie-cron-3.0.1-69.src.rpm
vixie-cron-3.0.1-69.src.rpm:
    Header V3 DSA signature: OK, key ID db42a60e
    Header SHA1 digest: OK
(ecbb244ab022ecd23114bb1d6c9bdeb74f8d9520)
    MD5 digest: OK (fb0a75eca1d526d391c36dc956c23bdd)
    V3 DSA signature: OK, key ID db42a60e
```

If you run this command on a package that does not verify, you'll see an error like the following:

```
# rpm --checksig xtoolwait-1.3-3.src.rpm
xtoolwait-1.3-3.src.rpm: (SHA1) DSA sha1 md5 (GPG) NOT OK (MISSING KEYS:
GPG#db42a60e)
```

Items that fail are listed in uppercase, such as DSA, while items that succeed appear in lowercase. In this example, the sha1 and md5 tests succeeded, while the DSA test failed. This failure does not necessarily mean that the package is not legitimate. This failure can mean one of three things:

1. The package was not properly signed in the first place. That is, it is a legitimate package but the package author did not properly sign the RPM.

2. The package has been modified in some way. That is, the package is not legitimate.

3. The RPM system has not been initialized with the public key from the package vendor.

From this error, you don't yet know whether the package is legitimate or not. The first step, though, is to check that you have imported the proper public key from the package vendor.

Importing public keys

The --import option to the rpm command imports the public key from a given vendor. The format for this key follows:

```
The following public key can be used to verify RPM packages built and
signed by Red Hat, Inc. using `rpm -K' using the GNU GPG package.
Questions about this key should be sent to security@redhat.com.

-----BEGIN PGP PUBLIC KEY BLOCK-----
Version: GnuPG v1.0.0 (GNU/Linux)
Comment: For info see http://www.gnupg.org

mQGiBDfqVEqRBADBKr3B16PO8BQOH8sJoD6p9U7Yy17pjtZqioviPwXP+DCWd4u8
HQzcxAZ57m8ssA1LK1Fx93coJhDzM130+p5BG9mYSPShLabR3N1KXdXAYYcowTOM
GxdwYRGr1Spw8QydLhjVfU1VS14xt6bupPbFJbyjkg5Z3P7B1UOUJmrx3wCgobNV
EDGaWYJcch5z5B1of/41G8kEAKii6q7Gu/vhXXnLS6m15oNnPVybyngiw/23dKjS
ti/PYrrL2J11P2ed0x7zm8v3gLrYOcue1iSba+8g1Y+p31ZPOr5ogaJw7ZARgoS8
BwjyRymXQp+8Dete0TELKOL2/itDOPGHWO7SsVWOR6cmX4V1RRcWB5KejaNvdrE5
4XFtOd04NMgWI63uqZc4zkRa+kwEZtmbz3tHSdWCCE+Y7YVP6IUf/w6YPQFQriWY
FiA6fD1OeB+B1IUqIw8OEqjsBKmCwvKkn4jg8kibUgj4/TzQSx77uYokw1EqQ2wk
OZoaEtcubsNMquuLCMWijYhGBBgRAgAGBQI361RyAAoJECGCGRgM3bQqYOhyYAnj7h
VDY/FJAGqmtZpwVp9I1itW5tAJ4xQApr/jNFZCTksnI+4O1765F7tA==
=3AHZ
-----END PGP PUBLIC KEY BLOCK-----
```

 For reasons of space, this is not a complete key.

You need to pass the name of the text file that holds the key to the rpm --import command, as shown following:

```
rpm --import key_file
```

 You must be logged in as the root user to import keys.

For example:

```
# rpm --checksig xtoolwait-1.3-3.src.rpm
xtoolwait-1.3-3.src.rpm: (SHA1) DSA sha1 md5 (GPG) NOT OK (MISSING KEYS:
GPG#db42a60e)

# rpm --import RPM-GPG-KEY

# rpm --checksig xtoolwait-1.3-3.src.rpm
xtoolwait-1.3-3.src.rpm: (sha1) dsa sha1 md5 gpg OK
```

This example shows an error message when trying to verify the key. Then, after importing the Red Hat public key, the verification works.

If, after importing this key, you still have problems, you can assume there are problems with the package. Many administrators will refuse to install such packages.

 You should be careful with packages that have signatures that do not verify.

To list the available keys, use a command like the following:

```
$ rpm -qa | grep -i gpg
gpg-pubkey-db42a60e-37ea5438
```

This example shows one key installed.

 You can erase this key as if it were a package, using the rpm -e command.

Getting the Red Hat public key

Strangely enough, the Red Hat public key is not installed when you install Red Hat Linux 8.0. If you need the key, the Red Hat public key is available on the root directory of all Red Hat Linux CD-ROMs, as shown in the following listing:

```
$ ls /mnt/cdrom/
EULA  GPL  README  RedHat/  RPM-GPG-KEY  SRPMS/  TRANS.TBL
```

Simply copy the RPM-GPG-KEY file to get the public key. Then use the rpm --import command with this key file.

 You can also download this key file from the Red Hat FTP site, at `ftp://ftp.redhat.com/pub/redhat/linux/8.0/en/os/i386/`.

Summary

This chapter covers options for the rpmbuild command that allow you to achieve a finer grain of control over how the command works. For example, the --short-circuit option tells the rpmbuild command to build just the stages you ask for. This helps when you have problems in one area of building an RPM and don't want to start over each time you try to see if the problem is solved.

The rpmbuild command also supports a set of -t options that work like the -b options, except the -t options try to build an RPM from a tar archive of sources (a tarball) instead of an RPM spec file. In this case, the rpmbuild command tries to work without a spec file.

The --rebuild option tells the rpmbuild command to install a source RPM, build the binary RPM, and clean out the installed source RPM. This provides quite a shortcut for installing binary RPMs from source RPMs.

RPMs should be signed to provide an extra level of authentication. This system isn't perfect, but it helps you verify that a package is from the person it says it is from and that the package has not been modified. You can check the signature on RPM packages you download. You can also, with some configuration, sign the packages you create.

Chapter 13

Supplemental Packaging Software

RPM IS INTENDED TO MAKE SYSTEM management easier, both for system administrators and other users who do all the day-to-day work of installing and removing applications and for developers and other users who do all the work of preparing applications for installation. For RPM packagers, the work involved in preparing an application for installation has two phases: first, the software must be compiled (if it is not written in an interpreted language such as Perl) and otherwise configured for the system on which it will be installed; then the RPM package of the software must be prepared by creating a spec file that properly packages it into an RPM. In contrast, packagers who choose to package applications in a simpler format, such as gzipped tarballs (compressed tar archives), have less work ahead of them, since they need only concern themselves with the first step.

After a packager has prepared an RPM package once, RPM makes the first step (compilation and configuration) easier when the packager has to package an updated version of the same software; RPM does a lot of work to track compilation commands, any needed patches, and any configuration modifications discovered to be necessary to prepare the software. Similarly, once an RPM spec file has been produced for an application, updating that spec file to support a newer version of that application is usually trivial. For these reasons, using RPM instead of a simpler, less end-user-friendly package format (such as gzipped tarballs) is a bit of a tradeoff for the packager; preparing an RPM of an application requires a little more initial time and work than preparing a gzipped tarball of that same application, but once created, the RPM package takes less time and effort to keep current than the gzipped tarball requires.

Packaging Aids

However, several helper tools are also available for RPM packagers. These tools can be used at various stages in the process of producing a high-quality RPM package to simplify the tasks that an RPM packager must perform. These tools include

syntax-highlighting modes for various text editors, making production and maintenance of spec files easier; macro packages for popular text editors, simplifying the
generation and maintenance of spec files; tools that generate spec files, simplifying
initial spec file creation; and debuggers that validate produced binary RPMs, helping
ensure that the spec file used to create the packages is accurate and high quality.

Using VIM spec plugins to improve spec file editing

Unix systems have traditionally shipped the legendary (or notorious, depending
upon your point of view) vi editor (pronounced *vee eye*) as their default text editor.
Vi was initially developed by Bill Joy in 1976 for BSD Unix. It eventually was
incorporated in AT&T System V Unix as well and later was mandated by the POSIX
1003 standards (which define what an OS must have to be Unix-compatible),
thereby conquering all facets of the Unix world.

The original vi source code is no longer freely available, but several clones of the
vi program have been created over the years. The most popular of these vi clones is
probably Vi IMproved, or VIM (www.vim.org). VIM is the standard vi implementation (meaning that when you type vi at the command prompt, the program you
really are running is vim) on many Linux distributions, including Red Hat Linux. It
is also freely available for most other Unixes and even for non-Unix systems such
as Microsoft Windows.

VIM is a fully backwards-compatible implementation of the original vi editor,
although it also offers many additional features that vi did not support. One VIM
feature that can be extremely useful when preparing spec files is colorized syntax
highlighting. VIM has an extensible interface through which it can be told about
the syntax used for files of various types. Once it understands a filetype's syntax, it
can color the various syntactic structures of that file in different ways. For example, when editing a Bourne shell script using VIM, comments are typically blue,
control statements (if, for, do, and so on) are yellow, variables are purple, and so
forth. Many people find this feature very useful, since a single glance reveals the
entire logical structure of the file. Furthermore, errors in the file (such as a missing
done statement failing to close a do loop in a Bourne shell script) are often immediately obvious when using such a colorizing editor.

Usually, VIM does not understand the structure of RPM spec files. When preparing
a spec file, VIM displays all text in the same color. A spec.vim syntax file is available
for VIM that makes VIM aware of the syntax used for RPM spec files. When this file
is used, the various structural components (%define, preamble statements, %build,
and so forth) are all colorized, making the logic of the spec file readily apparent.

The spec.vim file that provides VIM with an understanding of spec-file syntax is
bundled with newer versions of VIM, or it can be downloaded from the Internet.
Most RPM-based Linux distributions, including Red Hat Linux, ship this file with
VIM as part of their distribution and even automatically configure VIM to load this
syntax file any time an RPM spec file is being edited. When using VIM on a system
that does not automatically load spec.vim whenever spec files are edited, you
should download the spec.vim file (I tend to save such personal extensions in
~/etc/vim, but you can save it any place you prefer).

Download the spec.vim syntax file for VIM from `http://pegasus.` `rutgers.edu/~elflord/vim/syntax/spec.vim`.

Once downloaded, configure VIM to load your new syntax file. You can do this by putting the following in your ~/.vimrc file (assuming you have saved the file as ~/etc/vim/spec.vim; adjust the path as necessary if you saved it elsewhere):

```
augroup syntax
au! BufNewFile,BufReadPost *.spec  so ~/etc/vim/spec.vim
au  BufNewFile,BufReadPost *.spec  so ~/etc/vim/spec.vim
augroup END
```

This statement will instruct VIM to load the syntax file whenever a file named with a *.spec* extension is edited. You can now even customize the colors which VIM uses, if you like, by editing ~/etc/vim/spec.vim!

The VIM editor has hundreds of built-in commands for formatting text. If necessary, it can even be extended with new commands. Furthermore, these commands can be defined in FileType plugins, so that different commands are loaded depending upon the type of file being edited (just as different syntax matching can be used depending upon the type of file being edited). Gustavo Niemeyer has written a spec plugin, pi_spec, which defines various commands that can be used when working with RPM spec files. Currently, this plugin can be used to automate maintenance of the %changelog section of RPM spec files.

By default, the spec plugin provides a macro, spec_chglog, which is mapped to the <LocalLeader>-c key. Normally, the LocalLeader key in VIM is mapped to "\", a backslash character. This means you press \c to load the spec_chglog macro. If desired, you can instead map spec_chglog to a different key by putting a statement like the following in your ~/.vimrc file.

```
au FileType spec map <buffer> C <Plug>SpecChangelog
```

In this case, that statement would map the macro to the "C" key, but you can map it to a different key by replacing the "C" in the statement with whichever key or key combination you prefer.

The spec_chglog macro checks the %changelog in the spec file currently being edited and makes sure that the last entry in this %changelog was written today and was written by you. If it was, the macro adds a new item to the entry. If it was not written today, or was written today, but not by you, the macro adds an entirely new entry. Optionally, the macro also checks that the name, version, and release of the package are correct and will update the release if it is incorrect. In addition, the macro maps the percent key, %, making it usable in command mode in VIM to move quickly between sections within a spec file.

To help spec_chglog, you can define a few variables in your ~/.vimrc file to customize its behavior. The variable `spec_chglog_format` defines what the macro uses for new `%changelog` entries. If you do not define this variable, the macro will ask you for an e-mail address and construct it for you the first time you use the macro. Alternatively, you can customize it yourself by adding an entry like the following to your ~/.vimrc file.

```
let spec_chglog_format = "%a %b %d %Y Your Name <your@email.address>"
```

The preceding format is what Red Hat's developers use for Red Hat Linux spec files and results in a `%changelog` entry that looks like the following, with the user name and e-mail address changed to protect the innocent:

```
* Mon Apr 15 2002 Bob Marley <bob@marley.yow>
```

The variables in the `spec_chglog_format` control the time format that is used. If you want different time formats in your `%changelog` entry, you can replace the variables (using `%A` instead of `%a` would cause the full weekday name, such as "Monday", to be printed) using the documentation in the strftime(3) man page as a guideline.

By default, the macro will insert new entry items after existing items. For example, if I already have a `%changelog` entry for today that reads as follows:

```
* Mon May 6 2002 Bob Marley <bob@marley.yow>
- Updated to newest release
```

Then, using the macro to add a new entry for an additional patch I added will, by default, result in an entry that reads:

```
* Mon May 6 2002 Bob Marley <bob@marley.yow>
- Updated to newest release
- Added Solaris compile patch
```

If I want, I can instead have new items inserted before existing items, so that my second entry instead looks like

```
* Mon May 6 2002 Bob Marley <bob@marley.yow>
- Added Solaris compile patch
- Updated to newest release
```

To have new items inserted before existing items, simply add the following line to your ~/.vimrc file:

```
let spec_chglog_prepend = 1
```

Optionally, the macro can track version and release numbers in the `%changelog` entries automatically. Adding the line

```
let spec_chglog_release_info = 1
```

results in the first item in every changelog entry automatically reflecting the version and release, so that my %changelog entry might instead look like the following:

```
* Mon May 6 2002 Bob Marley <bob@marley.yow>
+ httpd-2.0.36-2
- Updated to newest release
- Added Solaris compile patch
```

If this feature is enabled, the macro automatically checks the version and release information to make sure that they have increased. If they haven't, it will offer to update them for you. Add the following line to your ~/.vimrc file to disable this feature, if necessary.

```
let spec_chglog_never_increase_release = 1
```

This spec plugin ships with newer versions of VIM. Both it and the VIM spec syntax highlighting extensions can be very useful for speeding spec file editing and debugging, and are well worth trying out if you are a VIM user.

You can find out more about VIM at www.vim.org.

Adding functions with emacs rpm-spec-mode

Of course, not everyone in the world uses VIM. Another commonly used editor is the emacs editor originally developed by Richard M. Stallman. Unlike vi, emacs is not considered an essential Unix component and is not always found installed on a Unix system, although it is bundled with just about every Linux distribution.

Over the years, two major emacs variants have emerged. GNU Emacs is produced by the Free Software Foundation and can be downloaded from www.gnu.org/software/emacs/emacs.html. XEmacs is based on GNU Emacs and is available from www.xemacs.org. Historically, the two differed in their user interfaces (XEmacs, as the name suggests, had an X Window interface, though GNU Emacs has one as well these days) and in some technical details of how they operated. Both are freely available under the terms of the GNU GPL, so you can download and try either or both if they are not already on your system.

See Appendix G for more on the GNU GPL, or General Public License.

Red Hat Linux includes RPMs of both GNU Emacs and XEmacs as part of the distribution, and most other Linux distributions will include one or both as well.

Like VIM, both GNU Emacs and XEmacs support syntax highlighting. They are also both extensible, having the ability to load mode files that add new commands and functions. Stig Bjørlykke has written a mode, rpm-spec-mode.el, which works with both GNU Emacs and with XEmacs to add many functions, making it easier to use when editing RPM spec files. Red Hat Linux includes and enables this mode in both GNU Emacs and XEmacs, as do many other Linux distributions.

You can download this emacs mode from `http://tihlde.org/ ~stigb/rpm-spec-mode.el`.

After downloading, you will need to put the following lines in your ~/.emacs init files (for GNU Emacs) or ~/.xemacs init files (for XEmacs) to instruct emacs to load rpm-spec-mode whenever a file with a `.spec` extension is being edited:

```
(autoload 'rpm-spec-mode "rpm-spec-mode.el" "RPM spec mode." t)
(setq auto-mode-alist (append '(("\\.spec" . rpm-spec-mode)) auto-mode-alist))
```

Once installed, rpm-spec-mode will provide emacs with additional support for editing RPM spec files. Figure 13-1 shows this mode in GNU Emacs, and Figure 13-2 shows this mode in XEmacs.

With this mode, emacs can do syntax highlighting of spec files, just like VIM. The mode file rpm-spec-mode.el contains the emacs instructions that specify what should be highlighted and what colors should be used for highlighting.

If you do not see syntax highlighting when you edit a spec file, your emacs session may or may not be currently configured to do syntax highlighting. First, make sure that the status bar at the bottom of your emacs window says (RPM-SPEC), indicating that rpm-spec-mode is being used. If it doesn't, double-check the rpm-spec-mode installation instructions. If the status bar does indicate that you are using rpm-spec-mode, also double-check that syntax highlighting (which, in emacs, is a global configuration option) has been enabled. In both GNU Emacs and XEmacs, the Options menu has a Syntax Highlighting option that must be enabled before emacs will colorize spec file syntactic structures.

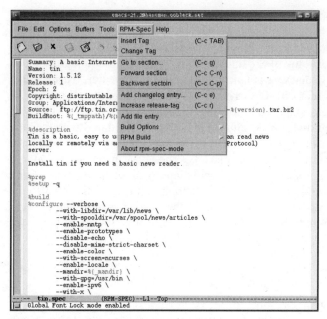

Figure 13-1: Gnu Emacs using rpm-spec-mode

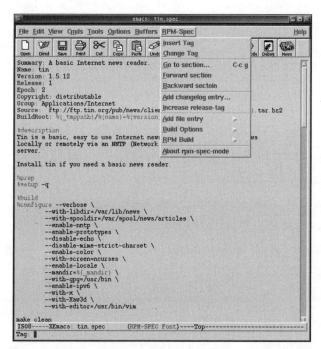

Figure 13-2: XEmacs using rpm-spec-mode

In addition to providing syntax colorization, rpm-spec-mode adds a variety of new functions to emacs that can be used to speed the process of creating or editing RPM spec files. These new functions appear on the RPM-Spec menu that is added to emacs by rpm-spec-mode. Many of the functions are similar to the functions added to VIM by the spec_chglog macro. Navigation functions to move quickly through a spec file are provided, so that Ctrl+C, Ctrl+N (press Ctrl+C followed by Ctrl+N) will move the cursor to the next major section of the spec file, while Ctrl+C, Ctrl+P will move the cursor to the prior major section of the spec file. Similarly, macros are also defined to increment the release tag (Ctrl+C, R) and the very handy option to add new %changelog entries (Ctrl+C, E). Like the VIM macros for adding %changelog entries, the rpm-spec-mode command checks to see if an entry already exists for today. If not, it adds a new entry, but if so, it just adds a new item to the existing entry. For %changelog entries to have the correct e-mail address, the emacs variable user-mail-address must be set correctly. If it is not set on your system, you can add the following line to your emacs initialization files:

```
(setq user-mail-address "your@email.address")
```

In addition to these basic functions, rpm-spec-mode offers more advanced spec file creation support. Opening a new buffer in emacs for a spec file that does not already exist automatically generates a skeleton spec file.

To further speed things up, emacs offers a number of macros for the main tasks in writing an RPM spec file. Table 13-1 lists these macros.

TABLE 13-1 MACRO COMMANDS FOR THE RPM SPEC MODE IN EMACS

Command	Function
Ctrl+C Tab	Adds a new tag to the spec file
Ctrl+C Ctrl+F F	Adds a new file to the %files section
Ctrl+C Ctrl+F C	Adds a new configuration file to the %files section
Ctrl+C Ctrl+F D	Adds a new documentation file to the %files section
Ctrl+C Ctrl+F G	Adds a new ghost file to the %files section
Ctrl+C Ctrl+D D	Adds a new directory to the %files section
Ctrl+C Ctrl+D O	Adds a new documentation directory to the %files section
Ctrl+C Ctrl+C U	Changes the umask in %defattr entries in %files
Ctrl+C Ctrl+C O	Changes the owner in %defattr entries in %files
Ctrl+C Ctrl+C G	Changes the group in %defattr entries in %files

Furthermore, rpm-spec-mode even adds macros to emacs that can be used to build RPMs from spec files without even having to exit emacs! Since the process of constructing spec files is often iterative (make new spec, build RPM from spec, find mistake, edit spec, build RPM from spec, find mistake, and so on), this capability of emacs to be used as an IDE for RPM package generation is extremely useful. Basic macros exist to do complete builds (Ctrl+C B to build a binary package, Ctrl+C S to build a source package, and Ctrl+C A to build both). Macros can also be used to execute various intermediate steps, such as the %prep stage (Ctrl+C P), the %build stage (Ctrl+C C), or the %install stage (Ctrl+C I). Various options of the build process can also be controlled, such as GPG-signing of generated packages.

If you are a user of GNU Emacs or XEmacs, you should definitely take the time to learn to use rpm-spec-mode. Being able to build packages from within the editor where you are editing the spec file that builds those packages is a great productivity gain for many people.

Validating and debugging spec files with rpmlint

Both VIM and emacs extensions help with the process of initially creating spec files and with the maintenance of existing RPM spec files. After a spec file has been created, and RPMs have been created using that spec, the binary RPMs generated from the spec can be validated using the rpmlint command. The name rpmlint comes from lint, the traditional Unix utility that can "sanity-check" C source code, looking for certain classes of common C coding mistakes. The idea behind rpmlint is similar; it processes binary RPMs, checking for certain common mistakes made by RPM packagers.

The rpmlint command currently ships with a wide variety of checks and is written using a modular interface so that additional checks can easily be added if needed. Currently, rpmlint can check that all binary files in the package are correct (making sure that a .noarch.rpm package does not contain binary files, that no binaries are being installed in /etc, that the binary file types in the package are appropriate for the package architecture, that shared libraries are configured correctly, and that all executables are stripped). It can also check the validity of files marked as configuration files in the RPM (ensuring that configuration files are only being installed in /etc, not in /usr) and that the package file complies with the distribution's policies for packages (checking things such as the compression of man pages and Info pages and the correctness of vendor and distribution fields in the package header).

In addition, rpmlint performs a variety of checks to ensure that the package complies with the Filesystem Hierarchy Standard (verifying that files are installed in their standard locations on the system), the Linux Standards Base (verifying that package-file naming is LSB-compliant) and that files have correct ownerships and permissions. Init scripts are double-checked (for packages that have init scripts) to ensure that the basic structure of the init script is correct and that appropriate %post and %preun configuration directives are being run to configure the init script on the system. %post, %pre, and %preun scripts are also double-checked (ensuring that only valid interpreters are specified for scripts and that scripts are written in valid syntax). The validity of the package itself is also checked in various ways (ensuring that the package is GPG-signed, that the package's source RPM is correctly prepared, that the package spec file uses correct syntax, and that all tags used in the package header are valid).

 To find out more about the Filesystem Hierarchy Standard, see `www.pathname.com/fhs/`. To find out more about the Linux Standards Base, see `www.linuxbase.org`.

Download `rpmlint` from `www.lepied.com/rpmlint`. It is written entirely in Python, so a Python interpreter is necessary to run it. Once installed, `rpmlint` can be configured on a system-wide basis, using the /etc/rpmlint/config file, or on a per-user basis, using the $HOME/.rpmlintrc file. This file can specify checks to perform, check output that should be ignored, and configuration options. Configuration options can be specified, listing what entries are valid for various fields in the RPM header, such as the Vendor and Packager fields. By default, Red Hat Linux ships with this configuration file set to validate packages to make sure they are suitable for Red Hat Linux; if packaging for a different distribution, this file might need to be modified.

Once `rpmlint` has been installed and configured, it can be run against RPMs. For example, rpmlint helps with creating packages, such as tin (a popular Usenet client) for Red Hat Linux, since it is not included with the distribution. After preparing a tin spec file, then building RPMs from that file, you can typically double-check them using `rpmlint`.

For example, when running `rpmlint` on a source RPM, you'll see output like the following:

```
$ rpmlint tin-1.5.12-1.src.rpm
E: tin no-packager-tag
W: tin invalid-license distributable
W: tin no-url-tag
W: tin strange-permission tin-1.5.12.tar.bz2 0664
W: tin obsolete-tag Copyright
$
```

For the most part, this package looks fine according to the `rpmlint` output. The permissions on the tin source code can be changed (0644 is the "preferred" permissions), and you might want to change my spec file to use the License tag instead of the now-obsolete Copyright tag. Similarly, you might want to add a URL tag to the package to point to the URL for the software.

When running `rpmlint` on a binary RPM, you'll see output like the following:

```
$ rpmlint tin-1.5.12-1.i386.rpm
W: tin invalid-vendor None
W: tin invalid-distribution None
E: tin no-packager-tag
W: tin invalid-license distributable
W: tin no-url-tag
$
```

With this output, the binary package looks fine. You should set a vendor, distribution, and packager, but you can ignore those warnings. Similarly, `rpmlint` warns because it does not recognize the license type used, "distributable". You can fix this, you can ignore this, or you can modify /etc/rpmlint/config so that `rpmlint` recognizes "distributable" as a valid license.

The sorts of validity checks that `rpmlint` can do make it valuable for ensuring the quality and consistency of RPMs. Most RPM-based Linux distributions validate their entire distribution using `rpmlint`. Using it for packages you prepare is a good idea as well.

Generating the %files section with RUST

For the most part, maintaining RPM spec files is relatively straightforward. Creating spec files from scratch, however, can be a little bit more challenging. Tools like rpm-spec-mode for emacs can help with the process, generating skeleton spec file templates that can be filled in, but these sorts of tools do not address the step that most new RPM packagers seem to find most difficult: generating the `%files` section. Creating a complete, accurate list of all needed files supplied by an application can be difficult, particularly when it is an application with which you are unfamiliar. Most software supports installation to a temporary location; if the software you are packaging allows this, generation of `%files` is (almost) as simple as using `BuildRoot` to install the application to a temporary directory, then running an `ls -1R` command in that subdirectory to see all the installed files and directories. Even then, though, the output from `ls -1R` must be cleaned up and converted into `%files` format for adding to the spec file. All of this takes time.

A couple of tools exist to reduce the amount of work needed for this stage of the process, automating the generation of the `%files` section of spec files. The most sophisticated of these toolsets is RUST.

Download RUST from www.rusthq.com.

RUST consists of two tools: crust and rust. The crust command provides a command-line tool that can create a chroot() jail, in which software can be built and installed, and then automatically generate a spec file that documents the files that were installed. This not only eliminates the need to generate a %files section for a spec file manually but also removes the need to modify software to support installation to a temporary location using BuildRoot, a sometimes difficult task.

The rust command provides a graphical front end to the crust command, as shown in Figure 13-3.

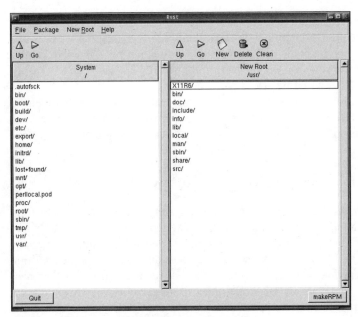

Figure 13-3: rust, a drag-and-drop spec file generator

The rust command provides a graphical interface that can be used to control crust and supports drag-and-drop creation of spec files. In the rust interface, two file trees are displayed. The left-hand tree displays the local file system, while the right-hand tree displays the file tree inside the crust chroot() jail. Files that should be packaged together can just be dragged from their current locations on the system (displayed in the left-hand tree) to their final destinations in the right-hand tree. You can then click the *makeRPM* choice to generate an RPM containing those files. Although not terribly useful for packages being generated from source code, this feature can greatly simplify creation of RPMs of applications that are only supplied in binary format (such as the Linux Adobe Acrobat reader).

RUST's rust application can be useful in some circumstances (providing new developers a graphical tool that can be used to generate binary RPMs), and crust is more generally useful for packaging difficult-to-package software that needs to be built and installed in a chroot() jail. Unfortunately, development of RUST appears to have stopped, so extension of RUST to become a more generally useful IDE for RPM generation is not likely to happen. However, the project is licensed under the GNU GPL (see Appendix G), so it might be resumed by another developer or team of developers.

setup.sh and MakeRPM.pl

Other tools that have been developed to simplify the process of creating an RPM spec file take an entirely different approach. Tools such as setup.sh, available from `www.mmedia.is/~bre/programs/setup.sh`, are intended to function as wrappers around the existing build commands (`./configure` and `make`) for software. These types of tools take the approach of using the standard build tools for software (since those tools must always be used to build the software, whether using RPM or compiling the software from a source tarball) and capturing the output to generate an RPM spec file automatically.

The MakeRPM.pl Perl script, available from `www.perl.com/CPAN/modules/byauthors/id/JWIED`, is another example of such an approach. MakeRPM.pl is a more specialized tool than setup.sh, as MakeRPM.pl is intended only for producing RPMs from Perl modules packaged in CPAN (`www.cpan.org`). It is implemented as a wrapper around the standard commands (`perl Makefile.PL` ; `make` ; `make test` ; `make install`) used to install Perl CPAN software.

MakeRPM.pl actually works quite well for its intended purpose – producing packages of CPAN modules. The setup.sh script is currently viewable mainly as a proof of concept, rather than being a generally universal automatic spec file generator. In the future, when spec files are likely to be representable using a formal closed-syntax grammar, it is possible that more generalized spec file generation tools will be developed. Until that time, however, some of the previously mentioned tools, particularly the VIM and emacs extensions, can provide assistance when manually generating spec files.

Manipulating package files with rpm2cpio

Normally, RPM packagers are concerned with taking source code or binary files, and producing an RPM that contains those files and can be used to install them on end-users' systems. Sometimes, packagers and end users find themselves in the opposite position, that of having a source or binary RPM package file and needing to extract its contents. An RPM can always be installed to access its contents (either source code, patches, and a spec file which get put under %_topdir for a source RPM, or software which gets put in system directories for a binary RPM), but that is often overkill. I frequently want to extract a single patch file, or the spec file, from a source RPM, but I don't really need to install the entire source RPM. Similarly, people often want to extract the contents of RPMs on systems that do not come with RPM, such as Solaris.

Fortunately, tools are available that can process RPM package files into a format from which their content can be extracted. Structurally speaking, RPM package files are compressed `cpio` archives that have additional binary data added to the beginning containing various meta-data about the package (specifying its architecture and OS, for example), a GPG signature if the package is signed, and so forth. If this binary data is removed from the beginning of the RPM package file, the remainder is a System V Release 4-style `cpio` file that can be manipulated using any reasonably complete `cpio` command. Several different tools, each sporting the name rpm2cpio, are available which can do this binary data removal, converting an RPM package file into a standard `cpio` archive.

RPM ships with an `rpm2cpio` utility that can be used to convert RPM package files to `cpio` files. (Chapter 3 introduces the `rpm2cpio` utility.) For example, if you have a source RPM package file and want to extract its files without having to install it, you can process it through `rpm2cpio`. The `rpm2cpio` command takes as input an RPM package file, and produces a `cpio` file on standard output. For example, to redirect the output to a file, use a command like the following:

```
$ rpm2cpio fluxbox-0.1.8-2.src.rpm > fluxbox-0.1.8-2.cpio
$
```

This command creates a cpio archive from the package. You can later use cpio commands on the output file. You can also pipe the output of `rpm2cpio` through the `cpio` command:

```
$ rpm2cpio fluxbox-0.1.8-2.src.rpm | cpio -i -d
656 blocks
$
```

This command extracts the contents of the package.

This `rpm2cpio` command is bundled with RPM and is installed on most RPM-based Linux distributions, including Red Hat Linux. However, it is less useful on systems that do not come with RPM, such as Solaris. This "standard" implementation of `rpm2cpio` is written in C, and so must be compiled before it can be used. Since most commercial Unix systems do not come with a C compiler by default (unlike Linux and other free Unixes, such as the BSD operating systems), compiling this `rpm2cpio` code can be a major undertaking.

Fortunately, `rpm2cpio` implementations are also available in a couple of other languages, in more easy-to-install formats for other operating systems, including as a Bourne shell script or a Perl script. The Bourne shell syntax should work on any reasonably modern Unix system (and even a few non-Unix systems; it also works on Microsoft Windows under cygwin, for example). The script in Listing 13-1 should be saved to a file named rpm2cpio.sh, marked executable, and copied to a directory in your path.

Listing 13-1: rpm2cpio as a Bourne Shell script

```
#!/bin/sh

pkg=$1
if [ "$pkg" = "" -o ! -e "$pkg" ]; then
    echo "no package supplied" 1>&2
    exit 1
fi

leadsize=96
o=`expr $leadsize + 8`
set `od -j $o -N 8 -t u1 $pkg`
il=`expr 256 \* \( 256 \* \( 256 \* $2 + $3 \) + $4 \) + $5`
dl=`expr 256 \* \( 256 \* \( 256 \* $6 + $7 \) + $8 \) + $9`
# echo "sig il: $il dl: $dl"

sigsize=`expr 8 + 16 \* $il + $dl`
o=`expr $o + $sigsize + \( 8 - \( $sigsize \% 8 \) \) \% 8 + 8`
set `od -j $o -N 8 -t u1 $pkg`
il=`expr 256 \* \( 256 \* \( 256 \* $2 + $3 \) + $4 \) + $5`
dl=`expr 256 \* \( 256 \* \( 256 \* $6 + $7 \) + $8 \) + $9`
# echo "hdr il: $il dl: $dl"

hdrsize=`expr 8 + 16 \* $il + $dl`
o=`expr $o + $hdrsize`

dd if=$pkg ibs=$o skip=1 2>/dev/null | gunzip
```

After you have marked this file as executable and placed it in your command path, you can use the script just like the C language implementation of rpm2cpio. This script also takes an RPM package file as input and produces a cpio file on standard output, and so should be used in conjunction with redirection or a pipe:

```
$ rpm2cpio.sh fluxbox-0.1.8-2.src.rpm | cpio -i -d
656 blocks
$
```

In this case, I piped the output to cpio, directly extracting it. I could have redirected the output of rpm2cpio.sh to a file instead.

In addition to the Bourne shell implementation of rpm2cpio, a version has been written in Perl by Roger Espel Llima. The Perl rpm2cpio implementation should work on any system that has a reasonably modern Perl interpreter. To use this version of rpm2cpio, the script in Listing 13-2 should be saved to a file named rpm2cpio.pl, marked executable, and copied to a directory in your path.

Listing 13-2: The Perl version of rpm2cpio, rpm2cpio.pl

```perl
#!/usr/bin/perl

# Copyright (C) 1997,1998,1999, Roger Espel Llima
#
# Permission is hereby granted, free of charge, to any person obtaining a copy
# of this software and any associated documentation files (the "Software"), to
# deal in the Software without restriction, including without limitation the
# rights to use, copy, modify, merge, publish, distribute, sublicense,
# and/or sell copies of the Software, and to permit persons to whom the
# Software is furnished to do so, subject to the following conditions:
#
# The above copyright notice and this permission notice shall be included in
# all copies or substantial portions of the Software.
#
# THE SOFTWARE IS PROVIDED "AS IS", WITHOUT WARRANTY OF ANY KIND, EXPRESS OR
# IMPLIED, INCLUDING BUT NOT LIMITED TO THE WARRANTIES OF MERCHANTABILITY,
# FITNESS FOR A PARTICULAR PURPOSE AND NONINFRINGEMENT.  IN NO EVENT SHALL THE
# SOFTWARE'S COPYRIGHT HOLDER(S) BE LIABLE FOR ANY CLAIM, DAMAGES OR OTHER
# LIABILITY, WHETHER IN AN ACTION OF CONTRACT, TORT OR OTHERWISE, ARISING FROM,
# OUT OF OR IN CONNECTION WITH THE SOFTWARE OR THE USE OR OTHER DEALINGS IN
# THE SOFTWARE

# (whew, that's done!)

# why does the world need another rpm2cpio?  because the existing one
# won't build unless you have half a ton of things that aren't really
# required for it, since it uses the same library used to extract RPM's.
# in particular, it won't build on the HPsUX box i'm on.

# sw 2002-Mar-6 Don't slurp the whole file

# add a path if desired
$gzip = "gzip";

sub printhelp {
  print <<HERE;
rpm2cpio, perl version by orabidoo <odar\@pobox.com> +sw
dumps the contents to stdout as a cpio archive

use: rpm2cpio [file.rpm] > file.cpio

Here's how to use cpio:
     list of contents:   cpio -t -i < /file/name
```

```
        extract files:    cpio -d -i < /file/name
HERE

  exit 0;
}

if ($#ARGV == -1) {
  printhelp if -t STDIN;
  $f = "STDIN";
} elsif ($#ARGV == 0) {
  open(F, "< $ARGV[0]") or die "Can't read file $ARGV[0]\n";
  $f = 'F';
} else {
  printhelp;
}

printhelp if -t STDOUT;

# gobble the file up
##undef $/;
##$|=1;
##$rpm = <$f>;
##close ($f);

read $f,$rpm,96;

($magic, $major, $minor, $crap) = unpack("NCC C90", $rpm);

die "Not an RPM\n" if $magic != 0xedabeedb;
die "Not a version 3 or 4 RPM\n" if $major != 3 && $major != 4;

##$rpm = substr($rpm, 96);

while (!eof($f)) {
  $pos = tell($f);
  read $f,$rpm,16;
  $smagic = unpack("n", $rpm);
  last if $smagic eq 0x1f8b;
  # Turns out that every header except the start of the gzip one is
  # padded to an 8 bytes boundary.
  if ($pos & 0x7) {
    $pos += 7;
    $pos &= ~0x7;          # Round to 8 byte boundary
    seek $f, $pos, 0;
```

Continued

Listing 13-2 *(Continued)*

```
    read $f,$rpm,16;
  }
  ($magic, $crap, $sections, $bytes) = unpack("N4", $rpm);
  die "Error: header not recognized\n" if $magic != 0x8eade801;
  $pos += 16;                # for header
  $pos += 16 * $sections;
  $pos += $bytes;
  seek $f, $pos, 0;
}

if (eof($f)) {
  die "bogus RPM\n";
}

open(ZCAT, "|gzip -cd") || die "can't pipe to gzip\n";
print STDERR "CPIO archive found!\n";

print ZCAT $rpm;

while (read($f, ($_=''), 16384) > 0) {
  print ZCAT;
}

close ZCAT;
```

After set up, rpm2cpio.pl works much like the C and Bourne shell versions, so the following command can be used to generate a `cpio` archive from an RPM package file:

```
$ rpm2cpio.pl fluxbox-0.1.8-2.src.rpm | cpio -i -d
CPIO archive found!
656 blocks
$
```

Depending upon the system you are on, one or more of these three `rpm2cpio` programs should work. All three are useful any time you want to extract a file or files from an RPM package file but do not actually need to install the RPM.

Summary

Creating RPM spec files and maintaining those files can be a difficult chore. A number of tools and add-ons for text editors have sprung up to help make this less of a chore.

Users of the two most common Linux text editors, vi and emacs, can use add-ons that understand the RPM spec file syntax. These add-ons help reduce errors and, though the use of macros, can speed development of spec files by automating some of the tasks.

The RUST tool provides a graphical interface for creating spec files that can simplify a lot of the work normally required.

Once you've created an RPM package, you can use the `rpmlint` command to flag missing, incomplete, or incorrect elements in your RPMs.

Another tool, called `rpm2cpio` in its various incarnations, allows you to extract files from an RPM package by taking advantage of the fact that RPM files use the `cpio` format internally. The `rpm2cpio` tools can output RPM data into the `cpio` format directly; you can then pipe the output to the `cpio` command to extract.

After all this help in making RPMs and spec files, the next chapter covers a set of best-practice guidelines to help avoid problems when making your RPMs.

Chapter 14

Packaging Guidelines

IN THIS CHAPTER

◆ Avoiding common mistakes

◆ Following good practices

RPM IS A COMPLEX SYSTEM that helps manage thousands of packages for a complex operating system. Furthermore, RPM is very, very flexible. This flexibility makes it important that you follow the rules to create packages the proper way. Otherwise, you'll face a host of problems with your RPMs. Following some best-practices guidelines will help you avoid future problems as you release RPM updates.

This chapter covers ways to avoid common problems as well as best-practice guidelines for creating your own RPMs.

Avoiding Common Problems

Developers creating RPMs seem to hit many of the same roadblocks. This section covers some of the most common problems faced by RPM users and package builders.

Never, never, never build RPMs logged in as the root user. See the "Building" section for details.

Scan the mailing lists

Many people have tried to solve a lot of serious problems that arise when using RPM, so if you are facing difficulties, chances are someone else has tackled those issues before. The RPM mailing list provides a technical forum for discussing RPM issues and problems. In many, if not most, cases, you can find answers to problems by scanning the mailing list archives.

You can also sign up for the mailing list so that you can send in requests and see the responses.

For details on viewing the RPM mailing list archives and signing up for the list, see `www.rpm.org/mailing_list/`. See `http://groups.yahoo.com/group/rpm-list/messages` for an archive of the list.

If you are working with RPMs and pushing the envelope for other operating systems or complicated packages, this list is definitely worth a look.

Before sending any messages, though, be sure to look through the message archives to see if the message has already been answered. You will save time waiting for a response if you can get an archived response right away.

You should also ask any questions in a way that will generate the most helpful responses. This includes:

- *Do your homework first.* Check to see if your question has already been answered by looking at the mailing list or newsgroup archives. In the end, this saves you the most time, as you don't have to wait for answers.

- *Describe the problem and the symptoms as clearly as possible.* After all, this is what you want help with.

- *Use clear subject headers.* This is the first part of your message that people will read. If you are not clear, the key people who could answer your questions may never even read your message. And, if they don't read the message, you will never get an answer.

- *Send your message in plain text, not HTML.* Do not include a separate HTML copy of your message. This just makes it harder to read, especially for people who read collected digests of mailing lists.

- *Make it easy for people to reply to you.* Include your e-mail address in your message. You might want to include a line like "Please send your reply to me at" and then provide your e-mail address.

These tips on asking questions come from the Internet document "How to Ask Questions the Smart Way" by Eric Steven Raymond and Rick Moen, available at multiple sites, including `www.owlriver.com/tips/smart`.

In addition to the RPM mailing list, there is also a Usenet newsgroup, named linux.redhat.rpm. You can read this newsgroup with any newsreading program.

Newsgroups are sometimes called discussion groups.

Use rpmbuild

In older versions of RPM, you called the `rpm -ba` command to build RPMs. With RPM 4.1, you must use the `rpmbuild` command. If you have the `rpmbuild` command available, even if you are running an older version of RPM, run `rpmbuild` instead of `rpm` to build your RPMs.

You'd be surprised at how such a simple item is one of the most-asked questions on the RPM mailing list. That's because the `rpm -ba` command, and the other `-b` options, no longer work in RPM 4.1. These options are supported by the `rpmbuild` command.

Don't try to defeat the system

If you are finding your spec files getting more and more complex, and that you are trying to disable RPM features, chances are you are trying to defeat the system. This is not a good idea.

The RPM system works in a certain way. You may not always agree with the way it works, but if you try to make it work in contrary ways, in most cases you'll end up fighting RPM to no avail.

There are certain rules, and more importantly, certain conventions, that RPMs should follow. The previous chapters in this section on building RPMs have outlined those conventions. Follow them. When you go against these conventions, you are really trying to defeat how the RPM system works.

Turn off automatic dependency generation

When you build an RPM, the `rpmbuild` command will automatically generate dependencies on Linux shared libraries and other system commands. You can turn this off if you need to, using a number of means.

You can disable the automatic generation of dependencies by placing the following directive in your spec file:

```
Autoreq: 0
```

A better approach, though, is to override the `%{__find_requires}` and `%{__find_provides}` macros, or just one of these as needed. You can null out either of these macros by adding commands like the following to your spec file:

```
%define __find_requires %{nil}
```

This approach is better because it allows you to override only the `requires` checks. In addition, you can get more specific and simply change how the automatic dependency checks are performed. For example, you can also change the definitions of these macros to perform normal dependency generation except for any problematic files or packages. These two macros resolve to shell scripts that perform the automated dependency checks, as you can see with the `rpm --eval` command:

```
$ rpm --eval "%__find_provides"
/usr/lib/rpm/find-provides
rpm --eval "%__find_requires"
/usr/lib/rpm/find-requires
```

You can override these scripts to filter out any dependencies that cause problems for your packages.

Don't list directories in %files

Unless you really mean it, don't list directories in your `%files` section in your spec files. That is because the `rpmbuild` program will automatically add all files in that directory to your RPM. If this is a system directory, such as /usr/bin, your RPM has now claimed ownership for all the files, regardless of the source package.

To avoid all files in the directory becoming part of the package, list the files explicitly, perhaps generating the list of files as the program builds.

If you do need a directory installed as part of your package, use the `%dir` directive, described in Chapter 10.

Handling circular dependencies

If two packages each depend on the other, you don't want each package's spec file to list the other in a `requires` section. If this occurs, the packages won't install without one of the force options, since each package will require the other to be installed first.

Chapter 4 covers how to install or upgrade packages while ignoring dependency checks. In general, you do not want to ignore these checks.

You can work around this issue by using the `PreReq` directive instead of `Requires`. For example, if package A depends on B and package B depends on A, you can place the following in the package B spec file:

```
PreReq: A
```

In addition, you can install both packages at the same time to avoid some of the problems with circular dependencies. Simply include both packages on the `rpm -Uvh` command line.

Following Good Practices

Working through problems is one thing. It's best, however, to set up an environment to help avoid problems all together. The following sections cover what are considered the best practices for creating RPMs.

Before you make an RPM, you should plan out what you intend to build and how it will be structured. As you build the RPM, you want to watch out for things that can go wrong, and work from a known clean environment.

Preparation

Before you start to make an RPM, you need to follow a few steps to ensure you have everything ready.

Create a Source RPM

Having a source RPM allows you to transfer all the sources for a package from one system to another, along with all the instructions coded in the spec file for actually building the binary package. This is very handy for keeping track of software, and it is also very important since you can regenerate the binary RPM at any time from the source RPM. In other words, make the generation of RPMs follow the RPM conventions and fit this into your normal software build process.

This means that for each RPM you want to build, you really need two: a source and a binary RPM. This isn't that hard to do, since you can easily make a source RPM into a binary RPM with the `rpmbuild` command.

Start with Pristine Sources

In addition to planning on making a source RPM, you should also start with pristine, unmodified sources for the application you plan to package as an RPM. Starting with pristine sources means you can reproduce the entire process and recreate the RPM from scratch if necessary. (Quality control and configuration management people really appreciate this.)

The pristine sources should be exactly the sources you got when you downloaded the application, or acquired it in house. This doesn't mean that you won't have to modify the sources eventually. For that, you create patches. The key is just to start the process with unmodified sources.

Some RPMs have nearly 100 patches that the `rpmbuild` command applies when building the RPM. That is a lot of patches, too many for most applications. Even so, the process is the same. Create a patch or patches for all the changes you need to make. You can easily specify patches in the spec file.

Chapter 10 covers the spec file.

Keeping your patches separate from the original sources makes it easier to reproduce the RPM from scratch, and makes it easier to integrate a new version of the
base software, since your code, in the form of patches, is separated from the base
software code.

Decide What Goes In Each Package

You don't have to stuff all your software into one RPM. Instead, you can often simplify your RPM by dividing it into two or three separate (but likely dependent)
RPMs.

For example, the RPM system itself has one RPM for the basic system, rpm, one
for developers of the RPM system, rpm-devel, and one for those building RPMs,
rpm-build. Yet another RPM provides the Python programming API, rpm-python.

Chapter 17 covers Python programming.

This last division is important. The Python RPM draws in as a dependency the
Python system itself. Adding this into, say, the core RPM package would needlessly
complicate the dependencies for that package.

When dividing your software into RPMs, keep two main issues in mind:

◆ You want to divide the software into RPMs that fit the model for users of
the system.

◆ You want to divide the software into RPMs such that the separate RPMs
are simpler to create and manage.

The RPM system follows these guidelines, especially the first. Few users will
extend the RPM system itself, which allows RPM team to shed this functionality
from the core RPM and contain it in rpm-devel. Those who build RPMs fit into a
different category than those who use RPMs since just about everybody needs to
use RPMs to install packages, but few users actually build RPMs. Again, the sepa-
ration works from a user's perspective.

You also want your package divisions to make each package easier to specify. You
can break particularly tough dependencies into smaller units and simplify things. If
the package division doesn't simplify things, then it may not be a good idea.

Create a Test RPM Database

You don't always have to work with the system RPM database. In fact, while developing RPMs, you probably don't want to change the system database.

If you have a test RPM database, you can install your RPMs into this test database. To do so, use the `--justdb`, `--dbpath`, `--prefix`, and `--badreloc` options. These options allow you to install an RPM into just the database, using a different database, with a different root file location (into a test directory, for example) and handle all files that were not marked for relocation, respectively.

 The `--test` option when installing also allows you to just test the install, not actually perform it.

Combined, all these options mean you can use an RPM database just set up for testing and that problems won't impact your working Linux systems. To make this work, though, you need a test RPM database.

To be rigorous, you should create the test RPM database from scratch from a known set of packages. This will allow you to exactly verify the behavior of your RPM under different system configurations. This is the best choice since you should install the packages under a known, and non-root, directory hierarchy to avoid having file problems with the working system.

If you want to cheat, you can copy your real RPM database to another directory and use that. Note that in this case, the file paths in the database will point to the real file locations on disk.

Regardless of how you create a test database, recreate the database each time you run a test, so that you are sure of a known starting state. Usually this is as simple as copying a master test RPM database into a directory you use for running tests.

Building

Building RPMs isn't as easy as it should be. You'll often need to try again and again to get the `rpmbuild` command to create a working RPM. This section covers best practices to follow when performing the actual build of the RPM.

Use Tools

Using tools can help speed up the RPM-making process, as well as give you a head start in learning how RPMs work. RPM-building tools such as the Red Hat plugin for the Eclipse Integrated Development Environment have proven really helpful.

Chapter 13 covers RPM-building tools. Appendix F covers the Eclipse Integrated Development Environment.

Even though so-called *real* Linux hackers can make a working virtual memory system with just the cat command, don't scoff at tools. Your time is too valuable.

Another useful tool is the gendiff program that comes with the RPM release. The gendiff program makes it easier to create patches by avoiding the need to keep a separate directory of the original sources. The gendiff program also works on all changed files within a directory, making a patch for everything you modified.

To work with gendiff, you first need to save a backup copy of each file you intend to edit prior to editing. Use a consistent file-name extension for the saved copies of the files, such as .orig, short for original. After you edit some files, run the gendiff command as follows:

```
$ gendiff directory_name .saved_extension > patch_name.patch
```

For example, if you saved the original files to a .orig extension, you can create a patch in a directory named src (short for sources) with a command like the following:

```
$ gendiff src .orig > mypatch.patch
```

The patch file mypatch.patch will contain all the differences detected for all files in the given directory.

Never Build RPMs as Root

Never, never, never build RPMs logged in as the root user. Always build your RPMS while logged in as a normal user. This is hard to remember since you must be logged in as root to install an RPM. And you'll want to test each RPM you create to see if it can install cleanly.

Even so, *never build RPMs logged in as the root user.* The RPM spec file has a number of scripts and commands. An error in any of these could cause damage to your system. This includes modifying files, removing files, or copying new contents on top of system files. The root user has permission to perform all these operations.

To avoid all this, build your RPMs while logged in as a normal user. Any problematic scripts should generate errors.

Create a Digital Signature

RPM 4.1 and later revisions place more importance on signing your packages. The rpm command will, by default, verify signatures on each package it reads.

Therefore, you should create a digital signature for your packages, if only to meet user expectations. In addition, you should place a copy of your digital signature on your organization's Web site and public key servers. Having multiple copies in multiple locations helps prevent malicious users from impersonating your keys.

Chapter 12 covers signing packages.

Copy Smartly

Your Linux distribution probably includes more than one CD-ROM chock full of RPMs. Each of these RPMs has a spec file. You can examine these spec files and see how others choose to build their RPMs. Rather than starting from scratch, you can copy declarations from these spec files into your spec file.

Not all these packages were made smartly. Some spec files, as you will see, are a large mess. Obviously, don't copy these. Look for clean spec files with clear directives.

Set Up the BuildRoot

A `BuildRoot` directive sets the location where your code will be built. The convention is for you to define a subdirectory beneath the `_tmppath` directory. For example:

```
BuildRoot: %{_tmppath}/%{name}-buildroot
```

Once set, `rpmbuild` defines the RPM_BUILD_ROOT environment variable to the value specified for the `BuildRoot`.

With the `rpmbuild` command, you can use the `--buildroot` option to specify a directory to use to override the `BuildRoot` directive in the spec file.

Using a `BuildRoot` set to a directory that normal users have write access to allows you to build the package logged in as a normal user. It also helps separate the contents of your package from those of other RPMs.

Always define a `BuildRoot`.

Add changelog entries for each new version

Each time you create a new version in RPM format, you should add an entry to the change log. This allows administrators to get a better idea about what changed from the previous version.

The change log can help people decide whether or not to upgrade a package. A log entry about a security fix, for example, provides useful information to users.

Define the Group For Your Package

Packages are categorized into groups. These group names, while not always the best, appear in the graphical tools such as the Red Hat package manager. If your application is a Linux shell program, then users will expect to find it in the System Environment/Shells group and not the Development/Languages or System Environment/Daemons groups. This is a rather small detail, but it helps users find your package in the huge array of Linux RPMs.

The official list of RPM groups is located in /usr/share/doc/rpm-4.1/GROUPS for RPM 4.1, and similarly-named directories for other RPM versions.

Summary

This chapter covers guidelines for avoiding problems when creating RPMs and following best practices to avoid future problems as well.

When trying to avoid common problems, your best starting point is the RPM mailing list and newsgroup.

For best practices, you should start at the very beginning when you are planning what to build into an RPM. Always start with pristine sources and then patch as needed. Your RPM should include the pristine sources and any necessary patches. You should always create a source RPM, so that you can reproduce your RPM anywhere.

When building RPMs, copy good examples of spec files, as this will get you going far more quickly than any other technique. Use tools to help automate parts of your RPM-building process.

Never build RPMs when logged in as the root user.

This chapter ends the section on building RPMs. The next section covers programming to the RPM APIs.

Part III

Programming RPM

Chapter 15

Automating RPM with Scripts

IN THIS CHAPTER

◆ Deciding when to program and when to script

◆ Examining RPM files with scripts

◆ Querying the RPM database with scripts

THE RPM COMMAND PROVIDES A very high-level view of package management. Most of the operations you need to perform require only a single invocation. Some of the command-line options to the `rpm` command tend to get very complex, however, especially for detailed queries. That's where scripting can help.

This chapter covers scripting, specifically shell scripting, with the `rpm` command, especially useful for newcomers to Linux scripting.

Scripting

Scripting allows you to quickly write new commands in a language, called a scripting language, that can help automate your work. Used heavily by system administrators and lightly by software developers, scripts can help remove some of the tedium from your day-to-day tasks. Scripts can also hold the complex query formats used with the `rpm` command so you don't have to remember them.

Scripts start out as text files. These text files hold commands in the scripting language. Most of these script file commands run commands installed on your system, such as `rpm`. To run a script, invoke a command, called an *interpreter*, that reads in the script file and executes the commands inside the script.

Programming is usually considered different from scripting, even though there are many similarities. Programs start out as text files. These text files hold commands in the programming language and sometimes, not often, calls to commands installed on your system. Programs generally involve more work than scripts and are generally larger, containing more commands.

Furthermore, most programs need to be compiled. A separate command parses the program text files and generates some form of machine code. Multiple pieces of a program may be linked together to form a command you can call from your shell prompt.

Some programming languages, such as Java or C#, are compiled to a generic bytecode format. A compiled Java program, for example, is the same no matter what the architecture. To run such a program, you need a runtime engine such as the `java` command provides. (*Runtime engine* is a fancy term for interpreter.)

Such differences between scripting and programming sometimes get in the way of performing real work. For example, I once worked with a group of people who were convinced that they were not programmers. They felt that programming was an art that was far beyond them. Yet, they wrote hundreds of kilobytes of scripts to create a sophisticated graphical interface for a Computer-Aided Design system. In my mind, they were programming (and doing quite well at it). In their minds, though, there was a clear distinction between scripting – what they could do – and programming, which was beyond them, they thought.

Don't get caught up in this. Use the right tool for the job.

Distinguishing Scripting Languages from Programming Languages

Experts differ regarding what defines a scripting language and what defines a programming language. It's clear that languages such as Python blur the old distinction between programming and scripting.

Originally, scripting was writing small files of commands that invoked other system commands. For example, you could write a script that wraps the Linux `file` command. Scripts were executed by scripting-language interpreters that parsed each command one at a time and then executed the command.

Modern scripting languages, such as Tcl, are parsed at runtime and compiled into an internal bytecode format. Once compiled, there is no real difference from a language associated with programming such as Java.

With a scripting language

◆ You generally don't have to compile the script in advance. The scripting language interpreter may compile the program, often to an internal byte code, but you don't have to invoke a compiler as a separate step.

◆ The facilities of the language generally provide a higher level and more abstract level of interaction with the system than with programming languages. For example, writing socket-based networking code in Tcl requires a lot less code than writing the same code in a programming language such as C. Tcl provides a more abstract view of networking; therefore, your code is a lot simpler.

◆ The commands in the scripting language are mostly the commands available to you on the command line. Scripting languages introduce their own commands, too.

◆ The language is generally identified as a scripting language. This is more consensus than anything else. Forth is considered an interpreted programming language, while Perl is considered a scripting language.

Table 15-1 lists some of the more common scripting and programming languages. Note that these are the generally accepted categories for these languages, not hard and fast rules. This should not stop you, for example, from writing programs in Perl or Python. The distinctions between programming and scripting have blurred in recent years.

TABLE 15-1 COMMON SCRIPTING LANGUAGES AND COMMON
          PROGRAMMING LANGUAGES

Scripting Languages	Programming Languages
Bash (Bourne Again shell)	Assembler
Csh (C shell)	BASIC
JavaScript	C
Ksh (Korn shell)	C++
Lua	C#
MS-DOS batch files	FORTRAN
Perl	Forth
Python	Java
Ruby	LISP
Sh (Bourne shell)	Modula-2, Modula-3
Tcl	Oberon
	Pascal

Deciding When to Program and When to Script

Just as the distinction between programming and scripting languages has blurred in the last few years, so have the guidelines for when you should program and when you should script. The simplest rule remains, though: Use whatever techniques make you productive. In the end, no one really cares if you call it a program or a script.

Even so, these guidelines may help:

◆ If you have to perform a lot of operations on a lot of RPMs, a program will likely perform much faster than a script that calls the `rpm` command over and over.

◆ If the task is relatively simple, scripting generally works best.

◆ If you are more experienced with a particular language, use it.

◆ If you need to perform complex operations, perhaps involving transactions, a program is probably the right way to go.

◆ In many cases, programming languages work better for creating graphical user interfaces, although Python and Perl offer graphical user interface toolkits, such as Perl/Tk or PyQt.

There isn't one right way to do it. Pick what works best for you.

This chapter covers shell scripting. Chapter 16 covers C programming. Chapter 17 covers Python scripting and programming, and Chapter 18 covers Perl scripting.

Shell Scripting Basics

For newcomers to scripting, don't worry. A script, in this case a shell script, is merely a text file with commands mostly the same as the commands you can type at the keyboard. I'll point out the differences.

The following sections quickly introduce scripting for those new to this venture.

Writing a script

For your first venture, enter the following script into a text file:

```
rpm -qa | grep rpm
```

This script has a two-part command. The `rpm -qa` part queries all RPM packages, as covered in Chapter 4. The `grep rpm` part finds only packages with *rpm* in their names. This is a very simple script, but it can serve to show how to work with scripts.

Save this file under the name listrpmpkgs, since this script lists RPM packages.

If you're new to Linux, you'll notice there's no program named Notepad.exe. There are, though, a plethora of Linux text editors to choose from. See Appendix F for a listing of Linux text-editing tools.

Running a script

Once you've entered a script, you can run it with the sh command, as shown following, passing the name of your script to the sh command:

```
$ sh listrpmpkgs
librpm404-devel-4.0.4-8x.27
librpm404-4.0.4-8x.27
rpm404-python-4.0.4-8x.27
rpm-4.1-1.06
rpm-devel-4.1-1.06
gnorpm-0.9-1
rpm-python-4.1-1.06
redhat-rpm-config-8.0-1
rpm-build-4.1-1.06
rpmrebuild-1.0-0
```

Type the command you have placed in your script at the command line. There should be no difference in the output. For example:

```
$ rpm -qa | grep rpm
librpm404-devel-4.0.4-8x.27
librpm404-4.0.4-8x.27
rpm404-python-4.0.4-8x.27
rpm-4.1-1.06
rpm-devel-4.1-1.06
gnorpm-0.9-1
rpm-python-4.1-1.06
redhat-rpm-config-8.0-1
rpm-build-4.1-1.06
rpmrebuild-1.0-0
```

Problems running scripts

The previous script example required the sh program, a Linux shell, to run the script. You also had to have the script file, such as listrpmpkgs, available. So, if you have stored the file in /home2/bin, to run the script, use the following command:

```
$ sh /home2/bin/listrpmpkgs
```

That's not very convenient. Furthermore, you always have to remember where you stored the script file listrpmpkgs. To make this command work better, you can turn your script into a command.

Turning a script into a command

To turn a script into a command, do three simple things:

1. Add a special magic comment to the start of the file so Linux recognizes your text file as a command script.

2. Change the permissions on the file so that it is marked as executable.

3. Copy the file to a directory located in your command path.

Shell scripts use a # to indicate a comment, text intended for human readers that can help explain the purpose of the script. By convention, Linux shells use a #! comment in the first line of a script file as a special marker that indicates the file is a shell script. The text that comes after the #! holds the name of the command that should be used to run the script. In almost all cases, that command should be /bin/sh for a shell script.

So edit the listrpmpkgs script again, and add the magic comment so that the file reads as follows:

```
#!/bin/sh
rpm -qa | grep rpm
```

Make sure the #! comment starts at the beginning of the first line.

Next, change the permissions on the script to mark it as an executable program. Use the chmod command to do this. The chmod command changes the file permissions. To see the permissions, run the ls -l command before changing the permissions:

```
$ ls -l listrpmpkgs
-rw-rw-r-- 1 ericfj  ericfj  31 Nov  7 20:02 listrpmpkgs
```

The first set of characters, the -rw-rw-r--, indicate the permissions in three batches: permissions for the file owner, the owner's group of users, and world (everyone else). The *rw* means read and write, and the *r* alone means read only for everyone not the owner and not in the owner's group.

To add the permission to execute the file for the file owner only, use the following command:

```
$ chmod u+x listrpmpkgs
```

In this command, the u stands for the user who owns the file (for historical reasons, an o stands for *others*, not owner). The +x means add the *x* permission, short for execute permission.

After running this command, you can see the revised permissions.

```
$ ls -l listrpmpkgs
-rwxrw-r-- 1 ericfj  ericfj  31 Nov  7 20:02 listrpmpkgs
```

 Use the man chmod command to see more information on this command.

You now have a command you can run locally. For example:

```
$ ./listrpmpkgs
librpm404-devel-4.0.4-8x.27
librpm404-4.0.4-8x.27
rpm404-python-4.0.4-8x.27
rpm-4.1-1.06
rpm-devel-4.1-1.06
gnorpm-0.9-1
rpm-python-4.1-1.06
redhat-rpm-config-8.0-1
rpm-build-4.1-1.06
rpmrebuild-1.0-0
```

The next step is to copy the file to a directory in your system command path. To see which directories are in your path, run the following command:

```
$ echo $PATH
/usr/local/bin:/usr/bin:/bin:/usr/X11R6/bin:/home/ericfj/bin:/usr/java/j2sdk1.4.0_01/bin
```

Pick one of these directories. The /usr/local/bin directory is a common place to share locally created commands. If this is a personal command for your own use only, a directory under your home directory will be better. In this example, the /home/ericfj/bin is one such directory.

Copy the script file to a directory in your command path, and you are ready to go.

If you use the C shell, `csh`, or the T C shell, `tcsh`, you need to run the `rehash` command to tell the shell to look again at the set of commands available in your command path.

Enter the following command:

```
$ listrpmpkgs
librpm404-devel-4.0.4-8x.27
librpm404-4.0.4-8x.27
rpm404-python-4.0.4-8x.27
rpm-4.1-1.06
rpm-devel-4.1-1.06
gnorpm-0.9-1
rpm-python-4.1-1.06
redhat-rpm-config-8.0-1
rpm-build-4.1-1.06
rpmrebuild-1.0-0
```

You have now extended the Linux command set with your own command.

Windows users may be used to the convention that program file names end in *.exe* and scripts end in *.bat* or *.cmd*. When you run these programs or scripts, you don't include the extension, *exe*, *.bat*, or *.cmd*. With Linux and Unix, though, the full file name is important, so if you name your script rpminfo.bat, you must type rpminfo.bat each time you run the script. That's why most Linux programs and scripts have no filename extension.

If you want to share your script with others, you should give them the right to execute it as well. You can do that with the following command:

```
$ chmod a+x listrpmpkgs
```

In this case, the a stands for all users.

Passing command-line options to your script

The listrpmpkgs script used so far isn't very useful. It performs one command and that's it. We cannot customize it without writing a new script.

One way to make a script more flexible is to allow it to use command-line options. Just like the rpm command accepts a zillion options, you can make your scripts accept options.

Shells define special variables for the command-line options passed to the shell. Table 15-2 lists these options.

TABLE 15-2 SHELL VARIABLES FOR COMMAND-LINE OPTIONS

Variable	Holds
$0	The name of the script itself, from the command line
$1	The first option
$2	The second option
$3	The third option
$4	The fourth option
$5	The fifth option
$6	The sixth option
$7	The seventh option
$8	The eighth option
$9	The ninth option
$*	All command-line options
$#	Holds the number of command-line options

Use $#argv in place of $# if you use the C shell to run your scripts.

You can use these variables to allow the user to pass the text to search for, instead of always searching for *rpm*. With this addition, your new script, renamed rpmgrep, follows in Listing 15-1:

Listing 15-1: rpmgrep

```
#!/bin/sh

rpm -qa | grep $*
```

This script now expects a command-line option that holds the text to search for. Mark this script as an executable; then you can run it as follows:

```
$ ./rpmgrep python
python-devel-2.2.1-17
gnome-python2-gtkhtml2-1.99.11-8
gnome-python2-canvas-1.99.11-8
gnome-python2-1.99.11-8
rpm404-python-4.0.4-8x.27
orbit-python-1.99.0-4
gnome-python2-bonobo-1.99.11-8
gnome-python2-gconf-1.99.11-8
libxslt-python-1.0.19-1
libxml2-python-2.4.23-1
python-optik-1.3-2
python-2.2.1-17
rpm-python-4.1-1.06
mod_python-3.0.0-10
python-tools-2.2.1-17
```

If you want to make this command available, copy it to a directory in your command path as described in the preceding section.

Examining RPM Files

When you work with a lot of RPM files, you'll find that you run the same commands over and over again for each new package you get. For example, you may want to see what capabilities a package requires. You can type in the rpm command each time, or write a short shell script with the necessary command-line options. Listing 15-2 shows this script.

Listing 15-2: rpmdepend

```
#!/bin/sh

rpm -qp --requires $*
```

This script expects the name of an RPM package file. Run the command as follows:

```
$ rpmdepend vim-common-6.1-14.i386.rpm
rpmlib(PayloadFilesHavePrefix) <= 4.0-1
rpmlib(CompressedFileNames) <= 3.0.4-1
/bin/sh
/usr/bin/awk
```

```
libc.so.6
libc.so.6(GLIBC_2.0)
libc.so.6(GLIBC_2.1)
```

Another common task I perform involves listing all the files in an RPM along with the descriptive information on the package. This can really help, since so many Linux packages have nondescriptive names such as dia and anaconda.

Listing 15-3 shows the rpminfo script.

Listing 15-3: rpminfo

```
#!/bin/sh

rpm -qilp $* | less
```

This script lists a potentially long set of lines, so the script pipes the output to the less command. For example:

```
$ ./rpminfo perl-XML-Dumper-0.4-22.noarch.rpm
Name        : perl-XML-Dumper              Relocations: /usr
Version     : 0.4                              Vendor: Red Hat, Inc.
Release     : 22                           Build Date: Tue 06 Aug 2002 01:53:30
PM CDT
Install date: (not installed)             Build Host: vegeta.devel.redhat.com
Group       : System Environment/Libraries  Source RPM: perl-XML-Dumper-
0.4-22.src.rpm
Size        : 10015                           License: GPL
Signature   : DSA/SHA1, Tue 06 Aug 2002 02:11:39 PM CDT, Key ID fd372689897da07a
Packager    : Red Hat, Inc. <http://bugzilla.redhat.com/bugzilla>
URL         : http://www.cpan.org
Summary     : Perl module for dumping Perl objects from/to XML
Description :
XML::Dumper dumps Perl data to XML format. XML::Dumper can also read
XML data that was previously dumped by the module and convert it back
to Perl.  Perl objects are blessed back to their original packaging;
if the modules are installed on the system where the perl objects are
reconstituted from xml, they will behave as expected. Intuitively, if
the perl objects are converted and reconstituted in the same
environment, all should be well.
/usr/lib/perl5/vendor_perl/5.8.0/XML/Dumper.pm
/usr/share/man/man3/XML::Dumper.3pm.gz
```

I use this script so that I know what files a package wants to install.

Querying the RPM Database

In addition to querying RPM files, you can script the commands you use to query the RPM database. This is most useful for the long commands with query formats, especially if you have a hard time remembering all the formats.

Querying for all packages installed at the same time

If you want to list all the packages that were installed with the same transaction ID as a particular package, for example, you can use a script like rpmtran, in Listing 15-4.

Listing 15-4: rpmtran

```
#!/bin/sh

tid=`rpm -q --qf "%{INSTALLTID}\n" $*`

rpm -q --tid $tid
```

This script uses the query format to get the transaction ID, or tid, for a particular package. It then passes this transaction ID to the rpm command to query for all packages installed with the same transaction ID.

For example:

```
$ ./rpmtran tcl
itcl-3.2-74
tclx-8.3-74
tcl-8.3.3-74
tix-8.2.0b1-74
tkinter-2.2.1-17
```

Reading HTML documentation for a package

You can combine the rpm command with other commands as well. For example, the rpm -qd command lists the documentation files with a package. If this documentation is in HTML format, you can display this documentation in a Web browser such as Mozilla. Furthermore, by convention, the starting page for HTML documentation should be a file named index.html. Listing 15-5 combines all these factors:

Listing 15-5: rpmmoz

```
#!/bin/sh

html_file=`rpm -qd $* | grep index.html | head -n 1 `
```

```
echo "Launching Web browser with $html_file"

htmlview $html_file &
```

This script searches for the documentation for a given package name, finds the first file named index.html, and launches the Web browser in the background to display this file, using the `htmlview` command which will likely run `mozilla` or your configured Web browser. When you run this command, you should see output like the following; then the Web browser should appear:

```
$ ./rpmmoz rpm-devel
Launching Web browser with /usr/share/doc/rpm-devel-4.1/apidocs/html/index.html
```

 This script does not check for errors. If there are no files named index.html, the script launches the Web browser anyway. You can fix this by changing the script to validate the html_file variable prior to launching the Web browser.

Where to Go from Here

This chapter just introduces the basics for shell scripting. There are many more things you can do. The online manual pages for the `bash` or `tcsh` commands provide a wealth of reference information on these shells.

A number of Web sites provide tutorials on bash, including `http://pegasus.rutgers.edu/~elflord/unix/bash-tute.html` and `www.linuxorbit.com/modules.php?op=modload&name=Sections&file=index&req=viewarticle&artid=459`. In addition, the Linux Documentation Project at `www.tldp.org/guides.html` provides a bash scripting guide, along with a number of bash- and shell-related how-to documents at `www.tldp.org/HOWTO/HOWTO-INDEX/howtos.html`.

Teach Yourself Linux, by Steve Oualline and Eric Foster-Johnson (John Wiley & Sons, 2000), introduces a number of Linux topics, including text editors and scripting, for those new to Linux. And *Graphical Applications with Tcl and Tk* (Hungry Minds, Inc., 1997) by Eric Foster-Johnson, covers another scripting language, Tcl/Tk.

Use your imagination. Any command that you run often or that is hard to type can be scripted. Furthermore, you can write complex scripts that automate some of the more tedious tasks you need to perform.

Summary

Scripting is the art of writing a set of commands into text files to speed up your work. Programming is the art of writing a set of commands into text files, compiling the text files, and getting paid more. Choosing when to program and when to script isn't always a clear-cut decision, but generally programs are move involved and complex, while scripts are shorter tools that automate your work. This chapter provides just a glimpse of all you can do with scripts and the RPM system.

Scripts work very well for capturing obscure syntax options for the rpm command, especially the query formats. You can figure out a command once and then save the command as a script to save time in the future.

Scripts aren't the best choice for all tasks, though. In many cases, you need to write a program to accomplish your goals. The next chapter delves into the RPM C programming API, rpmlib.

Chapter 16

Programming RPM with C

IN THIS CHAPTER

◆ Using the RPM C library

◆ Setting up a development environment

◆ Programming with the RPM C library

◆ The power of popt for command-line argument processing

◆ Comparing package files to installed packages

THE RPM C LIBRARY ALLOWS YOU to perform all the operations of the `rpm` command from within your own C or C++ programs.

The reason is simple: The `rpm` command was created using the RPM libraries. These same libraries are available for you to use in your own programs.

The `rpm` command itself is quick and, for the most part, simple. So, why would you want to write RPM programs?

There are many reasons, some of which are listed here:

◆ Speed: If you need to perform a task on many RPM files such as verifying a large set of files, then performing the task from one program will be a lot faster than launching the `rpm` command for each file.

◆ Custom options: If you need to do something the `rpm` command doesn't offer, or doesn't make easy, then you may want to write your own program.

◆ Convenience: If you need to make many packages quickly, with custom options, your best bet may be to create a program suited for your tasks. Before doing this, though, be sure to look into whether writing a shell script will handle your task adequately. You'll find writing RPM shell scripts goes much faster than writing whole programs.

◆ Installation programs: The Windows world has standardized on graphical installation programs such as InstallShield or InstallAnywhere. The RPM system, on the other hand, has focused on automated installation with the rpm command. You can combine the best of both worlds by writing a graphical installation program on top of the RPM system.

◆ Integration with environments: You may want to better integrate RPM with a Linux desktop environment such as GNOME or KDE.

♦ Working with other languages: This book covers programming RPM with C, the core language for the library, as well as the Python and Perl scripting languages. You can use the RPM library, though, to help bind with other languages such as Tcl, Ruby, or even C# (especially one of the C# implementations for Linux).

This chapter and the next cover RPM programming. This chapter covers the RPM C programming library, which provides low-level access to RPM functionality. The next chapter covers the RPM Python programming library, which provides a much higher-level of abstraction. If you are attempting to write a complex RPM program, your best bet is to try the Python API first. Even so, there is a lot you can do with the RPM C library.

Programming with the C Library

RPM C programs are C programs that call on functions in the RPM library, often called rpmlib. To use the rpmlib, you need to set up a C programming environment and install the rpm-devel package.

Setting up a C programming environment

At the very least, you'll need a C compiler, gcc, and a text editor. The easiest way to get the C compiler is to install the packages grouped under Software Development with the Red Hat package management tool.

See Chapter 8 for more on the Red Hat package management tool.

The gcc package requires a number of capabilities. Make sure you install all the necessary packages. Just about every Linux distribution includes gcc and everything you need to develop C programs, so this should not be a problem.

For text editors, you can use the vi or emacs text editors, or any of a number of graphical editors such as gedit.

Appendix F covers Linux text editors and development tools.

Once you have a C programming environment set up, you next need to get the RPM library for an RPM development environment.

Setting up the RPM programming environment

To program with the RPM library, you need to install the rpm-devel package. You must have a version of rpm-devel that matches your version of the rpm package. If you have Red Hat Linux, your installation CDs will also have the version of the RPM development package that corresponds to your system.

Your program should link against the same libraries that are used by the rpm command itself in order to insure compatibility, so make sure that the version of the rpm-devel package matches the rpm package itself. In most cases, the best bet is to use the RPM programs and libraries that come with your version of Linux.

You can also download the rpm packages from `ftp://ftp.rpm.org/pub/rpm/dist/`. This site includes versions of the RPM libraries going back to 1996, ancient history in terms of Linux.

The package you need is rpm-devel. If you installed Red Hat Linux 8.0, the package is rpm-devel-4.1-1.06. This package includes header files, documentation, and libraries.

Using the RPM Library

All C programs using the RPM library need to include the file `rpmlib.h`, which defines the core data structures, constants, and functions. One thing you'll quickly note is that the RPM C library accesses RPM data at a very low level. This is one reason why many developers are moving to Python for their RPM programs, since the Python RPM API presents a higher level of abstraction.

Chapter 17 covers programming RPM with Python.

In addition to `rpmlib.h`, the header file `rpmcli.h` defines a high-level API based on the command-line options to the `rpm` command. (The *cli* in rpmcli stands for *command-line interface*.) Table 16-1 lists other important RPM header files that make up the major subsystems of the RPM system.

TABLE 16-1 RPM SUB-SYSTEM HEADER FILES

File	Defines
rpmdb.h	RPM database access
rpmio.h	RPM input/output routines
popt.h	Command-line option processing

In addition, a number of header files define the major data objects in the RPM system and the functions that operate on these data objects. Table 16-2 lists these header files.

TABLE 16-2 RPM DATA OBJECT HEADER FILES

File	Defines
rpmts.h	Transaction sets
rpmte.h	Transaction elements (packages)
rpmds.h	Dependency sets
rpmfi.h	File information
header.h	Package headers

All the RPM include files are located in /usr/include/rpm on most versions of Linux.

You can use the rpm command and the queries introduced in Chapter 5 to determine exactly where the header files are located. Simply execute the following command:

```
$ rpm -ql rpm-devel
```

Examine the output of this command for include files.

Compiling and linking RPM programs

RPM programs using the rpmlib C API are the same as C programs everywhere. You need to include the proper header files that define the API calls you need, and link with the right set of libraries.

Include Files

The rpm include files are located in /usr/include/rpm, so you should add this directory to the set of directories that the C compiler looks in for include files with the -I command-line option. For example:

```
$ gcc -I/usr/include/rpm -c rpm1.c
```

 This also means that you can install the rpm header files in other directories as needed, and just change the -I command-line option.

To help debug problems, you probably want to add the -Wall (output all warnings) and -g (compile with debugging information) options. For example:

```
$ gcc -Wall -g -I/usr/include/rpm -c rpm1.c
```

Libraries

The main rpm library is librpm.a, or a shared version of this same library. To do most anything with RPM programming, you need to link in the following libraries, as listed in Table 16-3.

TABLE 16-3 REQUIRED RPM LIBRARIES

Library	Usage
Rpm	Main RPM library
Rpmdb	RPM database library
Rpmio	RPM input/output
Popt	Command-line option parsing library

If you are creating RPMs from your C programs, you also need to link in the rpmbuild library. To compile and link a simple RPM program, you need a command like the following:

```
gcc -I/usr/include/rpm -o program program.c -lrpmbuild \
      -lrpm -lrpmdb -lrpmio -lpopt
```

On some versions of Linux or on other operating systems, you'll likely need to link a set of helper libraries, as shown following:

```
gcc -I/usr/include/rpm -o program program.c -lrpmbuild \
        -lrpm -lrpmdb -lrpmio -lpopt -lelf -lbz2 -lz
```

If you have installed the rpm libraries in a non-standard directory, you need to use the -L option to specify where else to look for libraries. For example:

```
gcc -I/usr/include/rpm -o program program.c -L/opt/lib/rpm \
        -lrpmbuild -lrpm -lrpmdb -lrpmio -lpopt -lelf -lbz2 -lz
```

The -L option tells the cc compiler to look in the /opt/lib/rpm directory as well as in the standard locations such as /usr/lib.

Starting with RPM 4.2, you should just need to link in the rpm library. The other libraries will get pulled in automatically if needed.

Getting information on your RPM environment

A large part of the RPM system lies in system-specific configuration, including the platform you are running on, compatible platforms, and locations of various files. The RPM *rc* and macro systems support hundreds of options tuned to the specifics of your system, and any customizations you have configured.

Chapter 21 covers customizing RPM.

Your C programs need to access these RPM system settings to ensure that all data values are properly set up for your system architecture and installation. So, to start an RPM C program, you need to read in all the configuration files. To do this, call rpmReadConfigFiles.

```
int rpmReadConfigFiles(const char *files, const char *target);
```

The files parameter holds a colon-delimited list of files that make up your system's configuration. The target parameter holds the target platform. You can pass NULL for both these parameters to use the RPM defaults, which is generally what you want.

The `rpmReadConfigFiles` function returns a 0 on success, or -1 on errors.

Once you have read in the configuration files, you can access values in the configuration, or print it out.

Printing the Configuration

To print out the configuration, call `rpmShowRC`.

```
int rpmShowRC(FILE* output);
```

Pass in an output file to print the configuration to, such as `stdout`. For example:

```
rpmShowRC( stdout );
```

The `rpmShowRC` function always returns 0.

To control some of the output from `rpmShowRC`, and other RPM library functions, you can set the logging verbosity level by calling `rpmSetVerbosity`:

```
void rpmSetVerbosity(int level);
```

For example:

```
rpmSetVerbosity(RPMMESS_NORMAL);
```

Table 16-4 lists the verbosity levels from `rpmio/rpmmessages.h` going from least output to more output.

TABLE 16-4 OUTPUT VERBOSITY LEVELS

Level	Usage
RPMMESS_FATALERROR	Only critical error conditions and above
RPMMESS_ERROR	Only error conditions and above
RPMMESS_WARNING	Only warning conditions and above
RPMMESS_QUIET	Same as RPMMESS_WARNING
RPMMESS_NORMAL	Only significant messages
RPMMESS_VERBOSE	Verbose informational messages
RPMMESS_DEBUG	Debugging messages, and everything above

You can put together a simple RPM program such as the one shown in Listing 16-1.

Listing 16-1: rpm1.c

```
/* Show the rpmrc settings. */
#include <stdio.h>
#include <stdlib.h>

#include <rpmlib.h>


int main(int argc, char *  argv[]) {

    int status = rpmReadConfigFiles( (const char*) NULL,
                   (const char*) NULL);

    if (status != 0) {
        printf("Error reading RC files.\n");
        exit(-1);
    } else {
        printf("Read RC OK\n");
    }

    rpmSetVerbosity(RPMMESS_NORMAL);

    rpmShowRC( stdout );

    exit(0);
}
```

Compile this program with a command like the following:

```
$ cc -I/usr/include/rpm -o rpm1 rpm1.c -lrpm -lrpmdb -lrpmio -lpopt
```

When you run this program, you should see the contents of your configuration printed to the screen.

Expanding the Value of Macros

With all the *rc* and macro configuration files, the RPM system has a lot of values, usually called macros, that you can use to refer to settings. The term *macro* is used because the values can be more than simple strings. You can have one macro refer to the value of other macros, for example. The basic macro syntax is:

%name_of_macro

For example:

```
%_target
```

Most of the internal RPM macros start with an underscore, _.

You can expand a macro with the `rpm --eval` command:

```
$ rpm --eval %_target
i386-linux
```

You can also refer to a macro using the following syntax:

```
%{name_of_macro}
```

For example:

```
%{_target}
```

This syntax makes it easier to include a macro in combinations with other text and other macros, since it clearly delineates the macro name.

Chapter 21 covers macros in depth. In your C programs, your code will likely need to expand the value of macros to place data in the proper directories, determine the platform architecture, and so on.

Expanding Macros in Your Code

You can use `rpmExpand` to determine the value of system macros from within your C programs.

The `rpmExpand` function can expand the values of one or more macros, returning the expanded value. You can pass a variable number of parameters to `rpmExpand`, and you must terminate the list with a `NULL`:

```
char* rpmExpand (const char *arg,...);
```

You need to free the data returned by `rpmExpand` by calling `free`.

The program in Listing 16-2 takes the first command-line argument to your program (after the program name) and expands that argument as a macro.

Listing 16-2: rpmexpand.c

```c
/* Show some macro settings. */
#include <stdio.h>
#include <stdlib.h>

#include <rpmlib.h>
#include <rpmmacro.h>

int main(int argc, char * argv[]) {

    int status = rpmReadConfigFiles( (const char*) NULL,
                        (const char*) NULL);

    if (status != 0) {
        printf("Error reading RC files.\n");
        exit(-1);
    }

    char* value = rpmExpand(argv[1], (const char*) NULL);

    printf("Value of macro is [%s]\n", value);

    exit(0);
}
```

Compile and link this program as shown previously.

When you run this program, pass the name of a macro to expand. For example:

```
$ ./rpmexpand %_target
Value of macro is [i386-linux]
```

You can pass multiple macros together, as shown following:

```
$ ./rpmexpand %_builddir/%_target
Value of macro is [/usr/src/redhat/BUILD/i386-linux]
```

You can verify this program with the `rpm --eval` command, introduced previously:

```
$ rpm --eval %_builddir/%_target
/usr/src/redhat/BUILD/i386-linux
```

The Power of popt

Popt provides a powerful command-line processing library, allowing the `rpm` command to handle a variety of options in a very flexible way. You can use popt alone as a library in its own right, or use it combined with the rpm library to handle command-line options like those of the `rpm` command.

At its most basic, popt processes the command-line arguments to a C program, traditionally called `argc` and `argv`, into an option table that describes and contains all the option values.

The main advantage popt has over simpler libraries such as `getopt` lies in the ability to handle complex arguments and to define aliases. The `rpm` command supports three different behaviors for the `-i` option, depending on the context (install a package, get information on a package as part of a query, and perform the install stage of a source RPM, as part of `rpmbuild`).

The popt library supports both traditional Unix short options such as `-U` and the longer options common for GNU programs, especially on Linux, such as `--upgrade`. For the popt library, you can define both short and long variants for each option. In addition, command-line options may be individual flags, such as `-v` for verbose, or options that expect one or more data values as arguments, such as `-f`, which requires a file name.

Popt aliases

One of the most powerful features of popt is the ability to define aliases. A popt alias allows you to define one command-line option as an alias for a set of options. As its simplest, the `rpm` command-line options `--upgrade` and `-U` refer to the same action. You could define one as an alias for the other.

With rpm, the file /usr/lib/rpm/rpmpopt-4.1 (for RPM version 4.1) defines over 400 lines of popt aliases to configure the `rpm` command-line options. For example:

```
Rpm    alias -requires    --qf \
   "[%{REQUIRENAME} %{REQUIREFLAGS:depflags} %{REQUIREVERSION}\n]" \
   --POPTdesc=$"list capabilities required by package(s)"
```

This example defines `rpm --requires` as really a query using the `--qf` or `--queryformat` options covered in Chapter 5.

See Chapter 21 for more on defining popt aliases.

Programming with popt

To use popt in your programs, you need to fill in a table of options and then call poptGetContext. The poptGetContext function parses the command-line options and returns a poptContext, an opaque data type that you need to pass as a parameter to a number of popt functions. The poptContext holds the state of your command-line processing. This allows you to call the popt library with multiple sets of arguments. Each set will have an associate poptContext to keep all the data separate.

The basic poptGetContext function signature follows:

```
poptContext poptGetContext (const char * name,
    int argc,
    const char ** argv,
    const struct poptOption * options,
    int flags );
```

All the popt functions require the popt.h include file:

```
#include <popt.h>
```

The flags should be a bitmask of any options you require, including those listed in Table 16-5.

TABLE 16-5 FLAGS FOR poptGetContext

Flag	Meaning
POPT_CONTEXT_NO_EXEC	Ignore executable expansions
POPT_CONTEXT_KEEP_FIRST	Treat argv[0], the command name, as an option
POPT_CONTEXT_POSIXMEHARDER	Do not allow options to follow arguments

When done with a poptContext, you should free it by calling poptFreeContext:

```
poptContext poptFreeContext(poptContext context);
```

The call to poptFreeContext frees up the memory allocated for the context.

You can also fill in a `poptContext` from settings in a file with `poptReadConfigFile`:

```
int poptReadConfigFile(poptContext context,
    const char * file_name);
```

Filling in the Options Table

You need to pass in a table that defines all the possible options. This table is an array of structures, where each structure defines one option. The format for a single option follows:

```
struct poptOption {
    const char * longName;
    char shortName;
    int argInfo;
    void * arg;
    int val;
    const char * descrip;
    const char * argDescrip;
};
```

Going through this structure, the `longName` defines the long version of the option, such as "upgrade" for --upgrade. The `shortName` defines the short, one-character option, such as 'U' for an option of -U. You can place a null character, '\0', to specify no short option. With the `rpm` command, the --rebuilddb option has only a long name and not a short name, for example.

The `longName` is not preceded by the double minus sign. Similarly, the `shortName` is not preceded by the single minus sign.

The `descrip` field holds a short description of the option and the `argDescrip` field holds a description of the types of values it expects, or `NULL` if this option expects no values.

The `argInfo` field holds a flag that tells the popt library how to treat the option. At the very least, you need to define the type of the option. You can also define special processing flags. Table 16-6 lists the argument types in the options table.

TABLE 16-6 POPT OPTION TABLE ARGINFO ARGUMENT TYPES

Type	Value	Meaning
POPT_ARG_NONE	0	No argument data, just the option such as -v
POPT_ARG_STRING	1	arg treated as string
POPT_ARG_INT	2	arg treated as int
POPT_ARG_LONG	3	arg treated as long
POPT_ARG_INCLUDE_TABLE	4	arg points to a table
POPT_ARG_CALLBACK	5	arg points to a callback function
POPT_ARG_INTL_DOMAIN	6	sets translation domain
POPT_ARG_VAL	7	use value of val field for arg
POPT_ARG_FLOAT	8	arg treated as float
POPT_ARG_DOUBLE	9	arg treated as double

Use these constants, from the include file popt.h, in place of the actual numbers.

Depending on the type you define in the argInfo field, popt will interpret the generic pointer field, arg, in different ways. Using a pointer allows the popt library to automatically update your program variables based on the command-line option settings.

You can pass NULL for the arg field. In this case, the popt library will not set any values for you.

The POPT_ARG_NONE type indicates that this option has no argument. For example, the -v verbose option has no data. On the other hand, the POPT_ARG_STRING type indicates that the user should provide a string. For example, the -f option to the rpm command is expected to include a string argument, the name of the file to look up.

If the argInfo argument type is POPT_ARG_NONE, the popt library will set arg to 1 if the option is present on the command line. You should pass a pointer to an int if you want this set for you.

Popt Callbacks

The `POPT_ARG_CALLBACK` type indicates that the `arg` field holds a function pointer to a callback function of the following type:

```
typedef void (*poptCallbackType) (poptContext con,
    enum poptCallbackReason reason,
    const struct poptOption * opt,
    const char * arg,
    const void * data);
```

The callback `reason` will be one of the following `enum` values:

```
enum poptCallbackReason {
    POPT_CALLBACK_REASON_PRE    = 0,
    POPT_CALLBACK_REASON_POST   = 1,
    POPT_CALLBACK_REASON_OPTION = 2
};
```

The `data` field holds the value of the `descrip` field in the `poptOption` entry. You can cheat and stuff a pointer to arbitrary data into this field.

The callback function is most useful if you are using nested option tables. You can place your processing code for the nested options into a callback.

Special Option Table Flags

In addition to the types in Table 16-6, you can also define special bit flags that define extra processing information for each option. Combine these bit flags with the type values using a logical OR operation:

- ◆ The `POPT_ARGFLAG_ONEDASH` flag allows the `longName` to be used with one or two dashes, such as `-upgrade` or `--upgrade`.

- ◆ For bitmask options, the `POPT_ARGFLAG_OR`, `POPT_ARGFLAG_NOR`, `POPT_ARGFLAG_AND`, `POPT_ARGFLAG_NAND`, and `POPT_ARGFLAG_XOR` type flags tell the popt library to apply the given operation, OR, NOR, AND, NAND, or XOR, to the value if set. The `POPT_ARGFLAG_NOT` flag tells the popt library to negate the value first.

- ◆ You can also use the macros `POPT_BIT_SET` to set a bit and `POPT_BIT_CLR` to clear a bit.

- ◆ The `POPT_ARGFLAG_OPTIONAL` flag indicates that the argument value is optional.

- ◆ The `POPT_ARGFLAG_DOC_HIDDEN` flag tells popt to hide this option when displaying the help documentation. In other words, this is an internal option.

◆ The rarely used POPT_ARGFLAG_STRIP flag tells popt to consume an option and ignore it. This option is rarely used.

◆ The POPT_ARGFLAG_SHOW_DEFAULT flag tells popt to show the initial value of the argument for this option as a default when displaying a help message.

Magic Options

With RPM programs, developers usually round out the option table with three special options: POPT_AUTOALIAS, POPT_AUTOHELP, and POPT_TABLEEND. The POPT_AUTOALIAS option sets up a table of aliases:

```
#define POPT_AUTOALIAS { NULL, '\0', POPT_ARG_INCLUDE_TABLE, poptAliasOptions, \
                    0, "Options implemented via popt alias/exec:", NULL },
```

This option refers to the table, poptAliasOptions. You can use the POPT_ARG_INCLUDE_TABLE argInfo type to include another table of options. These options get filled in from popt aliases. In addition, within RPM programs, another table, rpmcliAllPoptTable, holds a set of options common to all RPM programs.

The POPT_AUTOHELP option supports standard help options. The POPT_AUTOHELP macro adds in automatic support for -?, --help, and --usage options.

```
#define POPT_AUTOHELP { NULL, '\0', POPT_ARG_INCLUDE_TABLE, poptHelpOptions, \
                    0, "Help options:", NULL },
```

The POPT_TABLEEND option defines an empty option to mark the end of the table. You must include an empty option to end the table, and POPT_TABLEEND makes this easy.

```
#define POPT_TABLEEND { NULL, '\0', 0, 0, 0, NULL, NULL }
```

The code in Listing 16-3, in the "Running a popt example" section later in this chapter, shows a full option table.

Parsing the Command-Line Options

Once you have set up a poptGetContext, you need to iterate over all the command-line parameters. To do this, call poptGetNextOpt:

```
int poptGetNextOpt(poptContext context);
```

If an error occurs, `poptGetNextOpt` returns a negative error code. If the context is at the end of the options, `poptGetNextOpt` returns -1. Table 16-7 lists the error codes:

TABLE 16-7 ERROR CODES FROM POPTGETNEXTOPT

Code	Meaning
POPT_ERROR_NOARG	Option requires an argument, but it is missing
POPT_ERROR_BADOPT	Argument could not be parsed
POPT_ERROR_OPTSTOODEEP	Aliases are nested too deeply
POPT_ERROR_BADQUOTE	Start and end quotation marks don't match
POPT_ERROR_BADNUMBER	Argument could not be converted to a number
POPT_ERROR_OVERFLOW	Argument number was too big or too small
POPT_ERROR_ERRNO	A system call returned an error in errno

Walking Through the Command-Line Options

In normal circumstances, `poptGetNextOpt` parses all the options and returns -1. If your needs are simple, you can use the pointers to the variables passed in the options table, described previously. If you need some special processing for options not handled by popt, that is, options of type `POPT_ARG_NONE`, then `poptGetNextOpt` returns the single-character option.

In this case, you can call `poptGetNextOpt` in a `while` loop. For example:

```
while ((option = poptGetNextOpt(context) ) {
    /* Do something... */
}
```

Inside your `while` loop, you can call `poptGetOptArg` to get the value of the argument:

```
char * poptGetOptArg(poptContext context);
```

You can restart the processing of the options by calling `poptResetContext`:

```
void poptResetContext(poptContext context);
```

The popt system is just looking for arguments that start with a dash, -. In most command-line applications, you may have a number of extra arguments at the end, such as a list of file names. The popt library doesn't process these, but can provide them to you.

Call `poptGetArg` to return the next extra argument:

```
char * poptGetArg(poptContext context);
```

Keep calling this function until it returns NULL.

Call `poptPeekArg` to look at the next argument but not mark it as being processed:

```
char * poptPeekArg(poptContext context);
```

Or, you can get the whole list of extra arguments by calling `poptGetArgs`:

```
char ** poptGetArgs(poptContext context);
```

Handling Errors

Inside your `while` loop processing the command-line arguments, you can call `poptBadOption` to get the option that was bad, and `poptStrerror` to look up the error message associated with the error.

For `poptBadOption`, you need to pass in the context, and a bitmask of flags. Normally, pass 0 for no flags or `POPT_BADOPTION_NOALIAS`, which tells popt to return the actual option, not a value defined in an alias. This makes `poptBadOption` return the option closest to, if not exactly the same as, what the user entered, which makes for better error reporting.

The `poptBadOption` function signature follows:

```
char * poptBadOption(poptContext context, int flags);
```

Pass the error number returned by `poptGetOptArg` to `poptStrerror` to get the standard error message for that option:

```
const char * poptStrerror(const int error_code);
```

You can combine these and print out an error with code like the following:

```
fprintf( stderr, "Error with option [%s]\n %s",
    poptBadOption(context, POPT_BADOPTION_NOALIAS),
    poptStrerror(error_code);
```

To print out a usage message, call `poptPrintUsage`:

```
void poptPrintUsage(poptContext context,
    FILE *output,
    int flags);
```

This function prints out the usage help information, which is a useful function when the user has called a program with incomplete or wrong options.

Running a popt example

Pulling this all together, you can use the popt1.c program, in Listing 16-3, as an example for using popt to process command-line options.

Listing 16-3: popt1.c

```
/* Processes command-line options. */

#include <stdio.h>
#include <stdlib.h>

#include <popt.h>

/* Data values for the options. */
static int intVal = 55;
static int print = 0;

static char* stringVal;


void callback(poptContext context,
    enum poptCallbackReason reason,
    const struct poptOption * option,
    const char * arg,
    const void * data)
{
    switch(reason)
    {
        case POPT_CALLBACK_REASON_PRE:
            printf("\t Callback in pre setting\n"); break;
        case POPT_CALLBACK_REASON_POST:
            printf("\t Callback in post setting\n"); break;
        case POPT_CALLBACK_REASON_OPTION:
            printf("\t Callback in option setting\n"); break;
    }
}
```

Continued

Listing 16-3 *(Continued)*

```
/* Set up a table of options. */
static struct poptOption optionsTable[] = {
 { (const) "int", (char) 'i', POPT_ARG_INT, (void*) &intVal, 0,
 (const) "follow with an integer value", (const) "2, 4, 8, or 16" },

 { "callback", '\0', POPT_ARG_CALLBACK|POPT_ARGFLAG_DOC_HIDDEN,
 &callback, 0, NULL, NULL },

 { (const) "file", (char) 'f', POPT_ARG_STRING, (void*) &stringVal, 0,
 (const) "follow with a file name", NULL },

 { (const) "print", (char) 'p', POPT_ARG_NONE, &print, 0,
 (const) "send output to the printer", NULL },

   POPT_AUTOALIAS
   POPT_AUTOHELP
   POPT_TABLEEND
};

int main(int argc, char *argv[]) {

    poptContext context = poptGetContext(
        (const char*) "popt1",
        argc,
        argv,
        (const struct poptOption* ) &optionsTable,
        0);


    int option = poptGetNextOpt(context);
    printf("option = %d\n", option);

    /* Print out option values. */
    printf("After processing, options have values:\n");

    printf("\t intVal holds %d\n", intVal);
    printf("\t print flag holds %d\n", print);
    printf("\t stringVal holds [%s]\n", stringVal);

    poptFreeContext(context);

    exit(0);
}
```

This example defines a callback but otherwise uses the simplest case for processing the command-line options. This program lets the popt library simply set the values into the option table. In most cases, you should avoid more complex command-line processing.

To compile popt programs, you just need the popt library. For example:

```
gcc -I/usr/include/rpm -o popt1 popt1.c -lpopt
```

When you run this program, try out the different options. For example, when you set all the options, you'll see output like the following:

```
$ ./popt1 -i 42 --print -f filename1
        Callback in option setting
        Callback in option setting
        Callback in post setting
option = -1
After processing, options have values:
        intVal holds 42
        print flag holds 1
        stringVal holds [filename1]
```

This command used two short options and one long. You can mix and match short and long options, as shown following:

```
$ ./popt1 --int 42 -p --file filename1
        Callback in option setting
        Callback in option setting
        Callback in post setting
option = -1
After processing, options have values:
        intVal holds 42
        print flag holds 1
        stringVal holds [filename1]
```

This example used a short option for print, -p, and long options for the other two options. The popt library also provides handy help and usage messages, using the option table macro POPT_AUTOALIAS. To get a help message, use --help or -?:

```
$ ./popt1 --help
Usage: popt1 [OPTION...]
  -i, --int=2, 4, 8, or 16     follow with an integer value
  -f, --file=STRING            follow with a file name
  -p, --print                  send output to the printer

Options implemented via popt alias/exec:
```

```
Help options:
  -?, --help                 Show this help message
  --usage                    Display brief usage message
```

Notice how the help descriptions from the options table are used.

 With some shells, especially the tcsh shell, you need to wrap a -? in single quotes. For example:

```
$ ./popt1 '-?'
```

The usage message is shorter, and you also get it for free:

```
$ ./popt1 --usage
Usage: popt1 [-i|--int 2, 4, 8, or 16] [-f|--file STRING] [-p|--print]
        [-?|--help] [--usage]
```

All in all, the popt library provides a handy library for processing command-line options and aliases, covered in Chapter 21.

Handling rpm command-line options

The RPM C library makes extensive use of popt for processing command-line arguments. Functions that set up the RPM library, such as rpmcliInit, which sets up the RPM command-line environment, require a table of poptOption entries that define the command-line options for your program.

To create a simple program that handles the standard rpm command-line options, set up the following options table:

```
static struct poptOption optionsTable[] = {

  { NULL, '\0', POPT_ARG_INCLUDE_TABLE, rpmcliAllPoptTable, 0,
       "Common options for all rpm modes and executables:",
       NULL },

    POPT_AUTOALIAS
    POPT_AUTOHELP
    POPT_TABLEEND
};
```

Then, initialize your program with a call to rpmcliInit:

```
poptContext rpmcliInit(int argc, char *const argv[],
    struct poptOption * optionsTable);
```

When you call `rpmcliInit`, it will set up all the variables for the standard rpm command-line options.

For example, to see if the verbose flag is turned on, call `rpmIsVerbose`:

```
int rpmIsVerbose();
```

When you are done with a program that called `rpmcliInit`, call `rpmcliFini` to clean up the global data:

```
poptContext rpmcliFini(poptContext context);
```

The call to `rpmcliFini` returns NULL.

Working with RPM Files

The RPM C library provides functions to read RPM files as well as query the RPM database. Going beyond querying, you can perform all the tasks that the `rpm` and `rpmbuild` commands do, since both these commands are written in C using the RPM library. That said, some tasks are much easier than other tasks. If you are writing a complex package installation program, or a program that keeps various systems up to date with regards to package versions, you may want to look at the Python RPM API instead of the C RPM library.

Chapter 17 covers the Python RPM API.

Opening RPM files

When working with an RPM file from within a program, the first thing you need to do is open the file. Use `Fopen`:

```
FD_t Fopen(const char * path,
    const char * fmode);
```

`Fopen` works like the standard C function `fopen(3)`.

The reason the RPM library wraps the input/output C library functions is to ensure portability to other operating systems. This is a fairly common technique.

Reading the RPM lead and signature

Once you have opened an RPM file, you can start to read header information, which is the most interesting information to most RPM programs. (You may also want to read the files in the RPM payload, for example.) Before you can start reading the header, though, you must read forward in the RPM file past the lead and signature.

 Chapter 3 introduces the lead and signature.

Even if your programs don't want to examine the lead or signature, you must read past to position the file offset properly for reading the header information. To read past the lead, call readLead:

```
int readLead(FD_t fd, struct rpmlead *lead);
```

The readLead function returns 0 on success or 1 on an error. It fills in an rpmlead struct:

```
struct rpmlead {
    unsigned char magic[4];
    unsigned char major;
    unsigned char minor;
    short type;
    short archnum;
    char name[66];
    short osnum;
    short signature_type;
    char reserved[16];
};
```

To read past the signature, call rpmReadSignature:

```
rpmRC rpmReadSignature(FD_t fd,
    Header * header,
    sigType sig_type);
```

The return code is one of the values listed in Table 16-8.

TABLE 16-8 RETURN CODES FROM RPMREADSIGNATURE

Code

RPMRC_OK

RPMRC_BADMAGIC

RPMRC_FAIL

RPMRC_BADSIZE

RPMRC_SHORTREAD

You can do more with the signature than merely reading past it, of course. Look in the online RPM documentation for more on verifying signatures.

After reading the signature, you can start to read the general header entries.

Reading header information

The header information includes the package name, version, pre- and post-installation scripts, and so on. To read in the RPM header, call `headerRead`. If successful, `headerRead` returns a `Header` object. You can then read data values from the Header.

```
Header headerRead(FD_t fd,
    enum hMagic magicp);
```

 When working with the RPM database, you will also use `Header` objects.

The trickiest thing about calling `headerRead` is that you must pass a special magic number flag. This value must be `HEADER_MAGIC_YES` if the header has a set of magic numbers, and `HEADER_MAGIC_NO` if not. If you guess incorrectly, `headerRead` will return an error. To get around this, you can compare the major number in the lead. For example:

```
Header header = headerRead(fd, (lead.major >= 3) ?
        HEADER_MAGIC_YES : HEADER_MAGIC_NO);
```

This snippet is one of the gems you'll find when you browse the RPM source code. Use the source.

To read values from the Header, call headerGetEntry. To call headerGetEntry, you pass in a Header and a tag ID. You get back the type of the tag, a pointer to the tag values, and a count of the number of values stored under this tag.

```
int headerGetEntry(Header header,
    int_32 tag,
    hTYP_t type,
    void **pointer,
    hCNT_t data_size);
```

The call to headerGetEntry returns a 1 on success, or a 0 on failure. On success, the pointer will point at the retrieved data, with the type parameter set to one of the following enum values:

```
enum  rpmTagType_e {
  RPM_NULL_TYPE = 0,
  RPM_CHAR_TYPE = 1,
  RPM_INT8_TYPE = 2,
  RPM_INT16_TYPE = 3,
  RPM_INT32_TYPE = 4,
  RPM_STRING_TYPE = 6,
  RPM_BIN_TYPE = 7,
  RPM_STRING_ARRAY_TYPE = 8,
  RPM_I18NSTRING_TYPE
}
```

If the type is RPM_STRING_ARRAY_TYPE or RPM_BIN_TYPE, you must free the pointer. Call headerFreeData to free the data:

```
void* headerFreeData(const void *pointer,
rpmTagType type);
```

You need to pass in the data pointer and the type flag. You can safely call headerFreeData for all types. The function will do nothing if the type is not set up to require freeing.

When you call `headerGetEntry`, you must identify the tag you want from the header. This tag is an identifier for the `--queryformat` tags introduced in Chapter 5. The file `rpmlib.h` lists the various tags, such as `RPMTAG_NAME`, `RPMTAG_VERSION`, and `RPMTAG_RELEASE`.

The following function shows how to read a string entry from a `Header`:

```
/* Function to read a string header entry. */
char* readHeaderString(Header header, int_32 tag_id) {

    int_32 type;
    void* pointer;
    int_32 data_size;

    int header_status = headerGetEntry(header,
        tag_id,
        &type,
        &pointer,
        &data_size);

    if (header_status) {

        if (type == RPM_STRING_TYPE) {
            return pointer;
        }
    }

    return NULL;
}
```

Pass the `Header` object and the ID of the tag to read. For example:

```
char* name    = readHeaderString(header, RPMTAG_NAME);
char* version = readHeaderString(header, RPMTAG_VERSION);
char* release = readHeaderString(header, RPMTAG_RELEASE);
```

To just get the name, version, and release number, you can call the utility function `headerNVR`, which has the following function signature:

```
int headerNVR(Header header,
    const char **nameptr,
    const char **versionptr,
    const char **releaseptr);
```

When you are through with a header, free it by calling headerFree:

```
Header headerFree(Header header);
```

The call to headerFree returns NULL, so you can use the call to set the original pointer to NULL to prevent accidental reuse. For example:

```
header = headerFree(header);
```

A shortcut to header information

You can read in a Header using the shortcut utility method rpmReadPackageFile:

```
int rpmReadPackageFile(rpmts ts,
    FD_t fd,
    const char *filename,
    Header *header);
```

You need to pass a transaction set to rpmReadPackageFile and an open file. The filename is just used for reporting errors. On success, rpmReadPackageFile fills in a Header object from the package file. The return value is 0 for success.

To get the necessary transaction set, you need to create one with rpmtsCreate, covered in the "Programming with the RPM Database" section, following.

In most cases, you should call rpmReadPackageFile in place of readLead, rpmReadSignature, and headerRead, since rpmReadPackageFile also verifies the package integrity.

Closing RPM files

When you're done with an RPM file, close it with Fclose:

```
int Fclose(FD_t fd);
```

Fclose acts much like the standard C function fclose(3). The FD_t is an RPM data type that is very similar to a FILE pointer.

The RPM I/O subsystem, defined with rpmio.h, includes functions that mimic (and in most cases wrap) the ANSI C stdio functions. These include: Fopen, Fclose, Fread, Fwrite, Ferror, Fflush, Fileno, and Fseek.

These functions wrap the ANSI C stdio functions to add new features. The Fopen function, for example, supports HTTP or FTP URLs in the place of a file name, so long as you append ".ufdio" to the mode.

Programming with the RPM Database

Many functions in rpmlib require a transaction set. In particular, accessing the rpm database is quite easy using a transaction set.

Create a transaction set by calling rpmtsCreate:

```
rpmts rpmtsCreate(void);
```

RPM uses transaction sets to bracket operations on the RPM database. As the RPM API evolves, transaction sets will become more and more important. Transaction sets also help in that the RPM library will automatically open the RPM database as needed.

When you are done with a transaction set, call rpmtsFree:

```
rpmts rpmtsFree(rpmts ts);
```

The call to rpmtsFree returns NULL.

Database iterators

Once you have a transaction set, you can iterate over the installed packages in the RPM database by creating an *iterator*. To do this, call rpmtsInitIterator:

```
rpmdbMatchIterator rpmtsInitIterator(const rpmts ts,
    rpmTag rpmtag,
    const void *keypointer,
    size_t keylen);
```

You need to specify which tag to iterate by, which in most cases will be the package name, RPMTAG_NAME, introduced previously. With the RPMTAG_NAME tag, you need to pass the name of a package to look for in the keypointer parameter. (The keypointer varies based on the tag you pass.)

For string data, you can pass 0 for the keylen parameter. For example, this call to rpmtsInitIterator looks for all packages named *sendmail*.

```
rpmdbMatchIterator iter;
iter = rpmtsInitIterator(ts, RPMTAG_NAME, "sendmail", 0);
```

The rpmdbMatchIterator allows you to iterate through a number of packages, in this case, all the packages that match a given name. After calling rpmtsInitIterator, the next step is to call rpmdbNextIterator:

```
Header rpmdbNextIterator(rpmdbMatchIterator iter);
```

This function returns the next package `Header` object in the iterator. The `Header` will be `NULL` if there are no more packages in the iterator.

If the `Header` is not `NULL`, you can get entries from it, as shown previously. You can use a while loop to go through all the matching packages. For example:

```
while ( (installed_header = rpmdbNextIterator(iter) ) != NULL) {
    /* Do something... */
}
```

 In future versions of the RPM library, `rpmtsNextIterator`, will replace `rpmdbNextIterator`.

You do not need to free the `Header` returned by `rpmdbNextIterator`. Also, the next call to `rpmdbNextIterator` will reset the `Header`.

You can customize how an iterator works by adding a pattern to the iterator with `rpmdbSetIteratorRE`:

```
int rpmdbSetIteratorRE(rpmdbMatchIterator iter,
    rpmTag tag,
    rpmMireMode mode,
    const char * pattern);
```

Calling `rpmdbSetIteratorRE` modifies the passed-in iterator to use the given pattern as a further test on the given tag. The mode parameter names the type of pattern used, which can be one of those listed in Table 16-9.

TABLE 16-9 TYPES OF PATTERNS FOR RPMDBSETITERATORRE

Type	Meaning
RPMMIRE_DEFAULT	Same as regular expressions but with \., .*, and ^..$ added
RPMMIRE_GLOB	Glob-style patterns using `fnmatch`
RPMMIRE_REGEX	Regular expressions using `regcomp`
RPMMIRE_STRCMP	String comparisons using `strcmp`

For more on these patterns, see the online manual pages for fnmatch(3), glob(7), regcomp(3), regex(7), and strcmp(3).

Free the iterator when done with `rpmdbFreeIterator`:

```
rpmdbMatchIterator rpmdbFreeIterator(rpmdbMatchIterator iter);
```

The call to `rpmdbFreeIterator` returns NULL.

Dependency sets

To compare package versions, create a dependency set. The `rpm` command, for example, uses dependency sets to compare package versions.

You could compare the version numbers directly, calling `headerGetEntry` to get the version and release tags, converting these strings to numbers and then comparing, but this would cause problems. The custom comparison is not as exact as the code in this section, especially since many packages have version numbers that are not true numbers, such as 1.12.4, with one too many decimal points. This makes the comparisons harder. In addition, there is more than just the version number to take into account. You need to deal with the Epoch value, as well as the release, too.

To handle all the complicated logic of comparing versions, you can use the code in this section, or call `rpmvercmp`. Do not try to compare version numbers with custom code.

To create a dependency set for a given package `Header`, call `rpmdsThis`. Calling `rpmdsThis` creates a dependency set that holds a triple of the package name, the Epoch/Version/Release information, and the flags.

```
rpmds rpmdsThis(Header header,
    rpmTag tagID,
    int_32 Flags);
```

For comparing packages, you can pass `RPMTAG_REQUIRENAME` for the `tagID`. The actual `tagID` here is ignored for the version check. What you do need, though, are flags to check whether another package is less than or equal to the Epoch/Version/ Release information in this dependency set. For this task, pass the following bit flags:

```
(RPMSENSE_EQUAL|RPMSENSE_LESS)
```

Once you have a dependency set, you can use the handy function rpmdsNVRMatchesDep to compare the *NVR*, or Name, Version, Release entries in the header of one package against the data in the dependency set.

```
int rpmdsNVRMatchesDep(const Header header,
    const rpmds dependency_set,
    int nopromote);
```

After checking the dependencies, rpmdsNVRMatchesDep returns 1 if the dependency overlaps, or 0 otherwise. In terms of comparing packages, 1 means that the package file is as old or older than the installed package, and 0 means that the package already installed is newer. Pass 1 to prevent promoting the Epoch value in the packages during the comparison.

The actual comparison is controlled by the call that creates the dependency set, especially the flags. Thus, passing flags of (RPMSENSE_EQUAL|RPMSENSE_LESS) to rpmdsThis set up the test as a less than or equal test.

 The RPM C API documentation marks rpmdsNVRMatchesDep as deprecated, to be replaced in the future.

You can also call rpmVersionCompare to compare the versions of two packages:

```
int rpmVersionCompare(Header header1, Header header2);
```

The return value is -1 if the header1 represents an older version than header2, 0 if the two headers represent the same version, and 1 if header1 represents a newer version than header2.

To get the name of the package from a dependency set, call rpmdsN:

```
const char* rpmdsN(const rpmds dependency_set);
```

You can use rpmdsN to get the name when calling rpmtsInitIterator if you are working with dependency sets when searching the RPM database.

Free a dependency set when done by calling rpmdsFree:

```
rpmds rpmdsFree(rpmds dependency_set);
```

As with other free functions, rpmdsFree returns NULL.

Comparing an RPM File to an Installed Package

You can pull together the RPM file and database discussions, shown previously, to create a number of RPM programs. A useful utility that shows the RPM C library compares a package file against installed packages, reporting whether the package in the RPM file represents a newer or older package than what was already installed.

Listing 16-4 shows such a program.

Listing 16-4: vercompare.c

```
/* Compares a package file with an installed package,
telling which one is newer.

Usage:
vercompare pkg_files+

Compile as
  cc -I/usr/include/rpm -o vercompare vercompare.c -lrpm -lrpmdb -lrpmio -lpopt

*/
#include <stdlib.h>

#include <rpmcli.h>
#include <rpmdb.h>
#include <rpmds.h>
#include <rpmts.h>

/* Set up a table of options using standard RPM options. */
static struct poptOption optionsTable[] = {

 { NULL, '\0', POPT_ARG_INCLUDE_TABLE, rpmcliAllPoptTable, 0,
      "Common options for all rpm modes and executables:",
      NULL },

  POPT_AUTOALIAS
  POPT_AUTOHELP
  POPT_TABLEEND
};

int main(int argc, char *  argv[])
{
```

Continued

Listing 16-4 *(Continued)*

```
poptContext context;
const char ** fnp;
rpmdbMatchIterator iter;
Header file_header, installed_header;
rpmts ts;
rpmds dependency_set;
FD_t fd;
rpmRC rpmrc;
int rc;

context = rpmcliInit(argc, argv, optionsTable);
if (context == NULL) {
    exit(EXIT_FAILURE);
}

ts = rpmtsCreate();


for (fnp = poptGetArgs(context); fnp && *fnp; fnp++) {

/* Read package header, continuing to next arg on failure. */
fd = Fopen(*fnp, "r.ufdio");

if (fd == NULL || Ferror(fd)) {
    rpmError(RPMERR_OPEN, "open of %s failed: %s\n", *fnp,
             Fstrerror(fd));
    if (fd) {
        Fclose(fd);
    }

    continue;
}

rpmrc = rpmReadPackageFile(ts, fd, *fnp, &file_header);
Fclose(fd);

if (rpmrc != RPMRC_OK) {
    rpmError(RPMERR_OPEN, "%s cannot be read\n", *fnp);
    continue;
}
```

```
    /* Generate "name <= epoch:version-release" depset for package.*/
    dependency_set = rpmdsThis(file_header, RPMTAG_REQUIRENAME,
              (RPMSENSE_EQUAL|RPMSENSE_LESS));

    rc = -1;        /* assume no package is installed. */

    /* Search all installed packages with same name. */
    iter = rpmtsInitIterator(ts, RPMTAG_NAME, rpmdsN(dependency_set), 0);

    while ((installed_header = rpmdbNextIterator(iter)) != NULL) {

        /* Is the installed package newer than the file? */
        rc = rpmdsNVRMatchesDep(installed_header, dependency_set, 1);

        switch (rc) {
        case 1:
        if ( rpmIsVerbose() )
            fprintf(stderr, "installed package is older (or same) as %s\n",
            *fnp);
        break;
        case 0:
        if ( rpmIsVerbose() )
            fprintf(stderr, "installed package is newer than %s\n",
            *fnp);
        break;
        }
    }


    /* Clean up. */
    iter = rpmdbFreeIterator(iter);

    dependency_set = rpmdsFree(dependency_set);

    if (rc < 0 && rpmIsVerbose() )
        fprintf(stderr, "no package is installed %s\n", *fnp);
    }

    ts      = rpmtsFree(ts);
    context = rpmcliFini(context);

    return rc;


}
```

The vercompare.c program shows reading in RPM package files as well as querying the RPM database. It introduces transaction sets, used extensively in the RPM API, and also dependency sets. You can use this program as a guide for making your own RPM programs.

When you run the vercompare.c program, pass the names of one or more RPM files. The vercompare.c program will extract the package name from the files, and then query the RPM database for matching packages. For each matching package, vercompare.c checks whether the installed package is newer than the RPM file, or at the same version or older. For example, if you have installed version 1.17-1 of the jikes package (a Java compiler), you can compare the installed version against RPM files. If you have a package that has a newer version, you should see output like the following:

```
$ ./vercompare -v  jikes-1.18-1.i386.rpm
installed package is older (or same) as jikes-1.18-1.i386.rpm
```

Note that the output is relative to the installed package.

If you compare against a file that has an older version of the package, you will see results like the following:

```
$ ./vercompare -v  jikes-1.14-1-glibc-2.2.i386.rpm
installed package is newer than jikes-1.14-1-glibc-2.2.i386.rpm
```

And, if you compare to an RPM file that holds the same package, you will see output as follows:

```
$ ./vercompare -v jikes-1.17-glibc2.2-1.i386.rpm
installed package is older (or same) as jikes-1.17-
glibc2.2-1.i386.rpm
```

You can change this aspect of the test by changing the flags passed to rpmdsThis.

 The vercompare.c program prints out nothing unless there is an error. Instead, it sets the program exit status based on the package version comparison. You can use this with automated tools, such as make, that check the exit status. If you want output from the program, pass the -v, verbose, option to the command, as shown in the previous examples.

The RPM cli or command-line interface functions, such as rpmcliInit, are based on the command-line options expected by the rpm and rpmbuild commands. You can use these functions to provide a high level of abstraction onto the RPM system. For example, to run the query options just like the rpm command, call rpmcliQuery.

```
int rpmcliQuery(rpmts transaction_set,
    QVA_t qva,
    const char **argv);
```

Set the QVA_t variable to point at the global variable rpmQVKArgs, which is set up from the global option table for the query mode, rpmQueryPoptTable. Pass rpmcliQuery a set of file names or package names. You can get these names in the given format by calling poptGetArgs, introduced previously.

To support the query options, you need the rpm query entries in your poptOption table. To get these options, add the following entry:

```
{ NULL, '\0', POPT_ARG_INCLUDE_TABLE, rpmQueryPoptTable, 0,
        "Query options (with -q or --query):",
        NULL },
```

With the rpmQueryPoptTable options, you can make a program that works like the rpm --query command using just the following code:

```
poptContext context;
QVA_t qva = &rpmQVKArgs;
rpmts ts;
int ec;


context = rpmcliInit(argc, argv, optionsTable);
if (context == NULL) {
    /* Display error and exit... */
}

ts = rpmtsCreate();

if (qva->qva_mode == 'q') {
    /* Make sure there's something to do. */
    if (qva->qva_source != RPMQV_ALL && !poptPeekArg(context)) {
        fprintf(stderr, "no arguments given for --query");
        exit(EXIT_FAILURE);
    }

    ec = rpmcliQuery(ts, qva, (const char **) poptGetArgs(context));
}

ts = rpmtsFree(ts);

context = rpmcliFini(context);
```

This code supports all the query options just like the rpm command. That's both good and bad. If you wanted everything exactly like the rpm command, chances are you could use the rpm command as is. But if you need to add RPM query support into your programs, this is probably the easiest way to do it.

With a small additional set of code, you can add support for all the --verify options to your program. You need to include the --verify command-line option definitions, which come from the global rpmVerifyPoptTable table:

```
/* Add in --verify options. */
{ NULL, '\0', POPT_ARG_INCLUDE_TABLE, rpmVerifyPoptTable, 0,
      "Verify options (with -V or --verify):",
      NULL },
```

You can then check for the verify mode, and support the options, with code like the following:

```
if (qva->qva_mode == 'V') {
    rpmVerifyFlags verifyFlags = VERIFY_ALL;

    /* Verify flags are negated from query flags. */
    verifyFlags &= ~qva->qva_flags;
    qva->qva_flags = (rpmQueryFlags) verifyFlags;

    /* Make sure there's something to do. */
    if (qva->qva_source != RPMQV_ALL && !poptPeekArg(context)) {
        fprintf(stderr, "no arguments given for --verify");
        exit(EXIT_FAILURE);
    }

    ec = rpmcliVerify(ts, qva, (const char **)
    poptGetArgs(context));
}
```

The workhorse function in this code is rpmcliVerify, a high-level function that performs all the --verify work done by the rpm command.

```
int rpmcliVerify(rpmts transaction_set,
    QVA_t qva,
    const char **argv);
```

Again, set the QVA_t variable to point at the global variable rpmQVKArgs, which is set up from the global option table for the query mode, rpmQueryPoptTable.

Putting this all together, Listing 16-5 shows a program that performs the same as the rpm command for the --query and --verify options.

Listing 16-5: rpmq.c

```
/*
rpm --query and --verify modes in standalone program.

Compile as
  cc -I/usr/include/rpm -o rpmq rpmq.c -lrpm -lrpmdb -lrpmio -lpopt

See option usage by invoking
  ./rpmq --help
*/
#include <stdlib.h>

#include <rpmcli.h>
#include <rpmdb.h>
#include <rpmds.h>
#include <rpmts.h>

/* Set up a table of options. */
static struct poptOption optionsTable[] = {

  { NULL, '\0', POPT_ARG_INCLUDE_TABLE, rpmcliAllPoptTable, 0,
        "Common options for all rpm modes and executables:",
      NULL },

  { NULL, '\0', POPT_ARG_INCLUDE_TABLE, rpmQueryPoptTable, 0,
       "Query options (with -q or --query):",
       NULL },

  /* Add in --verify options. */
  { NULL, '\0', POPT_ARG_INCLUDE_TABLE, rpmVerifyPoptTable, 0,
       "Verify options (with -V or --verify):",
       NULL },

    POPT_AUTOALIAS
    POPT_AUTOHELP
    POPT_TABLEEND
};


int main(int argc, char *  argv[])
{
    poptContext context;
    QVA_t qva = &rpmQVKArgs;
    rpmts ts;
    int ec;
```

Continued

Listing 16-5 *(Continued)*

```
context = rpmcliInit(argc, argv, optionsTable);
if (context == NULL) {
    poptPrintUsage(context, stderr, 0);
    exit(EXIT_FAILURE);
}

ts = rpmtsCreate();

/* Check for query mode. */
if (qva->qva_mode == 'q') {
    /* Make sure there's something to do. */
    if (qva->qva_source != RPMQV_ALL && !poptPeekArg(context)) {
        fprintf(stderr, "no arguments given for --query");
        exit(EXIT_FAILURE);
    }

    ec = rpmcliQuery(ts, qva, (const char **) poptGetArgs(context));
}
/* Check for verify mode. */
else if (qva->qva_mode == 'V') {
    rpmVerifyFlags verifyFlags = VERIFY_ALL;

    /* Verify flags are negated from query flags. */
    verifyFlags &= ~qva->qva_flags;
    qva->qva_flags = (rpmQueryFlags) verifyFlags;

    /* Make sure there's something to do. */
    if (qva->qva_source != RPMQV_ALL && !poptPeekArg(context)) {
        fprintf(stderr, "no arguments given for --verify");
        exit(EXIT_FAILURE);
    }

    ec = rpmcliVerify(ts, qva, (const char **) poptGetArgs(context));
}
else {
    poptPrintUsage(context, stderr, 0);
    exit(EXIT_FAILURE);
}

ts = rpmtsFree(ts);

context = rpmcliFini(context);

return ec;
}
```

There is not a lot of code in rpmq.c, as this program is mostly calling the high-level functions for the rpm command-line interface.

When you run the rpmq program, it performs the same tasks as the `rpm` command with the `--query` (or `-q`) and `--verify` (or `-V`) command-line options.

For example, rpmq supports query formats:

```
$ ./rpmq -q --qf "%{NAME} %{INSTALLTID:date}\n" jikes
jikes Fri 25 Oct 2002 06:49:38 PM CDT
```

Where to Go from Here

There is a lot more you can do with the RPM library; you're limited only by your imagination. The best way to get started is to follow the examples in this chapter and then try out some RPM programs on your own. After working with the RPM library for a while, you can delve into other RPM topics.

The RPM Web site, at `www.rpm.org`, has most of the available documentation on the RPM system. This site also includes official RPM released software.

One of the best ways to help find out about how to perform RPM tasks is to look at the source code for the `rpm` program itself. For this, download the rpm-src source RPM, too. To see the `rpm` command-line interface functions in action, look especially at tools/rpmcache.c and tools/rpmgraph.c, two relatively short RPM files that show how to take advantage of a number of short cuts. The source code for the Python and Perl bindings can also provide extra hints about the purposes of the RPM API calls.

The RPM Web site also has a cross-referenced set of HTML pages on the RPM programming API. The pages for version 4.1 of RPM are available at `www.rpm.org/rpmapi-4.1/`. A good starting page is `www.rpm.org/rpmapi-4.1/modules.html`, which lists a number of modules within the overall RPM library. This extra level of organization can help you locate the functions you need.

Summary

Everything you can do with RPM you can program in C. That's because the source code for the entire RPM system is available. In addition, the `rpm` and `rpmbuild` programs make use of a published API, called rpmlib, to access RPM functionality. You can use this library yourself.

The popt library, short for parse options, provides a lot of handy utilities for parsing very complex command-line options. You can use popt inside your own programs, even if you don't use the rest of the RPM functionality.

Most RPM programs start up by calling `rpmcliInit`, which sets up RPM variables for the large set of command-line options supported by most RPM commands.

Call `rpmReadPackageFile` to read in the `Header` object from a package file. You can also get `Header` objects for the packages installed in a system by initializing an iterator to iterate over a set of packages that meet a certain criteria.

This chapter covers a fairly low level of access to RPM functionality. The next chapter, on Python programming, shows a higher level of abstraction for working with RPM.

Chapter 17

Programming RPM with Python

IN THIS CHAPTER

◆ Using the RPM with Python

◆ Installing the necessary modules

◆ Programming with the RPM database

◆ Programming with RPM files

◆ Installing packages programmatically

PYTHON PROVIDES AN OBJECT-ORIENTED scripting language that is suitable for both short scripts and full applications. As an example, the Red Hat enterprise package management program, up2date, is written in Python. Up2date shows a complex application but also one with a good-looking user interface.

For RPM applications, the Python RPM module, rpm-python, provides a higher-level abstraction to RPM functionality than the C API introduced in Chapter 16, making it much easier to develop RPM applications in Python than in C. This is why more and more RPM tools are being written in Python.

 If you've never scripted with Python before, don't worry. The Python syntax is simple and easy to pick up. See the "Where to Go from Here" section at the end of this chapter for a list of some Python tutorials.

This chapter covers how to set up a Python development environment for RPM applications and how to access RPM functionality from Python. It covers how to query the RPM database as well as how to install or upgrade packages.

Setting Up a Python Development Environment

Setting up a Python development environment is much the same as setting up a C programming environment. You need to install a set of packages for general Python development, install a package that provides the Python API to the RPM system, and choose a program for editing your Python scripts.

Appendix F covers Linux text editors and development tools.

If you want to make a graphical user interface in your Python programs, you need to install a separate Python package.

Installing the base Python packages

The base Python package needed for developing applications is python. For RPM usage, you should install Python 2.2, not Python 1.5. That's because the RPM bindings for Python are moving to support only 2.2 and higher releases.

The Python package for RPM access is rpm-python. Install these as you would any other packages.

Chapter 4 covers installing packages.

Using Python for graphics

Python supports a number of different toolkits for creating graphical user interfaces. You need one of these toolkits if you want to create Python applications that sport a user interface instead of command-line tools. Among the most popular toolkits are PyGKT, PyQt, and Tkinter.

◆ PyGTK is a binding between Python and the GTK+ toolkit used by the GNOME desktop, one of two main desktop environments for Linux. (KDE is the other main desktop environment.) The Red Hat redhat-config-packages program uses PyGTK and sports a very good-looking user interface.

PyGTK provides full access to the GTK+ widgets such as menus, dialog windows, and buttons. Install the pygtk2 module for PyGTK. For more on PyGTK, see www.daa.com.au/~james/pygtk/.

◆ **PyQt** connects Python scripts to the Qt C++ user interface toolkit. Qt forms the base library used by the KDE desktop environment and KDE applications. As with PyGTK, PyQt allows you to access the rich widget set provided by the library.

Install the PyQt package for PyQt. For more on PyQt, see www. riverbankcomputing.co.uk/pyqt/.

◆ **Tkinter** is considered a standard part of Python and is based on the Tk (pronounced *teekay*) toolkit from the Tcl scripting language. The main advantages of Tkinter are that it is considered part of Python, meaning users are more likely to have it, and Tkinter works on multiple platforms, including Windows.

The main drawback of Tkinter is that the widget sets are not as rich as PyQt or PyGTK. For more on Tkinter, see www.python.org/topics/tkinter/.

After you've set up your environment and installed all the necessary packages, the next step is to start working with the Python API for RPM.

The Python API Hierarchy

The RPM Python API provides a high-level abstraction into RPM functionality divided into logical areas. Table 17-1 lists the main RPM types. In most cases, you need to begin with rpm and create a transaction set.

TABLE 17-1 PYTHON TYPES FOR RPM USAGE

Class	Covers
rpm	RPM base module into RPM API
rpmts	Transaction sets
rpmte	Transaction elements, a package in a transaction set
rpmmi	Match iterators, used for querying the RPM database
Rpmds	Dependency set
Rpmfi	File into set
Header	A package header

In general, the RPM Python API is well-integrated into the standard Python API. For example, you use the Python `os` class to read in RPM package files.

The examples in this chapter use the RPM 4.1 Python API. The API in previous versions is significantly different from the 4.1 version.

Programming with the RPM Database

Compared to the RPM C API, discussed in Chapter 16, the Python API is much simpler and requires many fewer programming statements to get your job done.

Just about every Python RPM script needs a transaction set. Create a transaction set with `rpm.TransactionSet`:

```
import rpm

ts = rpm.TransactionSet()
```

The transaction set will automatically open the RPM database if needed.

The code examples in this chapter follow the Red Hat conventions for naming variables, such as `ts` for a transaction set. This is to make it easier to read the Python examples in the RPM sources, along with Red Hat installer programs written in Python.

You will need a transaction set in just about every Python script that accesses RPM functionality.

Accessing the RPM database

Transaction sets provide a number of methods for working with the RPM database at the database level. Use these methods if you need to interact with the database as a whole, as opposed to accessing individual packages in the database. For example, you can initialize or rebuild the RPM database with these methods. You can also use a handy trick for accessing another RPM database instead of the default system database.

Setting the Database Location

A transaction set will open the RPM database assuming the default location. To specify a different RPM database location, call addMacro, as shown following:

```
rpm.addMacro("_dbpath", path_to_rpm_database)
```

You can work with more than one RPM database by setting the _dbpath macro, creating a transaction set, and then removing the macro. After doing this, you can create another transaction set for the default RPM database, allowing your script to work with more than one database. For example:

```
# Open the rpmdb-redhat database
rpm.addMacro("_dbpath", "/usr/lib/rpmdb/i386-redhat-linux/redhat")
solvets = rpm.TransactionSet()
solvets.openDB()
rpm.delMacro("_dbpath")

# Open default database
ts = rpm.TransactionSet()
```

This example uses the rpmdb-redhat package, which holds a database of all Red Hat Linux packages. The explicit call to openDB opens the RPM database. In most Python scripts, though, you do not want to call openDB. Instead, a transaction set will open the database as needed.

The call to delMacro removes the _dbpath macro, allowing the next call to TransactionSet to use the default RPM database.

Do not call closeDB on a transaction set. This method does indeed close the RPM database, but it also disables the ability to automatically open the RPM database as needed.

Initializing, Rebuilding, and Verifying the Database

The transaction set provides an initDB method to initialize a new RPM database. This acts like the rpm --initdb command.

```
ts.initDB()
```

The rebuildDB method regenerates the RPM database indices, like the rpm --rebuilddb command:

```
ts.rebuildDB()
```

The `rebuildDB` method regenerates the RPM database indices, like the `rpm --rebuilddb` command.

The `verifyDB` method checks that the RPM database and indices are readable by the Berkeley DB library:

```
ts.verifyDB()
```

Calling this method is the same as running the `db_verify` command on each of the database files in /var/lib/rpm.

See Chapter 5 for more on initializing, rebuilding, and verifying RPM databases.

Once you have a transaction set, you can start querying the RPM database.

Querying the RPM database

Call `dbMatch` on a transaction set to create a match iterator. As with the C API, a match iterator allows your code to iterate over the packages that match a given criteria.

A call to `dbMatch` with no parameters means to set up a match iterator to go over the entire set of installed packages. The basic format follows:

```
import rpm

ts = rpm.TransactionSet()

mi = ts.dbMatch()
for h in mi:
    # Do something with header object...
```

In this example, the call to `dbMatch` returns a match iterator. The `for` loop iterates over the match iterator, returning one header each time.

In addition to this syntax, you can call `next` on the match iterator to get the next entry, a header object that represents one package. For example:

```
import rpm


ts = rpm.TransactionSet()

mi = ts.dbMatch()
```

```
while mi:
     h = mi.next()
     # Do something with the header object
```

The explicit call to next on the match iterator will likely no longer be supported in a future version of the RPM Python API, since the PEP-234 (Python Enhancement Proposal) calls for one means or the other for iterating, but not both.

For example, Listing 17-1 shows a Python script to print out the name, version, and release information for all installed packages.

Listing 17-1: rpmqa.py

```
#!/usr/bin/python

# Acts like rpm -qa and lists the names of all the installed packages.
# Usage:
# python rpmqa.py

import rpm

ts = rpm.TransactionSet()

mi = ts.dbMatch()
for h in mi:

    print "%s-%s-%s" % (h['name'], h['version'], h['release'])
```

When you call this script, you should see output like the following, truncated for space:

```
$ python rpmqa.py
libbonoboui-2.0.1-2
attr-2.0.8-3
dhclient-3.0p11-9
file-3.37-8
hdparm-5.2-1
ksymoops-2.4.5-1
imlib-1.9.13-9
logwatch-2.6-8
mtr-0.49-7
openssh-clients-3.4p1-2
pax-3.0-4
python-optik-1.3-2
dump-0.4b28-4
sendmail-8.12.5-7
sudo-1.6.6-1
```

```
mkbootdisk-1.4.8-1
telnet-0.17-23
usbutils-0.9-7
wvdial-1.53-7
docbook-dtds-1.0-14
urw-fonts-2.0-26
db4-utils-4.0.14-14
libogg-devel-1.0-1
```

If you set the execute permission on this script, you can skip the explicit call to the python command. For example:

```
$ ./rpmqa.py
```

Examining the package header

The code in Listing 17-1 introduces the package header object, an object of the hdr class. This represents a package header, and contains entries such as the name, version, pre- and post-installation scripts, and triggers.

The hdr Class

You can access each entry in the header using Python's dictionary syntax. This is much more convenient than calling headerGetEntry in C programs. The basic syntax to access header entries follows:

```
value = h['tag_name']
```

For example, to get the package name, use the following code:

```
name = h['name']
```

You can also use a set of predefined RPMTAG_ constants that match the C API. These constants are defined in the rpm module. For example:

```
name = h[rpm.RPMTAG_NAME]
```

Using the rpm constants such as rpm.RPMTAG_NAME is faster than using the strings such as 'name'.

For header entries that hold an array of strings, such as the list of files in the package, the data returned is a Python list. For example:

```
print "Files:"
files = h['FILENAMES']
for name in files:
    print name
```

You can use file info sets to achieve more compact code. For example:

```
print "Files:"
fi = h.fiFromHeader()
print fi
```

The requires, provides, obsoletes, and conflicts information each appear as three separate but related lists for each set of information, with three lists for the requires information, three for the provides information, and so on. You can extract this information using Python dependency sets using the simple code following:

```
print h.dsFromHeader('providename')
print h.dsFromHeader('requirename')
print h.dsFromHeader('obsoletename')
print h.dsFromHeader('conflictname')
```

The rpminfo.py script in Listing 17-3 shows how to print out this information.

Printing Header Information with sprintf

In addition to using the Python dictionary syntax, you can use the `sprintf` method on a header to format data using a syntax exactly the same as the query format tags supported by the `rpm` command.

Chapter 5 covers query formats.

The basic syntax is as follows:

```
h.sprintf("%{tag_name}")
```

You can also use special formatting additions to the tag name. For example:

```
print "Header signature: ", h.sprintf("%{DSAHEADER:pgpsig}")
print "%-20s: %s" % ('Installed on', h.sprintf("%{INSTALLTID:date}") )
```

You can combine this information into functions that print out header entries with specific formatting. For example:

```
def nvr(h):
    return h.sprintf("%{NAME}-%{VERSION}-%{RELEASE}")
```

Note that you only really need to use sprintf when you need the format modifiers, such as date on %{INSTALLTID:date}. In most other cases, Python's string-handling functions will work better.

Querying for specific packages

When you call dbMatch on a transaction set object, passing no parameters means to iterate over the entire set of installed packages in the RPM database. You can also query for specific packages using dbMatch. To do so, you need to pass the name of a tag in the header, as well as the value for that tag that you are looking for. The basic syntax follows:

```
mi = ts.dbMatch(tag_name, value)
```

For example, to query for all packages named *sendmail*, use code like the following:

```
mi = ts.dbMatch('name', 'sendmail')
```

The call to dbMatch returns an rpmdbMatchIterator. You can query on any of the tags in the header, but by far the most common query is by name.

Some matches are fast and some are much slower. If you try to match on a tag that is indexed in the RPM database, the matches will perform much faster than for those tags that are not indexes. To determine which tags are indexed, look at the files in /var/lib/rpm. For example, Name and Requirename are files in /var/lib/rpm. These tags are indexed and will therefore match quickly.

Listing 17-2 shows an example Python script which queries for a particular package name and then prints out the name, version, and release for all matching packages.

Listing 17-2: rpmq.py

```
#!/usr/bin/python

# Acts like rpm -q and lists the N-V-R for installed
# packages that match a given name.
# Usage:
# python rpmq.py package_name

import rpm, sys

ts = rpm.TransactionSet()

mi = ts.dbMatch( 'name', sys.argv[1] )
for h in mi:

    print "%s-%s-%s" % (h['name'], h['version'], h['release'])
```

When you call this script, you need to pass the name of a package to query, which the python interpreter will store in sys,argv[1] in the call to dbMatch. For example:

```
$ python rpmq.py sendmail
sendmail-8.12.5-7
```

Printing information on packages

You can create the equivalent of the rpm -qi command with a small number of Python commands. Listing 17-3 shows an example. This script queries for a particular package name, as shown previously in Listing 17-2. Once a package is found, though, rpminfo.py prints out a lot more information, similar to the output from the rpm -qi command.

Listing 17-3: rpminfo.py

```
#!/usr/bin/python

# Lists information on installed package listed on command line.
# Usage:
# python rpminfo.py package_name

import rpm, sys

def printEntry(header, label, format, extra):
    value = header.sprintf(format).strip()
```

Continued

Listing 17-3 *(Continued)*

```
    print "%-20s: %s %s" % (label, value, extra)


def printHeader(h):

    if h[rpm.RPMTAG_SOURCEPACKAGE]:
        extra = " source package"
    else:
        extra = " binary package"

    printEntry(h, 'Package', "%{NAME}-%{VERSION}-%{RELEASE}", extra)

    printEntry(h, 'Group', "%{GROUP}", '')
    printEntry(h, 'Summary', "%{Summary}", '')
    printEntry(h, 'Arch-OS-Platform', "%{ARCH}-%{OS}-%{PLATFORM}", '')

    printEntry(h, 'Vendor', "%{Vendor}", '')
    printEntry(h, 'URL', "%{URL}", '')
    printEntry(h, 'Size', "%{Size}", '')
    printEntry(h, 'Installed on', "%{INSTALLTID:date}", '')

    print h['description']

    print "Files:"
    fi = h.fiFromHeader()
    print fi

    # Dependencies
    print "Provides:"
    print h.dsFromHeader('providename')
    print "Requires:"
    print h.dsFromHeader('requirename')

    if h.dsFromHeader('obsoletename'):
        print "Obsoletes:"
        print h.dsFromHeader('obsoletename')

    if h.dsFromHeader('conflictname'):
        print "Conflicts:"
        print h.dsFromHeader('conflictname')


ts = rpm.TransactionSet()
```

```
mi = ts.dbMatch( 'name', sys.argv[1] )
for h in mi:

    printHeader(h)
```

 You should be able to simplify this script. The extensive use of the `sprintf` method is for illustration more than efficiency. You generally only need to call `sprintf` when you need a format modifier for a tag. In the rpminfo.py script, `sprintf` was also used to ensure that all entries are text, which allows for calling `strip`.

The `printEntry` function takes in a header `sprintf` tag value in the format of `"%{NAME}"`. You can also pass in more complex values with multiple header entries, such as `"%{NAME}-%{VERSION}"`.

When you run this script, you need to pass the name of a package. You'll see output like the following:

```
$ python rpminfo.py jikes
Package           : jikes-1.18-1  binary package
Group             : Development/Languages
Summary           : java source to bytecode compiler
Arch-OS-Platform  : i386-Linux-(none)
Vendor            : (none)
URL               : http://ibm.com/developerworks/opensource/jikes
Size              : 2853672
Installed on      : Mon Dec  2 20:10:13 2002
The IBM Jikes compiler translates Java source files to bytecode. It
also supports incremental compilation and automatic makefile
generation,and is maintained by the Jikes Project:
http://ibm.com/developerworks/opensource/jikes/

Files:
/usr/bin/jikes
/usr/doc/jikes-1.18/license.htm
/usr/man/man1/jikes.1.gz

Provides:
P jikes
P jikes = 1.18-1
```

```
Requires:
R ld-linux.so.2
R libc.so.6
R libc.so.6(GLIBC_2.0)
R libc.so.6(GLIBC_2.1)
R libc.so.6(GLIBC_2.1.3)
R libm.so.6
R libstdc++-libc6.2-2.so.3
```

Refining queries

The `pattern` method on a match iterator allows you to refine a query. This narrows an existing iterator to only show the packages you desire. The basic syntax follows:

```
mi.pattern(tag_name, mode, pattern)
```

The two main uses of the `pattern` method are to query on more than one tag, such as the version and name, or to narrow the results of a query, using the rich set of pattern modes. The `mode` parameter names the type of pattern used, which can be one of those listed in Table 17-2.

TABLE 17-2 PATTERN MODES FOR THE PATTERN METHOD

Type	Meaning
rpm.RPMMIRE_DEFAULT	Same as regular expressions, but with \., .*, and ^..$ added
rpm.RPMMIRE_GLOB	Glob-style patterns using fnmatch
rpm.RPMMIRE_REGEX	Regular expressions using regcomp
rpm.RPMMIRE_STRCMP	String comparisons using strcmp

For more on these patterns, see the online manual pages for fnmatch(3), glob(7), regcomp(3), regex(7), and strcmp(3). The `pattern` method calls `rpmdbSetIteratorRE` from the C API, covered in Chapter 16.

To query for all packages starting with *py*, for example, you can use code like the following:

```
import rpm

ts = rpm.TransactionSet()

mi = ts.dbMatch()

mi.pattern('name', rpm.RPMMIRE_GLOB, 'py*' )

for h in mi:
# Do something with the header...
```

Listing 17-4 shows an example for glob-based querying.

Listing 17–4: rpmglob.py

```
#!/usr/bin/python

# Acts like rpm -q and lists the N-V-R for installed packages
# that match a given name using a glob-like syntax
#
# Usage:
# python rpmglob.py "package_fragment*"

import rpm, sys

ts = rpm.TransactionSet()

mi = ts.dbMatch()

if not mi:
    print "No packages found."
else:
    mi.pattern('name', rpm.RPMMIRE_GLOB, sys.argv[1] )

for h in mi:

    print "%s-%s-%s" % (h['name'], h['version'], h['release'])
```

When you run this script, you'll see output like the following:

```
$ python rpmglob.py "py*"
pyxf86config-0.3.1-2
python-devel-2.2.1-17
pygtk2-devel-1.99.12-7
pygtk2-libglade-1.99.12-7
pygtk2-1.99.12-7
pyOpenSSL-0.5.0.91-1
python-optik-1.3-2
python-docs-2.2.1-17
python-2.2.1-17
python-tools-2.2.1-17
```

In addition to working with the RPM database, the Python API also provides access to RPM files.

Reading Package Files

As you would expect, the Python API includes methods for working with RPM package files in addition to installed RPM packages. Most of these methods require a header object, which you can read from an RPM package file.

Reading headers from package files

Like the C function rpmReadPackageFile, the Python API provides a convenient way to read in a header object from an RPM package file. The hdrFromFdno method reads an RPM header from an open file descriptor. The basic syntax is:

```
h = ts.hdrFromFdno(fdno)
```

 The hdrFromFdno method uses Python's low-level file descriptors instead of the higher-level Python file objects. In the RPM C library, an FD_t is a FILE**. This could be bound to a Python class, but that is outside the scope of this chapter.

The following example shows a function that opens a file, reads in the RPM header, and then closes the file:

```
def readRpmHeader(ts, filename):
    """ Read an rpm header. """
    fd = os.open(filename, os.O_RDONLY)
```

```
        h = ts.hdrFromFdno(fd)

    os.close(fd)
    return h

ts = rpm.TransactionSet()

h = readRpmHeader( ts, 'n-r-v.rpm' )
```

The hdrFromFdno method raises a number of exceptions based on issues detected with the package files. The following example shows these exceptions:

```
def readRpmHeader(ts, filename):
    """ Read an rpm header. """
    fd = os.open(filename, os.O_RDONLY)

    h = None
    tryL
        h = ts.hdrFromFdno(fd)
    except rpm.error, e:
        if str(e) == "public key not available":
            print str(e)
        if str(e) == "public key not trusted":
            print str(e)
        if str(e) == "error reading package header":
            print str(e)
            h = None


    os.close(fd)
    return h

ts = rpm.TransactionSet()

h = readRpmHeader( ts, 'n-r-v.rpm' )
```

You can decide in your code whether the exceptions should stop processing or not.

Setting the verification flags

Starting with rpm 4.1, package files are verified automatically, which can cause problems, especially if you are working with older packages, or packages without proper digital signatures.

In most cases, the automatic verification is an advantage, since you can have greater confidence in the package files. However, you can call setVSFlags on a transaction set to change the default behavior.

```
ts.setVSFlags(flags)
```

For example, if you have problems with old packages that do not have proper signatures, you can use code like the following to ignore such checks:

```
# Set to not verify DSA signatures.
ts.setVSFlags(rpm.RPMVSF_NODSA)
```

Table 17-3 lists the flags you can pass to setVSFlags on a transaction set. These flags are bitmasks. You can *or* them together for more than one setting. You must do a binary *or*. Do not use the Python or keyword. Use | instead, for a binary *or* operation.

TABLE 17-3 FLAGS FOR SETVSFLAGS

Flag	Meaning
rpm.RPMVSF_NEEDPAYLOAD	Leave the file handle positions at the beginning of the payload.
rpm.RPMVSF_NOHDRCHK	Don't check the RPM database header.
rpm.RPMVSF_ NODSA	Don't check the header and payload DSA signatures.
rpm.RPMVSF_ NODSAHEADER	Don't check the header DSA signature.
rpm.RPMVSF_ NOMD5	Don't check the header and payload MD5 digests.
rpm.RPMVSF_ NORSA	Don't check the header and payload RSA signatures.
rpm.RPMVSF_ NOSHA1HEADER	Don't check the header SHA1 digest.
rpm._RPMVSF_NODIGESTS	Convenience to not check digests.
rpm._RPMVSF_NOSIGNATURES	Convenience to not check signatures.

To turn off all checks, you can pass -1 to setVSFlags:

```
ts.setVSFlasgs(-1)
```

Dependency Comparisons

Dependency sets, first introduced in Chapter 16 on C programming, allow you to compare the dependencies between two packages. One of the most common uses for this is to compare a package file against a version on disk to see if the package file holds a newer version of a package than the one installed.

You can call dsOfHeader on a header object to get the default dependency set for the header. Armed with dependency sets from two headers, you can compare the sets to see which package is newer using simple code like the following:

```
file_h  = ts.hdrFromFdno(fd)
file_ds = file_h.dsOfHeader()
inst_ds = inst_h.dsOfHeader()
if file_ds.EVR() >= inst_ds.EVR():
    print "Package file is same or newer, OK to upgrade."
else:
    print "Package file is older than installed version."
```

Pulling this all together, Listing 17-5 provides a Python script that compares a package file against an installed package, reporting on which is newer.

Listing 17-5: vercompare.py

```
#!/usr/bin/python

# Reads in package header, compares to installed package.
# Usage:
# python vercompare.py rpm_file.rpm
#

import rpm, os, sys

def readRpmHeader(ts, filename):
    """ Read an rpm header. """
    fd = os.open(filename, os.O_RDONLY)

    h = ts.hdrFromFdno(fd)

    os.close(fd)
    return h


ts = rpm.TransactionSet()
h  = readRpmHeader( ts, sys.argv[1] )
```

Continued

Listing 17-5 *(Continued)*

```python
pkg_ds = h.dsOfHeader()

for inst_h in ts.dbMatch('name', h['name']):
    inst_ds = inst_h.dsOfHeader()

    if pkg_ds.EVR() >= inst_ds.EVR():
        print "Package file is same or newer, OK to upgrade."
    else:
        print "Package file is older than installed version."
```

The Python script in Listing 17-5 is essentially the same as the longer C program vercompare.c in Listing 16-4 in Chapter 16.

This script takes in a package file name on the command line, loads in the header for that package, and looks up all packages of the same name installed in the RPM database. For each match, this script compares the packages to see which is newer.

You can modify this script, for example, to print out a message if a package isn't installed.

Installing and Upgrading Packages

With the RPM system, you have a lot of choices. You can install or upgrade packages with the rpm command. You can install or upgrade packages with special programs you write using the C API. And you can install or upgrade packages using the Python API. If you are writing a special program to install or upgrade packages, the Python API makes this task much easier. As with the C API, most of your work needs to be part of a transaction set.

To install or upgrade a package, you need to create a transaction set, build up the transaction with packages, which are stored as transaction elements within the transaction set, check for unresolved dependencies, reorder the transaction set based on the dependencies, and then run the transaction set. Running the transaction set installs or upgrades the packages. The following sections cover these steps.

Building up the transaction set

Package installs and upgrades need to be performed within the context of a transaction set. To install or upgrade a set of packages, you need to call addInstall with the package headers to install or upgrade. The basic syntax follows:

```python
ts.addInstall(header, key_data, mode)
```

When you call addInstall, you pass the header object along with arbitrary callback key data and a mode flag. The mode flag should be 'i' to install a package, 'u' to upgrade a package, or 'a' as a special code to make a package available for transaction checks but not install or upgrade the package. The 'a' flag is rarely used. In most cases, you should use 'u', just as in most cases, you should install packages with rpm -U instead of rpm -i.

The key_data parameter will get passed to the transaction set run callback, covered in the "Running the transaction" section later in this chapter.

To remove packages instead of install or upgrade, call addErase instead of addInstall:

```
ts.addErase(package_name)
```

To set up a package to be upgraded or installed, you can use code like the following:

```
h = readRpmHeader( ts, sys.argv[1] )

ts.addInstall(h, sys.argv[1], 'u')
```

This example expects a package file name on the command line (accessed with sys.argv[1]), and reads in the package header using the readRpmHeader function introduced previously.

The call to addInstall adds the header object (and the associated RPM package file) for an upgrade with the 'u' mode flag. The name of the package file, from sys.argv[1], is passed as the arbitrary data for the transaction set run callback function.

Transaction elements

Transaction sets are made up of transaction elements. A transaction element makes up one part of a transaction and holds one package per operation (install or remove) in each transaction set. That is, there is one transaction element per package per operation in the transaction set. You can iterate over a transaction set to get each transaction element. Once you have a transaction element, you can call methods on each element to check entries in the header as well as get dependency sets for the package.

Table 17-4 lists the informational methods you can call on a transaction element. Most of the methods listed in Table 17-4 return a single value.

TABLE 17-4 METHODS ON TRANSACTION SETS

Method	Returns
A	Returns package architecture
E	Returns package epoch
O	Returns package operating system
R	Returns package release number
V	Returns package version
N	Returns package name
NEVR	Returns package name-epoch-version-release
DS	Returns the package dependency set for a given tag
FI	Returns the file info set for the package

For more complex checking, the DS method returns the package dependency set for a given tag:

```
ds = te.DS(tag_name)
```

Pass one of 'Providename', 'Requirename', 'Obsoletename', or 'Conflictname' for the tag name. For example:

```
ds = te.DS('Requirename')
```

The FI method returns the file info set for the package:

```
fi = te.FI(tag_name)
```

For the FI method, you must pass a tag name of 'Basenames'.

As an example, Listing 17-6 shows how to iterate through a transaction set to get transaction elements.

Listing 17-6: te.py

```
#!/usr/bin/python

# Adds all package files on command line to a transaction
# and prints out the transaction elements.
# Usage:
```

```
# python te.py rpm_file1.rpm rpm_file2.rpm ...
#
import rpm, os, sys

def readRpmHeader(ts, filename):
    """ Read an rpm header. """
    fd = os.open(filename, os.O_RDONLY)

    h = ts.hdrFromFdno(fd)

    os.close(fd)
    return h



ts = rpm.TransactionSet()

# Set to not verify DSA signatures.
ts.setVSFlags(rpm._RPMVSF_NOSIGNATURES)

for filename in sys.argv[1:]:
    h = readRpmHeader(ts, filename)
    print "Installing %s-%s-%s" % (h['name'], h['version'], h['release'])
    ts.addInstall(h, filename, 'i')

print "This will install:"
for te in ts:
    print "%s-%s-%s" % (te.N(), te.V(), te.R() )

ts.check()
ts.order()

print "This will install:"
for te in ts:
    print "%s-%s-%s" % (te.N(), te.V(), te.R() )
```

The te.py script sets up a transaction and then prints out the elements, never completing the transaction. The purpose here is just to show what is in the transaction. The second set of printed output shows the results of the check and order methods, covered in the following section.

Checking and reordering the transaction elements

After you have called addInstall or addErase for each of the packages you want to install, upgrade, or remove, you need to call two methods to verify the transaction set and order all the elements properly. These two methods are check and order.

Checking the Dependencies

The check method checks the dependencies in a transaction set.

```
unresolved_dependencies = ts.check()
```

It returns None if all dependencies are resolved, or a complex tuple for each unre-solved dependency. In general, if the check method returns anything but None, you cannot perform the transaction.

On a dependency failure, check returns a complex tuple of the dependency information in the following format:

```
((N,V,R), (reqN, reqV), needsFlags, suggestedPackage, sense)
```

The first element is a tuple of the name, version, and release of the package you are trying to install. The next tuple holds the required name and required version or conflicting name and version. The version will be None if the dependency is a shared library or other file.

The needs flags tell you about the requirement or conflict. The value is a bitmask that can contain the following bit settings: rpm.RPMSENSE_EQUAL, rpm.RPM-SENSE_GREATER, and rpm.RPMSENSE_LESS. This tells you if the dependency is for a version of a package greater than 4.1, for example.

The suggested package names a package that solves the dependency. The pack-ages considered are those for which you call addInstall with a flag of 'a'. This value will be None if there is no known package to solve this dependency.

You can tell whether the dependency is a conflict or a requirement based on the sense value, one of rpm.RPMSENSE_CONFLICTS or rpm.RPMSENSE_REQUIRES.

For example, the following tuple shows a required package:

```
(('eruby-devel', '0.9.8', '2'), ('eruby-libs', '0.9.8'), 8, None, 0)
```

The following tuple shows a required shared library:

```
(('jpilot', '0.97', '1'), ('libpisock.so.3', None), 0, None, 0)
```

 This tuple format will likely change in future versions of RPM. This example shows the format in RPM 4.1. With each RPM release, check the online docu-mentation on the Python API to look for changes.

Transaction Check Method Callbacks

You can pass an optional callback function to the call to check. This callback gets called for each unresolved dependency in the transaction set. You can use this call-back to try to automatically bring in required packages, for example.

The basic syntax for the transaction check callback is:

```
def checkCallback(ts, TagN, N, EVR, Flags):
    # Do something...
```

You can use a `check` callback to automatically bring in packages that are required into a transaction set. You can bring in packages from the Red Hat RPM database package, which contains a database of all Red Hat packages, the rpmdb-redhat package. You can open the database from this package by using the trick described previously for opening transactions to more than one RPM database at a time. Simply set the `_dbpath` macro to `"/usr/lib/rpmdb/i386-redhat-linux/redhat"`, or the location of your rpmdb-redhat database, and create a transaction set. Your `check` callback can then search this extra database and add packages from that database into the current, real RPM database.

Your `check` callback can also attempt to find package files to resolve dependencies, from a disk directory or network archive for example. The following code shows a stub `check` callback that you can fill in to try to resolve dependencies. This callback sets up a format for finding unresolved packages in another RPM database, or elsewhere. You need to fill in the skeleton with the algorithm you want to actually resolve the dependencies.

```
def checkCallback(ts, TagN, N, EVR, Flags):

    if TagN == rpm.RPMTAG_REQUIRENAME:
        prev = ""
    Nh = None

    if N[0] == '/':
        dbitag = 'basenames'
    else:
        dbitag = 'providename'

    # What do you need to do.
    if EVR:
        print "Must find package [", N, "-", EVR, "]"
    else:
        print "Must find file [", N, "]"

    if resolved:
        # ts.addIntall(h, h, 'i')

        return -1

    return 1
```

Depending on the values passed to the callback, your code must either find a package itself or a package that provides a given file or capability to resolve the dependency. If you have another RPM database to look at, such as the rpmdb-redhat database, you can use dbMatch to find the necessary packages in that database. If, however, you are working with a directory of RPM files, you need to build up file names from the package name, version, and release.

Reordering the Transaction Set

You can add packages to a transaction set in any order. The order method reorders the transaction set to ensure that packages get installed or removed in the right order. The order method orders by a topological sort using the dependencies relations between objects with dependency comparisons.

 You must call check prior to order.

Running the transaction

After setting up the transaction set, perform the transaction by calling run. You need to provide two parameters:

```
ts.run(callback, client_data)
```

The callback parameter must be a Python function. The client_data is any data you want to pass to the callback. There may be more than one package in the transaction set, so this data should not be specific to a particular package.

 You must not pass None as the client_data or you will get a Python error.

Transaction run Method Callbacks

The callback you pass to the run method on a transaction set is essential. Your callback must work properly, or the transaction will fail. You must provide a callback.

Your callback will get called a number of times, mostly as a means to report progress. If you are writing a graphical user interface, for example, you can use the progress callbacks to update a visual progress meter.

The basic syntax for the transaction set `run` callback is:

```
def runCallback(reason, amount, total, key, client_data):
    # Do your stuff...
```

The `key` is the data you provided in the call to the `addInstall` method. The `client_data` is the data you passed to the `run` method.

Each time your callback is called, the transaction set will provide a reason flag. Table 17-5 lists the values for the reason parameter.

TABLE 17-5 TRANSACTION SET RUN CALLBACK REASON VALUES

Value	Reason
rpm.RPMCALLBACK_UNKNOWN	Unknown problem
rpm.RPMCALLBACK_INST_PROGRESS	Progress for installation
rpm.RPMCALLBACK_INST_START	Start of installation
rpm.RPMCALLBACK_INST_OPEN_FILE	Callback should open package file
rpm.RPMCALLBACK_INST_CLOSE_FILE	Callback should close package file
rpm.RPMCALLBACK_TRANS_PROGRESS	Transaction progress
rpm.RPMCALLBACK_TRANS_START	Transaction start
rpm.RPMCALLBACK_TRANS_STOP	Transaction stop
rpm.RPMCALLBACK_UNINST_PROGRESS	Uninstallation progress
rpm.RPMCALLBACK_UNINST_START	Uninstallation start
rpm.RPMCALLBACK_UNINST_STOP	Uninstallation stop
rpm.RPMCALLBACK_REPACKAGE_PROGRESS	Repackaging progress
rpm.RPMCALLBACK_REPACKAGE_START	Repackaging start
rpm.RPMCALLBACK_REPACKAGE_STOP	Repackaging stop
rpm.RPMCALLBACK_UNPACK_ERROR	Error unpacking package file
rpm.RPMCALLBACK_CPIO_ERROR	cpio error getting package payload

Your callback must handle at least two cases: a reason value of `rpm.RPMCALLBACK_INST_OPEN_FILE` and `rpm.RPMCALLBACK_INST_CLOSE_FILE`.

With the reason of rpm.RPMCALLBACK_INST_OPEN_FILE, you must open the RPM package file and return a file descriptor for the file. You need to keep this file descriptor in a global-scope or otherwise-accessible variable, because with the reason of rpm.RPMCALLBACK_INST_CLOSE_FILE, you must close this file.

Coding A Sample Callback

The following code shows a valid sample callback for upgrading and installing packages.

```
# Global file descriptor for the callback.
rpmtsCallback_fd = None



def runCallback(reason, amount, total, key, client_data):

    global rpmtsCallback_fd

    if reason == rpm.RPMCALLBACK_INST_OPEN_FILE:
        print "Opening file. ", reason, amount, total, key, client_data
        rpmtsCallback_fd = os.open(client_data, os.O_RDONLY)
        return rpmtsCallback_fd
    elif reason == rpm.RPMCALLBACK_INST_START:
        print "Closing file. ", reason, amount, total, key, client_data
        os.close(rpmtsCallback_fd)
```

This callback assumes that the call to addInstall passed client data of the package file name. This callback ignores the client_data passed to the run method, but this is a perfect slot for passing an object. You can use this, for example, to avoid having a global variable for the file descriptor.

Upgrading A Package

Listing 17-7 shows a simple Python script to upgrade or install a package.

Listing 17-7: rpmupgrade.py

```
#!/usr/bin/python


# Upgrades packages passed on the command line.
# Usage:
# python rpmupgrade.py rpm_file1.rpm rpm_file2.rpm ...
#
import rpm, os, sys


# Global file descriptor for the callback.
rpmtsCallback_fd = None
```

```
def runCallback(reason, amount, total, key, client_data):

    global rpmtsCallback_fd

    if reason == rpm.RPMCALLBACK_INST_OPEN_FILE:
        print "Opening file. ", reason, amount, total, key, client_data
        rpmtsCallback_fd = os.open(key, os.O_RDONLY)
        return rpmtsCallback_fd
    elif reason == rpm.RPMCALLBACK_INST_START:
        print "Closing file. ", reason, amount, total, key, client_data
        os.close(rpmtsCallback_fd)


def checkCallback(ts, TagN, N, EVR, Flags):

    if TagN == rpm.RPMTAG_REQUIRENAME:
        prev = ""
    Nh = None

    if N[0] == '/':
        dbitag = 'basenames'
    else:
        dbitag = 'providename'

    # What do you need to do.
    if EVR:
        print "Must find package [", N, "-", EVR, "]"
    else:
        print "Must find file [", N, "]"

    if resolved:
        # ts.addIntall(h, h, 'i')

        return -1

    return 1



def readRpmHeader(ts, filename):
    """ Read an rpm header. """
    fd = os.open(filename, os.O_RDONLY)
```

Continued

Listing 17-7 *(Continued)*

```
    h = ts.hdrFromFdno(fd)

    os.close(fd)
    return h


ts = rpm.TransactionSet()

# Set to not verify DSA signatures.
ts.setVSFlags(-1)

for filename in sys.argv[1:]:
    h = readRpmHeader(ts, filename)
    print "Upgrading %s-%s-%s" % (h['name'], h['version'], h['release'])
    ts.addInstall(h, filename, 'u')


unresolved_dependencies = ts.check(checkCallback)

if not unresolved_dependencies:
    ts.order()

    print "This upgrade will install:"
    for te in ts:
        print "%s-%s-%s" % (te.N(), te.V(), te.R())

    print "Running transaction (final step)..."
    ts.run(runCallback, 1)
else:
    print "Error: Unresolved dependencies, transaction failed."
    print unresolved_dependencies
```

This script expects the name of an RPM package file on the command line, and attempts to upgrade the package. (This will also install new packages.)

When you run the rpmupgrade.py script, you should see output like the following:

```
# rpm -q jikes
jikes-1.17-1


# python rpmupgrade.py jikes-1.18-1.i386.rpm
Upgrading jikes-1.18-1
This upgrade will install:
jikes-1.18-1
```

```
jikes-1.17-1
Running transaction (final step)...
Opening file.  4 0 0 jikes-1.18-1.i386.rpm 1
Closing file.  2 0 2854204 jikes-1.18-1.i386.rpm 1

# rpm -q jikes
jikes-1.18-1
```

This example shows that the package was upgraded after running the rpmup-grade.py script. Note that with an upgrade, the original package, jikes-1.17-1 in this case, is also added to the transaction set. With an install, this is not the case. That's because the original package is removed as part of the transaction.

If you run this script as a non-root user, you will likely see an error like the following:

```
$ python rpmupgrade.py jikes-1.18-1.i386.rpm
Upgrading jikes-1.18-1
This upgrade will install:
jikes-1.18-1
jikes-1.17-1
Running transaction (final step)...
error: cannot get exclusive lock on /var/lib/rpm/Packages
error: cannot open Packages index using db3 - Operation not permitted (1)
error: cannot open Packages database in /var/lib/rpm
```

If a package has a dependency on a file such as a shared library, you will see output like the following:

```
# python rpmupgrade.py jikes-1.17-glibc2.2-1.i386.rpm jpilot-0_97-1_i386.rpm
Upgrading jikes-1.17-1
Upgrading jpilot-0.97-1
Must find file [ libpisock.so.3 ]
Error: Unresolved dependencies, transaction failed.
(('jpilot', '0.97', '1'), ('libpisock.so.3', None), 0, None, 0)
```

If a package has a dependency on another package, you will see output like the following:

```
# python rpmupgrade.py eruby-devel-0.9.8-2.i386.rpm
Upgrading eruby-devel-0.9.8-2
Must find package [ eruby-libs - 0.9.8 ]
Error: Unresolved dependencies, transaction failed.
(('eruby-devel', '0.9.8', '2'), ('eruby-libs', '0.9.8'), 8, None, 0)
```

Where to Go from Here

The RPM bindings for Python are documented along with the C programming API. On a Red Hat Linux system, look in the file /usr/share/doc/rpm-devel-4.1/apidocs/ html/group__python.html to see the start of the Python-specific documentation.

Note that much of this online documentation covers the C functions that provide the Python bindings, not the Python API itself. But, if you examine the online information on objects listed as classes, such as rpmts, you can find the Python-specific documentation.

Furthermore, if you look into the .c files that make up the Python bindings, you can find PyMethodDef structure tables. These tables provide useful glimpses into the Python API.

To learn more about programming in Python, install the python-docs package. The python-docs package has a large set of online documentation for Python, including the official Python Tutorial. With Red Hat Linux, start at /usr/share/ doc/python-docs-2.2.1/html/tut/tut.html.

Other tutorials are available at http://diveintopython.org for the Dive Into Python tutorial for experienced programmers, and at http://py. vaults.ca/parnassus/apyllo.py/935043691.636055170 for the Vaults of Parnassus listing of tutorials.

Summary

This chapter introduces the high-level RPM API for Python programming. You can use this API from Python scripts to perform RPM functionality, just as you can write C programs using the RPM C API covered in Chapter 16.

In general, the Python API is simpler and requires fewer code statements than the corresponding functionality in the C API.

Just about all of your work with the Python API requires a transaction set, which you can get by calling rpm.TransactionSet.

To query the RPM database, call dbMatch on the transaction set object. To install or upgrade packages, call addInstall, check, order, and run on the transaction set.

The next chapter switches to another language for accessing the RPM system: Perl. With the rich set of APIs, you can write your RPM programs in C, Python, Perl, or any language that can call on code written in one of these languages.

Chapter 18

Programming RPM with Perl

IN THIS CHAPTER

◆ Using the RPM2 module to access information on package files

◆ Querying the RPM database from Perl

◆ Cross-referencing capabilities by the packages that provide and require capabilities

◆ Extracting information on packages

PERL IS ONE OF THE MOST POPULAR scripting languages. Used by system administrators, software developers, and a host of other users, Perl runs on many operating systems including Linux, Unix, and Windows. *Perl* stands for *Practical Extraction and Report Language*, or sometimes *Pathologically Eclectic Rubbish Lister*.

 In the same vein, *LISP* stands for *Lots of Irritating Single Parenthesis* and *COBOL* for *Completely Obnoxious Business Oriented Language*.

I began my book *Cross-Platform Perl* (John Wiley & Sons, 2000) by mentioning that when I first started learning Perl, I thought it was an evil plot. I still do. But it is a very *practical* evil plot. You can get a lot of work done with Perl, and quickly.

Because of a long history of text processing, Perl is especially popular among system administrators. Perl also supports add-on packages, called *modules*. You can find thousands of add-on modules for text processing, networking, and a plethora of other tasks. There are so many modules available that some people who don't like the Perl syntax script with Perl anyway, because the available modules save a lot of time.

See search.cpan.org, the Comprehensive Perl Archive Network, for a listing of many Perl modules.

This chapter covers working with RPM files and the RPM database using Perl. You can combine RPM usage with other Perl usage, such as generating HTML files or downloading RPMs over a network link.

Many of the RPM tools covered in Chapter 8 are written in Perl.

Getting and Using the Perl RPM Modules

A number of Perl RPM modules are available. No one module provides all the features you need, although with time, the Perl modules will consolidate into a few modules that most everyone uses. As of this writing, the RPM2 module, by Chip Turner of Red Hat, provides the most recent approach to working with the RPM system from Perl. This chapter covers the RPM2 module.

Red Hat Linux 8.0 comes with a perl-RPM2 package, which you need to install to use this module. Otherwise, you can download the module from www.cpan.org. Install this module, as well as the perl module, which provides the Perl language interpreter. Once you have this module installed and the perl package installed, you are ready to go.

The version of the perl-RPM2 package that ships with Red Hat Linux 8.0 has a bug in that it will not open package files that were created with the version of rpm that ships with Red Hat Linux 8.0. That is, the Perl module cannot read package files that ship with Red Hat Linux. You can read older package files, though. This problem only affects attempts to read .rpm files, not installed packages. The bug is related to reading signed packages but not having the GPG keys in the keyring. The latest version on search.cpan.org fixes this problem.

The RPM2 module contains Perl methods to work on two types of RPM objects: RPM files and installed packages.

Working with RPM Files

The RPM2 module provides a top-level object, RPM2, that acts as an entry point into the module. From the RPM2 object, you either open the RPM database, covered in the "Programming with the RPM Database" section, or open an RPM package file, covered here.

The first step in working with an RPM file is to open the file inside a Perl script.

Opening package files

The open_package subroutine opens an RPM package file and returns a header object (an RPM2::Header). The basic syntax follows:

```
my $header = RPM2->open_package( $filename );
```

For example:

```
my $header = RPM2->open_package("jikes-1.14-1-glibc-2.2.i386.rpm");
```

After you've opened a package, you can perform a number of query operations on the header object returned by the open_package subroutine.

Listing tags from the package

Each RPM package has information stored under a variety of tags, such as the package name under the NAME tag and the package long description under the DESCRIPTION tag.

These are the same tags introduced with the --queryformat option to the rpm command discussed in Chapter 5.

The tag subroutine returns the value of a given tag. For example, to get the name of the package, use the NAME tag:

```
use RPM2;

my $header = RPM2->open_package("jikes-1.14-1-glibc-2.2.i386.rpm" );

print $header->tag("NAME"), "\n";
```

Pulling this together, Listing 18-1 shows an example script that lists the name and one-line short summary of a package file.

Listing 18-1: rpmsum.pl

```perl
#!/usr/bin/perl

#
# Lists summary from an RPM package file
# Usage:
# rpmsum.pl package_name.rpm
#
use strict;
use RPM2;

my $header = RPM2->open_package( $ARGV[0] );

print $header->tag("NAME"), ": ", $header->tag("SUMMARY"), "\n";
```

Enter this script and name the file rpmsum.pl.

When you run this script, you need to pass the name of a package file on the command line. For example:

```
$ ./rpmsum.pl jikes-1.14-1-glibc-2.2.i386.rpm
jikes: java source to bytecode compiler
```

Convenience methods

The RPM2 module includes convenience methods for all RPM tags. This means you can use the method name in place of tag("NAME"). For example:

```perl
print $header->name(), ": ", $header->summary(), "\n";
```

Listing the name and version

The RPM2 module provides a handy subroutine for getting the NAME, VERSION, RELEASE, and EPOCH tags, often abbreviated as NVRE. The subroutine, as_nvre, returns a single string with these values in the standard format, with the values separated by minus signs.

Usually, the EPOCH tag has no value. If there is an EPOCH value, you will see it output first, and then a colon, and then the name, version, and release values. For example:

5:redhat-config-httpd-1.0.1-13

In this case, the EPOCH value is 5.

You can call this subroutine on any header object, or any package object to get the full name of the package. For example:

```
print $header->as_nvre(), "\n";
```

Checking whether the package is a source package

Another handy subroutine tells you if an RPM file represents a source RPM or a binary RPM. The is_source_package subroutine returns a true value if the package is a source package, and a false value otherwise.

The rpmpkg.pl script, shown in Listing 18-2, shows how to use the as_nvre and is_source_package subroutines.

Listing 18-2: rpmpkg.pl

```
#!/usr/bin/perl

#
# Queries RPM package file and prints
# out name and whether this is a source pkg.
# Usage:
# rpmpkg.pl package_name
#
use strict;
use RPM2;

my $header = RPM2->open_package( $ARGV[0] );

if ( $header->is_source_package() ) {
    print "Source package ",  $header->as_nvre(), "\n";
} else {
    print $header->as_nvre(), "\n";
}
```

Programming with the RPM Database

In addition to providing query routines for RPM files, you can also access the RPM database with the RPM2 package.

To access the RPM database, your Perl script must first open the database.

Opening the database

Open the RPM database with a call to open_rpm_db on the RPM2 object. For example:

```
my $rpm_db = RPM2->open_rpm_db();
```

You can also specify the directory where the RPM database resides. This is most useful for accessing a database in a non-standard location. For example:

```
my $rpm_db = RPM2->open_rpm_db( "-path" => "/var/lib/rpm" );
```

> The -path is normally used as a Perl bareword but is shown here as a string.

Once you have an RPM database object, you can call one of the find subroutines to find packages in most of the same ways as supported by the rpm -q command.

Finding packages

The find_by_name subroutine finds a package or packages by name. It returns a Perl list of the entries found. For example, if you installed more than one version of a package, find_by_name would return a list of all the packages at the different versions.

Similar to find_by_name, find_by_name_iter returns an iterator to iterate over the packages that match the query. The iterator approach is usually more efficient.

Iterating over packages

Iterators are important in the RPM2 package because they provide a more efficient interface to potentially large sets of packages, and because iterators more closely match the underlying C API. Furthermore, iterators are very easy to use. Simply call the next subroutine to move ahead to the next element, that is, the next package.

For example:

```
my $pkg_iter = $rpm_db->find_by_name_iter( "kernel" );

while (my $pkg = $pkg_iter->next() ) {

    # Do something ...
}
```

Listing 18-3 shows a script that acts much like the rpm -q command, without any other command-line options.

Listing 18-3: rpmname.pl

```perl
#!/usr/bin/perl

#
# Queries RPM database for given package.
# Usage:
# rpmname.pl package_name
#
use strict;
use RPM2;

my $rpm_db   = RPM2->open_rpm_db( "$^'path" => "/var/lib/rpm" );

my $pkg_iter = $rpm_db->find_by_name_iter( $ARGV[0] );

while (my $pkg = $pkg_iter->next() ) {

    print $pkg->tag("NAME"), "-", $pkg->tag("VERSION"), "\n";
}

$rpm_db->close_rpm_db();
```

When you run this script, you need to pass the name of a package to query. For example:

```
$ ./rpmname.pl kernel
kernel-2.4.18
```

Additional query subroutines

The find_by_name_iter subroutine finds a package by its name. The RPM2 module also supports a number of other query routines, listed in Table 18-1.

TABLE 18-1 RPM2 MODULE QUERY ROUTINES

Routine	Usage
find_all()	Returns a list with all the packages in the database
find_all_iter()	Returns an iterator over all the packages in the database

Continued

TABLE 18-1 RPM2 MODULE QUERY ROUTINES *(Continued)*

`find_by_file($filename)`	Finds all packages that own the given file, returning a list
`find_by_file_iter($filename)`	Finds all packages that own the given file, returning an iterator
`find_by_name($package_name)`	Finds all packages with the given name, returning a list
`find_by_name_iter($package_name)`	Finds all packages with the given name, returning an iterator
`find_by_provides($capability)`	Finds all packages that provide the given capability, returning a list
`find_by_provides_iter($capability)`	Finds all packages that provide the given capability, returning an iterator
`find_by_requires($capability)`	Finds all packages that require the given capability, returning a list
`find_by_requires_iter($capability)`	Finds all packages that require the given capability, returning an iterator

To verify the find routines, you can try the following script and compare the results with the rpm command. Listing 18-4 shows the script that finds what package provides a capability and also which packages require the capability.

Listing 18-4: rpmprovides.pl

```perl
#!/usr/bin/perl

#
# Queries RPM database for given package,
# listing what it provides and what other
# packages require the capability.
#
# Usage:
# rpmprovides.pl package_name
#
use strict;
use RPM2;
```

```
my $rpm_db    = RPM2->open_rpm_db();

my $pkg_iter = $rpm_db->find_by_provides_iter( $ARGV[0] );

print "Provides: ", $ARGV[0], "\n";

while (my $pkg = $pkg_iter->next() ) {
    print "\t", $pkg->as_nvre(), "\n";
}


# Now, what packages require this capability.

my $pkg_iter2 = $rpm_db->find_by_requires_iter( $ARGV[0] );

print "Requires: ", $ARGV[0], "\n";
while (my $pkg2 = $pkg_iter2->next() ) {
    print "\t", $pkg2->as_nvre(), "\n";
}

$rpm_db->close_rpm_db();
```

When you run this script with the name of a capability, you'll see output like the following:

```
$ ./rpmprovides.pl httpd
Provides: httpd
        httpd-2.0.40-8
Requires: httpd
        mod_perl-1.99_05-3
        5:redhat-config-httpd-1.0.1-13
        mod_python-3.0.0-10
        1:mod_ssl-2.0.40-8
```

The 5: in 5:redhat-config-httpd-1.0.1-13 and 1: in 1:mod_ssl-2.0.40-8 represent the EPOCH tag value.

To verify this script, run the rpm -q command to see if you get the same packages listed. For example:

```
$ rpm -q --whatprovides httpd
httpd-2.0.40-8

$ rpm -q --whatrequires httpd
mod_perl-1.99_05-3
redhat-config-httpd-1.0.1-13
mod_python-3.0.0-10
mod_ssl-2.0.40-8
```

In both cases, you see the same packages listed. You can use this technique to verify your scripts.

The find_by_provides_iter subroutine requires the name of a package, such as bash. You cannot pass a file name, such as /bin/bash, to get the name of the package that provides this capability (a file, really).

Getting information on packages

The tag, as_nvre, and is_source_package subroutines that worked on header objects read from RPM files, shown previously, also work with package entries returned from the RPM database.

For example, Listing 18-5 shows a script, rpminfo.pl, that prints out descriptive information about a given package.

Listing 18-5: rpminfo.pl

```
#!/usr/bin/perl

#
# Queries RPM database for given package and prints info.
# Usage:
# rpminfo.pl package_name
#
use strict;
use RPM2;

my $rpm_db   = RPM2->open_rpm_db( "-path" => "/var/lib/rpm" );

my $pkg_iter = $rpm_db->find_by_name_iter( $ARGV[0] );
```

```perl
while (my $pkg = $pkg_iter->next() ) {

    printInfo( $pkg );
}


$rpm_db->close_rpm_db();


# Prints info on one package.
sub printInfo {
    my($pkg)     = shift;

    print $pkg->as_nvre(), ", ", $pkg->tag("ARCH"), ", ",
        $pkg->tag("OS"),    ", ", $pkg->tag("PLATFORM"), "\n";

    print $pkg->tag("SUMMARY"), "\n";
    print "Group: ", $pkg->tag("GROUP"), "\n";
    print $pkg->tag("DESCRIPTION"), "\n";
    print "Vendor: ", $pkg->tag("VENDOR"), ", ", $pkg->tag("URL"), "\n";
    print "Size: ", $pkg->tag("SIZE"), "\n";
}
```

When you run this script, you'll see output like the following:

```
$ ./rpminfo.pl XFree86
XFree86-4.2.0-72, i386, linux, i386-redhat-linux-gnu
The basic fonts, programs and docs for an X workstation.
Group: User Interface/X
XFree86 is an open source implementation of the X Window System.  It
provides the basic low level functionality which full fledged
graphical user interfaces (GUIs) such as GNOME and KDE are designed
upon.
Vendor: Red Hat, Inc., http://www.xfree86.org
Size: 30552239
```

Listing the Installed Date

The installed date is a number value representing the number of seconds since the start of the Unix epoch, January 1, 1970, which predates the start of the Linux epoch by about 20 years. So, when you get the value of the INSTALLTIME tag, you'll see a meaningless number.

To make sense of this number, pass the value to the Perl localtime function. Listing 18-6 shows an example of this.

Listing 18-6: rpmdate.pl

```perl
#!/usr/bin/perl

#
# Queries RPM database for given package,
# prints out name, vendor, and date installed.
# Usage:
# rpmdate.pl package_name
#
use strict;
use RPM2;

my $rpm_db    = RPM2->open_rpm_db();

my $pkg_iter = $rpm_db->find_by_name_iter( $ARGV[0] );

while (my $pkg = $pkg_iter->next() ) {

    printDate( $pkg );
}

$rpm_db->close_rpm_db();



# Prints installation data for one package.
sub printDate {
    my($pkg)      = shift;

    my $date = localtime( $pkg->tag("INSTALLTIME") );

    printf("%-20s %-17s %s\n", $pkg->as_nvre(), $pkg->tag("VENDOR"), $date);
}
```

 The `printf` function in this script can do something the `rpm` command cannot do. Even with the `--queryformat` option, you cannot group multiple items and then set the size; with Perl, you can. Simply assign the multiple values to a string, or use the handy `as_nvre` subroutine, which gathers up to four tags together into one string.

When you pass the name of a package to this script, you'll see the date the package was installed. For example:

```
$ ./rpmdate.pl kernel
kernel-2.4.18-14     Red Hat, Inc.     Sat Oct  5 12:29:58 2002
```

Handling String Array Tags

Not only is the date stored in a format that adds complication to your script. A number of tags are string arrays, not scalar strings. This means you may see output that is all mashed together.

To help deal with this, the following subroutine takes in an array of strings and returns a string that is built using a passed-in delimiter:

```perl
sub arrayToString {
    my($sep)   = shift;
    my(@array) = @_;
    my($str);

    $str = $array[0];

    for ( $i = 1; $i < $#array; $i++ )
    {
        $str = $str . $sep . $array[$i];
    }

    return $str;
}
```

 Show your Perl expertise and earn extra points by implementing the `arrayToString` subroutine as a single Perl statement that uses the `join` function.

The following list shows the tags that are an array of strings:

◆ BASENAMES

◆ CHANGELOGNAME

◆ CHANGELOGTEXT

◆ DIRNAMES

◆ FILEGROUPNAME

- FILELANGS

- FILELINKTOS

- FILEMD5S

- FILEUSERNAME

- OLDFILENAMES

- PROVIDENAME

- PROVIDEVERSION

- REQUIRENAME

- REQUIREVERSION

 Chapter 5 covers more on these tags.

Listing the Files in a Package

The files subroutine provides a list of all the files in a package. Listing 18-7 shows how to access this list.

Listing 18-7: rpmfiles.pl

```perl
#!/usr/bin/perl

#
# Queries RPM database for given package,
# prints out the files in the package.
# Usage:
# rpmfiles.pl package_name
#
use strict;
use RPM2;

my $rpm_db   = RPM2->open_rpm_db();

my $pkg_iter = $rpm_db->find_by_name_iter( $ARGV[0] );

while (my $pkg = $pkg_iter->next() ) {

    printFiles( $pkg );
```

```
    }
$rpm_db->close_rpm_db();



# Prints installation data for one package.
sub printFiles {
    my($pkg)  = shift;

    my $files = arrayToString("\n", $pkg->files() );

    print "Files:\n", $files, "\n";
}

sub arrayToString {
    my($sep)   = shift;
    my(@array) = @_;
    my($str);

    $str = $array[0];

    for ( my $i = 1; $i < $#array; $i++ )
    {
        $str = $str . $sep . $array[$i];
    }

    return $str;
}
```

When you run this script, you'll see output like the following:

```
$ ./rpmfiles.pl jikes
Files:
/usr/bin/jikes
/usr/doc/jikes-1.17/license.htm
```

Comparing versions

The RPM2 module overrides the spaceship operator, <=>, to perform version comparisons between packages. The script in Listing 18-8 shows how to compare all local RPM files against the newest installed version of the same package if the package is installed.

Listing 18-8: rpmver.pl

```perl
#!/usr/bin/perl -w

#
# Compare versions of all *.rpm files against the
# latest packages installed (if installed)
#
# Usage:
# rpmver.pl
# This script looks for all *.rpm files.
#
use strict;
use RPM2;

my $rpm_db   = RPM2->open_rpm_db();

for my $filename (<*.rpm>) {
    my $h = RPM2->open_package( $filename );

    # Ensure we compare against the newest
    # package of the given name.
    my ($installed) =
        sort { $b <=> $a } $rpm_db->find_by_name($h->name);

    if (not $installed) {
        printf "Package %s not installed.\n", $h->as_nvre;
    } else {
        my ($result) = ($h <=> $installed);

        if ($result < 0) {
            printf "Installed package %s newer than file %s\n",
                $installed->as_nvre,
                $h->as_nvre;
        } else {
            printf "File %s newer than installed package %s\n",
                $h->as_nvre,
                $installed->as_nvre;
        }
    }
}
```

The sort { $a <=> $b } in front of the find_by_name call sorts all the packages of that name by the version number, so that the comparison is performed against the newest installed version of the package. The ($h <=> $installed) compares the header from the RPM file on disk against the newest installed version of the package.

When you run this script, you'll see output like the following, depending on which RPM files you have in the local directory:

```
$ perl rpmver.pl
Package acroread-4.0-0 not installed.
Package canvas-7.0b2.0-1 not installed.
Installed package jikes-1.18-1 newer than file jikes-1.14-1
Installed package SDL-1.2.4-5 newer than file SDL-0.9.9-4
Package ted-2.8-1 not installed.
```

Closing the database

When you are done with the RPM database, call close_rpm_db, as shown following:

```
$rpm_db->close_rpm_db();
```

Note that this call is not necessary, as the RPM2 module will close the database when the object, in this case $rpm_db, goes out of scope.

Where to Go from Here

One of the strengths of Perl is that there are so many add-on packages available. In addition, Perl is really strong in text processing. You can combine these strengths to provide cleaner output for RPM database queries, for example, avoiding the complex syntax for the --queryformat option to the rpm command. Perl can do more than the --queryformat option allows. For example, you can combine multiple values together into a Perl string and then format the output. The --queryformat option only allows formatting on each value individually, not groups of values.

In addition, you can combine one of the Perl templating modules, such as Text::Template or HTML::Template, to create an HTML page for a given package. You could use Perl to create formatted HTML pages for all the installed packages on your system, with HTML links to cross-reference all the dependencies.

Download these modules from the CPAN site, www.cpan.org.

This chapter covers the RPM2 module. Right now, the RPM2 module supports only querying packages and the RPM database. Future versions will likely add the ability to install, update, and remove packages.

In addition to this module, you can find an RPM module with RPM::Header and RPM::Database classes. Another module, RPM::Specfile, provides the ability to turn Perl modules, such as those stored on CPAN, into RPM packages. The RPM::Specfile module helps create an RPM spec file for a Perl module.

The Perl-RPM-Perlonly bundle provides an alternative version of the RPM::Header module written entirely in Perl with no usage of the C rpm library. This makes RPM access much easier on platforms for which you don't have the RPM system.

The RPM-Tools bundle includes RPM::Update, which compares the packages installed on your system (listed by calling `rpm -qa`) with the packages available on another system, that may be available only with a network link. This module can also update packages that are older than the designated master system. RPM::Make, also part of the RPM-Tools bundle, helps create RPM packages from a Perl script. This module does not support all the spec file options described in Chapter 10, but it can help you make simple packages.

You can download all these modules from the CPAN site.

Summary

This chapter introduces the `RPM2` add-on module to allow Perl scripts to access information on RPM package files and in the RPM database. To access an RPM file and query information about that file, you need to call the `open_package` subroutine. Once you've opened the file, you can call the `tag`, `as_nvre`, `is_source_package`, and `files` subroutines on the header object to query data about the package.

To access the RPM database, call `open_rpm_db`. Once you've opened the database, you can call one of the find subroutines, such as `find_by_name` or `find_by_name_iter`, to search for packages. The subroutines that have names ending with _iter_, such as `find_by_name_iter`, return an iterator object to iterate over the packages found. The other find subroutines, such as `find_by_name`, return a Perl list of the packages found.

You can then call the `tag`, `as_nvre`, and `files` subroutines on the package objects to query information about the packages.

When you are done with the RPM database, call `close_rpm_db`.

Part IV

Extending RPM

Chapter 19

Using RPM on Non–Red Hat Linuxes

IN THIS CHAPTER

- ◆ Dealing with RPM issues on other versions of Linux
- ◆ RPM standardization
- ◆ Working around RPM differences when installing RPMs
- ◆ Working around RPM differences when building RPMs
- ◆ Dealing with non-RPM-based Linux distributions

ALTHOUGH ITS NAME WAS ORIGINALLY the Red Hat Package Manager, RPM has been adopted by most major Linux distributions. With this adoption, RPM has moved from its Red Hat roots, and *RPM* now stands for the *RPM Package Manager*.

In addition, the RPM package format is being adopted by the *Linux Standards Base (LSB)*. The LSB defines a set of standards to help maintain compatibility for all Linux distributions.

See www.linuxbase.org for more on the LSB.

This chapter covers differences in how Linux distributions use RPM, ways to work around these differences, and also tools you can use for non-RPM distributions.

Troubleshooting RPM Installation Issues

The main RPM issues when dealing with installing RPMs on other versions of Linux are:

◆ Different versions of RPM itself

◆ Different divisions of software into packages

◆ Dealing with dependency issues

◆ Different install locations

The following sections expand on these issues.

Dealing with RPM versions

Red Hat Linux 8.0 ships with RPM version 4.1. Other distributions of Linux ship with other versions of RPM. Thus, one of the first commands you can run on another Linux distribution is the `rpm --version` command, to see what RPM version is in use and help identify any issues. For example:

```
$ rpm --version
RPM version 4.1
```

Once you know the RPM version, you can plan for any issues that arise from installing RPMs made with a different RPM version. For example, RPM 4.0 and higher inserts dependency information automatically into RPMs. If your Linux distribution runs RPM 3.*x*, you may need to disable some of the dependency checks, for example, if you want to install RPMs built under RPM 4.*x* onto an RPM 3.*x* system.

On installing RPMs, you can disable the dependency checks with the `--nodeps` option. If you do this, though, you should manually check that the dependencies are really met by your Linux installation.

On the other hand, if you want to install RPMs built on an RPM 3.*x* system onto an RPM 4.*x* system, you may need to deal with package signatures. RPM 4.*x* versions also automatically check for signatures. When installing packages on an RPM 4.*x* system, you can disable this feature with the `--nosignature` option.

Using these techniques, you should be able to install packages built with RPM 4.1 on systems that use RPM 3.*x* versions or vice versa.

Dealing with divisions of software into packages

There is no standardization as to how large applications are divided into packages on different Linux distributions. This means that dependencies between packages may differ.

If your dependencies are for packages provided with the Linux distribution, which includes a huge number of packages, you must address this issue. The package an RPM depends on may not exist and may not even be needed, on a particular Linux distribution.

If instead the dependencies are for files, especially shared libraries, you should be okay for the most part, unless the files are located in different directories.

The only real solution to this problem is to turn off dependency checks on installing, with the - -nodeps option. Then you must check manually that your system really does provide all the necessary dependencies. Use the techniques shown in Chapter 6 to verify all the dependencies are met on your system.

Using the - -nodeps option can lead to problems with your RPM database because you are installing packages by defeating the RPM system's safeguards for dependencies. Only use the - -nodeps option if you are really sure the dependencies are met on your system, even if from a different package than expected.

Dealing with dependency issues

One of the toughest areas to deal with is the problem of dependencies. This topic ranges from the very simple issue of installing a necessary package to complex issues of shared library versions or particular Perl modules.

Start with the simple case and make certain that you haven't failed to install a necessary RPM that provides the right dependency. In most cases, you can download a vendor-specific package from your Linux vendor, such as www.suse.com for SuSE Linux. Most Linux vendors provide HTTP or FTP sites with a large set of packages created for their distributions. If such a distribution-specific package solves a dependency issue, this is the easiest way around the problem.

After you verify that you haven't simply omitted a necessary package, move on to other potential explanations. Another issue involves shared libraries and ELF, or Extended Linking Format, symbols. A package may require an older or newer version of a shared library. Applications that are tied to a particular version of a shared library can cause problems, since you may not want to install incompatible versions of a shared library.

If the dependency is for a system-shared library, such as the shared C library, you can often recompile the package (rebuild from a source RPM) to get the package to use the newer or older version of the system library. This is possible because most Linux applications don't call on version-specific features of system shared libraries (some do, but most don't). If the dependency is for an application-shared library, this is more serious, since there were likely API changes that could impact the application. Install the package owning the application-shared library and again, try to rebuild the package from the source RPM.

You can use the `rpm -qf` command to query which package owns a given file. You can use the `rpm -q --whatprovides` command to query for which package provides a given capability. Chapter 6 covers more on dependencies.

Some packages are considered developer packages. These usually depend on some base package. For example, the rpm-devel package depends on the rpm package. The rpm-python package depends on both the rpm package and the python package (at particular version numbers as well).

This naming scheme of a *base* package and *base*-devel is used for Red Hat Linux packages, but may not be used for other vendor packages. In any case, you can solve this type of dependency by finding the relevant base packages that the package you are trying to install depends on. Consult the manuals that come with your Linux distribution or browse the online RPM repositories to see what naming conventions are used for your Linux distribution.

Many packages depend on scripting language interpreters, such as Perl. Sometimes the dependency is based on scripts used in a package, such as install or trigger scripts. You can have problems arise with the locations of these scripting interpreters. Perl, for example, is usually installed in /usr/bin/perl on most Linux systems. Another common location is /usr/local/bin/perl. In addition, packages may depend on particular add-on modules, especially Perl modules. With most versions of Linux released in the last few years, you should be able to override a Perl dependency with the `--nodeps` option as long as you have Perl installed.

File paths may also cause problems. For example, a file that a package depends on may be in a different location or owned by a different package. For this case, you can try to find the package that owns the file and make sure that package is installed. If your Linux vendor provides a pre-built RPM database of all packages, such as the rpmdb-redhat package, you can query this database to find out which package owns the file for that version of Linux.

Dealing with install locations

Linux vendors can install software anywhere. For example, some distributions place a lot of software under /opt instead of the more common /usr. From an RPM perspective, this is mostly an issue with file dependencies and the install location for packages. Evolving file system standards also help limit this issue.

You can attempt to relocate any package using the `--badreloc` option.

Chapter 4 covers the `--badreloc` option.

But whereas the `--badreloc` option will relocate the files in a package, it will not modify the contents of those files. So, any file inside a package that references files and directory locations may not work properly, since it may have the old, invalid, paths.

The only real way around this problem is to edit any script files that come with the package and contain hard-coded paths. If the paths reside inside binary executables, you need to get a source RPM for the package, patch the sources and then create a new RPM.

When all else fails, rebuild from the source package

When all of these techniques fail to install a package, you still have a fallback option. If you have the source RPM for a package, you can install the source RPM on the new system and then edit the spec file until you can rebuild a package that will install on your version of Linux.

For example, a set of Build Root Policy (brp) helper scripts are run at the end of the `%install` section in an RPM. These scripts perform tasks such as compressing man pages. The Mandrake brp scripts use bzip2 compression. Red Hat brp scripts use gzip compression. This is one case where rebuilding an RPM and then installing may work best.

Handling Problems Building RPMs

Given all these differences, how can you create RPMs while avoiding problems? With some work setting things up, you can create an RPM build environment that solves most vendor issues. This depends on taking a methodical approach to building your packages and using techniques to avoid vendor issues wherever possible.

When building RPMs, you will face many of the same problems – and solutions – as when installing RPMs. For example, due to the different ways Linux vendors divide software into packages, your RPMs will likely have issues defining the proper dependencies. There are also a number of issues that apply only when building RPMs.

The following sections cover the main issues when building RPMs.

Writing distribution-specific packages

One of the ways around all the differences between Linux distributions in RPM usage is to define distribution-specific packages. To do this, you create a separate package on each Linux distribution you support.

That's a lot of work. If possible, fit the differences into macros and use a single spec file to reduce some of this work. This technique works up to a point. Sometimes, your spec file becomes too complicated and you may decide that it is easier to create multiple spec files, one per Linux distribution.

One way to help make vendor-specific packages, or to see which RPM macros are defined on a given Linux distribution, is to look for an RPM that contains the distribution-specific RPM configuration. For example, on Red Hat Linux systems, the Red Hat RPM configuration is defined by the redhat-rpm-config package.

You can list the files in this package to see where Red Hat defines macros specific to their Linux distribution.

```
$ rpm -ql redhat-rpm-config
/usr/lib/rpm/redhat
/usr/lib/rpm/redhat/brp-compress
/usr/lib/rpm/redhat/brp-redhat
/usr/lib/rpm/redhat/brp-sparc64-linux
/usr/lib/rpm/redhat/brp-strip
/usr/lib/rpm/redhat/brp-strip-comment-note
/usr/lib/rpm/redhat/brp-strip-shared
/usr/lib/rpm/redhat/find-lang.sh
/usr/lib/rpm/redhat/find-provides
/usr/lib/rpm/redhat/find-requires
/usr/lib/rpm/redhat/macros
/usr/lib/rpm/redhat/perl.prov
/usr/lib/rpm/redhat/perl.req
/usr/lib/rpm/redhat/rpmrc
```

These files, such as /usr/lib/rpm/redhat/macros, show you what is specific to a given Linux distribution. You can then look at the macros defined in these files to identify settings for a particular distribution, in this case, Red Hat. Armed with this knowledge, you can better create portable RPM spec files.

Dealing with automatic dependency generation

One of the features in RPM 4.*x* is the automatic generation of dependencies. For a variety of reasons including different package layouts, different directory structures, or different versions of RPM, you may need to disable some or all of automatic generation of dependencies.

You can disable the automatic generation of dependencies by placing the following directive in your spec file:

```
Autoreq: 0
```

If you do so, you need to use the Requires: tag to manually define all requirements. This is not a good solution to the issue of automatic dependencies however. Most likely, you will need to override the %{__find_requires} and %{__find_provides} macros in order to filter out any unwanted dependencies.

These two macros resolve to shell scripts that perform the automated dependency checks, as you can see with the rpm --eval command:

```
$ rpm --eval "%__find_provides"
/usr/lib/rpm/find-provides
rpm --eval "%__find_requires"
/usr/lib/rpm/find-requires
```

You can override these scripts to filter out any dependencies that cause problems for your packages.

Dealing with different macros

Different Linux vendors define different macros in their RPM setup. This may mean not only different values for the macros, but different macro names as well. Because of this, it is best to define your own local set of macros when building RPMs.

As much as possible, depend on your own RPM macros. You can define your macros in terms of vendor-specific macros using conditional statements in your spec files, a topic covered in Chapter 11. You can also read examples in the "Build environment and macros" section of this chapter.

This really boils down to creating a disciplined RPM build environment.

Making relocatable packages

You should aim to make your packages relocatable so that users can install your packages into any directory. This makes it easier to deal with the locations chosen by different Linux distributions, such as /usr, /usr/local, or /opt, for installing add-on software.

Chapter 10 covers the spec file format. Chapter 11 covers making relocatable packages.

You can use the %{_bindir} macro in your spec files, which will help create per-distribution packages using the right settings.

In addition, you can define macros in your spec files that define the location for dependencies. You can then use the --define option to the rpmbuild command to define values for your macros that specify the locations for the dependencies.

This technique of setting up Linux distribution-specific macros can help solve a lot of problems with cross-platform RPMs.

Creating an RPM build environment

If you start with the idea that you want to build RPMs for multiple versions of Linux, you can set up an RPM build environment that cleanly separates most vendor-specific issues.

The key issues with the build environment are:

◆ Detecting the vendors

◆ Using macros to define a clean build process

◆ Handling different dependencies

Detecting Vendors

To make a clean build environment, you need to be able to detect the Linux vendor and make build settings based on this vendor. To help with this, many Linux vendors install a special file with the vendor name, or a special package with the vendor name. You can query for either of these.

For files, the convention follows:

```
/etc/vendor-release
```

For example:

```
$ more /etc/redhat-release
Red Hat Linux release 8.0 (Psyche)
```

For packages, the convention is vendor-release for a package name. For example:

```
$ rpm -q redhat-release
redhat-release-8.0-8
```

You can use either approach or simply define a macro for the vendor and use the --define option to set the macro. For example:

```
# rpmbuild -ba --define 'linuxVendor suse'
```

With this definition, you can use the macro %linuxVendor inside your spec files. It is generally easier, though, if your scripts can automatically detect the Linux vendor instead of having to define it manually. The manual approach works, though, if it becomes too much effort to detect the vendor automatically.

Build environment and macros

Once you can detect the Linux vendor, you can create macros based on the differences between Linux distributions that affect your applications.

Chapter 21 covers RPM macros.

The macros that specifically help you with platform differences include the %if .. %endif conditional. You can use this in combination with special macros you define. In addition, command-line options such as --with, --without, and --target allow you to control features and the build target within an RPM.

The %if macro allows you to specify a condition within your spec file. For example:

```
%if %{old_5x} && %{old_6x}
%{error: You cannot build for .5x and .6x at the same time}
%quit
%endif

%if %{old_5x}
%define b5x 1
%undefine b6x
%endif

%if %{old_6x}
%define b6x 1
%undefine b5x
%endif
```

You can also use %if to control settings such as the Requires:, as shown in the following example:

```
%if %{build6x}
Requires: util-linux, pam >= 0.66-5
%else
Requires: util-linux, pam >= 0.75-37, /etc/pam.d/system-auth
%endif
```

The --with command-line option defines a special macro starting with _with_. For example, the following command-line option defines a feature to use:

```
$ rpmbuild -bc --with ssh filename.spec
```

This example defines the macro _with_ssh to --with-ssh. This format was specially designed to work with GNU configuration. You can use this for conditional builds for platform-dependent issues.

The `--without` command-line option similarly defines a macro starting with `_without_`. The convention is that this option defines a feature the code should not use.

You can combine `--with` and `--without` to turn on and off features referenced in your spec files. For example:

```
./configure %{?_with_ssh}
```

This will pass the following command line if the `_with_ssh` macro is defined:

```
./configure --with-ssh
```

If this option is not defined, the command will be:

```
./configure
```

The `--target` option sets the spec file macros `%_target`, `%_target_arch`, and `%_target_os` . For example:

```
$ rpmbuild -bc --target ppc-ibm-aix /usr/src/redhat/SPECS/jikes.spec
```

Compatibility and Glue Packages

Not all Linux distributions are the same. Macros alone won't provide work-arounds for all the differences. You can, though, get a lot of mileage from compatibility and glue packages.

A *compatibility package* provides a legacy API on newer systems that no longer support the legacy API. By convention, compatibility packages are named with a leading `compat-` to signify their purpose.

For example:

```
$ rpm -q --qf "%{description}" compat-libstdc++
The compat-libstdc++ package contains compatibility Standard C++
```

Using a compatibility package allows you to create programs that use a least-common-denominator approach, programming to the oldest but most common APIs. As some Linux distributions eliminate the old APIs, compatibility packages can provide the missing APIs.

Similarly, a *glue package* provides a dependency that exists on some Linux distributions but not others. It glues together your package with the Linux distribution that is missing an essential capability.

With all this discussion of RPM and Linux differences, you might think that Linux is one big mess. That's not true. Linux maintains a high degree of compatibility among Linux distributions as well as among processor architectures. Most programs originally created for Linux on Intel-based architectures compile cleanly on Linux versions running on other processor architectures such as MIPS, SPARC, and ARM.

 A key point in both of these approaches is to separate the compatibility and glue packages from your main application packages. The application packages should be as clean of vendor issues as possible. Instruct your users to install the compatibility or glue packages as needed (based on their Linux distribution) along with the main application package or packages.

The main differences lie in how Linux vendors split up the huge number of files associated with Linux into RPM packages as well as which versions of tools like C compilers the vendors ship.

Dealing with Signatures

With SuSE Linux, or any Linux based on UnitedLinux 1.0, the RPM packages are signed with OpenPGP version 4, not 3, as used in RPM 4.1. This means that you must use some other, non-RPM means to extract the signatures from an RPM package, and then verify these signatures with gpg.

Dealing with Non-RPM-Based Linux Versions

The main Linux distributions that don't support RPM are the Debian GNU/Linux family and Slackware Linux. To help with these distributions, you can use a package-conversion tool called alien. Alien is a package that supports conversions between RPM and so-called alien package formats such as the dpkg (Debian GNU/Linux), slp (Stampede Linux), and tgz (Slackware Linux) formats.

You can use alien on your RPM-based Linux system to convert RPMs to some other format, such as the Debian dpkg. You can also use alien to convert other package formats into RPMs, depending on which way you need to go.

Standardizing RPMs

RPM is being considered as part of the Linux Standard Base, or LSB, 1.3. This will define a standard packaging format for Linux distributions, and over time reduce the RPM differences between distributions.

In addition, other efforts are underway to help unify the diverse Linux distributions, including the Filesystem Hierarchy Standard and the adoption of RPM by many Linux vendors.

Filesystem Hierarchy Standard

The FHS, or Filesystem Hierarchy Standard, defines the purpose of all the upper-level directories on Linux systems, such as /var and /usr/bin. This standard, along with the Linux Standard Base, or LSB, is driving Linux distributions to a greater degree of similarity.

The FHS helps by specifying where applications should get installed and which directories should be left to local administrators to manage. The FHS also defines the purpose of all Linux directories, giving vendors and application writers a better idea of where they should install their packages.

See www.linuxbase.org for more on the LSB. See www.pathname.com/fhs/ for more on the FHS.

RPM adoption

RPM has been adopted by a large number of Linux distributions. In addition, standardization efforts, both for RPM and for filesystem locations, are making Linux systems less varied. This means that over time, many of the RPM-related differences between Linux distributions will fade away, making it easier to create cross-platform RPMs.

Summary

This chapter covers differences in RPM versions between various Linux distributions, and techniques you can use to get around these differences. Each Linux vendor packages software differently, even if the vendor uses RPM. This can cause problems unless you write your spec files carefully. Inside your RPM spec files, you can use conditional elements as well as platform-based macro definitions to help create RPMs for multiple packages.

Some of the best conventions are to split the software in your applications from any compatibility or glue packages, separate packages that provide missing features for various flavors of Linux.

Standardization efforts such as the Linux Standard Base and Filesystem Hierarchy Standard are bringing Linux vendors closer and closer together. Widespread adoption of RPM by most Linux distributions also helps. Whereas this chapter covers RPM on other Linux distributions, the next chapter tackles RPM outside of Linux.

Chapter 20

RPM on Other Operating Systems

IN THIS CHAPTER

◆ Running RPM on other operating systems

◆ Bootstrapping RPM on other operating systems

◆ Setting up the RPM environment

◆ Creating non-Linux RPMs

◆ Setting up an RPM build environment

◆ Cross-building packages

RPM WAS ORIGINALLY DESIGNED on Linux and for most of its life has been a Linux-centric package management system. But most Linux programs are portable to most versions of Unix or Unix-like operating systems. Linux is, after all, a Unix-workalike operating system.

The RPM system is no exception. It has been ported to a number of operating systems, including quite a few Unix variants. The source code is freely available, so you can port RPM to other systems as well.

This chapter covers running RPM on non-Linux operating systems, including getting the RPM system in the first place, bootstrapping an RPM environment, and creating packages for other operating systems.

The first step is to get RPM for your system, or port RPM if it isn't already available.

Running RPM on Other Operating Systems

The RPM system, made up of mostly the `rpm` and `rpmbuild` commands, has been ported to a number of operating systems. There is nothing stopping you from running the RPM system on other platforms.

Other operating systems have their own native package management software. You may prefer the way RPM works, or merely want to standardize on RPM across all platforms you manage. There will always be a few issues, however, when running RPM on other operating systems. For example, operating system patches and updates are likely to be distributed in the operating system's native package management format, not RPM. Many applications will be updated also using the system's native package management format.

You will need to always keep in mind that there are two package management schemes in use: RPM and the native one. This issue has not stopped a great many people from using RPM on other systems, though, as shown by the list of platforms RPM has been ported to (see Table 20-1 for the list).

On the plus side, package management has always been one of the main areas where versions of Linux, Unix, and other operating systems differ, sometimes quite a lot. By using RPM, you can transfer your knowledge of package management from one system to another, saving valuable time and hassles. You will be able to update systems in the same manner, a big plus if you manage a diverse set of systems.

Another reason to use RPM on other operating systems is that in most cases, RPM provides far more capabilities than the native package management software. Following the RPM philosophy, each package can be separately verified, checked, and updated. Each package lists the other packages it depends on, and also lists the capabilities it provides. You can automate the installation and upgrade processes with RPM. You can also perform a lot of version and signature comparisons. All of this leads to a more secure, more robust system.

Many operating systems don't include these capabilities in the native package management software. This is why many users run RPM on other operating systems.

See Chapter 2 for more on the philosophy behind RPM.

If you decide to use RPM on a non-Linux system, the first step is getting RPM for your system, if it is available.

Getting RPM for your system

The first step to using RPM on non-Linux platforms is getting the RPM system for your platform. In most cases, this is a relatively easy step, as RPM has been ported to a great many platforms, as listed on the main RPM Web site.

Links to RPM versions for various platforms are listed at www.rpm.org/ platforms/.

Go to this site and download the versions for the platforms you need. Table 20-1 lists the platforms RPM has been ported to, as reported by the RPM site.

TABLE 20-1 AVAILABLE PLATFORMS FOR RPM

Platform	Notes
AIX	
AmigaOS	With GeekGadgets
BeOS	With GeekGadgets
FreeBSD	
HP-UX	10.20+, 9.04
IRIX	
Linux	Multiple platforms including Alpha, Intel, Motorola 68000, SGI MIPS, PowerPC, and SPARC
LynxOS	
MachTen	
MacOS X	
Mint	
NCS System V	
NetBSD	
OS/2	
OSF/1	3.2+
SCO OpenServer	5.0.2+
Sinix	
Solaris	Solaris for SPARC 2.4 and 8+, Solaris for Intel
SunOS 4.1.3	
Windows	Under Cygwin

Note that RPM has likely been ported to even more platforms. These are just the ones reported to the rpm.org site.

If you fix a bug in RPM on a non-Linux system, or if you port RPM to a new system, please report this to the rpm.org site maintainers, as well as make your work available for others. You never know, but someone else may fix a problem you're facing.

If Table 20-1 does not cover the platforms you need, you must compile and bootstrap the RPM environment for your platforms, as covered in the "Bootstrapping RPM on Other Operating Systems" section, following.

 Don't expect to find RPMs of the RPM system for these other platforms. If you did, there would be no way to install RPM. Instead, you'll find RPM packaged in a variety of formats, typically using a native bundling format for a given system, or at least a supported format. Compressed tar files are very common. RPM for IRIX systems come in IRIX tardist format.

If RPM is available for your system, download the package and follow any installation instructions that come with the package. For example, RPM for Solaris 8 requires the libiconv library, as well as the Solaris packages SUNWzlib and SUNWbzip. You must install these packages prior to installing RPM.

Each operating system will have similar requirements. Windows systems have a few extra requirements due to the fact that Windows is very different from Linux or Unix-like systems.

Running RPM on Windows

The version of RPM for Windows requires cygwin, originally the Cygnus port of many Unix tools to Windows. Now part of Red Hat, you can download the cygwin environment from the main cygwin site.

 Download cygwin from www.cygwin.com.

You can download a setup.exe program to install the environment on Windows. After installation, you can download the RPM system for Windows.

After you have RPM installed, you can set up your RPM system. If RPM wasn't already ported to your operating systems, however, you will need to bootstrap RPM on your platforms.

Bootstrapping RPM on Other Operating Systems

If you cannot find a version of RPM that has been ported to your platform, you can port it yourself. The RPM system usually isn't that hard to port to any platform that can appear like Unix or Linux systems, such as any platform that supports POSIX system calls or something like these system calls.

Don't be dismayed by the sheer size of the RPM package. Much of the RPM system was carefully designed to run across multiple platforms, so file access is abstracted to special portability routines. For example, RPM has been ported to both AmigaOS and BeOS, two non-Unix operating systems.

Downloading the RPM software

To bootstrap RPM on another operating system, download the RPM source code from the main RPM site.

You can download the RPM source code from `ftp://ftp.rpm.org/pub/rpm/dist/`.

Note that you probably do not want to download an RPM of the sources, since your platform won't have RPM available. In most cases, you'll want to download a tarred compressed archive, such as rpm-4.1.tar.gz for RPM version 4.1.

Extracting the software

If the system you plan to port RPM doesn't have the `tar` and `gzip` commands available, or something that supports these formats, then you need to find a way to extract the software.

Programs such as WinZip on Windows support extracting .tar.gz files. Your platform may have a similar program.

One way is to port the `gzip` and `tar` commands to your platform.

You can download the sources for `tar` and `gzip` from www.gnu.org.

Another way is to extract the sources on a platform with these commands available, such as a Linux platform. Then, create a file using a format supported by your operating system and transfer the files to the other system.

Once you have the RPM source code available on your target system, and all the files are extracted, you are ready to start porting. The first step is really simple: Read.

Reading the INSTALL file

In the main RPM source directory, you will see two very important files: README and INSTALL. Read them both. (You would be surprised at how many times people need to be told this.)

Of the two, the INSTALL file has much more detailed information on installing RPM on a new system. The INSTALL file describes the libraries required by RPM, provides tips on compiling RPM, and describes some of the set up work necessary after compiling the RPM system.

Some of the hardest parts of the RPM system to port, though, may be in the database, compression, and encryption calls, used as libraries by the RPM system.

Libraries required by RPM

Rather than invent everything from scratch, the RPM system makes use of a number of libraries, including those listed in Table 20-2.

TABLE 20-2 LIBRARIES USED BY RPM

Library	Purpose
Berkeley DB	RPM database, using db1 and db3
bzip2	Compression
gettext	International text lookup
gpg	For digital signatures
gzip	Compression
popt	Processing command-line options
zlib	Compression

Read through the INSTALL file to find out where you can download versions of these libraries. You may find that each library has its own set of dependencies, all of which you need to port to your target platform.

Tools for building RPM

In addition to the libraries listed in Table 20-2, RPM requires a number of GNU utilities for building RPM, including those listed in Table 20-3.

TABLE 20-3 TOOLS USED TO BUILD RPM

Tool	Usage
Autoconf	Builds configure scripts
Automake	Used with autoconf
GNU make	Used to control building the sources
Libtool	Used by the autogen.sh script

In addition to all this, RPM works best with the GNU C compiler, GCC, and the GNU make program, gnumake, or simply gmake.

 The source code for all the GNU tools is available at www.gnu.org.

Compiling RPM

After downloading the RPM sources, extracting all the files and installing all the prerequisite libraries, you are ready to start compiling RPM.

RPM includes quite a few subsystems, such as popt for parsing command-line options. Each of these subsystems requires some configuration. Most of this configuration is automated through the use of the autogen.sh script and the autoconf/automake tool used to create configure scripts.

The autogen.sh script is a Bourne shell script that checks for specific versions of necessary tools and libraries. After checking dependencies, the autogen.sh script calls different autogen.sh scripts in the beecrypt, libelf, popt, and zlib directories. When done with that task, the autogen.sh script calls `configure`.

Pass a command-line option of `--noconfigure` to disable the call to `configure`.

Edit the autogen.sh script if you are using different versions of the necessary tools. The autogen.sh script is coded to require the specific versions of these tools as were used originally to build the RPM package. In addition, your system may have libraries stored in different locations than those expected by the autogen.sh, so it's a good idea to edit this script and verify all the assumptions.

 One really big assumption in this script is that you have a Unix-like operating system. If not, you will need to determine how to set up the Makefiles manually. This requires a lot of trial and error while you edit the Makefiles and then see if you can build the software. Fix each problem that arises and try again.

When you are done with the autogen.sh script, you can use the following basic commands to create system-specific Makefiles, compile RPM and install the commands:

```
$ ./configure
$ make
$ make install
```

The `configure` script takes the Makefile.in files and uses these files as templates to create custom versions of Makefile.in files, tuned to your system. (The automake system starts with a Makefile.am file, creates an expanded Makefile.in file, and finally results in a Makefile tuned to your system.) If all else fails, you can copy each Makefile.in file to Makefile and then edit the Makefile to make one that will work on your system.

 See the GNU site, at www.gnu.org, for more on the autoconf and automake tools.

If the `make install` step fails, you can manually copy the RPM executables and scripts to a directory for system commands.

Handling problems

If RPM fails to compile or install, you can still work around many issues. The key is to find out what went wrong, fix the problem, and try again. You may go through this loop many times before RPM successfully compiles and installs.

Most problems can be solved by changing the configuration settings. If possible, change the inputs to the `configure` command to specify C compiler options, and so on, that you discover you need. You can then run the basic commands to build RPM again, but with any special options you discovered are necessary:

```
$ ./configure -any_options_set_here
$ make
$ make install
```

If you take this approach, you avoid having to edit a number of Makefiles (one in each source code subdirectory) by hand. You also have an easier time of switching to different command-line options as you determine more solutions to the compilation problems.

If this won't work, though, you can edit the Makefile.am file or the generated Makefile directly to add whatever settings are needed. For example, you may need to specify additional directories for libraries, or some C compiler compatibility option.

As you discover problems, remember you are not alone in porting RPM. Check the RPM mailing list, where the question of getting RPM going on other platforms comes up frequently.

For details on viewing the RPM mailing list archives and signing up for the list, see `www.rpm.org/mailing_list/`.

Setting Up the RPM System

Once you have RPM available on your platform, you need to set up the RPM system. This includes setting up the RPM database and creating an RPM environment.

Setting up the RPM database

After you have the RPM system available on your platform, you need to set up the RPM database. This usually involves two steps:

◆ Initializing an empty RPM database

◆ Populating the database with packages, especially for dependencies

Both steps are necessary.

Initializing an Empty RPM Database

After you have the RPM system installed on your platform, the next big step is to create an RPM database for your platform. You can make an empty database with the `rpm --initdb` command, as shown following:

```
# mkdir /var/lib/rpm
# rpm --initdb
```

The first command creates the default directory for the RPM database.

You may need to pass command-line options to specify a non-default location of the RPM database, such as the following:

```
# rpm --dbpath /location/of/your/rpm/database --initdb
```

Use a command like this one if you don't want to place the RPM database in its default location.

In addition, use the `-v` option to add more verbose output. This is very useful if errors occur. Use the `--root` option to specify a different root directory for RPM operations. Use the `--rcfile` option to specify a non-default set of *rc* files and the `--macros` option to specify a non-default set of macros.

 Chapter 21 covers RPM customization.

Initializing the RPM database creates the necessary structure for an empty database. You can then fill, or populate, the database with packages. In most cases, all you need to do is install packages to populate the RPM database, as each installed package gets added to the database.

Handling Dependencies for Packages Installed Without RPM

Each time you install a package, you populate the RPM database. This works well, as long as you have already installed all the dependencies for the packages you want to install.

On an operating system that is based on RPM, such as Red Hat Linux, all packages (except for some bootstrapping code) are installed with RPM. That means nearly everything on the system is defined in the RPM database. The RPM database then has a full knowledge of what you have installed and can properly handle dependencies. Thus, a failure to find a dependency means that you have not installed the requisite package that provides the needed capability.

On an operating system that is not based on RPM, however, such as Solaris or IRIX, most packages have already been installed by some means other than RPM.

That's because these operating systems use different native package-management techniques and different package formats.

It is very likely that RPM packages you want to install have dependencies that come from non-RPM packages. For example, the `rpm` program on Windows depends on the cygwin environment, yet this environment needs to be installed with a Windows setup.exe program, not with the `rpm` command.

To get around this problem, you need to populate the new RPM database with a package or packages that reflect the current system in order to properly handle dependencies. The main way to do this is to set up a virtual package.

Setting Up a Virtual Package

You can get around the problem of pre-existing software by building a virtual package that lists the system libraries — installed without RPM — in an RPM package. This way, the `rpm` command will find that the dependencies are installed, even if they were not really installed with RPM. You need to do this for all capabilities and system libraries installed outside of RPM control.

To help create such a virtual package, use the vpkg-provides.sh script from the scripts directory. The vpkg-provides.sh script searches a list of directories for shared libraries and interpreters (such as shells). The vpkg-provides.sh script then creates a spec file that lists all the files found, files that are managed outside of RPM. You can use this spec file to create an RPM and install the RPM using the `rpm` command to populate the RPM database.

The RPM spec file created by the vpkg-provides.sh doesn't really install any files, as all the files are already installed. Instead it makes a package that claims ownership for all these files so that RPM dependencies can function properly.

The vpkg-provides.sh script accepts three main command-line options: `--spec_header`, `--ignore_dirs`, and `--no_verify`.

The `--spec_header` option tells the script the name of the RPM spec file it should use as a header for the spec file it will produce. You need to provide the path to the file. For example:

```
# sh vpkg-provides.sh --spec_header /path/to/spec/file
```

You need to provide a spec file header to make a complete spec file. This header should contain the Summary, Name, Version, and Release settings, at least. Chapter 10 covers these spec file tags.

The `--ignore_dirs` option tells the vpkg-provides.sh script to ignore certain directories. You need to pass a list of `egrep` search patterns that identify the directories to ignore. Separate each pattern with a pipe character, |.

The `egrep` command may not be available on your system. It may be easier to edit the vpkg-provides.sh script and manually specify the directories to ignore.

The --no_verify option tells the vpkg-provides.sh script to skip the step of creating a script to verify checksums of all files in the package.

In addition to these main command-line options, you can also pass the following options to the vpkg-provides.sh script.

The --shlib_dirs option tells the vpkg-provides.sh script the directories to look for shared libraries. Pass a colon-delimited list of directories. For example:

```
# sh vpkg-provides.sh --spec_header /path/to/spec/file \
        --shlib_dirs "/bin:/usr/bin:/sbin:/usr/sbin:/usr/ucb:/usr/bsd"
```

The --interp_dirs option tells the vpkg-provides.sh script which directories to look in to find interpreters such as sh, bash, perl, wish (Tcl/Tk), and awk. The --interps option tells the vpkg-provides.sh script the names of the interpreter commands. Both these options expect a colon-delimited list.

The --find_provides option tells the vpkg-provides.sh script the name of the find-provides script to use, defaulting to /usr/lib/rpm/find-provides.

The vpkg-provides.sh script defines specific directories to look in for shared libraries and interpreters under various operating systems. You will most likely need to edit this section.

In fact, if you are working with a non-Unix system, or if you experience problems running the vpkg-provides.sh script, you can edit the file to remove the problematic commands. You can also create a new script in a scripting language supported on your system. The vpkg-provides.sh script is a Linux shell script. Linux and Unix systems should be able to run the script, but non-Unix systems likely won't have the commands and may also not support shell scripts at all. In an effort to be generic, the vpkg-provides.sh script does a lot of work. You can limit this by explicitly specifying directories and commands, for example. And if all else fails, you can create a virtual package manually (covered in the following section).

When complete, the vpkg-provides.sh script outputs a spec file, using the header you provided, and outputs a set of Provides: lines to specify what the package provides. It then outputs some empty definitions for the prep, build, install, and clean sections of the spec file.

For example, you can run the vpkg-provides.sh script with a command like the following:

```
$ sh ./vpkg-provides.sh --spec_header my_header.spec --find_provides
./find-provides --no_verify
```

If you run this script as a non-root user, you may get a number of permission errors as the vpkg-provides.sh script searches through system directories.

The script will then output your spec file header along with output like that shown in Listing 20-1.

Listing 20-1: Output from the vpkg-provides.sh script

```
Provides: /bin/sh
Provides: /bin/csh
Provides: /bin/ksh
Provides: /bin/perl
Provides: /bin/awk
Provides: /bin/nawk
Provides: /bin/oawk
Provides: /usr/bin/sh
Provides: /usr/bin/csh
Provides: /usr/bin/ksh
Provides: /usr/bin/perl
Provides: /usr/bin/awk
Provides: /usr/bin/nawk
Provides: /usr/bin/oawk
Provides: /sbin/sh
Provides: /usr/dt/bin/dtksh
Provides: /usr/xpg4/bin/sh
Provides: /usr/xpg4/bin/awk
%prep
# nothing to do
%build
# nothing to do
%install
# nothing to do
%clean
# nothing to do
%files
# no files in a virtual package
```

The vpkg-provides.sh script also outputs a package description that explains how the package was created. This is important so that you know this is a virtual package.

When done, use the rpmbuild command to create an RPM from the generated spec file.

Chapter 9 covers how to run the rpmbuild command, and Chapter 10 covers spec files in detail.

Creating a Virtual Package Manually

Even on Unix-like systems you may experience troubles with the vpkg-provides.sh script. That's simply because the vpkg-provides.sh script assumes a number of Unix and GNU utilities are available. In most cases, it will work best if you can fix what went wrong and run the vpkg-provides.sh script again.

If all else fails, though, you can create a virtual package spec file manually. Create a spec file starting with the Summary, Name, Version, and Release settings.

Looking at the output shown in Listing 20-1, you can create a `Provides:` statement for each shared library on your system, and each interpreter, such as shells. Add each statement to your spec file. For example:

```
Provides: libgen.so
```

Copy the prep, build, install, and clean sections exactly as they are in Listing 20-1. You can now run the `rpmbuild` command to create a virtual package. Install this package.

Creating the RPM environment

The RPM environment is made up of a large number of RPM settings and macro definitions. Run the `rpm --showrc` command to see the current environment settings on Linux:

```
$ rpm -showrc
ARCHITECTURE AND OS:
build arch            : i386
compatible build archs: i686 i586 i486 i386 noarch
build os             : Linux
compatible build os's : Linux
install arch          : i686
install os           : Linux
compatible archs      : i686 i586 i486 i386 noarch
compatible os's       : Linux

RPMRC VALUES:
macrofiles           : /usr/lib/rpm/macros:/usr/lib/rpm/i686-linux/macros:/etc/
rpm/macros.specspo:/etc/rpm/macros.db1:/etc/rpm/macros.cdb:/etc/rpm/macros:/etc/
rpm/i686-linux/macros:~/.rpmmacros
optflags             : -02 -march=i686
```

This output was truncated for space. As you can see, there are a lot of expected settings. You need to set up these same settings and macros, but with the proper values for the new system on which you are running RPM.

The files rpmrc.in and macros.in serve as the default templates used to create the rc and macro settings, respectively. These files are modified by the configure script to include values specific to the local operating system. You can edit these files as needed for your system, prior to installing RPM. That is, edit these files between calling the make command and the make install command.

Chapter 21 covers how to customize the RPM settings and macros, along with the popt aliases.

The INSTALL file in the RPM sources also describes some modifications you may want to make to the macros.

Creating Non-Linux RPMs

Once you have RPM set up on a system, you should be able to create RPMs using the rpmbuild command on that system.

Do not build RPM packages logged in as a root or Administrator user. If something goes wrong, rpmbuild could destroy files in your system. Remember that spec files can define a number of commands and shell scripts. Any of these could have an error that could cause major damage when run as a root user.

Before building RPMs with the rpmbuild command, though, you may want to customize the build environment to better reflect your system. You may also find it is too difficult to build most RPMs on the non-Linux system and instead focus on cross-building packages, should the rpmbuild command not work on the target systems.

This section covers topics related to building RPMs on or for non-Linux systems.

Setting up a build environment

In RPM terms, your build environment consists of the directories where you build RPMs, as well as the *rc* and macro settings that define all of the variables in an RPM-based system. To set up your build environment, you need to ensure that all the *rc* and macro settings reflect the true environment on your non-Linux system.

The rpm --showrc command, discussed previously in the "Creating the RPM Environment" section, lists the settings for your system. You can use this command to verify all the settings.

You may want to change some settings, such as the top directory where RPMs are built. By default, this setting is something like the following:

```
_topdir    %{_usrsrc}/redhat
```

See Chapter 21 for more on how to customize the *rc* and macro settings.

In most cases the `_topdir` setting on Red Hat Linux systems map to the /usr/src/redhat directory. Your system may not even have a /usr/src directory. Also you may not want to build RPMs in a redhat directory, which may cause confusion if you are building on a non-Red Hat Linux system.

See Chapter 19 for more information on setting up a build environment for RPMs. Chapter 19 focuses on other Linux systems, but many of the same techniques apply.

With a build environment set up, you should be able to create RPMs with the `rpmbuild` command. If this doesn't work, or is too difficult, then you can try cross-building packages.

Cross-building packages

You may find that it is too difficult to create RPMs on a given platform. It may be easier to build the RPMs on another platform, such as a Linux system, as if it were on the target platform. This is called cross-building packages, since you are building a package on one system specifically designed for another.

In most cases, the target platform is quite different from the system where you cross-build packages. Otherwise, you would likely just build the RPMs on the target platform.

The key issues with cross-building are the following:

◆ You must compile any executables with a cross compiler for the proper target platform.

◆ You must set the target platform in the RPMs you build.

◆ You must manage dependencies, and likely need to turn off the automatic generation of dependencies.

Setting up a cross-building environment is often more work than it is worth. If you can compile applications and build packages on the target system, do that. The cross-building option should be used only if you really cannot build packages on the target system. For example, many handheld or small-format computers lack the processor performance or memory to compile applications. These are good candidates for cross-building.

To compile executables for another platform, especially a platform with a different processor architecture, you need a cross compiler. A cross compiler runs on one system and produces executables for another.

Cross compilers are heavily used when working with embedded and small device systems. The embedded system may not have the processor power to compile applications, or it may simply be inconvenient to compile applications on the embedded system.

The Linux gcc compiler can act as a cross compiler if you install the right gcc add-on packages. See the GNU site for more on the gcc compiler.

You can download GCC and other GNU software from www.gnu.org.

In addition to compiling for the target platform, you need to ensure that the RPM is marked as being for the target architecture. If not, the rpm command will fail when trying to install the RPM on the target system.

You can set the target architecture with the --target option to the rpmbuild command. For example:

```
rpmbuild -bi --target arm-sharp-linux
```

This specifies a target CPU architecture of ARM, the vendor Sharp (which just happens to make an ARM-based Linux device) and the operating system of Linux. The basic format is:

```
cpu-vendor-os
```

See Chapter 12 for more on using the `--target` option to the `rpmbuild` command.

You must also turn off or correct any automatically generated dependencies in RPMs you build for other platforms. That is, any dependencies based on the operating system or architecture of the system you are cross-building on will likely not be found, or be found in a different location or format, on the target platform.

This is where the handy RPM feature of automatically building the dependencies does not work to your advantage. You can turn off this feature, however.

See Chapter 19 for information on how to turn off the automatic generation of dependencies.

You should turn off the automatically building of dependencies for any packages you cross build.

Using these techniques, you can build packages on one system for use on another, very different system. Due to the difficulties, you should only go this route if it becomes too difficult to use the `rpmbuild` command on the target systems.

Summary

With its superior package-management capabilities, especially for automated installations and upgrades, you may want to use RPM on non-Linux platforms. As the experience of many developers has shown, you can indeed use RPM on non-Linux platforms.

The rpm.org site maintains a listing of operating systems where developers have ported RPM. If you are lucky, you can download RPM for your operating system and start working right away. If you are not lucky, you will need to port RPM to your target system.

If RPM has been ported to your architecture, download the package and follow the installation instructions. If RPM has not been ported to your architecture, download the RPM sources and all prerequisite libraries. You may need to port each library to your architecture before you can even begin to port RPM.

The RPM sources use a configured build process that also requires some prerequisite tools. You need to get or port these to your architecture as well. Whew.

Once everything is in place, you can start the port of RPM. In many cases, you just need to figure out how to get RPM to compile and everything will fall into place. In other cases, you will need to work on each RPM subsystem to get it to build and run.

After you have RPM for your system, you need to initialize the RPM database with the `rpm --initdb` command. You can then start to populate your RPM database. Because a large number of libraries have already been installed on your system, you may need to create a virtual package that claims to provide these files. Installing such a virtual package will allow you to install other RPMs that may be dependent on system libraries.

Much of porting RPM to another platform depends on the RPM environment and how you need to customize that environment. The next chapter shows how to customize your RPM environment, on Linux or on other operating systems.

Chapter 21

Customizing RPM Behavior

IN THIS CHAPTER

◆ Defining RPM macros

◆ Configuring RPM settings

◆ Adding popt aliases

RPM PROVIDES A HIGH DEGREE OF customization in the form of basic settings, such as where your RPM database is located and the path to common commands like `setup` or `make`, to the ability to define new macros and command-line aliases. This chapter covers the three main ways to customize RPM behavior: RPM macros, RPM *rc* settings, and popt aliases.

Customizing with RPM Macros

Starting with RPM 3.0, RPM macros have replaced most RPM settings from the rpmrc files.

An RPM *macro* defines a setting to the RPM system. A macro can be defined as a static value, such as the directory where the RPM database is installed. A macro can also be defined in terms of other macros. Furthermore, a macro can be defined with parameters.

For example, the following defines two macros in a macro file:

```
%_usr        /usr
%_usrsrc     %{_usr}/src
```

In this case, the macro `%_usr` names the /usr directory. The macro `%_usrsrc` names the /usr/src directory, showing how to set a macro in terms of another macro.

The macro syntax is used in the query formats introduced in Chapter 5.

Defining macros

RPM provides a number of places you can define macros, including inside spec files (probably the most common usage), in special macro initialization files, and on the command line.

In each case, the syntax is slightly different.

Defining Macros in Spec Files

You can define macros in most places in a spec file. With spec files, use the %define syntax to define a macro, which uses the following syntax:

```
%define name(options)  body
```

The options are optional and can include the special values defined in Table 21-1.

TABLE 21-1 SPECIAL OPTIONS FOR MACROS

Option	Holds
%0	The name of the macro
%1	The first argument, after processing with getopt
%2-%9	Additional arguments
%*	All arguments, except for flags that have been processed
%#	Number of arguments

These options are similar to those for shell scripting.

Chapter 10 covers spec files.

In addition to these options, you can use a syntax of %{-a} to hold -a if an option of -a was passed. The syntax of %{-a*} indicates the value passed after the -a option.

You can assign a macro to the value returned by a shell command by using syntax like the following:

```
%(shell_command)
```

This is similar to the $(*shell_command*) syntax supported by bash.

Defining Macros in Macro Initialization Files

Inside a macro file, define macros with the following syntax:

```
%macro_name value
```

Macros defined for the RPM system start with an underscore. Some older macros are left without the leading underscore.

The macros defined with an underscore are not exported into rpm headers.

The %expand built-in macro will expand the value of something else, including executing a shell command. For example, the following sets the user's home directory to the %home macro:

```
%home            %{expand:%%(cd; pwd)}
```

Note that it is probably easier to simply set the %home macro in your per-user $HOME/.rpmmacros file to the name of your home directory rather than try to figure this out programmatically.

Defining Macros on the Command Line

The rpm command also lets you define macros with the --define option. The basic syntax is:

```
$ rpm --define 'macro_name value'
```

Do not place the leading percent sign, %, on the macro you define with `--define`.

You can evaluate a macro or a macro expression with `--eval`. For example:

```
$ rpm --eval %_usrsrc
/usr/src
```

Customizing Macros

You can add your own macro definitions, using the syntax shown in the "Defining Macros in Macro Initialization Files" section. These macros are read on each invocation of the `rpm` or `rpmbuild` commands.

To add your custom macros, you must edit one of the macro definition files. Table 21-2 lists the macro definition files and their usage.

TABLE 21-2 RPM MACRO FILES

File	Usage
/usr/lib/rpm/macros	Official RPM macros
/etc/rpm/macros	Per-system customizations
$HOME/.rpmmacros	Per-user customizations

Do not edit the /usr/lib/rpm/macros file, as this file gets overwritten when you upgrade to a new version of rpm.

Configuring RPM Settings

RPM includes hundreds of settings based on your current system architecture, environment, and which version of the RPM system you have installed. The old settings, called *rc* or *rpmrc* settings, are gradually being phased out by the newer, more consistent and more powerful macros.

You can still edit the *rc* settings, but in most cases you should edit macros instead.

Viewing the current settings

To view the current settings, use the `--showrc` command-line option:

```
$ rpm -showrc
ARCHITECTURE AND OS:
build arch            : i386
compatible build archs: i686 i586 i486 i386 noarch
build os              : Linux
compatible build os's : Linux
install arch          : i686
install os            : Linux
compatible archs      : i686 i586 i486 i386 noarch
compatible os's       : Linux


RPMRC VALUES:
macrofiles              : /usr/lib/rpm/macros:/usr/lib/rpm/i686-linux/macros:/etc/
rpm/macros.specspo:/etc/rpm/macros.db1:/etc/rpm/macros.cdb:/etc/rpm/macros:/etc/
rpm/i686-linux/macros:~/.rpmmacros
optflags                : -O2 -march=i686
```

This command displays the architecture and operating system information first, and then lists all the *rpmrc* values, shown here truncated for space.

Locating the rpmrc files

The `--showrc` option reads in all the rpmrc files from the various locations. By default, this is /usr/lib/rpm/rpmrc, /etc/rpm/rpmrc, and a file named .rpmrc (with a leading period) in your home directory.

These files are read in the order given, so that the later files can override settings in the earlier files.

The uses for these files are listed in Table 21-3.

TABLE 21-3 USES FOR THE RPMRC FILES

File	Holds
/usr/lib/rpm/rpmrc	RPM standard settings
/etc/rpm/rpmrc	Per-system configuration
$HOME/.rpmrc	Per-user configuration

The file /usr/lib/rpm/rpmrc gets overwritten each time you upgrade RPM. Do not customize this file.

You can override this list of files by calling the rpm or rpmbuild commands with the --rcfile option. This option expects a semicolon-delimited list of files to read in, in order. For example, if you are working on a 686-architecture Intel platform, you can create a file with the following setting:

```
optflags: i686  -g
```

Note that this disables optimization, so it is not a good setting. (The use of this value will make the result more visible.)

If you name this file .rpmnew and place it in your home directory, you can configure an alternate set of files with the --rcfile option and then evaluate the new optflags setting. For example:

```
$ rpm --eval "%{optflags}"
-O2 -march=i386 -mcpu=i686
$ rpm --rcfile $HOME/.rpmnew --eval "%{optflags}"
-g
```

This example shows the value before and after changing the configuration files.

When you use the --rcfile option, only the first file listed must exist. The rest of the files are optional. When you use the --rcfile option, however, the file /usr/lib/rpm/rpmrc is read first, and then the list of files you provide with the --rcfile option. The file /usr/lib/rpm/rpmrc is always used.

Changing settings

You can edit the per-user or per-system *rc* files to change the settings. The format of the rpmrc files is fairly simple but contains a few exceptions. The most basic format is:

```
setting: value
```

The settings get more complicated as the rpmrc syntax supports defining settings for multiple architectures at once. In that case, the typical format is:

```
setting: uname: value
```

The *uname* portion is replaced by a value that comes from the uname(2) system call, for example, i686 on a 686-class Intel architecture machine.

In most cases, your best bet is to copy an existing setting and modify it, rather than remembering all the exceptions.

Setting the optflags

One exception to the rule is the `optflags` setting, which controls C compiler options for optimization. The format for the `optflags` setting is:

setting: *arch value*

There is no colon after the architecture. For example:

```
optflags: i686 -O2 -march=i686
optflags: alphaev5 -O2 -mieee -mcpu=ev5
```

This example sets the optimization flags for an i686 system to `-O2 -march=i686` and an alphaev5 system to `-O2 -mieee -mcpu=ev5`. If your system is running on a 686-class processor, you will get one set of optimization flags. If your system is running on a V5 Alpha processor, you will get a different set.

Setting the Architecture Values

The `arch_canon` setting builds up a table of mappings between architecture names and the numbers used internally. The following example shows the Intel and SPARC architecture settings to 1 and 3 internally.

```
arch_canon:     athlon: athlon   1
arch_canon:     i686:   i686     1
arch_canon:     i586:   i586     1
arch_canon:     i486:   i486     1
arch_canon:     i386:   i386     1

arch_canon:     sparc:    sparc    3
arch_canon:     sun4:     sparc    3
arch_canon:     sun4m:    sparc    3
arch_canon:     sun4c:    sparc    3
arch_canon:     sun4d:    sparc    3
arch_canon:     sparcv9: sparcv9   3
```

The `arch_compat` setting builds a table of compatible architectures. The format is:

arch_compat: *arch: compatible_with*

This sets the given architecture arch as being compatible with another architecture. For example:

```
arch_compat: athlon: i686
```

This setting indicates that an athlon architecture is compatible with an i686. The table gets built up further with the following Intel-architecture compatibilities:

```
arch_compat: i686: i586
arch_compat: i586: i486
arch_compat: i486: i386
arch_compat: i386: noarch
```

The os_canon setting defines a table of operating system labels and internal numeric values. The basic syntax is:

```
os_canon: arch: name value
```

The arch comes from the uname(2) call. The name provides an RPM name for that operating system, and the value defines an internal numeric ID for that OS, for example:

```
os_canon:       Linux:  Linux   1
os_canon:       HP-UX:  hpux10  6
```

The buildarchtranslate setting defines the operating system settings to use as the build architecture. This value translates information from the uname(2) call to a value used by the arch_canon setting. For example:

```
buildarchtranslate: athlon: i386
buildarchtranslate: i686: i386
buildarchtranslate: i586: i386
buildarchtranslate: i486: i386
buildarchtranslate: i386: i386

buildarchtranslate: sun4c: sparc
buildarchtranslate: sun4d: sparc
buildarchtranslate: sun4m: sparc
buildarchtranslate: sparcv9: sparc
buildarchtranslate: sun4u: sparc64
```

Adding Popt Aliases

Popt provides a powerful library and RPM subsystem for handling the very complex RPM command-line options. You can customize your RPM usage by defining popt aliases for complex command-line arguments to the `rpm` or `rpmbuild` commands. A popt *alias* is a command-line option that expands to other command-line options.

This technique is used internally to define quite a few command-line options to the `rpm` and `rpmbuild` commands in terms of other, more complex options. Many of these aliases define simple command-line options in place of more complex query format options.

Chapter 5 covers the query format.

For example, the following entry defines the `--requires` and `-R` command-line options to the `rpm` command:

```
rpm  alias --requires   --qf \
   "[%{REQUIRENAME} %{REQUIREFLAGS:depflags} %{REQUIREVERSION}\n]" \
   --POPTdesc=$"list capabilities required by package(s)"
rpm  alias -R --requires
```

These options are set in the file /usr/lib/rpm/rpmpopt-4.1.

This is specific to RPM 4.1. Other releases of RPM use the same naming format but with the current RPM version number, such as 4.2 and so on.

Defining aliases

Defining aliases is pretty easy. The basic syntax is:

```
command_name alias option expansion
```

To create an alias for the `rpm` command, you use `rpm` for the *command_name*.

The command_name must be the name passed to the C poptGetContext function, covered in Chapter 16.

Follow this with alias and then the *option*. You will need separate aliases for the long and short options. The *expansion* defines the alias in terms of other already-defined command-line parameters.

You can define some complex aliases, such as the following one to display information about a package:

```
rpm  alias --info --qf 'Name        : %-27{NAME}  Relocations:
%|PREFIXES?{[%{PREFIXES} ]}:{(not relocateable)}|\n\
Version     : %-27{VERSION}       Vendor: %{VENDOR}\n\
Release     : %-27{RELEASE}   Build Date: %{BUILDTIME:date}\n\
Install date: %|INSTALLTIME?{%-27{INSTALLTIME:date}}:{(not installed)        }|
Build Host: %{BUILDHOST}\n\
Group       : %-27{GROUP}   Source RPM: %{SOURCERPM}\n\
Size        : % 27{SIZE}%|LICFNSE?{      License: %{LICENSE}}|\n\
Signature   :
%|DSAHEADER?{%{DSAHEADER:pgpsig}}:{%|RSAHEADER?{%{RSAHEADER:pgpsig}}:{%|SIGGPG?{
%{SIGGPG:pgpsig}}:{%|SIGPGP?{%{SIGPGP:pgpsig}}:{(none)}|}|}|}|}|\n\
%|PACKAGER?{Packager    : %{PACKAGER}\n}|\
%|URL?{URL         : %{URL}\n}|\
Summary     : %{SUMMARY}\n\
Description :\n%{DESCRIPTION}\n' \
 --POPTdesc=$"list descriptive information from package(s)"
```

Popt aliases get evaluated into Linux commands, so you can use pipes and other aspects of Linux shells in your aliases.

Look closely at the examples in the /usr/lib/rpm/rpmpopt-4.1 file. This is the most complete set of popt alias examples for RPM commands.

You can also define aliases that can set RPM macros, such as the following alias for setting the path to the RPM database:

```
rpm     alias --dbpath          --define '_dbpath !#:+'
```

In this example, !#:+ was defined to behave like a shell history-editing command. With popt, this means to grab the next command-line parameter and place it into the command defined for the alias.

To support the --help and --usage options, you can define the --POPTdesc and --POPTargs options to the alias as shown in the previous examples. These options also support internationalization.

All together, the popt alias setting is very close to the popt option table entries used with the C programming API.

Chapter 16 shows how to program with the popt library.

Customizing popt aliases

Like RPM macros and settings, popt aliases are defined in a cascading set of files. The official RPM aliases are defined in /usr/lib/rpm/rpmpopt-4.1 for rpm 4.1.

Do not modify this file! The RPM system depends on this file for proper functioning. Incorrect changes might disable many options to the rpm command.

Store per-system popt aliases in /etc/popt. Store per-user aliases in $HOME/.popt (with a leading period).

These files are shared by all applications that use popt.

For example, you can define an alias for rpm -qa that executes faster than the normal query all packages command, by turning off the tests for digest signature verification. To do so, add the following line to a file named .popt in your home directory:

```
rpm alias --qall    -qa --nodigest --nosignature
```

Once you set up this alias, you can run the following command in place of
`rpm -qa`:

```
$ rpm --qall
```

This should execute about one-third to one-half faster than the normal `rpm -qa`
command.

 Turning off the signature and digest tests means you are ignoring important
information that pertains to the integrity of your system. That is why the
alias shown here does not override the normal `-qa` option, and instead
defines a new `--qall` option.

Summary

This chapter shows the many ways you can customize RPM usage for your system
or your own personal environment. You can define RPM macros, which is the preferred way to make RPM settings. Or you can set RPM values in the older rpmrc
files, which are now mostly replaced by RPM macros.

Using popt, the powerful command-line option parser, you can define aliases to
add simple options that popt expands into whatever you define. Many of the `rpm`
command-line options are defined this way.

Part V

Appendixes

APPENDIX A
RPM Command Reference

APPENDIX B
Spec File Syntax

APPENDIX C
RPM Feature Evolution

APPENDIX D
RPM Package File Structure

APPENDIX E
RPM Resources

APPENDIX F
Linux Text Editors and Development Tools

APPENDIX G
Licensing RPM

Appendix A

RPM Command Reference

IN THIS APPENDIX

◆ `rpm` command

◆ `rpmbuild` command

THIS APPENDIX COVERS THE SYNTAX of the command-line options for the `rpm` and `rpmbuild` commands.

The rpm Command

The `rpm` command is the workhorse of the RPM system. The following sections cover options for the major operations with the `rpm` command.

Table A-1 lists the query options for the `rpm` command.

TABLE A-1 RPM QUERY OPTIONS WITH -Q OR --QUERY

Option	Usage
`-a, --all`	Query all packages
`-c, --configfiles`	List configuration files
`--changelog`	List changelog entries
`--conflicts`	List capabilities this package conflicts with
`-d, --docfiles`	List documentation files
`--dump`	Dump out extra information on files
`-f, --file filename`	Query for packages owning given file
`--filesbypapkg`	List all files in each selected package
`--fileid md5_id`	Query for the package with the given MD5 digest
`-g, --group group_name`	Query packages in the given group

Continued

TABLE A-1 RPM QUERY OPTIONS WITH -Q OR --QUERY *(Continued)*

Option	Usage
--hdrid *sha1_header_id*	Query for the package with the given header identifier number, in SHA1 format
-i, --info	Display a lot of package information including description
--last	Reorder the output of the rpm command to show the most recently installed packages first
--obsoletes	List capabilities this package obsoletes
-p, --package *rpm_file*	Query the given package file or files
--pkgid *md5_id*	Query for the package with the given MD5 package ID
--provides	List capabilities provided by package
querybynumber *number*	Query for the given entry, by number, in the RPM database
--qf, --queryformat *format*	Use the given query format for displaying the output
--redhatprovides *capability*	Look in rpmdb-redhat database for packages that provide the given capability
--redhatrequires *capability*	Look in rpmdb-redhat database for packages that require the given capability
-R, --requires	Lists packages and capabilities that this package depends on
--specfile *specfile*	Query the given spec file
-s, --state	Display the state of the listed files
--scripts	List scripts in the package
--tid *transaction_id*	Query for the package or packages with the given transaction ID
--triggeredby *package*	Query packages triggered by the given package
--triggers, --triggerscripts	List trigger scripts
--whatrequires *capability*	Query packages that require the given capability
--whatprovides *capability*	List packages that provide the given capability

Upgrade, freshen, and install options

Table A-2 lists the upgrade, freshen, and installation options for the rpm command.

TABLE A-2 RPM UPGRADE, FRESHEN, AND INSTALL OPTIONS

Option	Usage
--aid	Add any suggested packages to the list to install or upgrade
--allfiles	Install all the files, even if some might otherwise be skipped
--badreloc	Relocate files even if the package is not relocatable
--excludedocs	Skip the files marked as documentation
--excludepath *path*	Skip files that begin with *path*
--force	A short hand for --replacepkgs and --replacefiles
-h, --hash	Print hash marks, #, periodically while performing operation to provide some feedback
--ignorearch	Ignore the architecture listed in the package
--ignoreos	Ignore the operating system listed in the package
--ignoresize	Skip the check to see if there is enough disk space to install the package
--includedocs	Install files marked as documentation, turned on by default
--justdb	Just update the RPM database, do not modify any files
--nodeps	Skip verification of package dependencies
--nodigest	Skip verification of package and header digests
--nomd5	Skip verification of file MD5 checksums
--noorder	Do not reorder the list of packages to be installed based on dependencies
--nopost	Do not run post-install scripts
--nopostun	Do not run post-uninstall scripts
--nopre	Do not run pre-install scripts
--nopreun	Do not run pre-uninstall scripts
--nosuggest	Do not suggest packages for missing dependencies

Continued

TABLE A-2 RPM UPGRADE, FRESHEN, AND INSTALL OPTIONS *(Continued)*

Option	Usage
`--noscripts`	Do not execute scripts
`--nosignature`	Skip verification of package and header signatures
`--notriggers`	Do not execute trigger scripts
`--notriggerin`	Do not run trigger install scripts
`--notriggerpostun`	Do not run trigger post uninstall scripts
`--notriggerun`	Do not run trigger uninstall scripts
`--oldpackage`	Allow an upgrade to an older version of a package
`--percent`	Print out percentage of work completed as command executes
`--prefix` *directory*	Relocate package to *directory*, if package is relocatable
`--relocate` *old=new*	Relocate all paths that start with *old* to *new*, if relocatable
`--repackage`	Create a package from any files that would be erased
`--replacefiles`	Install package even if it replaces files from other packages
`--replacepkgs`	Install packages even if they are already installed
`--test`	Do not install or remove packages, just see if the command would work

Use `rpm -U` or `--upgrade` to upgrade, `rpm -i` or `--install` to install, and `-F` or `--freshen` to freshen a package.

Erase options

Table A-3 lists the erase, or package removal, options for the `rpm` command.

TABLE A-3 RPM ERASE (REMOVAL) OPTIONS WITH -E OR --ERASE

Option	Usage
`--allmatches`	Remove all versions of the packages; normally an error would occur if there is more than one package of the same name and you try to erase the package

Option	Usage
--nodeps	Skip verification of package dependencies
--noscripts	Do not execute scripts
--nopostun	Do not run post-uninstall scripts
--nopreun	Do not run pre-uninstall scripts
--notriggers	Do not execute trigger scripts
--notriggerpostun	Do not run trigger post uninstall scripts
--notriggerun	Do not run trigger uninstall scripts
--repackage	Create a package from any files that would be erased
--test	Do not install or remove packages, just see if the command would work

Signature options

Table A-4 lists the signature-related options to the rpm command.

TABLE A-4 RPM SIGNATURE OPTIONS WITH –K, --CHECKSIG, OR --IMPORT

Option	Usage
--addsign	Sign packages, same as --resign
--import *public_key*	Add given public key to the RPM database
--nodigest	Skip verification of package and header digests
--nosignature	Skip verification of package and header signatures
--resign	Sign packages

The --import option works on its own. The rest of the options work with one or more RPM packages.

Verify options

The rpm command can verify packages. This involves comparing all files installed by the package with the information in the RPM database, and looking for differences or missing files.

Table A-5 lists the verify options to the rpm command.

TABLE A-5 RPM VERIFY OPTIONS WITH -V OR --VERIFY

Option	Usage
-a, --all	Verify all packages
-f, --file *filename*	Verify packages owning given file
-g, --group *group_name*	Verify packages in the given group
--nodeps	Skip verification of package dependencies
--nodigest	Skip verification of package and header digests
--nofiles	Do not verify the files in the package
--nogroup	Do not verify the group owner
--nolinkto	Do not verify the link file attribute
--nomd5	Skip verification of file MD5 checksums
--nomtime	Do not verify the mtime attribute
--nomode	Do not verify the file mode (permissions)
--nordev	Do not verify the rdev attribute
--noscripts	Do not execute the verify scripts
--nosignature	Skip verification of package and header signatures
--nosize	Do not verify the file size
--nouser	Do not verify the owner of the file
-p, --package *rpm_file*	Verify the given package file or files
--specfile *specfile*	Verify the given spec file
--whatrequires *capability*	Verify packages that require the given capability
--whatprovides *capability*	Verify packages that provide the given capability

Database options

You can create a new, empty, RPM database as well as rebuild all the inverted lists used for quick access using the database options listed in Table A-6.

TABLE A-6 RPM DATABASE OPTIONS

Option	Usage
--initdb	Initialize database
--rebuilddb	Rebuild all the inverted lists from the Packages file

Miscellaneous options

These options can be used with any rpm command. Three of the options, --query-tags, --version, and --showrc, run on their own. The rest can be used with the other rpm options. Table A-7 lists these miscellaneous options.

TABLE A-7 MISCELLANEOUS RPM OPTIONS

Option	Usage
-?, --help	Print the popt help information for all the command-line options
--dbpath *path_to_rpm_db*	Use the given directory for the RPM database, instead of the default
-D, --define *'macro value'*	Define the given *macro* to hold the given *value*
-E, --eval *expression*	Print the evaluation of the given *expression*
--ftpport *port*	Use the given port number for FTP access
--ftpproxy *host*	Use the given host name as a proxy for FTP access
--httpport *port*	Use the given port number for HTTP access
--httpproxy *host*	Use the given host name as a proxy for HTTP access
--macros *file:file:file*	Read the given colon-separated files as the macro files to define RPM macros; only the first file must exist

Continued

TABLE A-7 MISCELLANEOUS RPM OPTIONS *(Continued)*

Option	Usage
--pipe *command*	Pipe the output of the rpm command to the given *command*
--querytags	Print the query tag names and exit
--quiet	Provide less output, normally show only errors
--rcfile *file:file:file*	Read the given colon-separated files as the rc files to define RPM settings; only the first file must exist
--root *directory*	Use *directory* as the top-level directory instead of /.
--showrc	Print the rpmrc and macro configuration and exit
-v, --verbose	Provide more verbose output
-vv	Provide even more verbose output, including debugging information
--version	Print the RPM version and exit

The rpmbuild Command

The rpmbuild command builds RPMs. Most of the options are duplicated. The options that begin with -b build from a spec file, and the options that begin with -t build from a compressed tar archive, commonly called a *tarball*.

Building from a spec file

Table A-8 lists the rpmbuild options for building RPMs from a spec file.

TABLE A-8 OPTIONS FOR BUILDING RPMS FROM A SPEC FILE

Option	Usage
-ba	Build all, both a binary and source RPM
-bb	Build a binary RPM
-bc	Build (compile) the program but do not make the full RPM, by executing the build commands through the %build section and stopping

Option	Usage
-bp	Prepare for building a binary RPM, by executing the build commands through the %prep section and stopping
-bi	Execute the build commands through the %install section and stop
-bl	Check the listing of files for the RPM
-bs	Build a source RPM only

Each of these options requires the name of a spec file at the end of the command line.

Building from a compressed tar archive

Table A-9 lists the rpmbuild options for working with a compressed tar archive.

TABLE A-9 OPTIONS FOR BUILDING RPMS FROM A COMPRESSED TAR ARCHIVE

Option	Usage
-ta	Build all, both a binary and source RPM
-tb	Build a binary RPM
-tc	Build (compile) the program but do not make the full RPM, by executing the build commands through the %build section and stopping
-tp	Prepare for building a binary RPM, by executing the build commands through the %prep section and stopping
-ti	Execute the build commands through the %install section and stop
-tl	Check the listing of files for the RPM
-ts	Build a source RPM only

Each of these options requires the name of a compressed tar archive at the end of the command line. The tar archive must contain a valid spec file inside the archive.

Rebuilding RPMs from source RPMs

You can use the rpmbuild command to rebuild an RPM from a source RPM with the options listed in Table A-10.

TABLE A-10 OPTIONS FOR REBUILDING RPMS FROM SOURCE RPMS

Option	Usage
--rebuild	Rebuild binary RPM from source RPM
--recompile	Recompile binary RPM from source RPM

Each of these options requires the name of a source RPM file on the end of the command line.

Customizing the build

You can customize the rpmbuild command with the options listed in Table A-11.

TABLE A-11 EXTRA BUILD OPTIONS FOR THE RPMBUILD COMMAND

Option	Usage
-?, --help	Print the popt help information for all the command-line options
--buildroot *directory*	Override the default root directory for building with directory
--clean	Remove the build tree after building
-D, --define 'macro value'	Define the given *macro* to hold the given *value*
--dbpath *path_to_rpm_db*	Use the given directory for the RPM database instead of the default
-E, --eval *expression*	Print the evaluation of the given *expression*
--macros *file:file:file*	Read the given colon-separated files as the macro files to define RPM macros; only the first file must exist
--nobuild	Don't really build anything, which really tests the spec file

Option	Usage
`--pipe` *command*	Pipe the output of the rpm command to the given *command*
`--quiet`	Provide less output, normally show only errors
`--rcfile` *file:file:file*	Read the given colon-separated files as the rc files to define RPM settings; only the first file must exist
`--rmsource`	Remove the sources after the build
`--rmspec`	Remove the spec file after the build
`--root` *directory*	Use *directory* as the top-level directory instead of /
`--short-circuit`	With the `-bc` or `-bi` options, jumps directly to the given stage and just executes that stage
`--showrc`	Print the rpmrc and macro configuration and exit
`--sign`	Sign the package with a GPG signature
`--target` *platform*	Build for the given platform. May not work if you don't have the other platform build commands, such as cross compilers, set up. Can work for Intel platforms with i386, i686, and so on.
`-v, --verbose`	Provide more verbose output
`-vv`	Provide even more verbose output, including debugging information
`--version`	Print the RPM version and exit

Appendix B

Spec File Syntax

IN THIS APPENDIX

◆ The package information tags

◆ Build sections

THE RPM SPEC FILE IS DIVIDED into two main parts: the package information tags, such as the name of the package, and the build sections, such as the commands to compile the software.

The following sections summarize the spec file syntax.

Package Information Tags

The package information tags contain most of the header tags that you can query with the rpm command. First and foremost, this includes a name.

The *name-epoch-version-release* tags, which form the NEVR used to identify packages, should all appear in your spec file, although you can skip the Epoch tag.

```
Name: name
# Epoch: 1
Version: version_number
Release: package_release_number
```

The optional Epoch tag provides an ordering for the version numbers (replacing the deprecated Serial tag). Use this tag if RPM cannot figure out the ordering of which release comes after another.

```
Epoch: 42
```

A number of tags allow you to define who made the package and under what conditions has the package been released:

```
Vendor: name_of_vendor
URL: URL_to_package_home
Copyright: package_copyright_message
Distribution: Linux_or_product_distribution
```

```
Packager: John Q. Smith <john.smith@somecompany.yow>
Group: group_for_categorizing_package
```

Use the `Group` tag to help users categorize your package.
The `Icon` tag allows you to provide a desktop icon for the package:

```
Icon: filename.xpm
```

A one-line summary is essential to tell users what your package is for:

```
Summary: one_line_description_of_package
```

You should also include a longer description section, marked by `%description`:

```
%description
Tcsh is an enhanced but completely compatible version of csh, the C
shell.  Tcsh is a command language interpreter which can be used both
as an interactive login shell and as a shell script command processor.
Tcsh includes a command line editor, programmable word completion,
spelling correction, a history mechanism, job control and a C language
like syntax.
```

In the description section, blank lines indicate paragraphs. Lines that start with a space are not formatted.

Comments

To help document your work, you can include comments (to yourself and others reading the spec file). Any line starting with a hash character, #, holds a comment. RPM will ignore comments.

```
# This is a comment.
```

In spec files, comments are used mostly to help explain your syntax choices to yourself should you view the spec file later.

Avoid using percent signs (%) in comments. They may get interpreted as RPM macros. See Chapter 10 for details.

Build settings

The `BuildArchitectures` tag names the architectures that a binary RPM will run on. See Chapter 21 for a description of the architecture settings. A special value of `noarch` indicates a package that is not dependent on a particular architecture, such as a Perl or Python script.

The `BuildPreReq` tag lists any prerequisites for building. For example:

```
BuildPreReq: ncurses-devel
```

The `Buildroot` tag names the temporary directory in which to build the package. For example:

```
Buildroot: %{_tmppath}/%{name}-root
```

Dependency tags

Dependency tags define all the dependencies for the package, as described in Chapter 6.

For each dependency, you can specify a capability name alone. For example:

```
Provides: capability_name
```

You can also provide a particular version number or indicate that your package has a dependency on a version larger or smaller than a given number. For example:

```
Requires: capability_name >= version_number
Requires: capability_name <= version_number
Requires: capability_name > version_number
Requires: capability_name < version_number
Requires: capability_name == version_number
Requires: capability_name = version_number
```

The ==and = act the same for dependencies. Both check for a version equal to the given number. You can provide multiple items, separated by commas. For example:

```
Requires: python >= 1.3, perl
```

For add-on modules for interpreters, especially Perl, you can use the following syntax to define capabilities:

```
Provides: perl(MIME-Base64)
```

This example provides the MIME-Base64 add-on Perl module.

You can also use or to specify more than one possibility. For example:

```
perl(IO-Wrap) == 4.5 or perl(IO-Wrap)-4.5
```

The `Provides`, `Requires`, `Obsoletes`, and `Conflicts` dependency tags all work the same for capability names and version numbers.

> You can also specify `BuildRequires` tags for capabilities necessary to build the package, not to install it. A `BuildConflicts` tag names capabilities that conflict for building, such as a particular version of the gcc C compiler.

Source files

The source and patch tags identify the source files used to build the binary package. The patch tags identify any patches used to modify the sources.

If you have more than one of a particular kind of tag, append a number. For example:

```
Source0: ftp://ftp.uk.linux.org/pub/linux/telnet-%{telnet_version}.tar.gz
Source2: telnet-client.tar.gz
Source3: telnet-xinetd
Source4: telnet.wmconfig
Patch1: telnet-client-cvs.patch
Patch5: telnetd-0.17.diff
Patch6: telnet-0.17-env.patch
Patch7: telnet-0.17-issue.patch
Patch8: telnet-0.17-sa-01-49.patch
Patch9: telnet-0.17-env-5x.patch
Patch10: telnet-0.17-pek.patch
```

Macros

You can define macros in your spec files to help control how the package gets built. The following section describes these macros.

Variable definition macros

The `%define` macro allows you to define new macros from within your spec file. A common usage is to define top-level directories with `%define` macros at the top of a spec file and then reference these directories throughout the file. For example:

```
%define  bindir  /bin
```

This allows you to change the setting in one place, which is very handy for directory paths used throughout your spec files.

See the section "Defining Macros in Spec Files" in Chapter 21 for more on this subject.

You can use this syntax for other things that may commonly change, such as version numbers. For example:

```
%define major 2
%define minor 2
%define patchlevel 7
Version: %{major}.%{minor}.%{patchlevel}
```

Table B-1 lists more special macros used within spec files.

TABLE B-1 SPECIAL SPEC FILE MACROS

Macro	Usage
%dump	Prints out macro values
%{echo:*message*}	Prints *message* to stderr
%{error:*message*}	Prints *message* to stderr and returns BADSPEC
%{expand:*expression*}	Like eval, expands *expression*
%{F:*file_exp*}	Expands *file_exp* to a file name
%global *name value*	Defines a global macro
%{P:*patch_exp*}	Expands *patch_exp* to a patch file name
%{S:*source_exp*}	Expands *source_exp* to a source file name
%trace	Toggles the printing of debugging information
%{uncompress:*filename*}	Tests if file *filename* is compressed. If so, uncompresses and includes in the given context. If not compressed, calls cat to include file in given context.
%undefine *macro*	Undefines the given macro
%{warn:*message*}	Prints *message* to stderr

Conditional macros

You can use a special syntax to test for the existence of macros. For example:

```
%{?macro_to_test: expression}
```

This syntax tells RPM to expand the expression if macro_to_test exists, otherwise ignore. A leading exclamation point, !, tests for the non-existence of a macro:

```
%{!?macro_to_test: expression}
```

In this example, if the macro_to_test macro does not exist, then expand the expression.

The %if macro performs an *if* test much like scripting languages. For example:

```
%if %{old_5x}
%define b5x 1
%undefine b6x
%endif
```

A %else allows you to specify what to do if the test is not successful. For example:

```
%if %{old_5x}
%define b5x 1
%undefine b6x
%else
%define b6x 1
%undefine b5x
%endif
```

Again, use an exclamation point to negate the test. For example:

```
%if ! %{old_5x}
%define b5x 1
%undefine b6x
%endif
```

You can use a && for an *and* test. For example:

```
%if %{old_5x} && %{old_6x}
%{error: You cannot build for .5x and .6x at the same time}
%quit
%endif
```

Built-in macros

The following macros are built into RPM and can help allow you to place your files in the right locations:

```
%_prefix          /usr
%_exec_prefix     %{_prefix}
%_bindir          %{_exec_prefix}/bin
%_sbindir         %{_exec_prefix}/sbin
%_libexecdir      %{_exec_prefix}/libexec
%_datadir         %{_prefix}/share
%_sysconfdir      %{_prefix}/etc
%_sharedstatedir  %{_prefix}/com
%_localstatedir   %{_prefix}/var
%_libdir          %{_exec_prefix}/lib
%_includedir      %{_prefix}/include
%_oldincludedir   /usr/include
%_infodir         %{_prefix}/info
%_mandir          %{_prefix}/man
```

Build Sections

After providing information about the package, you need to define the build stages, as described in Chapters 10 and 12.

Build preparation

The build preparation section sets the stage for the build. Usually this section has a `%setup` command. For example:

```
%prep
%setup -q
```

Build

The build section describes how to build the library or application. In most cases, the majority of the instructions are in the Makefile created by the prep section, leaving a build section something like the following:

```
%build
%configure
make
```

Installation

After building, the installation section holds the commands to install the library or application. For example:

```
%install
rm -rf %{buildroot}
%makeinstall
```

Clean up

The clean up section usually calls the make clean command to clean up the built files. For example:

```
%clean
rm -rf %{buildroot}
```

Install and uninstall scripts

RPM packages can run scripts prior to installation with %pre, and after installation with %post. You can also run scripts prior to an uninstall with %preun and after an uninstall with %postun. For example:

```
%post
/sbin/chkconfig --add ypbind

%preun
if [ "$1" = 0 ] ; then
    /sbin/service ypbind stop > /dev/null 2>&1
    /sbin/chkconfig --del ypbind
fi
exit 0

%postun
if [ "$1" -ge 1 ]; then
    /sbin/service ypbind condrestart > /dev/null 2>&1
fi
exit 0
```

File Tags

The `%files` tag lists the files your package should install. For example:

```
%files
%defattr(-,root,root)
/usr/X11R6/bin/xtoolwait
/usr/X11R6/man/man1/xtoolwait.*
```

You should mark configuration and documentation files with `%config` and `%doc`, respectively. For example:

```
%files
%defattr(-,root,root)
/sbin/ypbind
%{_mandir}/*/*
%config /etc/rc.d/init.d/*
%config /etc/yp.conf
%dir /var/yp
%dir /var/yp/binding
%doc README NEWS
```

Making relocatable packages

You can make a relocatable package by setting up one or more `Prefix` tags. For example:

```
Prefix: /usr
Prefix: /etc
```

Each file in the `%files` section must then start with one of the prefixes you provided. With this, installers can easily relocate the package with a command like the following:

```
# rpm --relocate /etc=/usr/etc file_name.rpm
```

The Change Log

The change log usually appears at the end of a spec file. It holds messages for each significant change. For example:

```
%changelog
* Fri Jun 21 2002 Bob Marley <marley@redhat.com>
- automated rebuild

* Tue May 08 2001 Peter Tosh <tosh@redhat.com> 1.3-1
- updated to 1.3
```

Appendix C

RPM Feature Evolution

ALTHOUGH RPM IMPLEMENTATIONS are largely compatible from version to version, RPM packagers must remember that RPM is a still-evolving program and that its developers are adding features to it with each new version. When producing RPM package files, packagers must keep in mind the audience that will be using the final RPM package files. They must decide which versions of RPM they intend the package to be used with and must use only the lowest common denominator set of features implemented in the oldest of the RPM versions they are targeting. As a quick reference, keep in mind the RPM features noted here and the RPM version in which they are introduced. In considering these revisions of RPM, the main releases of interest are RPM 2.5, RPM 3.0.5, RPM 4.0.4, and RPM 4.1.

RPM 2.5 is not widely used anymore; packages should target RPM 2.5 only if the intention is for the RPM package to install using absolutely all RPM versions.

RPM 3.0.5 is the final release of the 3.x series of RPM. It was the release of RPM shipped with Red Hat Linux 6.2 and older releases. It is still in wide use by other vendors as well. Cobalt's Linux distributions use an RPM implementation version based on RPM 3.0.5, for example. (Red Hat Linux was upgraded to RPM 4 via an errata.)

RPM 4.0.4 was used with the 7.x releases of Red Hat Linux, and RPM 4.1 first shipped with Red Hat Linux 8.0. Packages produced targeting RPM 3.0.5 should work with nearly all implementations of RPM still in use today. Packages produced targeting RPM 4.0.4 or RPM 4.1 will work only with recent RPM implementations.

RPM 2.5 is the oldest version of RPM that can, by any stretch of the imagination, still be considered in use. With RPM 2.5, most of the basic RPM features were in place, as well as more advanced functions such as triggers and support for internationalization of `Summary:`, `Description:`, and `Group:` tags in the RPM file header. RPM 2.5 was also the first version of RPM to use the RPM version 3 RPM file format.

RPM 2.5.3 added support for Epochs to the RPM header, implementing RPMTAG_EPOCH.

RPM 2.5.4 introduced the `%license` and `%readme` file types, which can be used in the RPM spec file to indicate license and README files.

RPM 2.5.6 added support for usage of the `Epoch:` keyword in the RPM spec file, allowing you to force an Epoch for your package. The `Epoch:` keyword replaced the older `Serial:` keyword, which semantically behaved similarly.

RPM 2.5.7 enforced the previously implied standard that the "-" character should not be used within the Version or Release fields in the RPM spec file.

RPM 2.90 introduced support for signing and verifying RPM package files using GPG, the GNU Privacy Guard.

RPM 2.91 allowed the usage of `Provides:` directives that defined absolute paths to provided files. Prior to RPM 2.91, `Provides:` could be used only for listing provided capabilities, not for using statements like `Provides: /path/to/file` to indicate provided files.

RPM 3.0.2 permitted usage of multiple `Provides:` lines for the first time, eliminating the need to combine all provided capabilities and files on the same line in the spec file.

RPM 3.0.3 added support for versioned dependencies. Prior to RPM 3.0.3, spec files could indicate that a package required another package or provided a specific capability, but they could not indicate the acceptable versions of the required package or which version of the capability the package provided.

RPM 3.0.4 introduced CompressedFileNames support to RPM. Prior to RPM 3.0.4, RPM packaged the absolute paths of all archived files within the package file. Package file headers contained statements such as

```
fileName #0:   /usr/bin/ar
fileName #1:   /usr/bin/as
fileName #2:   /usr/bin/gasp
fileName #3:   /usr/bin/gprof
```

With CompressedFileNames support, the RPM package file header instead stores the directory name, then just the base name of files within that directory. Package file headers now contain statements such as the following for a given directory with a number of files within that directory:

```
dirName #0:   /usr/bin
        baseName      dirIndex
#0       ar              0
#1       as              0
#2       gasp            0
#3       gprof           0
```

Each file entry now holds the file's base name within the directory, as well as an index number that refers to the directory entry. Since packages typically contain lots of files within the same directory, CompressedFileNames support results in significant memory savings when processing packages for installation.

RPM 3.0.5 added PayloadIsBzip2 support to RPM, allowing the data payload of RPM package files to be compressed using bzip2 instead of gzip. Even though

RPM now supports bzip2 compression of package files, this feature is rarely used in practice, since significantly more memory and time is required to install bzip2-compressed RPM package files than to install gzip-compressed RPM package files. RPM 3.0.5 also added support to RPM for manipulating existing RPM version 4 file format packages; packages produced with RPM 3.0.5 can only be RPM version 3 file format, however.

RPM 4.0 implemented several significant changes to RPM. RPM 4.0 created package files using RPM version 4 package file format. RPM 4.0 also switched from Berkeley db 1.85 to Berkeley db 3.1 as the database program used for creation and manipulation of the RPM database. The RPM package database file was renamed as well. The db3 package database file is /var/lib/rpm/Packages, and the older db1 package database file was /var/lib/rpm/packages.rpm. Changing the package database file name allowed old and new versions to co-exist if necessary, simplifying upgrades from older RPM releases to the new RPM 4.0 release. RPM 4.0 also introduced the PayloadFilesHavePrefix feature, changing the way archived files are named within the RPM package file. RPM package files contain a cpio archive of files. Prior to RPM 4.0, file names in the cpio archive were stored without a root prefix. With PayloadFilesHavePrefix, all file names within the cpio archive files now have a root prefix, such as ./usr/bin/ar. This modification made it possible for RPM package files to contain the root directory, "./". Additional sanity-checking was added to the RPM 4.0 spec file parser; beginning with 4.0, RPM no longer allows dangling symbolic links that contain the BuildRoot. This change eliminates a class of common mistakes made when producing RPMs. Finally, RPM 4.0 implicitly generates `Provides:` directives; whenever a package header is read, the `Provides:` directive `Provides: %{name} = %{epoch}:%{version}-%{release}` is automatically generated, ensuring that all packages explicitly provide themselves as a capability and removing the need to provide self-capabilities within the package spec file.

RPM 4.0.2 introduced the use of SHA-1 message digests to validate RPM header regions.

RPM 4.0.3 added the `%dev(type,major,minor)` spec file directive, allowing creation of device nodes. In addition, the `%configure` spec file directive now supported `-target` and `-host`, simplifying cross compilation when using RPM. The `%files` directive was extended by adding the `%exclude` subdirective that could be used to exclude files from inclusion. Finally, RPM 4.0.3 switched back to creating package files in RPM version 3 package file format by default, although it still supports RPM version 4 package file format as well.

RPM 4.0.4 provided PartialHardlinkSets support. RPM package files are sometimes created which contain multiple copies of the same file, stored as hard links to save space. Prior to RPM 4.0.4, RPM has always treated collections of hard links as an all-or-nothing proposition; all hard links were created, or else none were created. This behavior posed problems when some hard links in a set were tagged with attributes such as `%doc` or `%lang`, since rpm commands make it possible to install an RPM package file without installing any files with %doc attributes. Prior to RPM 4.0.4, doing so would break the hard link set, preventing creation of all hard links in the set. PartialHardlinkSet corrects this problem by allowing successful creation of subsets of the hard link set. RPM 4.0.4 also provided automatic generation of Perl module Requires: directives. find-requires now parses all packaged Perl scripts, generating any determined dependencies. In addition, RPM 4.0.4 provides transaction support for RPM.

RPM 4.1 adds separate header DSA and RSA signatures, allowing verification of RPM package headers.

Finally, when considering the RPM features required by your prepared package, remember that some required RPM features are specified manually within the package spec file, while others are automatically added by RPM during the RPM package file build process. For example, usage of versioned Requires: directives in a spec file will make the resulting RPM package file correctly installable only by RPM release 3.0.3 or later. Similarly, the preparation of any package using RPM release 4.0 or later will automatically produce RPM package files that can only be manipulated by releases of RPM that support the PayloadFilesHavePrefix feature. In the first case, you chose to produce packages that worked with RPM release 3.0.5 or later, but not with RPM release 2.5, by including a new directive in the package spec file. In the second case, however, you did not explicitly produce packages that work only with recent RPM releases. The simple fact that you built your RPM package using RPM release 4.0 means that you automatically used features that only RPM 4.0 and later releases understand. These automatic internal requirements are quite common in the later versions; as a result, the best practice is to decide the oldest version of RPM that you wish to support, then to build all packages using that version of RPM, keeping its feature set in mind as you prepare and build the packages.

Appendix D

RPM Package File Structure

IN THIS APPENDIX

- ◆ RPM package file structure
- ◆ RPM header entry formats
- ◆ Payload format

THIS APPENDIX DESCRIBES THE format of RPM package files. You can combine this information with C, Perl, or Python data structures to access the information. In all cases, you should access elements in an RPM file using one of the available programming libraries. Do not attempt to access the files directly, as you may inadvertently damage the RPM file.

Chapters 16, 17, and 18 cover programming with C, Python, and Perl, respectively.

The RPM package format described here has been standardized as part of the Linux Standards Base, or LSB, version 1.3.

The LSB 1.3 section on package file formats is available at www.linuxbase. org/spec/refspecs/LSB_1.3.0/gLSB/gLSB.html#PACKAGEFMT.

The Package File

RPM packages are delivered with one file per package. All RPM files have the following basic format of four sections:

♦ A lead or file identifier

♦ A signature

♦ Header information

♦ Archive of the payload, the files to install

All values are encoded in network byte order, for portability to multiple processor architectures.

The file identifier

Also called the *lead* or the *rpmlead*, the identifier marks that this file is an RPM file. It contains a magic number that the file command uses to detect RPM files. It also contains version and architecture information.

The start of the identifier is the so-called magic number. The `file` command reads the first few bytes of a file and compares the values found with the contents of /usr/share/magic (/etc/magic on many UNIX systems), a database of magic numbers. This allows the `file` command to quickly identify files.

The identifier includes the RPM version number, that is, the version of the RPM file format used for the package. The identifier also has a flag that tells the type of the RPM file, whether the file contains a binary or source package. An architecture flag allows RPM software to double-check that you are not trying to install a package for a non-compatible architecture.

The signature

The signature appears after the lead or identifier section. The RPM signature helps verify the integrity of the package, and optionally the authenticity.

The signature works by performing a mathematical function on the header and archive section of the file. The mathematical function can be an encryption process, such as PGP (Pretty Good Privacy), or a message digest in MD5 format.

The header

The identifier section no longer contains enough information to describe modern RPMs. Furthermore, the identifier section is nowhere near as flexible as today's packages require. To counter these deficiencies, the header section was introduced to include more information about the package.

The header structure contains three parts:

- ◆ Header record
- ◆ One or more header index record structures
- ◆ Data for the index record structures

The header record identifies this as the RPM header. It also contains a count of the number of index records and the size of the index record data.

Each index record uses a structure that contains a tag number for the data it contains. This includes tag IDs for the copyright message, name of the package, version number, and so on. A type number identifies the type of the item. An offset indicates where in the data section the data for this header item begins. A count indicates how many items of the given type are in this header entry. You can multiply the count by the size of the type to get the number of bytes used for the header entry.

Table D-1 lists the type identifiers.

TABLE D-1 HEADER TYPE IDENTIFIERS

Constant	Value	Size in Bytes
RPM_NULL_TYPE	0	No size
RPM_CHAR_TYPE	1	1
RPM_INT8_TYPE	2	1
RPM_INT16_TYPE	3	2
RPM_INT32_TYPE	4	4
RPM_INT64_TYPE	5	Not supported yet
RPM_STRING_TYPE	6	Variable number of bytes, terminated by a NULL
RPM_BIN_TYPE	7	1
RPM_STRING_ARRAY_TYPE	8	Variable, vector of NULL-terminated strings
RPM_I18NSTRING_TYPE	9	Variable, vector of NULL-terminated strings

Integer values are aligned on 2-byte (16-bit integers) or 4-byte (32-bit integers) boundaries.

Header Tags

Table D-2 lists the tag identifiers.

TABLE **D-2** HEADER ENTRY TAG IDENTIFIERS

Constant	Value	Type	Required?
RPMTAG_NAME	1000	STRING	Yes
RPMTAG_VERSION	1001	STRING	Yes
RPMTAG_RELEASE	1002	STRING	Yes
RPMTAG_SUMMARY	1004	I18NSTRING	Yes
RPMTAG_DESCRIPTION	1005	I18NSTRING	Yes
RPMTAG_BUILDTIME	1006	INT32	Optional
RPMTAG_BUILDHOST	1007	STRING	Optional
RPMTAG_SIZE	1009	INT32	Yes
RPMTAG_LICENSE	1014	STRING	Yes
RPMTAG_GROUP	1016	I18NSTRING	Yes
RPMTAG_OS	1021	STRING	Yes
RPMTAG_ARCH	1022	STRING	Yes
RPMTAG_SOURCERPM	1044	STRING	Optional
RPMTAG_FILEVERIFYFLAGS	1045	INT32	Optional
RPMTAG_ARCHIVESIZE	1046	INT32	Optional
RPMTAG_RPMVERSION	1064	STRING	Optional
RPMTAG_CHANGELOGTIME	1080	INT32	Optional
RPMTAG_CHANGELOGNAME	1081	STRING_ARRAY	Optional
RPMTAG_CHANGELOGTEXT	1082	STRING_ARRAY	Optional
RPMTAG_COOKIE	1094	STRING	Optional
RPMTAG_OPTFLAGS	1122	STRING	Optional
RPMTAG_PAYLOADFORMAT	1124	STRING	Yes

Constant	Value	Type	Required?
RPMTAG_PAYLOADCOMPRESSOR	1125	STRING	Yes
RPMTAG_PAYLOADFLAGS	1126	STRING	Yes
RPMTAG_RHNPLATFORM	1131	STRING	Deprecated
RPMTAG_PLATFORM	1132	STRING	Optional

Most of these tags are self-explanatory; however, a few tags hold special meaning. The RPMTAG_SIZE tag holds the size of all the regular files in the payload. The RPMTAG_ARCHIVESIZE tag holds the uncompressed size of the payload section, including the necessary cpio headers. The RPMTAG_COOKIE tag holds an opaque string.

According to the LSB standards, the RPMTAG_PAYLOADFORMAT must always be cpio. The RPMTAG_PAYLOADCOMPRESSOR must be gzip. The RPMTAG_PAYLOADFLAGS must always be 9.

The RPMTAG_OPTFLAGS tag holds special compiler flags used to build the package. The RPMTAG_PLATFORM and RPMTAG_RHNPLATFORM tags hold opaque strings.

Private Header Tags
Table D-3 lists header tags that are considered private.

TABLE D-3 PRIVATE HEADER TAGS

Constant	Value	Type	Required?
RPMTAG_HEADERSIGNATURES	62	BIN	Optional
RPMTAG_HEADERIMMUTABLE	63	BIN	Optional
RPMTAG_HEADERI18NTABLE	100	STRING_ARRAY	Yes

The RPMTAG_HEADERSIGNATURES tag indicates that this is a signature entry. The RPMTAG_HEADERIMMUTABLE tag indicates a header item that is used in the calculation of signatures. This data should be preserved.

The RPMTAG_HEADERI18NTABLE tag holds a table of locales used for international text lookup.

Signature Tags

The signature section is implemented as a header structure, but it is not considered part of the RPM header. Table D-4 lists special signature-related tags.

TABLE D-4 SIGNATURE-RELATED TAGS

Constant	Value	Type	Required?
SIGTAG_SIGSIZE	1000	INT32	Yes
SIGTAG_PGP	1002	BIN	Optional
SIGTAG_MD5	1004	BIN	Yes
SIGTAG_GPG	1005	BIN	Optional
SIGTAG_PAYLOADSIZE	1007	INT32	Optional
SIGTAG_SHA1HEADER	1010	STRING	Optional
SIGTAG_DSAHEADER	1011	BIN	Optional
SIGTAG_RSAHEADER	1012	BIN	Optional

The SIGTAG_SIGSIZE tag specifies the size of the header and payload sections, while the SIGTAG_PAYLOADSIZE holds the uncompressed size of the payload.

To verify the integrity of the package, the SIGTAG_MD5 tag holds a 128-bit MD5 checksum of the header and payload sections. The SIGTAG_SHA1HEADER holds an SHA1 checksum of the entire header section.

To verify the authenticity of the package, the SIGTAG_PGP tag holds a Version 3 OpenPGP Signature Packet RSA signature of the header and payload areas. The SIGTAG_GPG tag holds a Version 3 OpenPGP Signature Packet DSA signature of the header and payload areas. The SIGTAG_DSAHEADER holds a DSA signature of just the header section. If the SIGTAG_DSAHEADER tag is included, the SIGTAG_GPG tag must also be present. The SIGTAG_ RSAHEADER holds an RSA signature of just the header section. If the SIGTAG_ RSAHEADER tag is included, the SIGTAG_PGP tag must also be present.

Installation Tags

A set of installation-specific tags tells the rpm program how to run the pre- and post-installation scripts. Table D-5 lists these tags.

TABLE D-5 INSTALLATION TAGS

Constant	Value	Type	Required?
RPMTAG_PREINPROG	1085	STRING	Optional
RPMTAG_POSTINPROG	1086	STRING	Optional
RPMTAG_PREUNPROG	1087	STRING	Optional
RPMTAG_POSTUNPROG	1088	STRING	Optional

The RPMTAG_PREINPROG tag holds the name of the interpreter, such as sh, to run the pre-install script. Similarly, the RPMTAG_POSTINPROG tag holds the name of the interpreter to run the post-install script. RPMTAG_PREUNPROG and RPMTAG_POSTUN-PROG are the same for the uninstall scripts.

File Information Tags

File information tags are placed in the header for convenient access. These tags describe the files in the payload. Table D-6 lists these tags.

TABLE D-6 FILE INFORMATION TAGS

Constant	Value	Type	Required?
RPMTAG_OLDFILENAMES	1027	STRING_ARRAY	Optional
RPMTAG_FILESIZES	1028	INT32	Yes
RPMTAG_FILEMODES	1030	INT16	Yes
RPMTAG_FILERDEVS	1033	INT16	Yes
RPMTAG_FILEMTIMES	1034	INT32	Yes
RPMTAG_FILEMD5S	1035	STRING_ARRAY	Yes
RPMTAG_FILELINKTOS	1036	STRING_ARRAY	Yes
RPMTAG_FILEFLAGS	1037	INT32	Yes
RPMTAG_FILEUSERNAME	1039	STRING_ARRAY	Yes

Continued

TABLE **D-6** FILE INFORMATION TAGS *(Continued)*

Constant	Value	Type	Required?
RPMTAG_FILEGROUPNAME	1040	STRING_ARRAY	Yes
RPMTAG_FILEDEVICES	1095	INT32	Yes
RPMTAG_FILEINODES	1096	INT32	Yes
RPMTAG_FILELANGS	1097	STRING_ARRAY	Yes
RPMTAG_DIRINDEXES	1116	INT32	Optional
RPMTAG_BASENAMES	1117	STRING_ARRAY	Optional
RPMTAG_DIRNAMES	1118	STRING_ARRAY	Optional

The RPMTAG_OLDFILENAMES tag is used when the files are not compressed, when the RPMTAG_REQUIRENAME tag does not indicate rpmlib(CompressedFileNames). The RPMTAG_FILESIZES tag specifies the size of each file in the payload, while the RPMTAG_FILEMODES tag specifies the file modes (permissions) and the RPMTAG_FILEMTIMES tag holds the last modification time for each file.

The RPMTAG_BASENAMES tag holds an array of the base file names for the files in the payload. The RPMTAG_DIRNAMES tag holds an array of the directories for the files. The RPMTAG_DIRINDEXES tag contains an index into the RPMTAG_DIRNAMES for the directory. Each RPM must have either RPMTAG_OLDFILENAMES or the triple of RPMTAG_BASENAMES, RPMTAG_DIRNAMES, and RPMTAG_DIRINDEXES, but not both.

Dependency Tags
The dependency tags provide one of the most useful features of the RPM system by allowing for automated dependency checks between packages. Table D-7 lists these tags.

TABLE **D-7** DEPENDENCY TAGS

Constant	Value	Type	Required?
RPMTAG_PROVIDENAME	1047	STRING_ARRAY	Yes
RPMTAG_REQUIREFLAGS	1048	INT32	Yes
RPMTAG_REQUIRENAME	1049	STRING_ARRAY	Yes
RPMTAG_REQUIREVERSION	1050	STRING_ARRAY	Yes

Constant	Value	Type	Required?
RPMTAG_CONFLICTFLAGS	1053	INT32	Optional
RPMTAG_CONFLICTNAME	1054	STRING_ARRAY	Optional
RPMTAG_CONFLICTVERSION	1055	STRING_ARRAY	Optional
RPMTAG_OBSOLETENAME	1090	STRING_ARRAY	Optional
RPMTAG_PROVIDEFLAGS	1112	INT32	Yes
RPMTAG_PROVIDEVERSION	1113	STRING_ARRAY	Yes
RPMTAG_OBSOLETEFLAGS	1114	INT32	Optional
RPMTAG_OBSOLETEVERSION	1115	INT32	Optional

Each of these tags comes in triples, which are formatted similarly. The RPM-TAG_REQUIRENAME tag holds an array of required capabilities. The RPMTAG_REQUIREVERSION tag holds an array of the versions of the required capabilities. The RPMTAG_REQUIREFLAGS tag ties the two together with a set of bit flags that specify whether the requirement is for a version less than the given number, equal to the given number, greater than or equal to the given number, and so on. Table D-8 lists these flags.

TABLE D-8 BIT FLAGS FOR DEPENDENCIES

Flag	Value
RPMSENSE_LESS	0x02
RPMSENSE_GREATER	0x04
RPMSENSE_EQUAL	0x08
RPMSENSE_PREREQ	0x40
RPMSENSE_INTERP	0x100
RPMSENSE_SCRIPT_PRE	0x200
RPMSENSE_SCRIPT_POST	0x400
RPMSENSE_SCRIPT_PREUN	0x800
RPMSENSE_SCRIPT_POSTUN	0x1000

The RPMTAG_PROVIDENAME, RPMTAG_PROVIDEVERSION, and RPMTAG_PROVIDE-FLAGS tags work similarly for the capabilities this package provides. The RPMTAG_CONFLICTNAME, RPMTAG_CONFLICTVERSION, and RPMTAG_CONFLICTFLAGS tags specify the conflicts. The RPMTAG_OBSOLETENAME, RPMTAG_OBSOLETEVERSION, and RPMTAG_OBSOLETEFLAGS tags specify the obsoleted dependencies.

In addition, an RPM package can define some special requirements in the RPMTAG_REQUIRENAME and RPMTAG_REQUIREVERSION tags. Table D-9 lists these requirements.

TABLE D-9 SPECIAL PACKAGE REQUIREMENT NAMES AND VERSIONS

Name	Version	Specifies
Lsb	1.3	The package conforms to the Linux Standards Base RPM format.
rpmlib(VersionedDependencies)	3.0.3-1	The package holds dependencies or prerequisites that have versions associated with them.
rpmlib(PayloadFilesHavePrefix)	4.0-1	File names in the archive have a "." prepended on the names.
rpmlib(CompressedFileNames)	3.0.4-1	The package uses the RPMTAG_DIRINDEXES, RPMTAG_DIRNAME and RPMTAG_BASENAMES tags for specifying file names.
/bin/sh	NA	Indicates a requirement for the Bourne shell to run the installation scripts.

The payload

The payload, or archive, section contains the actual files used in the package. These are the files that the rpm command installs when you install the package. To save space, data in the archive section is compressed in GNU gzip format.

Once uncompressed, the data is in cpio format, which is how the rpm2cpio command can do its work. In cpio format, the payload is made up of records, one per file. Table D-10 lists the record structure.

TABLE D-10 CPIO FILE RECORD STRUCTURE

Element	Holds
cpio header	Information on the file, such as the file mode (permissions)
File name	NULL-terminated string
Padding	0 to 3 bytes, as needed, to align the next element on a 4-byte boundary
File data	The contents of the file
Padding	0 to 3 bytes, as needed, to align the next file record on a 4-byte boundary

The information in the cpio header duplicates that of the RPM file-information header elements.

Appendix E

RPM Resources

IN THIS APPENDIX

◆ Finding RPM sites on the Internet

◆ Accessing RPM newsgroups and mailing lists

THIS APPENDIX COVERS THE MATERIAL available on the Internet for working with RPM.

Finding RPM Sites

There is a wealth of RPM material online, although some of it is hard to find. The following sections list a number of RPM-related sites, divided by category. Note that as with any Internet sites, the sites listed may change or disappear.

The main rpm.org site

The main RPM site is `www.rpm.org`. This site provides the official distributions of the RPM software, as well as a lot of documentation online.

Table E-1 lists a number of useful links on this site.

TABLE E-1 LINKS ON THE RPM.ORG SITE

Link	Holds
`ftp://ftp.rpm.org/pub/rpm/dist/`	RPM software downloads
`ftp://ftp.rpm.org/pub/`	`rpm.org` download site
`www.rpm.org/cvs_help/`	Instructions for accessing the RPM CVS repository
`www.rpm.org/hintskinks/`	Tips for working with RPM
`www.rpm.org/hintskinks/bootstrap/`	Good tips on bootstrapping RPM to new platforms

Continued

TABLE E-1 LINKS ON THE RPM.ORG SITE *(Continued)*

Link	Holds
www.rpm.org/howto/	How-to documents for working with RPM
www.rpm.org/max-rpm/	Maximum RPM by Edward C. Bailey
www.rpm.org/RPM-HOWTO/	Good introductory tutorial
www.rpm.org/rpmapi-4.1/	API documentation

The main RPM FTP site, at `ftp://ftp.rpm.org/pub/`, includes the RPM distributions, as well as the Berkeley DB version 3 library, and the text of the book *Maximum RPM*. Download RPM software from `ftp://ftp.rpm.org/pub/rpm/dist/`.

RPM locator sites

A number of sites help you find RPMs for various applications. On the main sites, you can find specially built RPMs for a variety of Linux distributions. You can then download the RPMs made especially for your systems.

The main RPM-finding site is `rpmfind.net`, which offers a search engine as well as software you can run on your site.

The RPM PBone Search, at `http://rpm.pbone.net/`, is also very useful.

The `www.rpm.org/packagers/` site lists a number of places that package RPMs and provide them for downloading.

Many Java libraries and packages are available in RPM format from `www.jpackage.org/`.

Table E-2 lists a number of other RPM download sites.

TABLE E-2 RPM DOWNLOAD SITES

Site	Holds
rpmfind.net	Links to a huge number of RPMs, many specific to various Linux distributions
http://rpm.pbone.net/	RPM PBone search, useful for finding RPMs
www.rpm.org/packagers/	Lists a number of sites that provide RPMs for download

---

Site	Holds
`www.javapackage.org`	Many Java packages in RPM format
`http://plf.zarb.org/`	The Penguin Liberation Front has RPMs that for legal reasons cannot be included in the Mandrake Linux distribution.
`www.math.unl.edu/~rdieter/Projects`	Rex Dieter's RPM site
`www.rpmhelp.net`	Mandrake Linux RPMs
`www.aucs.org/rpmcenter/`	Edwin Chan's Red Hat RPMs
`www.owlriver.com/projects/links/`	Owl River Company RPMs

RPM tools sites

A large number of tools exist to help you work with RPMs. The following sites list some of the main tools:

◆ For the vim text editor, you can download a spec.vim syntax file from `http://pegasus.rutgers.edu/~elflord/vim/syntax/spec.vim`.

◆ For emacs, you can download an Emacs mode for spec files from `http://tihlde.org/~stigb/rpm-spec-mode.el`.

Appendix F lists links for a number of text editors.

◆ The rpmlint tool mentioned in Chapter 13 is available at `http://people.mandrakesoft.com/~flepied/projects/rpmlint/`.

Table E-3 lists a number of RPM-related tools and the sites you can find more information on the tools.

TABLE E-3 RPM-RELATED TOOLS

Tool	Site
apt-rpm	`ftp://ftp.conectiva.com/pub/conectiva/EXPERIMENTAL/apt/`
apt4rpm	`http://apt4rpm.sourceforge.net/`
AutoRPM	`www.autorpm.org`
AutoUpdate	`www.mat.univie.ac.at/~gerald/ftp/autoupdate`
current	`www.biology.duke.edu/computer/unix/current/`
kpackage	`www.kde.org`
MakeRPM.pl	`www.perl.com/CPAN/modules/by-authors/id/JWIED`
poldek	`http://poldek.pld.org.pl/`
rpm2html	`rpmfind.net/linux/rpm2html/`
rpmfind	`rpmfind.net`
RUST	`www.rusthq.com`
setup.sh	`www.mmedia.is/~bre/programs/setup.sh`
urpmi	`www.linux-mandrake.com/cooker/urpmi.html`

Programming sites

Only a few sites exist to help developers with programming for RPM. I maintain some quick links to RPM sites at `www.pconline.com/~erc/rpm.htm`. Most of these links are focused for programming with RPM.

The best sites for programming RPM are the online API documentation at `www.rpm.org/rpmapi-4.1/` for the RPM 4.1 release, and the `ftp.rpm.org/pub/rpm/dist/` site for downloading the RPM sources. There is a lot of documentation bundled with the source code.

Appendix F lists links for a number of Integrated Development Environments, or IDEs, aimed at programmers.

Sites related to RPM

If you try to make cross-platform RPMs, especially RPMs that should work for multiple versions of Linux, it is very important to follow the Linux standards for things like file placement and package formats.

The Filesystem Hierarchy Standard, or FHS, covers Linux directory layout at `www.pathname.com/fhs/`.

The Linux Standards Base is working on standardizing on the RPM package file format. See `www.linuxbase.org` for details.

Accessing RPM Mailing Lists and Newsgroups

The RPM mailing list provides the best source of technical RPM information. You can post questions and get quick, useful responses. If you are working with RPM, you should subscribe to this mailing list. For details on viewing the RPM mailing list archives and signing up for the list, see `www.rpm.org/mailing_list/`.

To help avoid unwanted commercial e-mail (in other words, spam), you need to register with a user name and password to subscribe to the mailing list or view the archives.

A Usenet newsgroup, named linux.redhat.rpm, also provides a forum for asking RPM-related questions. You can read this newsgroup with any newsreading program.

Appendix F

Linux Text Editors and Development Tools

IN THIS APPENDIX

◆ General text editors

◆ C-specific tools and integrated development environments

◆ Python-specific development tools

LINUX INCLUDES A NUMBER OF TEXT EDITORS and integrated development environments (IDEs), going from plain old text editors all the way up to sophisticated tools. These tools are suitable for shell scripting, C, Python, and Perl programming, along with a plethora of other uses. Linux makes extensive use of text files, especially for configuration data, so Linux has always included a number of text editors.

This appendix lists a number of tools for those who have not yet set up an RPM development environment on Linux. Note that choosing an editor or IDE is mostly a matter of personal taste. Programmers will often engage in raging battles over the superiority of text editors and other programming tools. Before searching around too far, try out what you have installed on your system and see if that works for you.

Note that Internet sites may change or disappear, so you may have to search to find these tools.

General Text Editors

Linux distributions include a number of text editors with varying sets of features. The two most common editors are vi and emacs, which come with virtually all Linux distributions. These editors are good for UNIX- or Linux-savvy developers, but generally have a steep learning curve for developers used only to Windows.

If you come from Windows, try gedit, kedit, or kate. These text editors open a graphical window on your desktop, making them appear more or less like the Windows Notepad.exe. All three offer more features than Notepad.exe, however.

You may not have installed any of these editors, but all are available as part of Red Hat Linux. You can install vi, emacs, gedit, kedit, or kate from the packages that come with your Linux distribution.

To start one of the editors, enter a command like the following:

```
$ gedit listrpmpkgs &
```

The ampersand, &, launches the program in the background. Replace gedit with the editor you choose.

Programming Text Editors

In addition to general-purpose text editors, Linux sports a large number of text editors with special features for programming, such as syntax highlighting. The extended version of vi, called vim, includes a number of add-ons that can help you with C programming tasks. Emacs also includes a wide array of features to help programming. Both of these editors can act as development environments with a bit of configuration. As mentioned previously, both come with most Linux distributions.

I also like an editor called nedit and another one called jedit. The jedit editor is written in Java, so that it runs the same on Windows and Linux, a big win if you must work on multiple platforms. (Emacs and vim have versions that work on Windows, too, along with Linux.) If you use jedit, you must have a Java runtime environment installed.

Download nedit from www.nedit.org. Download jedit from www.jedit.org. Download Java runtime environments from Sun at http://java.sun.com/j2se/downloads.html or IBM at www.ibm.com/java/jdk/ and select the IBM Developer Kit for Linux.

Integrated Development Environments for C Programming

If you want more of a graphical environment, Red Hat Linux ships with KDevelop, an IDE for C and C++ programming.

Anjuta provides a GTK/GNOME-based IDE, an alternative to the KDE-based KDevelop. KDevelop, however, supports KDE, GNOME, Qt, and text-mode C and C++ applications.

Download Anjuta from www.anjuta.org.

The Eclipse IDE, while mostly used for Java development, has a C and C++ mode called CDT, for C/C++ Development Tools. Eclipse is important because Red Hat provides an RPM-building plug-in to Eclipse.

 Download Anjuta from www.anjuta.org. Download Eclipse from www.eclipse.org and the Eclipse CDT from www.eclipse.org/tools/downloads.html.

Integrated Development Environments for Python Programming

As with C programs, Python scripts are made up of text files holding Python commands, so you need a text editor or some sort of development environment for creating Python programs. Any of the tools listed so far will work fine for developing Python applications. The key requirement is the ability to control tabs and indenting, since this is crucial to Python syntax.

IDLE, a graphical console and editor, supports creating Python applications. This is considered part of Python. IDLE requires the Python-tools package.

In addition, you can choose from Python-focused tools such as Bicycle Repair Man, a refactoring tool, or Boa Constructor and Black Adder, two Python IDEs.

 Boa Constructor is available from http://boa-constructor.sourceforge.net. Black Adder is a commercial tool available at www.thekompany.com.

The Eclipse IDE, mentioned previously, supports a number of Python add-ons. Combined with the C and C++ tools, and plug-ins for building RPMs, Eclipse brings together most everything you need for Python development on Linux.

 Eclipse is available at www.eclipse.org, and Python add-ons at http://sourceforge.net/projects/pyeclipse, http://sourceforge.net/projects/pe4eclipse, or http://www.kalab.com/freeware/pythoneclipse/pythoneclipse.htm.

This is really just the tip of the iceberg when it comes to Python tools. You can find many more available on the Internet.

A large listing of Python editing tools appears at `http://www.python.org/cgi-bin/moinmoin/PythonEditors`.

Appendix G

Licensing RPM

WHEN INCORPORATING SOMEONE ELSE'S existing code into your software project, you should always examine the license of the code carefully, make sure you understand its implications, and make sure you are willing to abide by them. You also need to make sure you have the legal right to incorporate the other code in your project. This is true for commercial code and commercial projects, and it is equally true for freely licensed code and free software projects.

RPM itself and most discussed helper applications (rpmlint, rpm-spec-mode, and so forth) are free software, meaning that the programs themselves are available without cost. In addition, most of these tools are considered open source software, which means the source code for the applications are also available.

These facts do not mean that they are unlicensed software, or that their source code can be used in any desired fashion. RPM and these helper applications are made freely available in both source and binary formats under the terms of the GNU Project's General Public License (GPL). The terms of the GPL are reproduced here, and should be consulted before incorporating any source code or binaries licensed under the GPL into your projects. Essentially, the GPL states that you can use GPL'ed source code or binaries for any purpose, so long as you always give those same rights (including access to your program's source code) to any users to whom you give software derived from GPL'ed source code (though a lawyer should be consulted to obtain an analysis of the implications of the GPL on your project, should you decide to use GPL'ed code in any commercially licensed project you might undertake).

The GNU General Public License

Version 2, June 1991
   Copyright (C) 1989, 1991 Free Software Foundation, Inc.
   675 Mass Ave, Cambridge, MA 02139, USA
   Everyone is permitted to copy and distribute verbatim copies of this license document, but changing it is not allowed.
Preamble
The licenses for most software are designed to take away your freedom to share and change it. By contrast, the GNU General Public License is intended to guarantee your freedom to share and change free software--to make sure the software is free for all its users. This General Public License applies to most of the Free Software Foundation's software and to any other program whose authors commit to using it.

(Some other Free Software Foundation software is covered by the GNU Library General Public License instead.) You can apply it to your programs, too.

When we speak of free software, we are referring to freedom, not price. Our General Public Licenses are designed to make sure that you have the freedom to distribute copies of free software (and charge for this service if you wish), that you receive source code or can get it if you want it, that you can change the software or use pieces of it in new free programs; and that you know you can do these things.

To protect your rights, we need to make restrictions that forbid anyone to deny you these rights or to ask you to surrender the rights. These restrictions translate to certain responsibilities for you if you distribute copies of the software, or if you modify it.

For example, if you distribute copies of such a program, whether gratis or for a fee, you must give the recipients all the rights that you have. You must make sure that they, too, receive or can get the source code. And you must show them these terms so they know their rights.

We protect your rights with two steps: (1) copyright the software, and (2) offer you this license which gives you legal permission to copy, distribute and/or modify the software.

Also, for each author's protection and ours, we want to make certain that everyone understands that there is no warranty for this free software. If the software is modified by someone else and passed on, we want its recipients to know that what they have is not the original, so that any problems introduced by others will not reflect on the original authors' reputations.

Finally, any free program is threatened constantly by software patents. We wish to avoid the danger that redistributors of a free program will individually obtain patent licenses, in effect making the program proprietary. To prevent this, we have made it clear that any patent must be licensed for everyone's free use or not licensed at all.

The precise terms and conditions for copying, distribution and modification follow.

TERMS AND CONDITIONS FOR COPYING, DISTRIBUTION AND MODIFICATION

0. This License applies to any program or other work which contains a notice placed by the copyright holder saying it may be distributed under the terms of this General Public License. The "Program", below, refers to any such program or work, and a "work based on the Program" means either the Program or any derivative work under copyright law: that is to say, a work containing the Program or a portion of it, either verbatim or with modifications and/or translated into another language. (Hereinafter, translation is included without limitation in the term "modification".) Each licensee is addressed as "you".

   Activities other than copying, distribution and modification are not covered by this License; they are outside its scope. The act of running the Program is not restricted, and the output from the Program is covered only if its contents constitute a work based on the Program (independent of having been made by running the Program). Whether that is true depends on what the Program does.

1. You may copy and distribute verbatim copies of the Program's source code as you receive it, in any medium, provided that you conspicuously and appropriately publish on each copy an appropriate copyright notice and disclaimer of warranty; keep intact all the notices that refer to this License and to the absence of any warranty; and give any other recipients of the Program a copy of this License along with the Program.

   You may charge a fee for the physical act of transferring a copy, and you may at your option offer warranty protection in exchange for a fee.

2. You may modify your copy or copies of the Program or any portion of it, thus forming a work based on the Program, and copy and distribute such modifications or work under the terms of Section 1 above, provided that you also meet all of these conditions:

   a) You must cause the modified files to carry prominent notice stating that you changed the files and the date of any change.

   b) You must cause any work that you distribute or publish, that in whole or in part contains or is derived from the Program or any part thereof, to be licensed as a whole at no charge to all third parties under the terms of this License.

   c) If the modified program normally reads commands interactively when run, you must cause it, when started running for such interactive use in the most ordinary way, to print or display an announcement including an appropriate copyright notice and a notice that there is no warranty (or else, saying that you provide a warranty) and that users may redistribute the program under these conditions, and telling the user how to view a copy of this License. (Exception: if the Program itself is interactive but does not normally print such an announcement, your work based on the Program is not required to print an announcement.)

   These requirements apply to the modified work as a whole. If identifiable sections of that work are not derived from the Program, and can be reasonably considered independent and separate works in themselves, then this License, and its terms, do not apply to those sections when you distribute them as separate works. But when you distribute the same sections as part of a whole which is a work based on the Program, the distribution of the whole must be on the terms of this License, whose permissions for other licensees extend to the entire whole, and thus to each and every part regardless of who wrote it.

   Thus, it is not the intent of this section to claim rights or contest your rights to work written entirely by you; rather, the intent is to exercise the right to control the distribution of derivative or collective works based on the Program.

   In addition, mere aggregation of another work not based on the Program with the Program (or with a work based on the Program) on a volume of a storage or distribution medium does not bring the other work under the scope of this License.

3. You may copy and distribute the Program (or a work based on it, under Section 2) in object code or executable form under the terms of Sections 1 and 2 above provided that you also do one of the following:

a) Accompany it with the complete corresponding machine-readable source code, which must be distributed under the terms of Sections 1 and 2 above on a medium customarily used for software interchange; or,

b) Accompany it with a written offer, valid for at least three years, to give any third party, for a charge no more than your cost of physically per-forming source distribution, a complete machine-readable copy of the corresponding source code, to be distributed under the terms of Sections 1 and 2 above on a medium customarily used for software interchange; or,

c) Accompany it with the information you received as to the offer to dis-tribute corresponding source code. (This alternative is allowed only for noncommercial distribution and only if you received the program in object code or executable form with such an offer, in accord with Subsection b above.)

The source code for a work means the preferred form of the work for making modifications to it. For an executable work, complete source code means all the source code for all modules it contains, plus any associated interface definition files, plus the scripts used to control compilation and installation of the executable. However, as a special exception, the source code distributed need not include anything that is normally distributed (in either source or binary form) with the major components (compiler, ker-nel, and so on) of the operating system on which the executable runs, unless that component itself accompanies the executable.

If distribution of executable or object code is made by offering access to copy from a designated place, then offering equivalent access to copy the source code from the same place counts as distribution of the source code, even though third parties are not compelled to copy the source along with the object code.

4. You may not copy, modify, sublicense, or distribute the Program except as expressly provided under this License. Any attempt otherwise to copy, modify, sublicense or distribute the Program is void, and will automati-cally terminate your rights under this License. However, parties who have received copies, or rights, from you under this License will not have their licenses terminated so long as such parties remain in full compliance.

5. You are not required to accept this License, since you have not signed it. However, nothing else grants you permission to modify or distribute the Program or its derivative works. These actions are prohibited by law if

you do not accept this License. Therefore, by modifying or distributing the Program (or any work based on the Program), you indicate your acceptance of this License to do so, and all its terms and conditions for copying, distributing or modifying the Program or works based on it.

6. Each time you redistribute the Program (or any work based on the Program), the recipient automatically receives a license from the original licensor to copy, distribute or modify the Program subject to these terms and conditions. You may not impose any further restrictions on the recipients' exercise of the rights granted herein. You are not responsible for enforcing compliance by third parties to this License.

7. If, as a consequence of a court judgment or allegation of patent infringement or for any other reason (not limited to patent issues), conditions are imposed on you (whether by court order, agreement or otherwise) that contradict the conditions of this License, they do not excuse you from the conditions of this License. If you cannot distribute so as to satisfy simultaneously your obligations under this License and any other pertinent obligations, then as a consequence you may not distribute the Program at all. For example, if a patent license would not permit royalty-free redistribution of the Program by all those who receive copies directly or indirectly through you, then the only way you could satisfy both it and this License would be to refrain entirely from distribution of the Program.

If any portion of this section is held invalid or unenforceable under any particular circumstance, the balance of the section is intended to apply and the section as a whole is intended to apply in other circumstances.

It is not the purpose of this section to induce you to infringe any patents or other property right claims or to contest validity of any such claims; this section has the sole purpose of protecting the integrity of the free software distribution system, which is implemented by public license practices. Many people have made generous contributions to the wide range of software distributed through that system in reliance on consistent application of that system; it is up to the author/donor to decide if he or she is willing to distribute software through any other system and a licensee cannot impose that choice.

This section is intended to make thoroughly clear what is believed to be a consequence of the rest of this License.

8. If the distribution and/or use of the Program is restricted in certain countries either by patents or by copyrighted interfaces, the original copyright holder who places the Program under this License may add an explicit geographical distribution limitation excluding those countries, so that distribution is permitted only in or among countries not thus excluded. In such case, this License incorporates the limitation as if written in the body of this License.

9. The Free Software Foundation may publish revised and/or new versions of the General Public License from time to time. Such new versions will be similar in spirit to the present version, but may differ in detail to address new problems or concerns.

Each version is given a distinguishing version number. If the Program specifies a version number of this License which applies to it and "any later version", you have the option of following the terms and conditions either of that version or of any later version published by the Free Software Foundation. If the Program does not specify a version number of this License, you may choose any version ever published by the Free Software Foundation.

10. If you wish to incorporate parts of the Program into other free programs whose distribution conditions are different, write to the author to ask for permission. For software which is copyrighted by the Free Software Foundation, write to the Free Software Foundation; we sometimes make exceptions for this. Our decision will be guided by the two goals of preserving the free status of all derivatives of our free software and of promoting the sharing and reuse of software generally.

NO WARRANTY

11. BECAUSE THE PROGRAM IS LICENSED FREE OF CHARGE, THERE IS NO WARRANTY FOR THE PROGRAM, TO THE EXTENT PERMITTED BY APPLICABLE LAW. EXCEPT WHEN OTHERWISE STATED IN WRITING THE COPYRIGHT HOLDERS AND/OR OTHER PARTIES PROVIDE THE PROGRAM "AS IS" WITHOUT WARRANTY OF ANY KIND, EITHER EXPRESSED OR IMPLIED, INCLUDING, BUT NOT LIMITED TO, THE IMPLIED WARRANTIES OF MERCHANTABILITY AND FITNESS FOR A PARTICULAR PURPOSE. THE ENTIRE RISK AS TO THE QUALITY AND PERFORMANCE OF THE PROGRAM IS WITH YOU. SHOULD THE PROGRAM PROVE DEFECTIVE, YOU ASSUME THE COST OF ALL NECESSARY SERVICING, REPAIR OR CORRECTION.

12. IN NO EVENT UNLESS REQUIRED BY APPLICABLE LAW OR AGREED TO IN WRITING WILL ANY COPYRIGHT HOLDER, OR ANY OTHER PARTY WHO MAY MODIFY AND/OR REDISTRIBUTE THE PROGRAM AS PERMITTED ABOVE, BE LIABLE TO YOU FOR DAMAGES, INCLUDING ANY GENERAL, SPECIAL, INCIDENTAL OR CONSEQUENTIAL DAMAGES ARISING OUT OF THE USE OR INABILITY TO USE THE PROGRAM (INCLUDING BUT NOT LIMITED TO LOSS OF DATA OR DATA BEING RENDERED INACCURATE OR LOSSES SUSTAINED BY YOU OR THIRD PARTIES OR A FAILURE OF THE PROGRAM TO OPERATE WITH ANY OTHER PROGRAMS), EVEN IF SUCH HOLDER OR OTHER PARTY HAS BEEN ADVISED OF THE POSSIBILITY OF SUCH DAMAGES.

END OF TERMS AND CONDITIONS

Appendix: How to Apply These Terms to Your New Programs

If you develop a new program, and you want it to be of the greatest possible use to the public, the best way to achieve this is to make it free software which everyone can redistribute and change under these terms.

To do so, attach the following notices to the program. It is safest to attach them to the start of each source file to most effectively convey the exclusion of warranty; and each file should have at least the "copyright" line and a pointer to where the full notice is found.

> <one line to give the program's name and a brief idea of what it does.>
> Copyright (C) 20yy <name of author>
>
> This program is free software; you can redistribute it and/or modify it under the terms of the GNU General Public License as published by the Free Software Foundation; either version 2 of the License, or (at your option) any later version.
>
> This program is distributed in the hope that it will be useful, but WITHOUT ANY WARRANTY; without even the implied warranty of MERCHANTABILITY or FITNESS FOR A PARTICULAR PURPOSE. See the GNU General Public License for more details.
>
> You should have received a copy of the GNU General Public License along with this program; if not, write to the Free Software Foundation, Inc., 675 Mass Ave, Cambridge, MA 02139, USA.

Also add information on how to contact you by electronic and paper mail.
If the program is interactive, make it output a short notice like this when it starts in an interactive mode:

> Gnomovision version 69, Copyright (C) 20yy name of author
> Gnomovision comes with ABSOLUTELY NO WARRANTY; for details type 'show w'. This is free software, and you are welcome to redistribute it under certain conditions; type 'show c' for details.

The hypothetical commands 'show w' and 'show c' should show the appropriate parts of the General Public License. Of course, the commands you use may be called something other than 'show w' and 'show c'; they could even be mouse-clicks or menu items — whatever suits your program.

You should also get your employer (if you work as a programmer) or your school, if any, to sign a "copyright disclaimer" for the program, if necessary. Here is a sample; alter the names:

> Yoyodyne, Inc., hereby disclaims all copyright interest in the program 'Gnomovision' (which makes passes at compilers) written by James Hacker.
>
> <signature of Ty Coon>, 1 April 1989
> Ty Coon, President of Vice

This General Public License does not permit incorporating your program into proprietary programs. If your program is a subroutine library, you may consider it more useful to permit linking proprietary applications with the library. If this is what you want to do, use the GNU Library General Public License instead of this License.

Index

Symbols

\ backslash, 253

-- double minus signs, 38

\# hash mark
   comments, 179, 450
   printing while command works, 36

\#! hash mark, exclamation point, 288

- minus sign, 38

() parentheses, 203, 204, 212

% percent sign, 179, 450

<=> spaceship operator, 385–386

[] square brackets, 83–84

_ underscore, 305

A

address, Internet. *See* URL (Uniform Resource Locator)

administrators
   files, manipulating (`rpm2cpio`), 263–268
   `%files` section, generating with RUST, 261–263
   functions, adding with emacs rpm-spec-mode, 255–259
   installing, removing, and upgrading applications, 4
   root
      caution against building RPMs, 167, 173, 278
      permissions when installing packages, 35
   `setup.sh` and `MakeRPM.pl`, 263
   spec file editing, improving with VIM plugins, 252–255
   spec files, validating and debugging (`rpmlint`), 259–261

AIX, 235–236

aliases
   customizing, 433–434
   defining, 431–433
   errors, handling, 314–315
   table, 312
   usefulness, 307

Alpha processor architecture, testing, 227

Anjuta, 482–483

anonftp (anonymous file transfer)
   installation triggers, 112–115, 215–217

Apache Web server
   installing, 4–5
   upgrading, 15

API (Applications Programming Interface)
   legacy compatibility issues, 400
   Python, 341–342
   simple database, 95

applications
   build instructions, spec file, 455
   C integrated development environment, 482–483
   installing, removing, and upgrading, 4–5
   opening RPM files within (`Fopen`), 319
   packages and, 8
   utilities, overcoming installation problems, 6

architecture
   conditionals based on, 226–228
   multiple CPU, 17–18
   names and numbers, mapping (`arch_canon`), 429–430

continued

continued

continued

continued

P

continued

R

continued

continued